IN 1937

IN 1937

BY

ALVIN C. EURICH

AND

ELMO C. WILSON

NEW YORK

HENRY HOLT AND COMPANY

EDITORIAL FOREWORD

Shortly after *In 1936* rolled from the press I met a man. He has a headline name. He is wise in the way of the world wags. Speaking of that book and its authors, he said: "A grand job, and I'll tell you why. This world gets more complex every day. As complexity grows we become more ignorant, baffled, jittery. The only way we can catch up, clarify, and calm down is to have the many fragments of world events knit for us into the organic pattern they really make but that is hard to see. This Eurich and Wilson have done. The book stays always by me." The same idea, put in other words, has been much repeated by students and by professional and business men and women.

As the copy for *In 1937* came to my desk, I was struck by the growth in power of the authors, not to simplify but to make clear the drama of world life in this year. The book is richer than last year's volume. With the addition of C. Marshall Muir's chapter on religion I think it complete and satisfying. It says more in less space, the writing is lean, hard, alive. The editor's work has thus been again a privilege. He, too, feels less ignorant for having read it.

MALCOLM S. MACLEAN

PREFACE

A year ago, upon publication of *In 1936,* a number of our friends and readers were gracious enough to inquire whether we planned to write a similar volume each year. *In 1937,* the second in the series, is a partial answer. Again we tried to present the major and significant trends of the year, not merely a chronology of isolated events. In a very real sense, the current volume follows the previous one just as the news it records is an outgrowth of the past. *In 1937* is a companion and supplementary volume to *In 1936.* Nevertheless we have attempted to give the background of the major events of the year so that the volume can be read with understanding independently of the previous one.

As for *In 1936* we are greatly indebted to the sources which simplified the writing of *In 1937: The New York Times, Time, News Week, Literary Digest, The Nation, The New Republic,* and other periodicals that are generally regarded as reliable sources of news and intelligent in their interpretation of trends.

Also we owe a deep debt of gratitude to our collaborators, three of whom continued to work on chapters for which they assumed primary responsibility in 1936: Gerald Hill on The Score for Music, Edgar W. Weaver on Books and Publishing, and Alice Albert Eurich on Stage and Screen. New collaborators for

vii

In 1937 are likewise thorough students in the fields for which they have written: Reverend C. Marshall Muir of Pittsburgh on Religion and Leroy Turner on Art. In addition, H. W. Bernard assisted with the chapter on Business Wavers. Malcolm S. MacLean in his capacity as editor gave generously of his time and fertile suggestions. We are grateful for the contributions of these collaborators and others who have shared in one way or another in giving birth to *In 1937*.

A. C. E.
E. C. W.

Minneapolis, Minn.
Evanston, Ill.
January 1, 1938

CONTENTS

PART I. THE NATIONAL SCENE

ix

PART III. LITERATURE AND THE ARTS

MISCELLANEOUS

PART I

THE NATIONAL SCENE

CHAPTER I

ROOSEVELT VS. HUGHES, McREYNOLDS, BUTLER, ET AL.

1787 U. S. CONSTITUTION: 1937

The story of American government and politics in 1937 was the story of a historic battle—a smashing, bruising fight between the tradition of checks and balances and a newer theory maintaining that because of the almighty power of the check there could be no satisfactory balance. It was a fight which was to split the nation wide open as it had not been rent for a generation, occupy the time and attention of the Federal legislature for six months, and pit Democrat against Brother Democrat to cripple the greatest majority any Democratic President had ever won in Congress.

At the center of the fight, with the conflict raging all around it, stood the Supreme Court of the United States. But as the nine aging members of this "third arm" of the Government settled comfortably into their sacrosanct seats at the first session of the new year, no flicker of apprehension showed in their calm faces. They knew well that the eyes of much of the nation were upon them. Before spring they would sit in judgment on laws which formed the very core of a New Deal. For three years now they had been reviewing proposals of the new planners. On constitutional

3

grounds they had found invalid the NRA, the AAA, the Guffey Coal Act, and many another pet experiment launched by an administration desperately trying to raise a nation from Depression depths with a program combining recovery with reform. They had grown used to being sniped at after unpopular decisions. The "Nine Old Men" could even smile faintly when they were branded "Nine Old Menaces." But they were not prepared for the "open season" which was to be declared on them within five weeks after the new year.

False Security. The Supreme Court had been lulled into a feeling of false security by the apparent mellowing of their severest critic, Franklin Delano Roosevelt. After blasting them as reactionary holdovers from a "horse and buggy" age in the spring of 1935, the President had deliberately refrained from direct criticism of the Court all during the national campaign of 1936. He had spoken often of things he intended to do in his second term. And some of these plans were sure to bring him into conflict with the Supreme Court. In his platform there had been mention of a "clarifying amendment" to be pushed if necessary to make the New Deal effective. But even in his opening address to Congress early in January the President gave no hint of any plan to "reform" the judiciary. He seemed rather at that time to be "courting" the Court, spoke of his hope that the judicial branch of government would "do its part in making Democracy successful." Nor did listeners in Congress detect any hint of what was to come in these words, also in his opening message: "With a better understanding of our purposes and a more intelligent recognition of our needs as a nation, it is not to be assumed that there will be a prolonged failure to bring legislative and judicial actions into closer harmony."

The Bolt from the Blue. Then, on the fifth of February, like a bolt flashed the Presidential message advising Congress that most members of the Supreme Court were too old for their jobs, should either be forced to quit or have additional judges appointed to take some of the burdens from their aging shoulders.

The Chief Executive pointed out that each Federal judge now had to handle nearly half again as many cases as in 1913, that congestion and delay resulted. The Supreme Court was laboring under a heavy burden. "Its difficulties in this respect were superficially lightened some years ago by authorizing the court in its discretion to refuse to hear appeals in many classes of cases. This discretion was so freely exercised that in the last fiscal year although 867 petitions for review were presented to the Supreme Court it declined to hear 717 cases. . . ."

In righteous indignation the Chief Executive thundered that "age" was the cause for this failure on the court's part to hear 87 per cent of the cases brought before it.[1] "In exceptional cases judges, like other

[1] While the message was being read to Congress mimeographed copies were brought to the justices of the Supreme Court as they were hearing a case. Their ages as they either chuckled or snorted at its contents: Chief Justice Charles Evans Hughes, 74; Pierce Butler, 70; Willis Van Devanter, 77; James C. McReynolds, 75; Owen J. Roberts, 61; George Sutherland, 74; Louis D. Brandeis, 80; Benjamin N. Cardozo, 66; Harlan F. Stone, 64.

men, retain to an advanced age full mental and physical power. Those not so fortunate are often unable
to perceive their infirmities. They seem to be tenacious
of the appearance of adequacy. . . . Modern com-
plexities call for the constant infusion of new blood
in the courts, just as it is needed in executive functions of the Government and in private business." (In
an earlier message to Congress the President had already suggested a plan for reorganizing the executive
branch of the Government.) "A lowered mental or
physical vigor leads men to avoid an examination of
complicated and changed conditions. Little by little
new facts become blurred through old glasses fitted, as
it were, for the needs of another generation."

Court "Reforms." Both to speed up justice and
to rejuvenate it then, Franklin Roosevelt proposed the
following changes in the federal judiciary: (1) Give
the Chief Justice power to assign temporarily lower
court justices from one court to another when dockets
grow crowded; (2) Appoint a $10,000 a year "proc-
tor" to watch for this congestion in the lower courts
and recommend transfers of judges and other steps to
relieve it; (3) Let any decision on the constitutionality
of a law be appealed directly to the Supreme Court,
there to take precedence over other cases so that the
constitutionality of laws could be determined in a
hurry; (4) Appoint additional judges in all Federal
courts without exception where there are incumbent
judges of retirement age (70) who have served on the
bench ten years and who do not choose to retire or
resign; (5) Appoint one new member to the Supreme

Court for every justice 70 or over who refused to retire.

A Shocked Nation. Forgotten almost immediately by the general public were all but the last of the President's proposals. Even after four years of watching changes sweep over their Federal Government with the speed of light, Mr. Citizen was not prepared for the shock of a proposal to reach up into the Olympian heights and "tamper" with the Supreme Court of the United States. Their history and civics books had taught them to think of the court as a thing apart, a collection of supermen cloistered in a holy vacuum dispensing awesome justice based on absolute truth and irrefutable learning. Now the supermen were being branded tottering incompetents who should make way for new blood.

Startled expressions on the faces of many New Deal leaders in Congress were proof they also were shocked, had not been consulted. One who had been in the know was Attorney General Homer Cummings. As the President's legal adviser it was he who had assured the Executive that his proposals did "not raise any issues of constitutional law." And it was he who convinced Mr. Roosevelt there was plenty of precedent for his plan to bring the Supreme Court to heel.

Precedent. The Constitution of the United States did not stipulate how many justices there should be. Starting with 6 members in 1789, the Court had been reduced to 5 in 1801, increased to 7 in 1807, to 9 in 1837, to 10 in 1863, reduced to 8 in 1866, then raised back to 9 in 1870, at which figure it had stood for 66 years. With a few notable exceptions these changes had been motivated by growth of court business. John Adams had attempted to retain Federalist control of the judiciary after Jefferson's forces had captured control of the executive and legislative branches in the elections of 1800-01. He whipped through the lame duck Congress a bill to reduce the court from 6 to 5 members, thus forestalling a Jefferson appointment. Again in 1866 Congress reduced the court to prevent President Andrew Johnson from appointing new justices who might nullify the reconstruction acts which had been saddled on the South after the war between the states. A congressional act of 1869 restored the membership to 9, but it was not increased to this number until the following year when President Grant needed an additional justice to "pack" the Court in favor of the Legal Tender Acts which had provided for the issuance of "greenback" currency during the war.

"Packing." But precedent or no precedent, legal or not, the President's proposals brought down on his head the fiercest denunciation of his career. His critics of the past four years hastened to shout "I told you so's" from platform, microphone and editorial page. They had contended all along that the Squire of Hyde Park aspired to be a Mussolini. Here, then, was proof of his dictatorial ambitions in this bald-faced attempt to bring the third arm of Government under his thumb, to "pack" the Supreme Court with hirelings who would jump to his whip-cracking. Six of the justices were seventy or over. It was no accident that 5 of the 6 were the confirmed conservatives who had stood shoulder to shoulder to veto one New Deal law after another. Did anyone suppose that the six new judges whom the President would appoint would be anything but partisans of his who would rubber stamp his laws regardless of constitution or legal precedent?

Liberal's Dilemma. This kind of talk was to be expected from the opposition—the Liberty Leaguers and "economic royalists" whose attacks the President had fattened on since March of 1933. What the President had not foreseen, however, was the sour expressions his plan produced on the faces of some of his staunch "liberal" friends, loyal supporters who had fought and bled with him to introduce many another New Deal reform, who even agreed with him wholeheartedly that SOMETHING should be done about the Supreme Court. Toughest poser for most of these New Dealers was, "Would you have approved such a plan had Herbert Clark Hoover introduced it, or would you have denounced it with all the vigor at your command as a thoroughly reprehensible trick to destroy the American system of checks and balances?"

These liberals worried also about establishing a precedent which, even though conceived from highest motives by the present administration, might be the root of much evil if and when the reactionaries should return to power and employ the same dodge. Others among them felt that such a fundamental change in the governmental system should result only from a decision by the people, favored a constitutional amendment to limit the power of the court by (1) empowering Congress by a two-thirds vote to override Supreme

Court decisions; or (2) requiring more than a simple majority of the justices to concur in order to invalidate a law; or (3) clarifying the commerce clause of the constitution which had proved the stumbling block on which so much New Deal legislation had tripped.

Faced by the dilemma of blindly supporting a President whose views they did not share on this single issue, or deserting him and thereby casting their lot with his enemies, others among these New-Dealers-till-now simply sent up a plaintive cry to "Give us time to think this thing through."

The President's Case.   In rebuttal to these objections which rose on all sides from foe and hitherto friend alike, the Chief Executive and his supporters stoutly maintained that the past four years had amply demonstrated the need for liberalizing a Supreme Court consistently out of step with the other two governmental arms.   Furthermore, the overwhelming vote in favor of the administration the previous fall had been a "mandate" to revamp the court in the quickest and most direct way constitutionally possible.   Amendments took too long—witness the Child Labor amendment which had been kicking about in state legislatures and constitutional conventions since 1924.   (The opposition countered with figures to show that since 1880 the average time required to ratify a constitutional amendment had been 16 months, pointed to the speed with which the Repeal of Prohibition had been effected.)   Also, said the President, tongue in cheek, there was always the off chance that the Supreme Court would declare unconstitutional an amendment limiting its powers. Laughing off the charges that he hungered for autocratic power, and denying any intention of placing "spineless puppets" on the bench, the President at the same time raised the issue of the power which rested in the hands of a single member of the Supreme Court who could and did topple the balance to produce 5-4 decisions outlawing acts of the national legislature.

Democratic Victory Dinner. Just a month to the day after he introduced his court plan—a month during which debate had raged in the halls of Congress, in the press, wherever men and women gathered together —the President seized the occasion of the Democratic victory dinner at Washington's Mayflower hotel to go before the people in a nationwide radio address. In fighting tones he presented his case as no one but the "best radio personality in the world" could.

"As yet there is no assurance that the three-horse team of the American system of government will pull together. If three well-matched horses are put to the heavy task of plowing a field where the going is heavy, and the team of three pull as one, the field will be plowed. If one horse lies down in the traces or plunges off in another direction, the field will not be plowed."

He rehashed the efforts of the administration to effect both recovery and reform since it assumed office, warned that much teamwork was still necessary, and finished with a clarion challenge for immediate action.

"Here is one-third of the nation ill-nourished, ill-clad, ill-housed—NOW!

"Here are thousands upon thousands of men and

women laboring for long hours in factories for inadequate pay—NOW!

". . . If we would keep faith with those who had faith in us, if we would make democracy succeed, I say we must act—NOW!"

Too Late. Shrewder political advisers might have told the occupant of the White House he had waited too long. Had he made his proposals eighteen months before when the national miseries he spoke of were closer to public consciousness his task would have been far easier. Now a large section of the nation had grown fatter. Returning boom conditions in industry, decent farm prices, a rising stock market had produced a sense of well-being which refused to take note of ever-increasing relief rolls. The critical conditions the President spoke of were being glossed over. Many of his listeners were too prone to agree with the dour comment of the New York *Times:* ". . . If the country now faces a crisis, it is a constitutional crisis, and it is of the President's own making."

"Substantially the Same Elements." So when Mr. Roosevelt in the victory dinner speech declared that resistance to his court plan came from "substantially the same elements of opposition" as had opposed all the other New Deal measures, he erred. In the next six months he was to find his strongest opposition coming from some of the "same elements" who had in fact been his enthusiastic supporters during his first term. It was because the President's friends led the opposition that a shrewd Republican minority was able to remain quietly in the background and let a great Democratic majority fight its heart out in intra-party strife which by the following July had so hopelessly ruined party harmony that the 75 Democratic senators voted 38 to 37 on the election of their own leader in the upper house.

Compromises. During the first six weeks after the court plan was introduced it was anyone's guess as to whether the bill incorporating the President's ideas would pass the Congress, with the odds being slightly in the bill's favor. In the Senate however it was soon evident that the "talent" was on the opposition's side. Republicans Borah and Johnson teamed, as they had so often in the past, to denounce the plan from the start. But, more important, so did Democrats Wheeler, Bones and Burke. And many another Democrat who had been an administration supporter right down the line refused to commit himself on this issue until the "visibility" was better.

Still, even those who denounced the plan most bitterly were anxious at the start to work out some form of compromise. Nebraska's Senator Burke, later the leader of the anti-Court plan bloc, proposed a constitutional amendment to allow justices to retire on full pay at 70 and require them to do so at 75. Senator Norris thought an amendment requiring more than a simple majority of the court to invalidate legislative acts might be feasible. Senators Wheeler and Bones favored an amendment to permit a two-thirds vote of Congress to override the judiciary's veto of a law. Senate Majority Leader Joe Robinson, charged with the task of jamming the plan through the upper house and fearful of pitfalls ahead, indicated that he personally would be willing to accept 75, rather than 70, as the age of superannuation.

Retirement Bait. As retirement bait for some of the Supreme Court's septuagenarians the Senate voted 76 to 4 in favor of the Sumners-McCarran bill previously passed by the House providing that justices who had been on the federal bench 10 years or more might retire at 70 on full pay.

The President signed this bill but refused to compromise one whit on his original demands. Nor would he permit the less controversial provisions of his plan to be submitted to Congress apart from the "rejuvenation" clauses.

Senate Judiciary Committee Hearings. Meanwhile the Senate Judiciary committee began hearings. Assistant Attorney General Robert H. Jackson scored early for the administration when he reminded the committee that in the 71 years between the adoption of the constitution and the Civil War the Supreme Court nullified only two acts of Congress on constitutional grounds. In the 72 years since the end of the war and the end of the Court's last term under the Hoover administration it had invalidated 60 Federal laws. But in the three years since the beginning of Roosevelt's first term the Court had acted 12 times to knock out acts of the national legislature.

Dean Leon Green of Northwestern University's law school, the author of a treatise in the *New Republic* holding the sit-down strike legal, spoke in favor of the court plan. Though not called to Washington, Minnesota's law dean, Everett Fraser, also championed the plan. Dean Young Berryman Smith of Columbia's law school found the Court situation "manifestly unsatisfactory," and calling for "corrective action." But he argued also for the right of the people to have their say in any such drastic change. His constructive suggestion was that Congress might set a national date for elections to state conventions which might speedily vote on some sort of amendment which would reduce the Court's veto powers.

Another law dean brought to Washington by the opposition was Michigan University's Henry M. Bates, who spoke against the bill. Professor Erwin N. Griswold of Harvard admitted that of the two methods of getting rid of judges—shooting and retiring—the latter method had the advantage of being "much more genteel."

The Hughes Letter. Obviously impressive to the committee was the letter from Chief Justice Hughes read by Senator Wheeler early in the hearings. The Chief Justice insisted that the Court was "fully abreast of its work" and declared that "An increase in the number of justices of the Supreme Court apart from the question of policy, which I do not discuss, would not promote the efficiency of the Court." Shrewdly reserving his trump card for the end of the letter, Justice Hughes mildly observed, "On account of the shortness of time I have not been able to consult with the members of the Court generally with respect to the foregoing statement, but I am confident that it is in accord with the views of the justices. I should say, however, that I have been able to consult with Mr. Justice Van Devanter and Mr. Justice Brandeis, and I am at liberty to say that the statement is approved by them."

The effectiveness of the Hughes letter lay not so much in the denial by the Chief Justice that age or anything else was cutting down the Court's efficiency, as in the revelation that the most consistent and most revered liberal on the high court, Justice Brandeis— the man who had done his best to persuade his fellows on the bench to find New Deal legislation constitutional whenever possible—was dead set against the Court bill.

The only other public word from the members of the Court during the controversy was an informal talk by Justice McReynolds at his college fraternity banquet (Phi Delta Theta) in which he urged good sportsmanship in accepting legal decisions. In an attempt to even the score the administration resurrected the only ex-member of the Court still alive, John Hessin Clarke, who went on the radio to declare that the Court proposals were "plainly within the powers granted to the Congress and therefore clearly Constitutional."

The Court Goes New Deal. Nothing further was said by any member of the Court past or present, but remembering the old saw that actions speak louder than words, the nine old men went methodically to work at the task of killing off the plan in the most effective way possible. Suddenly there appeared to be five instead of three New Dealers on the Court.

Students following the Court decisions the past three

years had generally classified members as follows: Conservatives—McReynolds, Van Devanter, Sutherland, Butler, Roberts; Liberals—Cardozo, Brandeis, Stone. The bushy-bearded Chief Justice was difficult to classify, but his vote had been with the conservatives more often than not.

At the very end of 1936 the Court had supported the administration in upholding the Gran Chaco embargo voted by Congress in May, 1934, to stop shipment of arms to warring Bolivia and Paraguay. But Justice Sutherland, reading the majority opinion, had taken pains to point out that while the President might enjoy a deal of freedom in matters of foreign policy, this freedom did not extend to domestic affairs. On only two other big cases had the Court held in favor of the President and his social planners, the TVA and Gold Clause decisions, as against a long procession of decisions which amputated one branch of the New Deal after another.

Minimum Wage Law Decision. Then, without the slightest warning, the Court on a single Monday (March 29) arched a "Who's-an-old-fogie-now" look in the direction of the White House, and handed down three liberal decisions on legislation which lay at the very heart of the administration's program. The first upheld the Washington state minimum wage law for women. Since 1923 the Court had been finding minimum wage laws for women clearly unconstitutional. Only the previous spring, in a case involving a similar statute in New York, the majority opinion had thundered that such a law deprived an employer of "liberty

without due process of law." And on a rehearing of
the same case in September, 1936, the same five justices
had refused to change their minds. Strangely enough,

("*The Birmingham Age-Herald*")
Did Someone Insinuate Senility?

however, they had at the same time agreed to hear the
Washington case involving the same principle.

A Wenatchee, Washington, hotel man had paid his
chambermaid $12 a week. State law set $14.50 as
minimum. The chambermaid sued. The case moved
slowly up to the highest court. Now five justices

headed by the Chief Justice reversed the court's previous stand. Mr. Hughes disposed of the "due process" argument by finding that "The constitution does not speak of freedom of contract. It speaks of liberty and prohibits the deprivation of liberty without due process of law. In prohibiting that deprivation the constitution does not recognize an absolute and uncontrollable liberty. . . ." ". . . The exploitation of a class of workers who are in an unequal position with respect to bargaining power . . . is not only detrimental to their health and well-being, but casts a direct burden for their support upon the community. What these workers lose in wages the taxpayers are called upon to pay. The bare cost of living must be met."

Frazier-Lemke. The second decision with which the administration could find little fault on that last Monday in March involved the right of the Federal Government to extend aid to the farmer. Early in the President's first term Senator Frazier and Representative Lemke of North Dakota had authored an act permitting a hard-pressed farmer to declare himself bankrupt and keep his farm by having it appraised at its current value, paying this sum to his creditors within five years. In May, 1935, the Supreme Court had declared this relief measure unconstitutional. Then the act was revamped, passed by Congress and now was being tested again before the Court. The majority of the Court found the changes satisfactory, declared it constitutional. The new act enabled the bankrupt farmer to keep his property only three years, meanwhile paying his mortgagee a "reasonable rent." Thus, in the old act the mortgage holder had been deprived of his property rights; in the act as amended he had not.

Railway Labor. On the same day came a ringing decision upholding some of the administration's favored ideas on labor, and giving a hint of what was to come in the test of the Wagner Labor Relations Act. The Railway Labor Act was passed in 1926 and amended in 1934. It compelled collective bargaining, empowered a majority of employees to elect their sole bargaining representative, provided machinery for mediation and adjustment of labor disputes, and was the model from which the Wagner Act was drawn. The Virginian Railway tried to bargain with a company union of its shop employees despite the fact that a majority of them had voted to have an A. F. of L. union represent them.

Justice Stone, speaking for the majority, found that "The peaceable settlement of labor controversies, especially where they may seriously impair the ability of an interstate rail carrier to perform its service to the public, is a matter of public concern," and thus a proper field for federal legislation.

Roberts Turns the Tide. These liberal decisions, all of them 5-4, were made possible because the Chief Justice swung his vote with those of Cardozo, Brandeis and Stone. But had he not been able to bring one of the former conservatives over with him, the story would have been different. For some reason now Justice Owen J. Roberts began to find more reason and justice on the side of the liberals. He switched his vote, and made possible the series of decisions which upheld one

New Deal act after another through the spring, as the President and his advisers struggled to keep their Court plan alive under a counter offensive against which they had no defense.

Wagner Act. It was the Wagner Act decision which really counted out the Court plan. The Wagner or National Labor Relations Act had been passed in the spring of 1935 as an attempt to set down a bill of rights for labor. It attempted to outlaw the company union by declaring that the employer might not dominate, interfere with or contribute financial or other support to the formation or administration of any labor organization. Nor could an employer discriminate against an employee because he belonged to a union. The act declared further that the employer must bargain with representatives chosen by the majority of his employees, and that a representative so chosen had the right to act for all employees. A National Labor Relations Board of three members appointed by the President was created by the act. Their job was to supervise labor elections, hear complaints of unfair practices, and issue orders to those accused of unfair practices.

This, then, was labor's "magna carta" which had been roundly damned by employers throughout the length and breadth of the land, and universally disregarded by them on the grounds that it was clearly an unconstitutional invasion of their rights.

Many observers were convinced it was because he was so sure this act would be nullified by the Supreme Court that the President had determined to increase the liberal representation on the High Court.

Five employers challenging the act were finally permitted to develop their arguments, and the Court on April 12 ruled on all five at once. A unanimous decision held against the challenge of the Virginia & Maryland Coach Co. to the National Labor Relations Board's ruling that 18 employees discharged for union activities should be reinstated. But the Coach Co., a bus line, was admittedly engaged in interstate commerce which Congress had the constitutional right to regulate.

It was not so clear, however, that the Fruehauf Trailer Co., the Friedman-Harry Marks Clothing Co. of Richmond, Virginia, and the Jones & Laughlin Steel Co. were engaged in interstate commerce. Yet the Court ordered their compliance with the ruling of the Labor Board made under provisions of the Wagner Act. Chief Justice Hughes: "We think it clear that the National Labor Relations Act may be construed so as to operate within the spirit of constitutional authority. . . . Discrimination and coercion to prevent the free exercise of the right of employees to a self-organization and representation is a proper subject for condemnation by competent legislative authority. The Congressional authority to protect interstate commerce from burdens and obstructions is not limited to transactions which can be deemed to be an essential part of the flow of interstate or foreign commerce. . . . When industries organize themselves on a national scale, making their relations to interstate commerce the dominant factor in their activities, how can it be maintained that their industrial labor relations consti-

Received in Senate
Aug. 12, 1937.

The White House,
19

To the
Senate of the United States.

I nominate Hugo L. Black
of Alabama to be an Associate Justice
of the Supreme Court of the United States.

Franklin D Roosevelt

THE SUPREME COURT IN THE NEWS

Top Left: Justice Van Devanter retires (Acme). *Top Right:*
Hugo L. Black nominated (Acme). *Bottom:* The Court poses
with its new member (Wide World).

LABOR MARCHES ON

Top Left: William Green insists on A.F.L. supremacy (Acme).
Top Right: John L. Lewis listens while Philip Murray explains
steel strike (Life Magazine). *Bottom:* Henry Bridges in a wist-
ful mood (Life Magazine).

tute a forbidden field into which Congress may not enter when it is necessary to protect interstate commerce from such paralyzing consequences of industrial war?"

The fifth test case involved the dismissal by the Associated Press of Morris Watson because of active work in the Newspaper Guild, union of newspaper men. The NLRB considered the case and ordered his reinstatement. The Associated Press refused, maintaining that the Wagner Act was in violation of the first amendment to the constitution guaranteeing freedom of the press because it deprived them of their right to fire an employee. Unless it could determine for itself the partiality or bias of its editorial employees, it could have no assurance that its news reports, sent out to papers all over the nation, would be free from prejudice.

But Justice Roberts, still hewing to the liberal line, found that employee Watson was fired not because of furnishing biased news but because of union membership. He informed the A.P. that the act did not compel it to employ anyone, nor did it require the association to retain in its employ an incompetent or anyone whose writings reflected bias. The act permitted a discharge for any reason other than union activity or agitation for collective bargaining.

Herndon Case. On April 26 the Court struck another blow for liberalism when it set aside the conviction of Angelo Herndon, Negro Communist who led a hunger march on Atlanta's court house in the summer of 1932, and who had been convicted by an Alabama court of "inducing others to join in . . . combined resistance to the lawful authority of the state" under an old Reconstruction law which was dragged out, dusted off and used for the first time since its enactment 66 years before. Again Roberts' vote made a 5-4 decision.

Social Security. Pausing in its consideration of New Deal laws for a breather, the Court upheld the Louisiana state tax on chain stores, granting the right of the state to tax on the basis of number of stores in the whole national chain rather than on those within the state borders only.

Then, in a final nose-thumbing gesture, the Court in its last week of deliberations before adjournment for the summer upheld the social security law. On May 27, the "five musketeers" found the unemployment insurance provisions of the act constitutional. They were joined by two others for a 7-2 decision validating the old age annuity part of the law. Then, to make the sweep clean, the Court voted 5-4 to uphold the Alabama unemployment insurance law passed to conform to the Federal law.

Unemployment insurance, under the act, was financed by a Federal levy on payrolls. Ninety per cent of this tax was turned over to the states to the payers' credit if and when the state enacted an unemployment insurance law satisfactory to the Federal Government. The Charles C. Steward Machine Co., suing for refund of such taxes collected by the Government, maintained that the act unconstitutionally "coerced" states into setting up unemployment insurance —for otherwise they lost the tax money.

On his 67th birthday Justice Cardozo read the decision. "During the years 1929 to 1936, . . . the number of unemployed mounted to unprecedented heights . . . at times the peak was attained of 16 million or more. Disaster to the breadwinner meant disaster to the dependents . . . the states were unable to give the requisite relief. . . . The problem had become national. . . . It is too late today for the argument to be heard with tolerance that in a crisis so extreme the use of the moneys of the nation to relieve the unemployed and their dependents is a use for any purpose narrower than the promotion of the general welfare. . . . The statute does not call for a surrender by the states of the powers essential to their quasi-sovereign existency. . . . The Social Security act is an attempt to find a method by which all these public agencies may work together to a common end."

This same reasoning disposed of the Alabama case, and provided the basis for the opinion, also read by Cardozo, validating the payroll taxes for old age annuities. Lawyers were quick to note that for the first time in the history of the nation the Court had upheld the power of Congress to raise taxes for the "general welfare."

Adjournment. Glancing back over its record during 1937 as it prepared to adjourn June 1, the Supreme Court could point to not having overruled the New Deal on a single major case. That the President continued to insist on the "reform" of the Court then was, in the opinion of a large section of the press, like the act of a drowning man pushing his rescuer under water as soon as he got his own feet on solid ground again.

In Spite Of or Because Of?   Just as stoutly, however, the administration's friends contended that it was

("*The Chicago News*")

A Yachtsman in the Doldrums.

"because of" the whip hand held by the Executive over the Court that its members had scurried to change their views, that there was no assurance that once this whip hand was relaxed they would not revert to their old reactionary opinions. In any case, the President shortly after the Court adjournment sternly told his press conference the Court could expect no let-up on his part. He accused it of sins of omission which upheld his contention that it was not wholly fit for its job. It had refused to prevent the suit of 19 utilities against TVA from going to trial in the lower courts. It had refused requests to permit cases involving legislative acts to be appealed directly to the Supreme Court without going through the Circuit Court of Appeals. It had refused to decide six cases on which it had heard arguments, holding them over for the fall term, and it had done nothing when a judge in Pennsylvania had enjoined Government attorneys from bringing suit in New York against the Aluminum Co. of America. The fight must go on.

Signs of Weakening. Yet there were definite signs that now for the first time the administration was beginning to doubt its strength. In a press conference early in June, Majority Leader Joe Robinson, the man who had borne the brunt of the fight for the President's plan in the Senate, admitted that "during the last few months some changes have occurred which modify the situation. . . ."

Senate Judiciary Committee Vote. Meanwhile the fight had been going very badly for the administration in the Senate judiciary committee hearings. On April 28, Senators McCarran of Nevada, Hatch of New Mexico, and O'Mahoney of Wyoming climbed down off the fence to join the opposition. From that date on, the tone of the committee's report was never in doubt.

Three weeks later it voted 10 to 8 against the plan, and defeated by the same vote a compromise proposal of Kentucky's Senator Logan to increase the court temporarily if justices over 75 did not retire.

In strong tones the committee recommended the "rejection of this bill as a needless, futile and utterly dangerous abandonment of Constitutional principle. It would not banish age from the bench nor abolish divided decisions. It would not affect the power of any court to hold laws unconstitutional. . . . It is a proposal without precedent and without justification. . . . It is a measure which *should be so emphatically rejected that its parallel will never again be presented to the free representatives of the free people of America.*"

"Harmony" Week-end. The Court plan was now as dead as the dodo. Vice President Garner indicated his disgust with the determination to keep it alive by quitting Washington for his Uvalde Texas ranch home in mid-June, leaving no word as to when he would return. Burke, Wheeler, and O'Mahoney were damning the plan with every breath, lining up more and more of their colleagues. Gradually it was made clear to the administration that there was no assurance any one of the compromise plans which might have passed easily earlier in the session would now receive a favorable vote in Congress. The Democratic breech was so wide that Republicans stood around the lobbies of Congress rubbing their hands in glee at the best news they had had in four years. And the split was showing up among members of the party outside Congress

as well. Even the President's good friend the governor
of New York, Herbert H. Lehman, denounced the plan
in a letter to Senator Wagner.

To repair his party lines the President staged a
"harmony" week-end party at the Jefferson Islands
club in Chesapeake Bay to muster support for the "reasonable compromise" he now felt he would have to
accept. Senator Robinson then introduced the compromise originally sponsored by Senators Hatch and
Logan which would have (1) provided one extra justice for each member over 75, (2) forbidden the appointment of more than one additional justice in any
calendar year, (3) refused to permanently enlarge the
Court, since as judges over 75 retired they would not
be replaced unless the Court had fewer than nine members.

Last Rites. Joe Robinson, working like a nailer in
the Washington heat, finally got 51 Senators to pledge
their support to this compromise. But when it reached
the Senate floor the bitterest debate since the original
plan was hatched broke out. Etiquette went unob-
served as Senators all but climbed down each other's
throats. Then suddenly, on the evening of July 14,
Joe Robinson died of a heart attack. His last rites
were symbolic of the burial of the Court plan which
he had done his best to make into law. Senators who
had been pledged to support the compromise now considered themselves released. More of them were alienated from the plan after the President personally
selected Kentucky's Alben Barkley to succeed Robin-

son. Many of the Old Guard were anxious that Mississippi's Pat Harrison be honored with this post. The

("*The Omaha World-Herald*")
Aid for the Hungry Elephant.

President had his way, but the vote among Democratic senators was 38 to 37.

Finally John Garner came back from Texas to take a hand at settling the whole affair. At his request the bill was rewritten in memorandum form by the judiciary committee. Then the original bill was quietly laid to its final rest. Senators voted 70 to 20 to return it to the judiciary committee, whence it would never again emerge.

New Court Bill. The end of the great battle was as dramatic as was the message which started it. When the revised bill emerged on the Senate floor as the Sumners Judicial Procedure Bill it made no change whatever in the Supreme Court. It did provide for direct appeal to the Supreme Court where the constitutionality of a law is questioned. It also gave the Attorney General authority to argue the government's side in such cases even though the Government might not be a party to the issue. It provided also that senior circuit judges might assign judges from one district to another to help clear up an accumulation of work.

Senator McCarran introduced the new bill. Presiding, Vice President Garner then asked if there were any amendments. McCarran introduced four short ones designed to make the intervention of the Attorney General mandatory in cases where constitutionality of laws was challenged. As the four were read the Vice President pounded his desk and shouted, "Without objection the amendment is agreed to. . . . Without objection the amendment is agreed to. . . ." Then, without interrupting the rhythm of his gavel he shouted, "Without objection the bill as amended is passed."

Under Senate rules one shout of "I object" could have stopped these steamroller tactics, but none of the flabbergasted senators spoke up. The House approved the Senate bill and the Supreme Court battle was finished. Only time would tell whether the battle lines would continue as sharply drawn on issues to follow. But wounds were deep, animosities bitter, and it would take all of the President's famed personal charm and persuasive political powers to mend his party's broken fences.

L'AFFAIRE BLACK

His task was no easier after his appointment of Alabama's Senator Hugo Black to the Supreme Court.

On the very day the Senate judiciary committee was voting 10 to 8 against the Court plan conservative Justice Willis Van Devanter announced his retirement from the Court under the provisions of the new Sumners-McCarran law promising him full pay of $20,000 a year for the rest of his life. After 26 years on the High Court the 78-year-old justice had had enough. Perhaps the knowledge that the defection of Justice Roberts to the side of the Court liberals placed him definitely among the minority may have made his job less satisfying. When the nine members filed out in adjournment June 1 he took off his robe for the last time, retreated to his Maryland farm.

Robinson Boom. Immediately the Senate "nominated" Joe Robinson for the vacant post. The Majority leader had fought bitterly for the Court plan, and even the Opposition felt that his efforts should be rewarded by the President. But the President made no move to "confirm" the "nomination." Joe Robinson was 65, not far from the age at which the President considered judges superannuated. Also, although he had worked like a Trojan for administration measures, the President, as well as his Senate colleagues, knew that the Arkansan's heart had not been fully in the New Deal. He had in fact broken tradition only that spring by stepping out of his role as Majority Leader to take the floor in a violent denunciation of the administration's own relief proposals. But his eligibility was settled for all time by his death in July.

Black Nomination. After infuriating some in the Senate by intimating he might not nominate a successor to Van Devanter until after Congress had adjourned, the President finally on August 12 sent to the Senate the name of another of its members, Hugo Black of Alabama. The Alabaman had been in the Senate for eleven years. There he had allied himself with progressives and radicals and proved his mettle as one of the ablest inquisitors in Congress.

Yct Hugo Black had come to the Senate largely because of the support of one of the nation's most reactionary organizations, the Negro-hating, Catholic-and-Jew-baiting Knights of the Ku Klux Klan. A tradition known as "Senatorial courtesy" makes it a foregone conclusion that any member of the upper house nominated for the High Court will be confirmed as a matter of course. So there was little doubt that the nomination of Senator Black was tantamount to confirmation. Crusty old Senator Borah bobbed up with a legal technicality based on the contention that no vacancy in the court actually existed, since Van Devanter's retirement left him, in theory at least, subject to call for service.

Senators Copeland and Burke raised the issue of Black's support from the Klan, asserting they were in receipt of telegrams from responsible parties accusing the nominee of belonging to the hooded order. But they were shushed by their colleagues, some of whom asserted they knew for a fact the Alabaman was not a Klansman and never had been. And Senator Black maintained a positively oppressive silence at this attempt to dig into the details of his early political career. Nor did the President pay any heed to this scandal-mongering.

The Senate confirmed the appointment 63 to 16 only five days after they received Black's name. The new justice took the secret oath of office in the Supreme Court and sailed for Europe with Mrs. Black.

Scandal! While the President's first Supreme Court appointee was vacationing abroad, the Pittsburgh *Post-Gazette,* owned by New Deal-hating publisher Paul Block, sent Reporter Ray Sprigle to Birmingham, political bailiwick of Black before he came to the Senate. By some hook or crook Sprigle got access to the records of the Ku Klux Klan. In mid-September he released a series of stories syndicated throughout the land with documentary evidence to show that (1) Hugo Black had joined a Birmingham post of the Klan in 1923; (2) after obtaining the support of the Klan in the Senatorial primaries of 1925 he wrote a letter of resignation from the order; (3) after winning the primary which meant election in Democratic Alabama he attended a Klan meeting where he reaffirmed his loyalty to Klan principles and accepted a gold card purporting to make him a life member.[1]

In "millennium" type the press of the nation screamed the scandal. All the bitterness of the Court fight was revived and redoubled. Senators who had opposed the confirmation roared their "I told you so's" loud enough to be heard 'round the world. Many of those who had stoutly championed the new justice now hastened to state publicly that they certainly would never have voted to confirm him had they known he was a Klansman. The "Imperial Wizard" of the Klan, a Georgia dentist named Hiram Evans, helped matters very little with the cryptic statement that "Black is not now a member."

Badgered by his press conferees for a statement, President Roosevelt admitted that, like the late Will Rogers, all he knew was what he read in the papers, said he had not heard from Justice Black, and that he would have nothing to say so long as the justice remained abroad. He added, however, that he had not known Black was a member of the Klan when he sent his nomination to the Senate. He turned a deaf ear to demands that he request the new justice to resign. Efforts on the part of a large section of the press to make Black's position so untenable he would be forced to resign were also fruitless. In his London hotel the Alabaman refused to commit himself on a course of action, refused to comment on the Sprigle articles, re-

[1] Also presented with a life membership card was the new Alabama Governor Bibb Graves who, following Black's elevation to the Supreme Court, appointed his wife, Dixie, to the Senate vacancy.

fused even to receive reporters. Instead he went calmly ahead browsing among second-hand bookstores while the tempest raged on this side of the Atlantic.

Radio Confession. Unhurriedly Justice and Mrs. Black came home on a slow boat, arriving in Norfolk, Va., September 29. Here he was affability itself to the press, but would make no statement other than to intimate that he might present his case to the nation over the radio. Three days later he delivered a brief, eleven-minute address over a nationwide hookup declaring he had decided to break precedent and speak to the nation because attacks made on his appointment threatened to kindle the fires of religious bigotry with a resulting "catastrophe" to the political and social life of America.

He cited his long liberal record in the Senate and his friendship for members of the faiths and races the Klan attacked. But he made no attempt to deny the accusations in the Sprigle articles, nor did he denounce the Klan itself.

"I did join the Klan. I later resigned. I never rejoined. . . . I have never considered and I do not now consider the unsolicited card given me shortly after my nomination to the Senate as a membership in the Ku Klux Klan. I have had nothing whatever to do with it since that time. . . ."

On the Bench. Reaction to the radio apology was varied. A large part of the 30,000,000 listeners were willing to accept at its face value the statement that the Justice was no longer a Klansman. Others were clearly of the opinion that "once a Klansman, always a

Klansman." Those who had most bitterly opposed the
President's Court plan pointed derisively to the fact
that after fighting for six months to get permission to
appoint more liberals to the Court, the President had
in his first appointment chosen a man who had belonged
to an organization whose very name was anathema to
the liberals of the nation.

But on October 4 Justice Black took his seat on the
high court.

Final Challenges. In a final attempt to prevent the
ex-senator from serving on the Supreme Court bench,
two motions were introduced to unseat him on the first
day he appeared with his new colleagues. The first, introduced by Lawyer Patrick Henry Kelley, reiterated
Senator Borah's claim that no vacancy existed. The
second, brought by a former Assistant Attorney General, Albert Levitt, challenged Black's eligibility because the retirement law, passed during his service in
the Senate, in effect increased the compensation of Supreme Court justices. And the Constitution says that
"no Senator or Representative shall, during the term
for which he was elected, be appointed to any civil office
the emoluments whereof shall have been increased during such time."

A week later Chief Justice Hughes announced to a
crowded court room that the petitions of Kelley and
Levitt were denied on the grounds that neither man had
a "sufficient interest" in Justice Black's appointment to
warrant their bringing the actions. Thus, there was
left open a tiny crack through which someone who
might demonstrate "sufficient interest" might at some

later date unseat the justice, but the best bet, as the court settled slowly into its routine, was that the Alabaman was to be a member of the High Court until his death or until that fatal day a few years distant when, having reached the hoary age of 70, he must keep faith with his appointer by retiring to live as best he might on $20,000 per annum.

1937-38 TERM

Biggest question in the minds of Americans scrutinizing the High Court as it opened its 1937-38 term was how far would the apparent new Liberal majority go toward revamping the traditional interpretations of the nation's laws—both old and new. The 1934-35 and 1935-36 terms had clung sternly to time-honored interpretations. The 1936-37 term had closed in a veritable orgy of decisions departing sharply from old paths. Would the 1937-38 session go even further in proving the "elasticity" of the Constitution?

Scottsboro. But by the end of 1937 the Supreme Court had handed down no history-making decisions of the sort which emblazoned front pages the previous spring. Nor was there absolute proof that the Liberal majority established the spring before would continue to hang together.

In a review of the case of Heywood Patterson, one of the nine Negroes convicted by Scottsboro, Ala., courts of raping two white girls, the Court, with Justice Black taking "no part in the consideration and decision of the application," refused to set aside the Alabama court's decision and sentence of 75-years imprisonment. The Scottsboro Defense Committee, with Samuel Leibowitz as chief counsel, indicated they would continue the fight to free Patterson.

Tax Decisions. In two tax decisions the Court voted 5-4 to deny the right of the Federal Government to tax bonuses given employees of the Universal Oil Products Company, and 6-3 that the state of Iowa could levy taxes on income from what had previously been declared tax-exempt bonds of the State and its political subdivisions.

In two far more important tax decisions handed down early in December, the Court by 5-4 opinions (Black voting with the majority) held that the state of Washington and West Virginia were entitled to levy upon the gross income of contractors on Government dams in the Kanawha and Ohio Rivers, and at Grand Coulee. The significance of these decisions lay in the possibility that the High Court might be on the way to revising the entire theory of tax immunity, that cases involving the right of the Federal Government to tax State employees' salaries, soon to be argued, might be decided for the Government by the same line of reasoning. Justice Hughes, in reading the two decisions, declared that the State tax levied on the Government contractors had not imposed an unconstitutional burden upon the Government. Thus the way might be open for modification of the long-established rule under which a State Government had been barred from taxing an instrumentality of the Federal Government, and vice versa.

Anti-trust. On the same day as the Government dam decisions, the Government won a victory when the Court set aside the injunction of a New York court, granted the Justice Department permission to proceed with its case against the Aluminum Co. of America, involving violation of the Sherman Anti-trust Law.

Gold Clause. In mid-December the Government won another important victory in the 6-3 decision sustaining the power of the Treasury to call gold clause Liberty Loan bonds for redemption in currency without paying interest to their original date of maturity. But the edge had already been taken off this decision by the original test of the Government's devaluation program wherein the Court had found for the Government in 1935.

NEW DEAL TESTS TO COME

There remained many New Deal innovations as yet untried before the Supreme Court. There were countless other laws which, invalidated by previous Supreme Courts, would be brought to test again, as had the minimum wage law for women. Occupying the spotlight among anticipated new term decisions, were those concerned with the newly-won rights of Labor, as evidenced in the Wagner Labor Relations Act, and with the right of the Federal Government to enter directly into competition with the public utilities, as it was doing in the TVA area and in a number of other spots throughout the nation.

CHAPTER II

LABOR GAINS SITTING DOWN

Labor discovered, perfected, rejected a new weapon during 1937. Curiously enough, when for the first time since Depression thousands of workers found themselves willing and able to stand on their own feet, they sat down. They sat down in droves. And for a while their sitting baffled an entire nation which failed to recognize in this new mass hysteria essentially the same fleeting components present in the chain letter craze, the miniature golf epidemic, and the Empress Eugenie hat.

For like its predecessors, the Sit-Down mania reached an amazing peak in an incredibly short time. As it spread like windblown flame across the land, it swept into industry on all fronts. Having its greatest success in the mass-production belt line type of industry, it also leaped into utterly unorganized labor. Negress wet nurses of Chicago who didn't know a union from an onion, and who thought John L. Lewis was heavyweight boxing champion, sat down in hospital ante rooms until their demands were met. In Kansas City the freshly dead lay rotting above ground as members of the gravediggers union squatted on their shovels demanding better working conditions, higher pay.

Workmen sat down because others were doing it. It just appeared to be a good idea at the time.

("Kladderadatsch," Berlin)

Sit-down Strike in America.

Fifty Million Frenchmen Had Been Right. Variously credited with originating in a Hungarian mine where miners in 1934 refused to come above ground until their wage demands were met, to a group of rubber workers in Akron, Ohio, to numerous other sources, it was nonetheless obvious that the immediate inspiration for the sit-down came across the Atlantic from France, where workers had achieved gains never before equaled in French labor history by refusing to work while refusing also to quit their places of employment. With a Labor government in power in Paris headed by Socialist Léon Blum, workers had been sure of sympathetic treatment. They got it, and with it a forty-hour week, paid vacations, many other concessions.

If it had worked in France, why not here?   Here also Labor could now count on a national administration and many state governments which, owing much to Labor votes, (United Mine Workers contributed $500,000 to the Democratic campaign) would look with a kindly eye on the workers' struggles for betterment, would not be too critical of the means employed.

Polishing the Weapon.   American ingenuity brought the new labor technique to a high peak of efficiency. Organizers were taught how the proper sit-down should be conducted. While employers stormed and threatened, their employees whiled away their time playing checkers tournaments, listened to speakers from among their ranks, put on skits, staged parties, worked at making comfortable beds from the best of curiously assorted materials. "Arsenals" of bolts, bits of pipe, whatever weapons were available, were stationed near windows where they would be ready to meet the onslaught of strikebreaker or militiaman.   Wives and sweethearts organized "emergency brigades" to supply food for the stay-ins, formed picket lines, even brandished clubs at those who would oust their men from company property.

Human Versus Property Rights. Employers, throwing their hands heavenward in a "What is the world coming to" gesture, cried out against the new weapon as illegal trespass, a violation of their property rights. Union leaders contended that "human rights" came before property rights. One lone law dean, Leon Green of Northwestern University, even maintained there was nothing illegal about the sit-down, that new methods had brought new employer-employee relationships which in turn must bring a new interpretation of the common law.

Congress Sits on Sit-Down. For weeks the Congress of the United States avoided the issue like the plague. New Jersey's Governor Harold G. Hoffman of Hauptmann trial fame warned that "if necessary the entire resources of the state" would be called into play to rout sit-downers in his state. Connecticut's liberal Governor Wilbur L. Cross declared there would be no sit-down strikes in the state so long as he was governor. And Vermont became the first state to pass a law specifically outlawing the sit-down.

But it was late in March before California's Senator Hiram Johnson rose to advise his senatorial colleagues that "the most ominous thing in our national economic life today is the sit-down strike." Then James Hamilton Lewis, Illinois' red-bearded senior senator, followed with the solemn warning that was being echoed across the land by newspaper and radio commentator: "In every hour and condition such as now surrounds this our government there awaits another Hitler and there lurks in the shadows another Mussolini."

Now Senator Wagner rose to expound his opinion that the sit-down, while being illegal under present laws, was not immoral, and that it was an inevitable result of the employers' defiance of the Labor Relations law that bore his name.

As the debate began to draw out more and more senatorial oratory, South Carolina's James F. Byrnes suddenly proposed an amendment to the Administration-sponsored Guffey Coal act, declaring it to be "the public policy of the United States that no employee of any producer of coal whose employment had been terminated, or who for any reason has ceased to work for such producer, shall remain upon the property . . . after he has received a written notice from such producer to leave such property."

This broke down the bars which had been making the subject taboo among Congressmen, and in the next few days 54 senators rose to give their views on the sit-down. The Administration succeeded in defeating the Byrnes amendment, but only after Majority Leader Joe Robinson had promised that a separate sit-down resolution would get early consideration. A few days later a resolution was passed by both houses which condemned the use of the new type of strike, but which also condemned the employers as a class for wholesale evasion of the Labor Relations Act.

End of an Epidemic. Meanwhile the fad had already begun to lose its popularity. Police had learned new and effective ways to deal with sit-downers. When, early in April, angry farmers, swinging club and fist, battered in the doors of the great chocolate plant at Hershey, Pennsylvania, to oust sit-downers and restore the market for their milk, Mr. Average Middle Class American approved. Public opinion, which had been inclined to keep an open mind in the early days of the mania, now began to veer definitely in the direction of "law and order." Shrewd publicity disseminated by corporation public relations counsel with figures and pictures showing damage caused by workers who had occupied plants helped to fan the flame of public resentment. By spring it had just about run its course. But while at its peak it was the most effective offensive weapon Labor had developed since the strike itself was invented, and without it John L. Lewis would never have been able to claim a membership of 4,000,000 in his C.I.O. as the year 1937 closed.

Industrial Unionism. Similarly, without the split between Lewis and William Green and the ensuing formation of the Committee for Industrial Organization to recruit for unionism workers in the mass production industries, the sit-down would not have found such fertile fields in which to blossom. Because William Green, President of the American Federation of Labor, and a majority of delegates at the Federation convention in the fall of 1935 voted no on A. F. of L. Vice President Lewis' proposal to bring together into single unions the unskilled workers in the great steel, automobile,

("*The St. Louis Post-Dispatch*")

"Boys, we'd better go out and stop it!"

rubber, glass and other mass production industries, Mr. Lewis resigned his high office in a huff, set to work organizing these workers on his own hook under the banner of an organization he styled the Committee for Industrial Organization.

GENERAL MOTORS

Among unions which flocked to join Lewis in the C.I.O. was the United Automobile Workers International, a relatively small industrial union which, under a militant program during 1937 was to blossom out into the third largest in the country. Prime requisite in the auto union's program for building up its prestige among the several million workers in this traditionally non-union industry was recognition by the manufacturers. The drive for this recognition began in the latter part of 1936. Striking swiftly at the automobile industry's most vulnerable link, U.A.W. staged a series of sit-downs in Detroit's Midland Steel Products Co. (makers of frames for Ford, Chrysler and others), Bendix accessories plant at South Bend, Indiana, Kelsey-Hayes Wheel Co. of Detroit, other manufacturers whose products kept the great automobile assembly lines running. With unfilled orders piling up and the prospect of the most prosperous season since the Depression, one after another of the parts makers conceded the union's recognition demands, agreed to pay raises.

By December, 1936, the union felt strong enough for a frontal attack on the industry itself.

Strike Spreads Quickly. Late in the year Leader Lewis, taking advantage of a series of spontaneous sit-downs which had broken out in several General Motors plants, delivered an ultimatum to the corporation to abolish the piece work system and the speed-up; institute a six-hour day, 30-hour week, minimum wage, and seniority system; and recognize the United Automobile Workers as the sole collective bargaining agent for all General Motors employees. When General Motors refused, key men in General Motors plants "sat down," stopped more of the great assembly lines, defied courts and law officers to remain in possession of 20 of the company's 69 plants for the 44-day duration of the strike.

Appealing to the courts, General Motors got Circuit Judge Edward D. Black to grant an injunction ordering the sit-downers to evacuate two Fisher body plants in Flint, Michigan, the storm center of the strike. The court order was hooted out of existence by striker and bystander alike when union investigators uncovered evidence that the good judge was a heavy holder of General Motors stock. A second injunction granted by Judge Paul V. Gadola was also disregarded by strikers who wired Governor Frank Murphy of Michigan they would die rather than obey it. The governor, with his political future at stake, saw to it that the men were given no opportunity to die martyrs' deaths, ordered the sheriff not to enforce the order nor the subsequent writ summoning union leaders for contempt of court.

The corporation's claims that only a small minority supported the strikers who could nonetheless close huge plants were given force by the organization of the Flint Alliance, which purported to have a membership of several thousand workmen opposed to the union's activities, and unwilling to have Lewis' men represent them in collective bargaining. Clashes between this group and strike sympathizers forced the governor to send virtually the entire state militia into Flint before the strike was ended.

Mediation.[1] Secretary of Labor Frances Perkins sent one of her ace mediators into the area to negotiate a settlement. He could do nothing against the union leaders' insistence on being recognized as sole collective bargaining agent in the industry, and the refusal of General Motors President Alfred P. Sloan and Executive Vice President William Knudsen to listen to such a proposal. A truce was arranged by Governor Murphy when the strike was about three weeks old, was quickly ended when United Automobile Workers President Homer Martin, an ex-preacher from Kansas, resented the corporation's promise to the Flint Alliance that it would not forget the non-union workers, and would "stand ready always to discuss with your group or any group of our employees any question without prejudice to anyone." "Doublecrossed," shouted Martin, and after having already arranged evacuation of two plants, told sit-downers in the others to sit tight.

Washington Front. Now Secretary Perkins summoned union and company leaders to Washington. Three days after negotiations began in her office, John L. Lewis wrecked them by deliberately trying to force the President of the United States to desert his place on the sidelines and grab up the union's banners. In a blast to the press he declared that Labor, at the request

---

[1] The year's most notable example of mediation occurred in October, when the National Mediation Board set up by the Railway Labor Act settled a threatened strike of Railway brotherhoods. Union representatives accepted the Board's award of an average wage increase of 6½ per cent, in place of the 20 per cent they had been demanding.

of the Administration, had "helped the President repel the economic royalists" in the last election. "The same economic royalists now have their fangs in Labor, and Labor expects the Administration to support the auto workers in every legal way in their fight."

General Motors President Sloan refused to continue the negotiations after Lewis' statement. The President mildly rebuked the C.I.O. leader in his press conference the next morning for making "headlines" which were "not in order." But when Sloan refused to return to Washington, the President more than evened the score by spanking the General Motors executive. ". . . I was not only disappointed in the refusal of Mr. Sloan to come to Washington, but I regarded it as a very unfortunate decision."

Dividends. Perhaps Mr. Sloan felt he was too busy watching his profits decline to return to the nation's capital. In December, during one peak week before the strike got under way, General Motors had turned out 53,000 automobiles. In the first week of February only 500, mostly trucks, rolled off the assembly lines. Result: a cut in quarterly dividends from fifty to twenty-five cents a share.

White House Intervention. Finally, after the impasse had lasted for more than a month, a telephone call came from the White House. The President of the United States authorized Governor Murphy to call a conference of opposing leaders in his, the President's, name. And after eight days of almost uninterrupted negotiation, with the President telephoning daily to insist on some sort of settlement, Governor

Murphy crammed peace terms down the disputants' throats, enabling 135,000 workers to return to work in mid-February, six weeks after the strike's beginning.

Settlement. In the court room of Judge George Murphy, brother of the governor, John L. Lewis and William Knudsen scratched their names to a settlement the principal provisions of which were as follows:

(1) The union called off the strike; (2) both sides would keep the peace, with no coercion, no recruiting of union members on company property, no further court action by the company (Three days after the settlement negotiations opened Judge Gadola had issued a writ ordering the arrest of the sit-downers and fifteen union officials for contempt of court. Again Murphy ordered the sheriff to ignore the judge's orders.); (3) negotiations would begin immediately on the grievances of the union as to the speed-up, wages and hours, with production being resumed at once; (4) General Motors agreed to recognize the automobile workers union as collective bargaining agent FOR ITS MEMBERS.

Who Won? To sideline observers the settlement terms looked very much like a defeat for John L. Lewis and his auto workers. They were forced to give in on their demand for "sole" collective bargaining rights for the entire industry. The corporation had offered to grant them bargaining rights for their own members before the strike ever started. On the other hand the union, controlling only a minority of the industry's employees, had obtained a signed contract with a member of the traditionally non-union automobile industry, distinctly a leg up for organized labor. But the union's principal gain was contained, not in the formal settlement terms, but in a letter written by Executive Vice President Knudsen to Governor Murphy. In it he declared that whereas the corporation could not "deny to any group of our employees the rights of collective bargaining," it had no intention of deliberately bargaining with other groups "for the purpose of undermining the position of this particular union," and agreed that "WITHIN A PERIOD OF SIX MONTHS FROM THE RESUMPTION OF WORK we will not bargain with or enter into agreements with any other union or representatives of employees or plants on strike in respect to . . . matters of general corporate policy . . . without first submitting to you [Governor Murphy] the facts of the situation and gaining from you the sanction of any such contemplated procedure as being justified by law, equity or justice toward the group of employees so represented."

The strike period had enabled union organizers to swell membership ranks enormously. Now they saw in Knudsen's letter a promise of a six months' grace period during which they could build up their union to a point where they would control a majority of the industry's workers. After that they might call an election as provided under the National Labor Relations Act, and with the vote of a majority of the workers in their favor, demand their legal right to be sole collective bargaining agents for all the employees.

With neither side able to claim complete victory

then, as good a guess as any was that the real winner had been Michigan's governor, whose astute handling of the strike launched a boom which many thought might lead him to the White House in 1940.

Back to Work. Sit-downers evacuated the twenty struck plants immediately upon hearing the settlement terms and the Knudsen letter. When they returned to work it was to find an increase of five cents an hour in their wages, announced by General Motors the day of the settlement. Although sporadic "wildcat" or unauthorized sit-downs continued to break out in the plants in succeeding weeks, United Automobile Workers President Martin gradually browbeat his men into accepting his leadership and living up to the signed contract.

Oshawa Agreement. After obtaining the agreement with General Motors in this country, the auto union now turned its attention across the border to Oshawa, Ontario, where a Canadian subsidiary of the corporation maintained a large plant. Demands for hour and wage changes and union recognition were refused by the company. A strike of General Motors employees was called. In contrast to the stand of Michigan's governor, Premier Mitchell Hepburn of Ontario jumped into the fray on the side of the corporation, declaring that "illegal sit-downs" promoted by "foreign agitators" would not be tolerated. Although two of his ministers resigned, he got his cabinet to decide to grant no relief to strikers. He refused to confer with U. S. union officials even when Union President Martin threatened to call a sympathetic strike in

LABOR IN ACTION

Top: Ford employees attack C.I.O. leader Frankensteen (Wide World). *Bottom:* Pickets "stopping" employee in steel strike (Acme).

LABOR STRIFE

Top: Ten strikers die when police "shoot to kill" (Life Magazine). *Right:* Embattled women help their mates (Life Magazine).

all the corporation's plants in the United States. Finally, late in April after the strike had lasted sixteen days, the Premier agreed to treat with local union officials, but not with officers from the United States. The settlement which followed upped wages from five to seven cents an hour, reduced hours from 50 to 44.

If Governor Murphy had vastly improved his political status in Labor-conscious Michigan, Premier Hepburn had also greatly heightened his popularity among Canadians who had been inclined to "view with alarm" the rising tide of Labor across the border, and who cherished the traditional concept of property rights.

CHRYSLER

With the General Motors contract under their belts, the U. S. union leaders now directed their guns toward Chrysler. Negotiations between the corporation and union leaders early in March were deadlocked when President Walter P. Chrysler refused the union's demand for sole collective bargaining rights—the same goal it had failed to achieve in the General Motors strike. In the case of Chrysler, however, the union claimed (and the company did not try to refute) the support of a substantial majority of the company workers. Unlike the General Motors strike also, the union made no wage and hour demands. Chrysler had upped wages ten per cent the day before the General Motors strike ended. The issue was solely one of recognition, then, and Chrysler refused to grant the union's demands in this regard.

Calling on the experience gained in the last two

months, Auto Union Leader Homer Martin called a sit-down which closed all Chrysler plants in the Detroit area, throwing 55,000 employees out of work.

Just Another Injunction. Chrysler did what General Motors had done—went to court and got an injunction. But by now strikers had learned they could safely thumb their noses at this legal instrument. Ordered to evacuate its men from the eight struck plants within 48 hours, the union responded by gathering some 30,000 roaring sympathizers in giant picket lines around the Chrysler properties. At the end of the 48-hour period a warrant was issued for the arrest of the sit-downers. But this time the sheriff needed no command from the governor to prevent him from carrying out the warrant. Eyeing the belligerent workers guarding plant windows and doors, he figured it would require an army of at least 30,000 men to storm the plants. Not having any such force at his command, he concluded that discretion was the better part of valor.

The "Great Mediator." Governor Murphy, who had been taking a well-earned vacation in Florida after establishing a reputation as the "Great Mediator" in the General Motors strike, rushed back to Detroit to summon Lewis and Chrysler to a conference. In return for a promise not to resume operations in his factories until after final negotiations were over, John L. Lewis agreed to evacuate the struck plants at once. U.A.W. President Martin spent twelve solid hours haranguing sit-downers before they all marched out. Then, after eleven days of negotiation, a settlement was reached. Again Lewis had been unable to put over his demand for sole bargaining rights. Walter Chrysler had stood pat, as had Alfred Sloan. Again Lewis could point to a signed contract for the union. But that contract read: "The corporation agrees to bargain with the union as the collective bargaining agency for such of its employees as are members of the union." The contract further provided that the company would not discriminate against union members nor promote or finance rival unions. But the union also promised not to coerce employees to join, nor to permit its members to take part in any sit-down or other strike in any Chrysler plant for one year—the life of the agreement.

The Chrysler strike was settled in mid-April, more than five weeks after it started. Meanwhile sit-downs had developed in Reo and Hudson plants. Day after the Chrysler agreement was reached Governor Murphy settled these two strikes on the same terms.

Sole Collective Bargaining Rights. A few weeks later, after the Wagner Labor Relations Act had been upheld by the Supreme Court of the United States, a labor election was held among employees of Packard Motor Company. Here the auto union won a four to one majority, and for the first time was granted the right to be the only collective bargaining agency for the employees of an automobile manufacturer.

FORD

It was no accident that the auto union had left until last its drive on Ford Motor Company. The tightly-controlled, family-owned concern was far less vulnerable than its contemporaries. The aging founder of a system of mass-production which had brought the automobile down out of the luxury class and revolutionized countless other manufacturing industries which copied his belt line assembly methods breathed fire at the very mention of unionism. Even after contracts with the auto union were signed by General Motors and Chrysler, Henry Ford declared, "We'll never recognize the United Automobile Workers Union or any other union." And if union leaders doubted his fighting ability they had only to check back through the records of the NRA to discover that he had defied the United States government for two years and got away with it. He had said his company would never join the National Recovery Administration, and it never had.

Ford paid high wages, had in fact been chiefly responsible for the high wages which prevailed in the entire industry. He had instituted a $5.00 minimum daily wage at a time when such pay was considered the height of foolhardiness by most employers in the land. Yet the union complained that he demanded highest efficiency from his men, forbade them to talk on the assembly line, had no scruples about laying them off for long periods during slack seasons, and fired his employees if he found they had joined a union.

Battle of River Rouge. So "Ford is next," was the cry of union leaders as soon as the Chrysler contract was signed. Sit-downs had broken out in several Ford plants during the winter, but had been settled in short order. The union had not been ready to take on its bitterest foe in the automobile industry. But in mid-May offices were set up in Dearborn, Michigan, home of the great Ford industries, and a Ford Organizing Committee began signing up members. The blandishments of the union organizers were countered by printed "Fordisms" written by the founder and distributed among his employees. "Figure it out for yourself," he wrote. "If you go into a union, they have got you and what have you got?"

Union organizers advised employees they should be demanding an $8.00 six-hour day. A group of them, including Richard T. Frankensteen, a former college football star, were severely beaten up by Ford company guards as they began distributing literature containing these demands in front of the Dearborn River Rouge Ford plant. Harry Bennet, Ford man in charge of the company guards, disclaimed all responsibility for the beating, contending that regular employees, not the company guards, had turned on the handbill distributors after they had been goaded and called "scabs." Cameramen on the scene, however, were able to get clear pictures of the mauling, from which it was possible to identify the Ford guards.

United Automobile Workers then brought charges against the company before the National Labor Relations Board, and at the union convention late in August delegates unanimously adopted a motion calling for a special assessment of $1 a member to raise a war chest to carry the fight to Ford.[1]

[1] The Labor Board ruled Ford guilty of violating the Wagner Act in a decision handed down Dec. 24. The manufacturer planned to appeal to the Supreme Court.

"BIG STEEL"

The one U. S. industry the mere mention of which had made Labor leaders see red for almost half a century was Steel. Back in 1892 the Amalgamated Association of Iron, Steel and Tin Workers was one of the strongest unions in the land. It had an iron-clad wage contract with the great Carnegie Steel Company. The contract expired in that year, and in arranging a new one the steel company proposed a wage cut. The union refused, and Andrew Carnegie's right hand man, Henry Clay Frick, who was managing the company in his chief's absence, refused to negotiate, threw up a barbed wire fence around the plant and locked the workers out.

When the men surrounded the plant in Homestead, Pennsylvania (seven miles from Pittsburgh), refusing to permit strikebreakers to enter, Frick sent to New York for 300 Pinkerton detectives. On a misty dawn in July these imported strikebreakers came stealthily up the Monongahela river on a barge. As the first Pinkerton man stepped ashore someone fired a shot. The detectives then opened fire and one of the bloodiest battles in U. S. Labor history was on. By five o'clock that afternoon three detectives and seven workers lay dead, hundreds of others lay wounded, battered and broken.

At the governor's orders the Pennsylvania state militia poured into the town, protected the strikebreakers, and finally starved the union into abject submission. Amalgamated's power was broken, and for

44 years it barely kept alive as the steel industry refused to recognize or treat with any labor union.

"Remember Homestead."   In the breast of John L. Lewis that humiliating Labor defeat rankled until he determined to humble the industry as it had humbled the union.   Here were a half million workers, of which only a paltry 7,000 were unionized.   In June 1936 he served notice on the steel masters that a drive was on which would not stop until they were again ready to sign union contracts.   Dumping $500,000 into the laps of startled old Amalgamated Iron, Steel and Tin union officials, he then formed the Steel Workers Organizing Committee, appointed his ablest lieutenant, Phillip Murray, to head the drive.

A giant mass meeting was staged near the scene of the battle with the Pinkertons, and with a cry of "Remember Homestead," organizers poured into the steel towns loaded with application blanks.   By the end of 1936 C.I.O. claimed 200,000 new recruits for the steel union and the industry braced itself for the greatest industrial battle of the generation, the attack on what John L. Lewis termed the "crouching lion in the pathway of Labor."

Carnegie-Illinois Capitulates.   Then suddenly and without warning came the astounding news late in February that, without the breaking of a single picket's head, an agreement had been reached between the Steel Workers Organizing Committee and Carnegie-Illinois Steel Corporation, biggest steel-producing unit in the world, and, what was even more significant, the biggest

subsidiary of the biggest anti-union force in the world
—United States Steel. Actually signed by Phillip Mur-

("*The New York Times*")

"Green" with Envy?

ray and Benjamin F. Fairless, president of Carnegie-
Illinois, the contract had apparently been agreed to
earlier at a friendly across-the-table session between
Lewis and Myron C. Taylor, U. S. Steel's board chairman. Those with long memories recalled that Mr.

Taylor had paid a visit to the White House early in the year.

First Contract Since 1892. The contract, to last until February 28, 1938, (1) upped steel workers' wages from a basic $4.20 to $5 a day, lowered the work week from 48 to 40 hours (this the steel corporation was only too glad to do because of the Walsh-Healy act preventing the U. S. government from buying anything produced under a work week in excess of 40 hours), (2) included the customary promises by the union not to recruit members on company property in return for which the company agreed not to discriminate against union employees nor interfere with union recruiting, (3) and recognized the Amalgamated Association of Iron, Steel and Tin Workers as the bargaining agent for its members among the corporation's 120,000 employees.

The simplest explanation for the capitulation of the U. S. Steel could be found in the fact that its business was booming. A strike might set back production weeks or months, cost the industry millions. Furthermore, in a seller's market such as it was entering, the increased costs resulting from the raised wages and lessened hours might be passed along to the consumer. This it did immediately by upping steel prices from $3 to $8 a ton.

C.I.O.'s Greatest Victory. The steel contract was C.I.O.'s greatest victory since its organization. Workers now flocked to join its unions. Sixty-five hundred new applications were entered within two days after the agreement. John L. Lewis' prestige was at its highest

peak, and Myron C. Taylor's "industrial statesmanship" (so-called by Mr. Lewis) strengthened the C.I.O.
position on the automobile and other fronts.

"LITTLE STEEL"

When U. S. Steel deserted steel's united front to
sign up with C.I.O., the "independent" companies in
the industry fell all over each other rushing to put into
effect in their plants the same wage and hour terms
agreed to by Taylor and Lewis.   But they made no
secret of the fact they considered they had been "sold
down the river."   Furthermore, the greatest among
these independents—Bethlehem, Republic, Youngstown
Sheet & Tube, National, Crucible, Inland, and American Rolling Mill—emphatically refused to sign any
sort of written contract with the union.

The Wagner Labor Relations Act, by now validated
by the Supreme Court, forced them to bargain collectively with representatives of their employees.   They
contended, however, that there was nothing in the act
which required them to put any agreement resulting
from such bargaining into writing.   They contended
that the union was not a legally responsible organization, that its signature on a contract meant nothing,
could not be enforced.   They also were well aware that
their signatures on contracts with the union would be
another great asset for the C.I.O. in its drive to capture
the majority of the steel industry's 550,000 workers.
And they anticipated a demand by the union for a
closed shop (plant in which all workers must belong
to the union) in Carnegie-Illinois when the contract

with that U. S. Steel subsidiary expired the following February. It might cost them millions, but if they could lick the union in a test of strength, thereby lessening its prestige, they might postpone or possibly prevent the evil day when Amalgamated would act for all their workers, saddle them with the dreaded closed shop.

Jones & Laughlin Poll. With the U. S. Steel agreement under his belt, Lewis was in no mood to rest on his laurels. One-fourth of the steel industry's output came from these eight great independents. Two hundred thousand workers were in their employ. Striking in the one independent where their organizers had been most successful in recruiting members, the Steel Workers Organizing Committee presented the management of Jones & Laughlin with a demand for a union contract. When the company refused, workers in the Aliquippa, Pennsylvania, and Pittsburgh plants walked out. (High fences surrounding plants, plus efficient company guards, plus inaccessibility of plants to a food supply made the sit-down technique ill-suited to the steel industry.) The strike lasted only 36 hours. Then the company agreed to permit the National Labor Relations Board to poll its workers on their preference for a bargaining agent, abide by the poll results. The vote showed 70 per cent of the workers favoring the union. This bound Jones & Laughlin to recognize Amalgamated as the SOLE bargaining agency, whereas the contract with U. S. Steel had given the union bargaining rights for its own members only.

This overwhelming vote scared several of the inde-

pendents into signing agreements on the terms nego-
tiated with "Big Steel," but Republic, Bethlehem, Inland, Youngstown, stood pat.

Strike in "Little Steel." Late in May Phillip Murray, head of the Steel Workers Organizing Committee,
got the nod from Lewis, called the strikes in "Little
Steel" which were to produce the year's bitterest bloodiest Labor battles.

Republic Steel's rough and ready President Tom
Girdler took charge of the company forces as generalissimo. His resolute refusal to "sign anything" spurred
his fellow steel officials to resist with every means at
their disposal the series of strikes which spread
through their plants. In some plants workers sympathetic with the management were quartered on the job
—a version of the stay-in used against Labor. Strikers
fired on planes bringing food to these workers, piled
ties on tracks to prevent supplies entering the plants.
Attempts to mail food and supplies to workers remaining in the plants were met by refusal of local post-
masters to accept such "unusual" shipments. Republic
protested to Postmaster General Farley against this
interference with the U. S. mails, causing a Senate investigation in which the highlight was Tom Girdler's
testimony that Phillip Murray was a "liar," and Senator Guffey of Pennsylvania "didn't know what he was
talking about."

Martial Law. Ohio Governor Martin L. Davey
clapped Youngstown under martial law when rioting
between strikers and company sympathizers killed two,
wounded 25. Forty thousand sympathetic coal miners

then threatened to march on Youngstown, were finally called off by John L. Lewis.

The feeling between striker and strikebreaker became so ugly at the Bethlehem plant in Cambria, Pennsylvania, that Governor George H. Earle asked Bethlehem's Board Chairman Eugene Grace to close the plant. When Grace refused, the governor ordered the plant closed.

Vomiting Gas. At Monroe, Michigan, the city election commission claimed to have polled the workers in the Republic plant in that city, reported a majority anxious to return to work. American Legionnaires then joined the mayor and police in opening the plant by force, using vomiting gas to rout the pickets.

Chicago Massacre. Bloodiest fighting of the six-weeks' strike occurred at the Republic plant in South Chicago. For two days crowds of strikers had been marching on the plant, trying to force its closing. Police drove them off with their night sticks. On the third day a mob estimated at 1,500 gathered for a new onslaught, began hurling rocks and steel bolts. Police drew guns and charged, firing into the crowd. When the smoke cleared away seven lay dead or dying, 100 others were carried away to hospitals.

Paramount News filmed the riot, then refused to release it for weeks on the ground it might cause more riots. Chairman Robert M. La Follette of the Senate Civil Liberties Investigating Committee subpoenaed the film, showed it to his committee and other Congressmen, declared publicly after investigating the massacre that there had been no provocation by strikers sufficient to justify the brutality of the police.

Paul Y. Anderson, writing in the St. Louis *Post Dispatch* after seeing the film, declared, "It made me want to go out and bite a policeman. . . . Without apparent warning, there is a terrific roar of pistol shots, and men in the front ranks of the marchers go down like grass before a scythe. . . . Instantly the police charge on the marchers with riot sticks flying. . . . In one scene . . . a policeman gives a fallen man a final smash on the head before moving on to the next job."

Mediation. By mid-June, Labor Secretary Perkins was ready to step into the strike picture with a mediation board appointed by her and comprised of the dean of the Wisconsin Law School, Lloyd K. Garrison, Undersecretary of Labor Edward F. McGrady, and Charles P. Taft, II, progressive son of the late Chief Justice and President.

Mediation got off to a bad start immediately when Girdler informed the board, which he considered definitely pro-Labor, that he and his friends would sign nothing. It broke down completely when the steel men gave no indication of weakening in their "standpatism."

Then Republic and Youngstown Sheet & Tube announced they were reopening their plants in spite of hell, highwater and pickets.

"Stop This Butchery." At this ultimatum armies of pickets began swarming into Mahoning and Trumbull counties in Ohio, location of the plants the operators were determined to reopen. John L. Lewis telephoned Secretary Perkins to "stop this contemplated butchery!" Finally President Roosevelt intervened directly to wire Girdler and Youngstown's President Frank Purnell in the "name of public safety" and a "reasonable and peaceful settlement" not to reopen.

Governor Davey followed up the Presidential request by sending 4,800 national guards into the troubled area with orders to keep closed plants shut, permit those already operating to continue to operate free from interference other than lawful picketing, disarm all persons not officers of the law, and keep non-residents out of the area.

"Right to Work Is Sacred." Governor Davey, who was hailed by Labor leaders when he first sent troops into the strike sector, was roundly damned by them a few days later when he announced that the right to work was as sacred as the right to strike, ordered troopers to protect all workers who wanted to return to their jobs. Governor Earle then withdrew his troopers from Cambria, permitting the great Bethlehem plant there to reopen. This broke the strike's backbone.

Dynamiting of plant water supplies in Youngstown and Canton did the union forces no good, even though a C.I.O. organizer was "purged" from the union for his part in the Canton affair. And the conviction of four union members for bombing the Republic plant at Warren, Ohio, was another black eye for the strikers. "Back-to-work" sentiment was growing stronger and stronger.[1] One after another this sentiment forced the

[1] Many of the steel workers got back to work just in time to be laid off, as the business recession forced plant after plant to close its doors.

opening of plants. When Indiana's Governor Town-
send finally patched up a truce between SWOC and
Youngstown Sheet & Tube Co., making only a few
changes in the company's policy regarding vacations,
no struck plants remained closed, and even the most
class-conscious striker was ready to admit that the
strike in "Little Steel" had failed.

LABOR'S HOUSE DIVIDED

Far more serious to Labor as a whole than the loss
of the Little Steel battle was the fact that the close of
1937 found trade unionism in America still split right
down the middle.   John L. Lewis might counter this
last defeat by pointing to the agreement with "Big
Steel," still the major part of the industry, and also to
the impressive gains during the year on other mass
production Labor fronts—oil, glass, rubber, automobile, mining.   But so long as the strength of C.I.O.
and A. F. of L. was being sapped by civil war, all these
gains might well prove evanescent, might easily be
wiped out by anti-Labor forces shrewdly playing one
faction off against the other.

Counter-offensive. Late in May, 1937, Green issued a call for a counter-offensive against the powerful
organizing drive of the C.I.O. which was continuing
undiminished, and daily seducing more unions from
the Federation ranks. Representatives of 102 national
and international unions met in special session at Cincinnati and mapped a plan of battle which included:
(1) Doubling dues members pay the Federation (thus
raising them to 2 cents a month) to raise a war chest.

(2) Hiring of 100 new organizers for a drive on all fronts to offset C.I.O. gains. (3) Requiring all local unions to join city central bodies and state Federations. Many local unions had joined C.I.O. even though their national officers remained loyal to the A. F. of L. (4) Ousting from city central bodies and state Federations all unions which had affiliated with C.I.O.

Keynoting that "the first dual movement occurred in Heaven itself, a place where harmony and peace prevailed," President Green declared that "There are men in mass production industries appealing for admission to the A. F. of L. now. Up to this time I have said no. But the clock has struck and the hour is here. We are going to give them a home in the A. F. of L. if they will come in." These fighting words fell a little flat on the ears of those with long memories. Admission of the mass production workers into the Federation had been precisely what had started all the shooting. It was because Green had refused to adopt this course eighteen months earlier that Lewis had pulled out.

Dualism. On the other hand, Green now felt that his accusations that Lewis had been trying all along to set up a dual organization had been proved, and he justified his action as self-defense. In March the executive officers of C.I.O. announced that they had decided to "issue certificates of affiliation to national, international, state, regional, city central bodies, and local groups whenever it is deemed such action is advisable." This resolution formally set C.I.O. up as a rival of A. F. of L.

Immediate result of the Federation special session was the "purge" of those local unions which had gone over to C.I.O. New York City expelled 46 unions with a membership of 250,000, and 27 were ousted in Chicago.

Pacific Coast Rivalry. Perhaps the bitterest example of C.I.O.-A. F. of L. rivalry was still being fought out on the Pacific coast as the year ended. As President of the Pacific Coast District of the International Longshoremen's Association, a radical young Australian named Harry Bridges had been given the nod by Lewis to bring all workers in any way connected with west coast shipping under C.I.O. banners. But the Pacific coast had long been the domain of Seattle's Dave Beck, the hardboiled regional executive of the Teamsters Union which had remained loyal to the A. F. of L. When Bridges began extending his organizing drive to the warehousemen, who stood midway between the longshoremen and the teamsters in the shipping picture, Beck got the A. F. of L. to award his teamsters jurisdiction over the warehousemen. In the warfare which followed Beck finally ordered his teamsters to cease trucking all goods handled by the Bridges longshoremen, and during the early fall of 1937 a virtual embargo of the entire waterfront developed. Harassed shippers in San Francisco, Seattle and other ports found this problem almost as knotty as the strike of maritime workers which had stopped all shipping on the Pacific coast in the fall of 1936.

Dave Beck also challenged the C.I.O. in the Pacific northwest's great lumber industry. In October the National Labor Relations Board designated the C.I.O. woodworkers' union as the bargaining agency for the logging camps and sawmills. The A. F. of L. refused to recognize the validity of this decision, and called a boycott on C.I.O. lumber. A. F. of L. carpenters refused to use the lumber, and Beck's teamsters would not haul it. Oregon's Governor Charles H. Martin and Portland's Mayor Joseph K. Carson then denounced the Labor Board and demanded that it withdraw from the scene unless it could enforce its decisions. The closed lumber mills, with their thousands of employees out of work, added greatly to Oregon's relief load as winter came on.

National Labor Relations Board. The difficulties faced by the National Labor Relations Board in the Pacific northwest were an indication of the stormy life the Board had led since its inception. Employers generally had refused to take its orders seriously until the Wagner Labor Relations Act, which established the Board, was validated by the Supreme Court in the spring of the year. By this time its job had been vastly complicated by the split within Labor. Toughest jobs it had in 1937 were those of deciding whether C.I.O. or A. F. of L. unions should be the bargaining agents in various industries.

That this could not be done without making enemies was attested by the fact that the Board was denounced by both C.I.O. and A. F. of L. conventions in October. Many employers turned to the A. F. of L. unions as the more conservative of two evils, and tried to sign contracts which would bar the C.I.O. from invading the ranks of their workers. A typical example of this was the case of the National Electric Products Corp. at Ambridge, Pa. For months C.I.O. and A. F. of L. unions had battled for control of the company's 1,600 workers. Then suddenly the company signed an exclusive bargaining contract with the A. F. of L. calling for a closed shop. This meant that every C.I.O. man in the shop had to join the A. F. of L. union and have dues deducted from his pay. To strengthen their position, the A. F. of L also obtained a court order demanding that the company live up to its contract. C.I.O. appealed to the Labor Board, which ruled the contract null and void. The company was then on the spot trying to decide which of two Federal agencies to obey—Court or Labor Board. Indications were that the case would be carried to the Supreme Court, which in the next twelve months would be called on to solve many such problems involving the jurisdiction of the new Board.[1]

MOVES TOWARD PEACE

Conventions. When the A. F. of L. met in annual convention at Denver early in October, while Green continued to blast Lewis as a traitor with "consuming" political ambitions, and Lewis, from the C.I.O. convention which met at the same time in Atlantic City, termed the A. F. of L. leader a "frightened little boy,"

[1] Members of the NLRB: Chairman Joseph W. Madden, 47-year-old former law professor at Cornell, Stanford, Chicago, other universities; Donald W. Smith, Philadelphia lawyer and son of a steel worker; Edwin S. Smith, former employment manager of Boston's famed Filene department store, and Massashusetts Commissioner of Labor and Industries.

there were strong undercurrents in both organizations working for peace.

Peace Offers. C.I.O. came through strategically with the first offer. Its leaders sent a telegram to Denver suggesting that 100 men from each organization be appointed as a peace committee. A. F. of L. refused to agree to this, but offered to have its "permanent peace committee" of three men headed by George M. Harrison, president of the Railway Clerks brotherhood, meet a smaller C.I.O. group. Finally 10 C.I.O. officers, headed by Steel Workers Organizing Committee Chairman Philip Murray, met the A. F. of L. group in discussions which began in the closing days of October.

Again C.I.O. was first with a plan. Lewis' forces offered to return to the Federation if they could remain as an autonomous division with sole jurisdiction over its own and future industrial unions which it demanded the right to organize in certain fields. C.I.O. also suggested that a national joint A. F. of L.-C.I.O. convention be called immediately to ratify the agreement.

Green's men refused this plan, offered their own which was turned down just as flatly by C.I.O. The A. F. of L. plan demanded (1) the twelve C.I.O. unions which were formerly A. F. of L. members in good standing return to the Federation; (2) the 20 newly chartered C.I.O. unions be amalgamated with corresponding Federation unions on terms to be settled at a conference; (3) the C.I.O. be *dissolved*.

Trouble with the C.I.O. plan, from Mr. Green's standpoint, was that (1) if Lewis' claims to a membership of 4,000,000 were exact, the entrance of that number into his organization as a unit under Lewis' control would mean complete domination of the Federation by the "autonomous" C.I.O., since the A. F. of L. could claim a membership of only 3,800,000. For under A. F. of L. rules of one convention delegate for every hundred members Lewis would have Mr. Green outvoted. (2) If C.I.O. were granted the right to organize and control industrial unions in the mass production industries, certain A. F. of L. unions such as the machinists and electricians, which had members in these industries, would have their toes stepped on. Thus the issue was no longer one of industrial versus craft unionism so much as it was one of personal and individual union power.

Pressure from Above and Below. Although the peace conference which began late in October broke down a few days later when neither faction would yield on any important issues, there was still strong reason to believe that the breach might be closed. The rank and file in Labor were becoming more and more convinced that petty jealousies were keeping their forces divided, and undoubtedly both Green and Lewis were also being subjected to gentle pressure from above. The President of the United States had made no secret of his desire to see the fight ended.

Face to Face. On December 2 the two men came together for a two-day conference at Washington, D. C. But apparently nothing was gained by this meeting. Lewis left the conference room growling that the status quo still existed, and the peace negotiations were turned back to the original committee. Meanwhile there were indications that the business recession, which had hit the steel, automobile, and other mass production industries hardest, was weakening the C.I.O. position. Thousands of workers in these industries had been laid off during the fall, had no money for union dues. Some observers reasoned that the A. F. of L., well aware of this condition, was less willing than ever to make any concessions. Another cause of glee among A. F. of L. chieftains was the trouble in one of C.I.O.'s biggest unions, the United Automobile Workers. President Homer Martin was having a tough time keeping control of his organization against the onslaughts of the more radical members led by Vice President Wyndham Mortimer. This intra-union strife not only gave C.I.O. a black eye throughout the nation, but undoubtedly played a part in the defeat of the C.I.O. candidates in the Detroit elections of city officials. Here, for the first time, C.I.O. entered politics directly. Its candidate for mayor, Patrick O'Brien, was defeated by the conservative Richard W. Reading, who got belated A. F. of L. support, and none of the C.I.O. nominees to the city council was elected.

Still Divided. Representatives comprising the original peace committee met again December 21, but ran up against the same old stone wall of stubbornness on both sides. This time they called it quits, announced no future peace meetings, and leaders loudly shouted that henceforth the fight would be to the death.

CHAPTER III

THE PRESIDENT AND THE 75th CONGRESS: FROM LOVE FEAST TO FREE-FOR-ALL

"THE SECOND NEW DEAL"

Starting as a love feast, the first regular session of the 75th Congress wound up as a free-for-all. Beginning its deliberations with the greatest Democratic majority the country had ever seen—76 Senators out of 96; 331 out of the 435 Representatives—the Congress which was supposed to inaugurate the "Second New Deal" degenerated into a free-swinging Battle Royal. Actual legislative accomplishments could be transcribed on a single page; its record of unfinished business filled volumes.

With the smaller Democratic majorities in the 73rd and 74th Congresses the New Deal had been stormily brought into being. In the hectic days of the 73rd, 27 major laws were passed to carry the Federal Government into the hinterland of territory it had never before explored. The "alphabetical" agencies had popped like startled rabbits out of a Congressional hutch whose caretakers reveled in the strong leadership coming from the White House, had no shame about voting on bills they did not pretend to understand. The AAA, NRA, CWA, HOLC, CCC, TVA and a host of other untried ventures had been launched

78

in the bubbling-over atmosphere of that first of the
New Deal Congresses. And the sessions of the 74th
had plunged confidently into such fields as national
labor relations, social security, banking reform—albeit

("*The Akron Beacon Journal*")

Is There Life Left in the Old Baby?

theirs was partly a job of patching up damage done the experimental program by an "unreconstructed" Supreme Court.

Repair work was also scheduled to occupy a part of the time of the 75th Congress, but because its members got all tangled up in bitterness it accomplished little beyond the patchwork. Three things could be blamed for this do-nothing course: (1) a President, re-elected by an overwhelming plurality, refused to rest on his oars, goaded his great party majority ever onward until it reared back on its haunches in its own version of a sit-down strike; (2) a Supreme Court issue which crossed party lines, gave rise to a flood of angry oratory lasting from February to July (see Chapter I); (3) a suddenly re-awakened Congressional interest in economy.

A "Mandate." When 27,700,000 voters returned Franklin Delano Roosevelt to the White House in November 1936, he interpreted this overwhelming vote as a "mandate" to go full speed ahead with the program of social reform which he had begun during his first term with a "New Deal" for the American people. Yet between the election and the opening of Congress in January there had developed a false hope among many of the President's conservative opponents that now finally he was ready to rest on his oars, to forsake change for consolidation. Perhaps his comparatively mild attitude toward the Supreme Court during the campaign proper, his admissions that some phases of his program might have been improved by more deliberation, his indications that it might be necessary to overhaul a few of the early experiments, gave birth to this wishful thinking. Perhaps also his post-election statement to Hyde Park neighbors: "Now I am going back to do what they call balance the budget," had fed these hopes.

State of the Union. But 1937 was only a few days old before all such yearnings after an "era of good feeling" were rudely jarred out of the national mind. Change, or at least attempt at change, was still to be the order of the day. Even the President's state-of-the-union opening address to Congress, mild in itself, emphasized departure from the traditional.

"For the first time in our national history a President delivers his annual message to Congress within a fortnight of the expiration of his term of office," said the Chief Executive. The 20th amendment to the Constitution, fathered by Nebraska's George Norris, had pushed the inauguration date ahead six weeks, provided for an earlier end to the President's first term.

Inauguration. And when on January 20 Franklin Roosevelt had stood bareheaded in a drenching rain to receive the oath of office from Chief Justice of the Supreme Court, Charles Evans Hughes, he had again given at least a broad hint of the course he intended to follow in the next four years. "The test of our progress is not whether we add more to the abundance of those who have much; it is whether we provide enough for those who have too little." Still concerned with that underprivileged one-third of the nation, the President was indicating he had no intention of treading water now. It was sink or swim with the program he had mapped out. And if by the end of 1937 the Second New Deal was fighting heavy seas against the headwinds of a rebellious Congress it was evidence of no real change in the Skipper's course.

Messages to Congress. Day after day he shot new ideas to Congress in sharply-outlined messages. Because he felt that he and the rest of the executives were not doing as good a job as they might, he called for authorization to completely reorganize the executive branch of the Federal Government. While flood waters were roaring over thousands of square miles in eastern states he urged Congress to adopt the report of his National Resources Committee recommending a six-year $5,000,000,000 program of co-ordinated public works to provide flood control, drainage, grade crossing elimination—10,000 other projects. He flashed the lightning bolt court reform plan.

When he beat Alf Landon to the draw the previous fall by suggesting crop insurance for farmers he had set a committee to studying this Biblical idea. Late in February the committee's report was ready and sent to Congress as a Presidential message. Stressing the need for legislation to replace the outlawed NRA, he had urged a statute to establish minimum wages, maximum work weeks. And he had asked Congress to duplicate his beloved TVA experiment in six other areas throughout the nation so that the entire country might be divided into seven great regional areas for purposes of national planning, flood control, conservation, and cheap electric power.

All these things he asked Congress to do. But an

uncertain and unwieldy Democratic majority supported by a tiny Republican minority balked, bogged down, and refused to do any of them.

OLD BUSINESS

Foreign Relations. Yet the speed with which Congress began its work as it convened January 5 belied its later pace. A peace-minded population was demanding that the American munitions industry stop fattening on the civil war in Spain. Under the Neutrality Act passed the year before the President could declare an embargo on arms shipments whenever he should decide that war existed between two or more nations. But in the case of Spain the war was between two factions within one country. Framers of the Neutrality law had not foreseen this possibility.

"Quarantining" Spain. So when Robert Cuse, dealer in second-hand war equipment, demanded a license to export $2,777,000 worth of used airplanes, uniforms, other war implements to Loyalist Spain, the unhappy State Department was forced to issue the license late in December 1936. But within 24 hours after the 75th Congress met Senator Key Pittman, Chairman of the Foreign Relations Committee, had introduced a resolution forbidding such shipments and providing a $10,000 fine and five years in prison as the maximum penalty for disobedience. A few hours later the bill had passed the Senate 81 to 0. And in the House only one objection to the act was raised. Minnesota's Farmer Laborite John T. Bernard registered a lone "Nay" because he sympathized with the

Spanish Loyalists so strongly he wanted to make a gesture of friendship toward them.

Meanwhile, as the Congress hustled through the Spanish embargo, Robert Cuse was desperately trying to rush his war supplies out of the New York harbor before the Congressional resolution became law. His ship, the *Mar Cantabrico,* was finally cleared and got beyond the three-mile limit before the law went into effect, but only after two American flyers, Bert Acosta and Gordon K. Berry, had tried and failed to attach the cargo on the grounds that the Spanish Loyalist Minister of Marine, Indalecio Prieto, owed them back wages for piloting Loyalist warplanes against the Rebels.

Neutrality. The Spanish munitions act added another page to the recently adopted "Neutrality" policy of this country, but failed to solve the problem of what was to happen to the Neutrality Act itself when it expired May 1. Passed originally in August of 1935 as a stopgap to stave off all chance of U. S. entanglement in a European mêlée which threatened to develop just then out of the Italo-Ethiopian fracas, the act had been extended for another year by the 74th Congress which had been unable to agree on any significant changes. Principal provision of the act as first passed was the embargo on war shipments to belligerents. Two amendments in 1936 placed a similar embargo on loans and credits to warring nations and exempted from the embargoes nations in this hemisphere at war with a non-American power. But the 1936 act established no permanent policy, was to expire again in a year.

What Senators Gerald P. Nye, Bennett Champ Clark and others among the ardent "isolationists" wanted was a permanent act. They wanted also an extension of the embargo against belligerents to include certain raw materials which, while not strictly implements of war, were nonetheless as essential to the prosecution of a war as guns and shells. And they further contended that U. S. steamers carrying a raw material like oil, for example, to one warring power might be as likely to attract torpedoes from the submarines of the other fighting nation as a boatload of bombs. Result: damage to U. S. property; injury to U. S. citizens; violation of "national honor"; WAR!

But from the shipping interests came howls that they were willing to run their own chances. From the international "co-operationists" came cries that a raw material embargo would be tantamount to an alliance with the wealthy powers against the poor. And from the President and the State Department came the objection that the Executive should have more freedom in foreign affairs than these automatic embargoes afforded him.

"Cash and Carry." Finally Congress adopted a compromise suggested by the financier and wartime chairman of the war industries board, Bernard Baruch. All the old provisions were included in what was to be a permanent neutrality act. But an entirely new "cash and carry" clause was added which was calculated to decrease the chance of an incident leading to war arising out of an attack on U. S. shipping, while not completely cutting off American export production for nations at war. When the President decided a state

"Are you fellows having a war?"

LABOR WINS AND LOSES

Top Left: Tom M. Girdler, the man who beat the C.I.O. (Wide World). *Top Right:* Chrysler cheerful after strike is settled (Acme). *Bottom:* Governor Murphy and strike leader Mortimer mark end of auto strike (Wide World).

ROOSEVELT AT WORK AND PLAY

Top Left: Vice-President Garner sits up to make sure of election (Life Magazine). *Top Right:* "My friends . . ." (Acme). *Bottom:* Democrats hold pow-wow at Jefferson Island (Wide World).

of war existed he could name such raw materials as he considered useful for war purposes, and forbid American ships to carry these materials. Furthermore, if foreign vessels wished to transport such materials to the warring nations, title to the goods must pass to the purchaser from the American seller before the goods might leave the United States. Since loans to belligerents were forbidden, this meant cash on the counter. The act was passed by both houses and rushed by plane to the President, who was fishing in the Gulf of Mexico. He signed it on the last day of April.

Isolationists screamed that, far from meaning neutrality, this provision was in reality a dangerous form of alliance with those nations which, possessing big navies and merchant marines, might come to our ports for our goods. Republicans grumbled at another extension of the President's powers. And cynics suggested that pressure from the shipping interests would prevent this clause from being invoked, make it a dead letter. Their cynicism seemed partly justified the following fall when the President refused to recognize that a state of war existed in the Far East, invoked no part of the Neutrality Act against either China or Japan.

Big Army, Bigger Navy. Meanwhile the army and the navy, contemptuous of efforts to legislate the nation out of war, saw to it that a billion dollars was appropriated for defense—a new peacetime high. For the navy, Congress appropriated $516,258,808 to be spent in the next fiscal year, $130,000,000 of it for construction of two battleships ($50,000,000 apiece), eight new destroyers, and four submarines.

All told the military appropriations totaled $609,-799,217. Of this $194,536,063 would be devoted to civil functions of the War Department, including rivers and harbors improvement.

Helium. In contrast to the big military and the neutrality programs the Congress took one short step in the direction of international co-operation when it passed a bill permitting the peace-time export of helium. Owning a virtual monopoly on this rare element, the United States had borne sharp criticism both at home and abroad when the great *Hindenburg,* world's biggest dirigible, exploded in mid-air as it was settling over the Lakehurst field on its first trip of the year from Germany to America early in May. No satisfactory explanation for the tragedy which cost the lives of 11 passengers and 21 of the crew was ever obtained, but one thing stood out crystal clear in the subsequent investigation. Had the airship been inflated with non-inflammable helium instead of the highly explosive hydrogen, the disaster would never have occurred. Under the new law, if the hard-pressed German government could scrape up enough foreign exchange to buy the enormously expensive helium, they need fear no explosion in the sister ship of the *Hindenburg* already in building when the fatal crash occurred.

LABOR

Coal. The Neutrality Act of 1937 had been simply a job of patching and amending a law, the spade work on which had been done during the previous year and a half. Another revising and revamping job done by the 75th Congress was the Guffey-Vinson Bituminous Coal Act. An earlier act bearing the same name and designed to stabilize the sick coal industry and insure producers a return sufficient to maintain union wage and hours standards, had been found unconstitutional by the Supreme Court. The High Court saw a violation of state's rights in the Act's attempts to regulate hours and wages of miners.

The new Act aimed only to regulate interstate commerce in bituminous coal. To do so it created a National Bituminous Coal Commission with powers to draft a coal code dealing with the right of the worker to bargain collectively, to fix prices and marketing arrangements. A tax of 19½ cents per ton was imposed on bituminous coal with the provision that it would be refunded to producers who complied with the code regulations. Without the labor provisions which had made it odious to the high court, Congress hoped the new Act would stand the tests of legality, hoped also that it would satisfy John L. Lewis' United Mine Workers, the union which had brought such strong pressure for its passage. Senator James Byrnes of South Carolina almost succeeded in incorporating in the new Act a direct slap at Mr. Lewis, when he proposed attaching to it an amendment outlawing the sit-down strike, thereby touching off a fiery debate which ended only in a separate resolution being adopted by the Senate condemning the sit-down. (See Chapter I.)

Railroad Pensions. Another New Deal law which the Supreme Court had seen fit to outlaw was an act setting up a pension system for rail employees. When the Social Security Act was passed in 1935, giving all but a few classes of workers a chance at an annuity when they reached 65, the railroad, Railway Express and Pullman employees were specifically excluded. Now these 1,500,000 workers were dealt with in a Railroad Retirement Act which made them eligible for pensions after 30 years or more of service. Modeled after the Social Security Act, a separate but related Rail Pension Tax Extension Act would finance the pension funds by taxing employers' payrolls and workers' wages. Pensions, when the railway men received them, would be generally much higher than those paid under the Social Security Act, with the possibility of a top of $120 a month.

Old Powers Renewed. Also among the old business taken up by Congress were several special emergency presidential powers due to expire during 1937. The first of these, the President's power to fix the gold content of the dollar anywhere between 50 and 60 per cent of its old weight, and to use a $2,000,000,000 Stabilization Fund to keep the dollar on an even international keel, was extended until June 30, 1939.

Renewed also for three years was the President's power to make reciprocal trade agreements with foreign nations, and empowering him to reduce tariffs as

much as 50 per cent without Congressional approval.
Sixteen such agreements had been arranged since the
power was granted in 1934, and the State Department
pointed with pride to the fact that trade with the
nations affected had increased $500,000,000 in that
time. In August Russia became the 17th nation to
sign up under a pact which obligated the Soviet government to increase its U. S. purchases from $30,000,-
000 to $40,000,000 in the next twelve months. In
return the United States granted Soviet Russia most-
favored-nation treatment for the first time. Pennsylvania coal operators set up a howl because the agreement wiped out a special $2-a-ton tax on Russian coal
and coke, but were appeased when the Soviets guaranteed not to ship more than 400,000 tons of coal to
this country during the coming year.

Congress also voted to extend the Reconstruction
Finance Corporation, only one of the New Deal agencies which antedated the New Deal itself. Under
Hoover-appointee Jesse Jones, the RFC had bolstered
shaky banks and industries by loaning $6,300,000,000
to private borrowers by the end of 1936. Of this
amount it had recovered $4,300,000,000, with a profit
of $150,000,000. But to relief and other Federal agen-
cies RFC had loaned $3,000,000,000, recovered only
$1,000,000,000. Despite contentions of Republicans
and conservative Democrats that many of its loans still
outstanding were absolutely uncollectable, the RFC
was granted a new lease on life to last until June 30,
1939. Extended for the same period were four subordinate credit agencies—Commodity Credit Corpora-

tion, Export-Import Bank, Electric Home and Farm
Authority, and RFC Mortgage Corporation.

Another New Deal agency voted two years more of
life was the Public Works Administration, which, however, was told to get its affairs in order against the
last day of June 1939 when it would pass out of
existence. To carry on projects already under way
$259,000,000 was appropriated, but it was to begin
no new projects.

A better fate was reserved for the Civilian Conservation Corps, the most popular among New Deal
relief agencies. After some byplay between the House
and the Senate during which Director Robert Fechner's salary was reduced from $12,000 to $10,000 by
Senators who didn't see why he should receive more
than they did, the CCC was made a permanent agency
of government. Enrollment was limited to 300,000 at
any one time.

NEW BUSINESS

Courts. To Franklin D. Roosevelt the most important single item of new business on the Congressional calendar for 1937 was revision of the nation's
judicial system. But because he and a majority of
Congressmen disagreed rather violently on the need
for the type of revision he suggested, judiciary changes
were restricted to two mild enactments. When the
sound and fury of the Court fight had subsided only
the Supreme Court Retirement Act and a Judicial
Procedure Act had been passed. (See Chapter I.)

HOUSING

The President liked to give as the reason why the Supreme Court must be brought into line the fact that it was continually throwing a wrench into administration efforts to do something for that "one-third of the population which was ill-housed, ill-fed and ill-clothed." The 75th Congress, while denying him the opportunity to "reform" the Court, undertook to do something for the "ill-housed."

Of new experiments launched by the 75th Congress perhaps the most significant was a large-scale plan to build decent homes for slum dwellers in cities civic and socially minded enough to want to co-operate.

Almost as dear to the heart of Senator Robert Wagner as the Labor Relations and Social Security Acts which bore his name was a national housing program he had been trying for two years to get through Congress. Prime purpose of this program was elimination of the city slums which breed filth, crime and disease. In 1935 his bill died in committee. In 1936 it was passed by the Senate, never reached the floor of the House. Introduced again in the 75th Congress, it was whittled down, hedged around with amendments, and finally passed in the closing hours of the session as the Wagner-Steagall Housing Act.

Two Ways to Clear Slums. Under its terms localities wishing to wipe out their slums might apply for aid from a new Federal Housing Authority set up in the Department of Interior. They could elect one of two ways to get Government funds for replacing old tenements with neat new low-rental dwellings.

(1) They might obtain a Federal loan up to 90 per cent of the cost of the project if they agreed to repay the loan within 60 years. But because the cost of the new building would in all probability be such that the low rents to be asked tenants would not meet both the cost of operation of the building and the cost of retiring the Government loan, the Government would make an annual subsidy of 3½ per cent of the cost of the project—providing the locality matched 20 per cent of this subsidy either in cash, tax allowances or services.

(2) The locality might obtain from the Federal Housing Authority an outright grant of 25 per cent of the cost of the slum-clearance project if the locality could make a similar grant of 20 per cent. In addition to the 25 per cent grant, the Government might then allot from Federal relief funds a sum equal to 15 per cent of the cost of the project to be spent for labor. In case this plan was elected by the locality there would, of course, be no annual subsidy from the Government.

Instead of the $700,000,000 asked by Senator Wagner, the Act appropriated $26,000,000 for the first fiscal year to get the program under way, authorized the Housing Authority to issue its own bonds (guaranteed by the United States) up to $100,000,000 the first year and $200,000,000 in each of the two succeeding fiscal years.

Homes for Whom? Who would be eligible to live in these new homes when they were completed? In general only the poorest of the poor—the bottom percentage of that "one-third of the nation" which the President referred to as "ill-housed, ill-fed, and ill-clothed." The Act provided that only those families whose incomes were less than five times their rent would be admitted. And rents in the slum-clearance projects would probably average about $5 per room.

As the program began to get under way in the fall of 1937 President Roosevelt appointed Senator Wagner's good friend Nathan Straus administrator of the new Housing Authority.

Bonneville Dam. Inadequate though the Housing Act might be, if the President had his way and Federal funds held out, more of the material comforts of life would be made available to great sections of the United States which because of geographical remoteness, and because they lacked cheap electric power, offered very poor living standards. Under his administration great dams to provide irrigation, flood control and cheap electric power had sprung up all over the continent. To Congress he sent a special message asking that the nation be divided into seven administrative regions, of which the Tennessee Valley would be one, to co-ordinate a great program to jack up living standards as they had been lifted in the TVA area.

Although Congress shelved his message for future consideration, they did pass an Act providing for the completion of a great dam already under way. The Bonneville Dam Act authorized the Secretary of War to complete, maintain and operate Bonneville Dam on the Oregon River.[1] It further provided for the creation of a Columbia River Administration to supervise distribution of "surplus" power in Oregon and Washington. The Supreme Court the previous winter had upheld the right of the Government to sell "surplus" electric power produced as a result of its efforts to control soil erosion, check floods, etc. The larger question of whether Uncle Sam could manufacture and sell power beyond what might be a surplus had not yet been settled by the end of 1937.

AGRICULTURE

For Agriculture also Congress had a prize package. A national scandal which the New Deal had done little to eliminate because of its dependence upon conservative Southern Democrats for political support was the shocking conditions among a class known as sharecroppers. The sharecropper worked his small plot of land for a landlord who advanced him seed and living necessities against the expected crop return. Often the advance for food and clothing took the form of scrip good only at the landlord's store at prices set by the landlord. Only by living in hovels of the worst sort and subsisting on a diet of cornmeal and sow belly could the cropper, in many instances, sustain his own and his family's lives. Thousands of them considered it a banner year if their portion of the harvested crop enabled them to pay off their bill at the landowner's store. Thousands of others ended the year still in

[1] Appointed Administrator of the Bonneville project was James D. Ross, Seattle municipal power man.

debt and in a state of virtual peonage, since they would get short shrift from state and county officials if they tried to leave the land before their accounts were squared. Besides, most of them being Negroes who knew only the growing of cotton, there were few places where they might go to improve their lots.

During 1935 and 1936, Communists, Socialists, and labor leaders invaded Arkansas and neighboring states where conditions were worst, organized the Southern Tenant Farmers' Union. Bloody riots developing out of attempts to break up union meetings spotlighted this desperate social problem.

Farm Tenant Act. Pressure to relieve the share-croppers finally produced the Bankhead-Jones Farm Tenant Act which authorized the Secretary of Agriculture to make 3 per cent loans, running for 40 years, to tenant farmers for purchase of farms. Similar loans could be obtained also for buying livestock and farm equipment. But instead of $50,000,000 asked for by the bill's sponsors, an economy-minded Congress allotted only $20,000,000 to begin operations, created a Farmers' Home Corporation to administer the program. Best bet was that this amount would accomplish very little toward blotting out the sharecropper scandal.

More Help for Farmers. A bill appropriating $50,000,000 for crop, feed and seed loans which had been vetoed by the President the year before was resurrected, repassed and this time signed by Mr. Roosevelt, who had had the error of his ways pointed out by farm lobbyists. Also given the President's O.K.

was the Farm Credit Act, broadening the list of eligible purposes for which Federal farm land loans might be made. And to guard against resumption of uncontrolled and unplanned farm production, the authority of the Federal Government to pay farmers for "not growing" crops was extended. Originally, under the AAA, these benefit payments were for "reducing acreage." Then, after the Supreme Court vetoed the AAA, the payments were continued for "soil conservation," Secretary of Agriculture Wallace had discovered he could use Federal funds to pay a farmer to retire land from production for the purpose of increasing the soil's fertility, whereas the Constitution apparently gave him no right to pay the farmer for simply cutting down his acreage. But the Soil Conservation Act, passed shortly after the invalidation of the AAA, had provided that after December 31, 1937, the individual states would disburse Federal funds provided for these benefit payments. Because only a few states had set up machinery for making the payments, Congress now decided that until December 31, 1941, the Federal Government would continue to pay out such funds direct to the farmer.

Sugar. To another large agricultural bloc Congress tendered assistance in the form of an act to replace the Jones-Costigan Sugar Control Act due to expire December 31, 1937. The Act had established a quota system limiting raw sugar imports and imposing a ½ cent per pound processing tax, receipts from which were paid out in cash benefits to beet and cane growers. Result of this law had been to keep the price of sugar in this country about three times that on world markets.

Sugar refiners, not content with simply extending the Jones-Costigan Act, proposed now in a new bill to impose strangling restriction on the importation of refined sugar from American territories—Hawaii and Puerto Rico—and to reduce in like manner the quotas of Cuba and the Philippines. When the President angrily threatened to veto the bill because of the new restrictions, a compromise was worked out which, while not satisfactory to the Chief Executive, was signed by him lest his veto stop also the benefit payments to beet and cane growers. The new Act empowered the Secretary of Agriculture to determine each year the amount of sugar needed for consumption in continental United States and to fix quotas for domestic and foreign countries on the basis of 55.59 per cent for the former and 44.41 per cent for the latter. The domestic quota was divided as follows: domestic beet sugar, 41.72 per cent; mainland cane sugar, 11.31; Hawaii, 25.5; Puerto Rico, 21.48; Virgin Islands, 0.24. The foreign quota division: Cuba, 64.41; Philippines, 34.70; other foreign countries, 0.24.

BUSINESS

Price Maintenance. Because many states had enacted statutes permitting contracts between manufacturers and retailers of trade-marked articles which guaranteed against price-cutting on these articles by the retailers, and because these state laws conflicted with the Federal Sherman Anti-Trust Act designed to prevent monopoly, Congress passed the Tydings-Miller

Resale Price Maintenance Act late in the session to amend the Sherman Act. The amendment recognized the legality of such contracts.

MONEY MATTERS

The Budget. If the Court plan sank a wedge in the Democratic majority in Congress, certainly the issue of Federal spending drove the wedge deeper. Those New Dealers who had contended all along that reform and recovery must go hand in hand, with reform always on the right hand, and that recovery would follow as a natural result of priming the economic pump with huge Government expenditures, were now met by a solid phalanx of their own friends who had begun to be worried about a thirty-five billion dollar deficit.

Even the President, who had once said that the Federal debt might go to fifty or seventy-five billion without cause for worry, began in 1937 to talk economy in tones he had not used since his campaign of 1932 when he had promised to cut Government expense "twenty-five per cent." He had been optimistic in his first budget address to Congress early in January. Booming business, agricultural recovery, and a decrease in unemployment made it seem possible at that time that a "layman's balance" might be effected for the Federal budget in the coming fiscal year if relief expenditures could be kept down to $1,500,000,-000. Yet the nation, knowing the notoriously poor reputation Mr. Roosevelt had gained as a prophet on matters of Federal finance, kept its fingers crossed.

Disappointing income tax returns forced the President to revise his figures in April, at which time he estimated that the 1938 budget would be out of balance by $418,000,000. Urging Congress to effect economies of $300,000,000 to $400,000,000, he said: "And while I recognize many opportunities to improve social and economic conditions through Federal action, I am convinced that the success of our whole program and the permanent security of our people demand that we adjust all expenditures within the limits of my budget estimate."

Yet by the following October 18 another revision was necessary. A stock market which had dived to 1931 levels, eliminating millions in income taxes for the year, coupled with Congressional expenditures on which the Chief Executive had not planned, would boost the 1938 deficit to $695,240,000, according to Treasury estimates. (See Chapter IV.)

End of Fiscal 1937. When the fiscal year 1937 ended on July 31, its balance sheet also caused wry faces among the administration. Although the deficit for the year was almost $2,000,000,000 less than in 1936 and the lowest since the New Deal took office, it was still $2,811,318,000. Savage spring floods had put an unexpected drain on relief funds. Federal revenue had not lived up to expectations, and instead of a total national debt of $35,026,000,000 as predicted by the President in January, the debt had climbed to $35,400,000,000 in round numbers.

When the President, after telling Congress in April the Federal deficit would be larger than he had anticipated earlier in the year, at the same time requested an appropriation of $1,500,000,000 to carry the burden of relief during the coming fiscal year, he stirred up a hornet's nest. Earlier in the session, when the First Deficiency bill calling for $790,000,000 to carry Relief through to the end of fiscal 1937, funds appropriated the year before not having been sufficient, the House haled Relief Administrator Harry Hopkins on the carpet, demanded to know what steps, if any, were being taken to get the Government out of the Relief business. Mr. Hopkins promised that WPA rolls then (in February) numbering 2,200,000 would be cut to 1,600,000 by June.

Congress had then obediently passed the Deficiency bill. Then when eastern floods devastated hundreds of square miles, made thousands temporarily homeless, Congress appropriated another $20,000,000, set up a Disaster Loan Corporation to make loans to flood victims. But as the President prepared to introduce his Relief bill for the coming fiscal year, he was visited by a group of his own administration leaders, including Majority Leader Senator Joe Robinson, who declared flatly that Relief spending would have to be reduced. So when the request came for $1,500,000,000 a roar went up from a section of Congress that this amount was too high. Senator Byrnes was among the most vocal in damning the request. He insisted that

$1,000,000,000 should be plenty for Relief, demanded retrenchment all along the line in the budget, and suggested that a flat ten per cent be knocked off estimates for all expenditures except funds for retirement of the public debt.

On the other hand, some among the House liberals were denouncing the Relief proposal as shockingly inadequate. Responding to the pressure from organizations like the Workers' Alliance, union of unemployed and Relief workers, they demanded an appropriation of at least $2,000,000,000 and preferably $2,500,000,000.

When the administration bill finally emerged on the floor of the House and it was apparent it would pass in the amount requested by the President, disgruntled Congressmen determined to get all they could for their own states and districts, while at the same time depriving the President of his power to allot the funds as he wished. Amendment after amendment earmarked millions for flood and drought control, roads, public works, until over $500,000,000 had been allocated for political pork. One amendment even lopped $2,000 off Harry Hopkins' salary. Administration leaders had to filibuster to keep the amended bill from passing. Finally Floor Leader Sam Rayburn, after a talk with the President, was able to assure Congressmen that no section of the country would be slighted in the spending of Relief funds. The House then passed the bill without any of the amendments.

But the battle went on in the Senate, with Robinson leading the fight against the bill of his own administration. Senator Byrnes, not having had any success with his suggestion to reduce budget estimates a flat ten per cent, now suggested that local communities be required to pay 40 per cent of Relief projects where they were financially able to do so. Senator Robinson fell in with this idea. When the President indicated he was unwilling to force communities to take a "pauper's oath" to get Federal funds, Robinson suggested a compromise amendment in which the communities would pay 25 per cent unless the President personally waived the requirement. Jumping into Robinson's role as Majority Leader, Senator Alben Barkley rallied administration forces to beat the Robinson amendment 58 to 34, but among the 34 were 24 Democrats, including such powers in the party as Harrison, Byrnes, Pittman, Bankhead, Clark, and Connally. The bill was passed late in June in the form desired by the President, giving him power to allocate funds as he saw fit. But the bitterness of the debate and the vote on the restricting amendments were again indicative of how wide the breach in the Democratic majority had grown.

TAXES

When the 75th Congress wound up its work it had appropriated all told the sum of $9,389,488,983 for Relief, regular expenses of Governmental departments, continuation of New Deal experiments of one sort or another, and for the few new experiments set in motion. This marked a drop of almost a billion dollars from the record of the previous session. But the last session of the 74th Congress had passed an important tax bill which had been banked on to up Federal revenue sharply. During the regular session of Congress in 1937 no important new taxes were devised.

Nuisance Tax. The so-called "Nuisance Tax" imposed in 1932 was extended until 1939. These taxes on gasoline, theater admissions, sporting goods, matches, radio sets, chewing gum, mechanical refrigerators and a long list of other things were expected to yield about $650,000,000 a year. The measure which extended these taxes also continued for two years three-cent postage.

Tax Loophole Revenue Act. The only other tax measure adopted by Congress was one designed to plug up loopholes in existing income tax statutes. After the President had been forced to revise his budget estimates because revenue from taxes had not increased as he had been led to believe it would, he set the Treasury Department to hunting an explanation. Suddenly one day late in May, Mr. Roosevelt told his press conference he had traced down the reason for the disappointing tax returns. About 150 of the nation's wealthiest men employed various dodges, some of which were perfectly legal, to evade or avoid payment of income taxes. Well-known to the American public was the case the Treasury had been preparing against Pierre S. DuPont and John J. Raskob. Selling each other stocks to establish losses for purposes of reducing income tax payments, the two financiers had later regained their original securities in another two-way sale.

Among other tax-avoiding devices used by the

wealthy were the following: (1) setting up personal holding companies in the Bahamas, Panama, Newfoundland from which tax money could not be extradited; (2) forming partnerships with wives and children, thus splitting income several ways to escape high surtaxes; (3) incorporating yachts, town houses, country estates, racing stables so that their operating losses could be claimed as deductions from income.

Quoting from the late Justice Holmes to the effect that "taxes are what we pay for civilized society," Mr. Roosevelt declared that apparently too many individuals were trying their best to get civilization at a discount. He proposed that the Treasury be authorized to conduct an investigation of these practices for the purpose of devising ways to circumvent individuals employing these dodges.

Tax Avoiders and Evaders. Congress, however, preferred to conduct the investigation itself, did so during June and July, but refused to listen to Republican Congressman Hamilton Fish, Jr.'s, impudent demands that the Roosevelt family's tax payments be examined. Among prominent persons who were revealed as guilty of the practices exposed by the Treasury were Jacob Schick, the retired army officer who invented the electric razor bearing his name, and who was assigning his royalties from its sale to a Bahama corporation. Jules S. Bache, prominent New York financier and philanthropist, was another tax avoider. And the movie actor Charles Laughton had escaped heavy taxes on his earnings in this country by having them assigned to his British holding company.

To end these pretty practices then, Congress late in the session passed an act which amended existing income taxes. Best estimates were that this Tax Loophole Revenue Act would bring in an additional $100,-000,000 to the Federal Government.

Tax Revision Demands. Meanwhile industry wailed that the taxes already in existence were strangling recovery at the source. Singled out for bitterest attacks were the capital gains tax, and the corporate surplus tax passed the year before as an attempt to force huge industrial surpluses out into dividends where they could be reached by the income tax.

ADJOURNMENT

These were the significant accomplishments of the first regular session of the 75th Congress. But even before adjournment, which finally came to the weary heat-ridden legislators on August 21, there were rumors circulating in the halls on Capitol Hill that the occupant of the White House across the way was to make them pay for mutilating or killing most of his measures by summoning them in special session during the fall. But unless time, the great healer, could close the raw wounds opened by the intra-Congress warfare of the previous eight months, the President's job of leadership would be no easier with a special session than it had been during the regular one. For the closing hours in the Senate were given over not to consideration of legislation but to furious exchanges of personal animosity. Night before adjournment Pennsylvania's Joseph Guffey had gone on the air to castigate leaders of the group which had produced the breach in the Democratic majority.

"Political ingratitude carries with it its own punishment both swift and effective," he threatened.

This promise of political reprisal caused Senators Burke, O'Mahoney, and Holt to roast the Pennsylvanian in highly vituperative language, and as the gavel fell for the last time, Montana's Burton K. Wheeler was shaking a trembling finger at Guffey, challenging him to "Lay on, Macduff, and damned be he that first cries, Hold, enough."

EXECUTIVE CHANGE

While a stubborn Congress was resisting change in its domain the Chief Executive was making alterations which needed no legislative say-so.

Diplomatic Shuffle. All year long he was shuffling his staff of diplomats and revamping the state department. Sending Anthony J. Drexel Biddle Jr. to Poland as Minister, he appointed Florence Jaffray Harriman to the job of Minister to Norway previously held by Drexel Biddle. Mrs. Harriman thus became the second woman to hold ministerial rank, Ruth Bryan having resigned the year before from the Denmark post, following her marriage to the Danish Captain Rohde. In July a third woman was added to the foreign service staff when Margaret M. Hanna, a minor official in the state department for 41 years, became consul in Geneva.

Other changes saw Ambassador Hugh S. Gibson being shifted from Brazil to Belgium, Jefferson Caffery going from Cuba to Brazil, J. Butler Wright to Cuba from Czechoslovakia. Leland Harrison went from Rumania to Switzerland and Hugh R. Wilson came back from Switzerland to become Assistant Secretary of State along with George S. Messersmith who was recalled from Austria. Grenville T. Emmet was transferred from the Netherlands to Austria where he died in October a few weeks after arriving on the new job.[1] Wilbur J. Carr, after a long career in Washington, was shifted from his position of Assistant Secretary of State to that of Minister to Czechoslovakia.

Assistant Secretary of State Sumner Welles was elevated to Under Secretary; Assistant Secretary Walton Moore was named Counselor to the State Department.[2]

Philippines. Early in the year the former Governor of Indiana, former National Commander of the American Legion, and potent politician, Paul V. McNutt, was appointed High Commissioner to the Philippines to replace Frank Murphy, who had returned to be elected Governor of Michigan. The new Commissioner got off on the wrong foot almost immediately by insisting that at state dinners in Manila, Filipinos toast him before their President, Manuel Quezon.

Cabinet Additions. Another former Legion Commander, Louis Arthur Johnson, was singled out for

[1] Another who died in the foreign service was James T. Marriner, U. S. Consul to Syria, shot by a crazed Syrian-American who thought the Consul was preventing him from returning to the U. S., where he had become a naturalized citizen.

[2] Late in the year Ambassador to Germany William E. Dodd, who had made no secret of his disgust with the Nazi regime, resigned. Hugh R. Wilson took his place.

honor by the President. He was named Assistant Secretary of War.

To fill the post of Under Secretary of the Treasury vacated the year before by the resignation of T. Jefferson Coolidge who differed with New Deal fiscal policies, Roswell F. Magill was induced to leave his job as Professor at Columbia University.[1]

Secretary James. The White House secretariat also came in for considerable change during the year. Early in January the President's 29-year-old eldest son James was named a special administrative assistant to handle his father's relations with the press. The following spring he was upped to full secretary rank, and in October his importance was enormously increased when his father chose him to act as buffer between the President and 18 of the largest independent and emergency agencies. Heads of these agencies would henceforth take their problems first to "Jimmy," who would then present them to his father.

Also promoted with son James to full secretary rank in the White House secretariat were Assistants Marvin McIntyre and Stephen Early.

Resignations and Appointments. With sincerest regret the President accepted the resignation of John G. Winant from the job of Chairman of the Social Security Board, appointed in his place another Board member, Arthur J. Altmeyer.

Rural Electrification Administrator Morris L. Cooke also retired to private life.

---

[1] Edward F. McGrady resigned as Assistant Secretary of Labor early in the fall to become R.C.A.'s labor relations director. Another fall resignation for business reasons returned Josephine Roche to her Colorado coal mines from the post of Assistant Secretary of the Treasury in charge of public health.

Eugene Vidal, under fire much of the time since his appointment as first director of the Bureau of Air Commerce, established in 1933 as a subdivision under the Department of Commerce, resigned in mid-winter to go into private aviation. In his place the President appointed Dr. Fred D. Fagg Jr., Northwestern University's authority on air law. But after thoroughly revamping the Bureau, Dr. Fagg announced in October that he would return the next year to Northwestern to become Dean of the School of Commerce. He would carry on, however, until June, 1938, before taking over the Deanship.

To fill two vacant posts on the tariff commission Franklin Roosevelt in April named Florida's former Congressman William J. Sears and Henry F. Grady of California.

James L. Houghteling, husband of the President's cousin Laura Delano, was appointed Commissioner of Immigration in July.[1]

FOREIGN AFFAIRS

During the early months of 1937 there was much talk of a secret ambition on the part of the President to sponsor a move toward world peace. His role as the "Good Neighbor" at the Buenos Aires Pan-American conference the previous December had been well received, and it was rumored that he had been bitten

[1] Another relative of the President's who went on the Federal payroll in 1937 was Mrs. Warren Delano Robbins, wife of the late cousin of the President who had been Minister to Canada. She was placed in the State Department to have charge of decorating diplomatic and consular establishments abroad.

by a great urge to extend his pacific efforts beyond the western hemisphere.[1]

Canadian Visitors. When first Canadian Prime Minister William L. Mackenzie King, and then Governor General of Canada Lord Tweedsmuir visited the White House in March and April, their sojourns were pointed to as evidence of the fact that while Congress was struggling to perfect an isolationist policy, the Chief Executive was looking toward more co-operation in world affairs.

Belgian Premier at White House. Belgium's Premier Paul Van Zeeland also paid a visit to the White House in June. Ostensibly here to receive an honorary degree from Princeton University, his alma mater, the shrewd young Belgian was believed generally to have more than degrees up his sleeve when he came to this country. Reports circulated that he was the agent of the European democracies sent to sound out the United States on the question of participating in a world economic conference.

End of Isolation. By the fall of 1937 it became apparent that all the rumors were not idle. Three things done by Franklin Roosevelt woke Americans with a bang to the realization that isolationism was not to be the credo of the administration, and caused many to

---

[1] In July the President signed eight treaties and conventions which had been drafted at the Buenos Aires congress and ratified by the Senate. Gist of these was that American nations would consult together when peace was threatened, resist intervention in their affairs by united forces, keep their noses out of each other's affairs, and, if war did break out between any two of them, the others would stay neutral. Since only two other American states had ratified the conventions, however, it might be a long time before they were put into operation.

wonder what all the shouting had been about during
the fight to pass a so-called Neutrality Act.

First, the President refused to invoke the arms embargo against warring China and Japan, as provided
in the Neutrality Act. Only thing he did was to forbid U. S. owned ships to carry arms, ammunition or
implements of war to either belligerent. (See Chapter IX on China.) Next, in a stirring speech at Chicago early in October, he declared that "peace loving
nations must make a concerted effort in opposition to
those violations of treaties . . . which today are creating a state of international anarchy and instability
from which there is no escape through mere isolation
or neutrality."

And finally, the President had accepted an invitation to send delegates to a Nine-Power conference
called to take measures to end the rape of China by
Japan. Indeed there was strong reason to believe that
the Brussels conference of the signers of the pact
guaranteeing the independence of China had actually
been promoted by the President and his state department. At least Great Britain's Foreign Secretary Anthony Eden lay the responsibility for convening the
conference at the door of the United States when questioned about it in the House of Commons.

That the Brussels conference would prove a dismal
failure was almost a foregone conclusion before its disillusioned representatives opened the first session. But
European democracies might still get some cheer from
the fact that Uncle Sam had come across the Atlantic

to talk over world problems with them.   And when the
President indicated that his choice for Ambassador to
the Court of St. James to succeed Robert W. Bingham,
who died in mid-December, would be his all-around
handyman, Joseph P. Kennedy, both Europe and
America wondered whether the principal task of Mr.
Kennedy would not be to devise a working arrangement between the two great English-speaking Democracies.

SPECIAL SESSION

Fall of 1937 had barely begun, however, when it became embarrassingly apparent to the President and his
administration that international co-operation would
have to wait on the more immediate job of promoting
a little better co-operation from that elusive abstraction known as the business cycle.

Northwest Trip.   Late in September Mr. Roosevelt
set out on a two weeks' jaunt through the Northwest,
presumably to find out how this section of the nation
had reacted to his Court defeat and the actions of Congress in the last few months.

But when he returned to Washington early in October, it was to find the nation's capital jittery over what
appeared to have all the earmarks of a new business depression.   (See Chapter IV.)   Distracted officials were
hearing complaints from business that the decline in
sales and production were a direct reflection of the
New Deal's policy of badgering business with one reform or threat of reform after another, that the SEC
regulations were curtailing normal trading on stock ex-

changes, that Federal taxes were stifling investment
and expansion, and that industry generally was so
frightened over the national debt and over what "Socialistic" move the administration might make next
that confidence in the future of the profit system in
America had been utterly shattered. Yet there were
some who were crying just as loudly that it had been
the recent "threat" of a balanced budget and reduced
Government spending which had brought on the new
decline euphemistically termed the "recession."

Business Conferees. After summoning Congress to
a special session to convene Nov. 15, the President settled down in his White House study to receive a constant parade of Government officials and business men,
each with his views as to the causes of the economic
decline, and some few with concrete proposals to remedy the situation.

Recovery Program. Out of these meetings came a
five-point recovery program: (1) Stimulation of Housing, to give a leg up to the industries which supply
building materials, and which were sinking fastest into
the doldrums. In a message to Congress late in November the President pointed out that between 1930
and 1937 the average annual number of houses built in
the United States had been 180,000, while in the seven
years prior to 1930 the average had been 800,000. To
remedy this appalling lag he proposed that Congress
boost the insurable limit for a Government guaranteed
loan from 80 to 90 per cent of a property's appraised
value on properties valued at not more than $6,000.
Thus a person with only $600 might obtain a guaran-

teed loan permitting him to build a $6,000 home. He also suggested that interest rates and service charges on these loans be reduced to as low as 5 per cent, that more money be made available for private building of large-scale housing developments, and that insurance be renewed on loans for repairing and modernizing old dwellings—this part of the Federal Housing Act having been allowed to lapse in April when the building boom appeared under way.

Both houses passed bills including the important housing proposals made by the President, but slight differences between the House and Senate measures necessitated a conference which had not smoothed out the differences as the session closed.

(2) Retrenchment of Government spending to restore confidence in the financial stability of the Government. In a speech before the Academy of Political Science on the eve of the opening of the special session, Treasury Secretary Morgenthau surprised his listeners by coming out flatly in favor of a balanced budget through reduction of Federal expenditures. Two weeks later the President asked Congress to slash $112,000,000 which had already been granted to states for road building during the coming year. But most Congressmen knew that, in an election year, road funds are valuable vote-getters, and refused to believe that this was the best place to economize.

(3) Immediate purchase of needed Government supplies for which funds had already been appropriated. The President indicated that $245,000,000 would be spent in this manner to stimulate business.

(4) Revision of taxes which were retarding business expansion. In his opening message to Congress Mr. Roosevelt urged that taxes be eased, particularly those which were hard on smaller businesses. And Senate Finance Chairman Pat Harrison took the lead in modifying the tax on undistributed corporate surplus. As the special session ended, Congress was still wrestling with the problem of satisfying the objections of business against this tax and the capital gains tax.

(5) Encouragement of construction for repair and expansion by public utilities. An estimated $3,200,-000,000 in such construction had been postponed, according to utilities heads, because of the "general feeling" that the New Deal was determined to embark on a large-scale program of Government-operated power plants all over the nation.

Unemployment Census. This program, it was confidently expected, would give business the shot in the arm it needed and put thousands back to work. An estimated 400,000 had been added to the lists of the unemployed in November alone, and pessimists feared that January would find the total unemployed in the nation back up to 9,000,000. To discover just how many were out of work, the President appointed Republican John D. Biggers to conduct a census. Cards were mailed to 31,000,000 homes in the nation, to be filled out and returned to Washington by anyone partly or wholly unemployed. These results will be checked by door-to-door counts in sample cities to establish the average percentage of error, with complete tabulations ready March 1, 1938. But if unemployment gained all winter, results obtained from a November census would mean little. Experts advised a similar sample every few months for a year or more.

Both Reform and Recovery. The President soon revealed this recovery program to the nation, but he also made it clear in his opening message to Congress that he was by no means ready to abandon reform. The two must still go hand in hand, even though he might now be willing to smile a trifle more sweetly on recovery. Even when he emphasized the need for tax revision for "smaller business," he could not resist the temptation to spank business lightly once more with the admonition that "if private enterprise does not respond, government must take up the slack."

Specifically, in that opening message, he asked Congress to enact four statutes, all of which he had requested previously: (1) Crop control; (2) Wages and hours regulation for industry; (3) Reorganization of the executive branch of the Government; (4) Regional planning by dividing the nation into seven great areas in which agencies like the TVA would operate.

The hell-raising spirit notable in Congress during the regular session was unabated when its members returned to Washington. And it was heightened by the fact that Congress convened ready to go to work on the crop control bill, the first item of business under a political bargain the President had made in the closing days of the regular session, and discovered that the administration leaders had no bill ready.[1]   The Senate

[1] Because the bumper crop in cotton had driven prices down to 10 cents a pound by August, the President, at the earnest behest of Con-

SUPREME COURT UPHOLDS LABOR

Top Left: Senator Wagner congratulates himself (Acme). *Top Right:* The stock exchange goes on "as usual" (Acme). *Bottom:* NLRB and its counsel reading decision (Acme).

SCIENCE IN 1937

Top: New Frisco Golden Gate Bridge completed (Acme). *Center:* The expedition to pre-historic Shiva in the Grand Canyon (Wide World). *Bottom:* Mellon's temple for industrial research (Wide World).

and House agricultural committees simply had not gotten around to preparing their separate bills. This would not have been serious but for the fact that the closing hours of the regular session had produced another political bargain. To prevent a threatened filibuster to keep Congress in session until passage of the Wagner Van Nuys anti-lynching bill (already approved in the House) Majority Leader Barkeley had agreed to permit the anti-lynching bill to come up early in the next session.

Crop Control. The complicated 97-page Senate crop control bill included provisions, to begin with the 1938 crops, for Department of Agriculture control of production of wheat, corn, cotton, tobacco, and rice. For wheat and corn the plan aimed to give a bushel of either the same purchasing power it had between 1909-1914—defined by the bill as a "parity price." Every bushel sold over Department of Agriculture marketing quotas would be taxed 50 per cent of its price—provided that two-thirds of the farmers affected, who were to be given a vote on the matter, approved of the plan. Secretary of Agriculture Henry A. Wallace's "evernormal granary plan"—storing grain in bumper years, releasing it in lean years—would also apply to wheat and corn. For cotton and tobacco farmers the bill pro-

gressmen from the cotton states, ordered the Commodity Credit Corp. to make loans of 9 or 10 cents a pound on the new crop, and to pay farmers the difference between what they eventually got on the market for their cotton and 12 cents a pound. For this he got a promise from Congressmen to make crop control legislation the first item of business in the next session. He felt that only if the next year's crop could be limited would the farmers get a price high enough to enable them to repay the loans.

vided both penalties for overproduction and soil conservation payments to induce them to retire part of their acreage to soil-building crops. And for rice there were to be quotas based on domestic consumption of this crop.

Most glaring omissions from the bill were any statement of its probable cost, and of how the money to finance the program was to be raised. Before Congress convened, the President had emphatically stated that any new legislation, including the crop bill, should stay within the budget limits, or be "backed 100 per cent by additional . . . taxes." Estimates of the bill's cost ranged from $750,000,000 to $1,000,000,000, but few Congressmen believed that the program could be held within the $500,000,000 already budgeted for crop control.

The House bill, although differing from the Senate measure in the matter of control—leaning more heavily on voluntary rather than compulsory co-operation by the farmer, and providing milder penalties for quota violations, followed the Senate bill in outline, and also failed to indicate cost or means of financing. Both houses passed their separate bills a few days before the special session adjourned, but there remained the difficult task of ironing out Senate and House differences in conference before crop control might become law.

Fair Labor Standards. Other measures requested by the President in his opening message fared little if any better than the crop bill by the end of the special session. Several times he called in Administration leaders to urge the passage of the Fair Labor Stand-

ards, or wages and hours bill. As the Black-Connery
bill, this attempt to revive some of the features of the
outlawed NRA had passed the Senate the summer before. It proposed to bar from interstate commerce all
products: (1) of child labor—under 16,[1] (2) of a
manufacturer who used labor spies and strike breakers,
(3) produced in violation of certain wage and hour
standards to be fixed by a Labor Standards Board
whose job it would be to determine fair standards in
various regions throughout the country.

After passing the Senate during the regular session
the bill was bottled up in the House rules committee,
where a majority of Republicans and conservative
Democrats who opposed it kept it pigeon-holed. The
committee simply refused to report the bill out for consideration, and the only way it could be forced out was
by a petition signed by 218 of the House's 435 members. The signatures were finally obtained by Chairman of the House Labor committee Mary T. Norton,
but meanwhile the bill had been scored from all sides.
Southern Democrats were opposed to it because it
would in all probability reduce the wage differential

[1] Despite a letter from the President to governors-elect of 19 states
early in January urging them to ratify the child labor amendment,
the year ended with only 28 of the required 36 states having approved the amendment. Most opposition to it came from the Catholic church, which feared it might be stretched to give the Federal
government jurisdiction over pupils in parochial schools, the press,
which feared for its newsboys, and the farmers. In June Senator
Vandenberg introduced a new amendment which he hoped would
eliminate some of the objections to the original one. The original
amendment read: "The Congress shall have the power to limit, regulate, and prohibit the labor of persons under 18 years of age."
Senator Vandenberg's amendment: "The Congress shall have the
power to limit and prohibit *for hire* the employment of persons under
16 years of age."

which enabled their industries to undersell northern competitors. From the opposite end of the economic pole William Green, A. F. of L. chief, opposed the bill because it failed to establish a definite minimum wage and maximum work week. He demanded a 40-hour week and a 40-cent an hour wage minimum for the nation at large. But again, the House effectively sidetracked the bill by voting to send it back to the committee in the last week of the special session. And it was extremely doubtful that it would be resurrected again in the regular session.

Seven TVA's. The bill to create seven regional agencies, of which the TVA would be one, to undertake national planning in their respective spheres, cope with flood control, soil erosion and other conservation problems, and distribute electric power, was also suspended in mid-air as the session ended.

Executive Reorganization. Because the President felt unable to cope with the mass of detail he was constantly asked to face, because the enormous growth of executive function under the New Deal had tended to make this arm of the Federal Government topheavy, and because he was having difficulty holding his crack administrators against the lure of better-paying jobs in industry, Franklin Roosevelt had asked Congress early in the regular session to authorize reorganization of the executive.

"Goose Egg" Session. Congress never got around to acting on executive reorganization in the special session. In fact it completed no important legislation whatever. But Congressmen might reply with some

justification to the charges of a "goose egg" session
that much spade work had been accomplished which
would smooth the way for both houses in the next regular session.[1]

[1] Any future "smoothness," however, would depend on how successful Franklin Roosevelt was in regaining control of his party.
Republicans made constant and successful efforts to seduce the conservative Democrats into the ranks of the opposition. They played
up the "dictator" angle for all it was worth, contending that the
President intended to seek a third term. The President refused to
comment directly on the third term question. He did, however, say
that he had a great ambition to get back to private life. On the
other hand, Democratic Publicity Chief Charles Michelson declared
in November, ". . . with the world in such a turmoil as it is today
outside of this continent, it cannot be forecast whether the American
people would permit him to lay down his burden in view of possible eventualities."

Trouble with the G.O.P. in 1937 as in 1936 was that it had no one
leader on whom it could rely to beat Franklin Roosevelt if he should
decide to violate tradition (no law) by running for a third term.

Herbert Hoover and Alf Landon both saved their party embarrassment by declaring themselves out of the running for 1940. Ex-
President Hoover tried to promote a plan for a mid-term Republican
convention in 1938, but was squelched by the National Committee.
The New York City elections returned to office Mayor Fiorello H.
LaGuardia with Republican backing. The stocky mayor defeated his
Tammany opponent, Jeremiah T. Mahoney, by a record-breaking
vote which was highly significant in marking the first time Tammany
had been whipped twice in succession by a "reform" mayor. But
LaGuardia had been a "Fusion" candidate, had received votes of
many besides Republicans, and after the election announced his membership in the new radical American Labor Party. The young racket-
buster, Thomes E. Dewey, had also won in the New York elections,
gaining the District Attorney's office against a Tammany opponent.
He might be a national figure in time, but only after more age, experience, and political seasoning.

As the year ended Republican leaders were trying desperately to
unite their forces behind the ousted president of the University of
Wisconsin, Glenn Frank. Perhaps 1938 might reveal him as the
G.O.P. "white hope."

CHAPTER IV

BUSINESS WAVERS

The business outlook at the dawn of 1937 was favorable. Men and women in all walks of life were optimistic. Not only was business on the upswing but the trend was so marked that John Q. Public was not so much concerned about maintaining recovery as controlling a boom. The market was favorable to commercial activity. True, clouds were in the business sky— labor unrest was serious, credit control caused concern, and tax forcing dividends proved an irritant—but these disturbances were not highly threatening. The abdication of the British King, the election of France's first "out-and-out" Leftist government, crises in the Far East and the revolt in Spain caused some uneasiness but not much alarm. At home America's most serious drought, a $100,000,000 rate decision against the railroads, and a boost in the margin required on stocks, all seemed unfavorable to business.

In spite of these events, forecasters estimated that the national income of $63,799,000,000 for 1936—itself a gain of nine billions, or sixteen per cent over 1935—would reach seventy billions in 1937. More specifically, continued gains for automobiles, building construction, steel production, and other indices of business activity were forecast. The future was not clear but the pattern was definite. Optimism prevailed.

The Government and Business. During the past few years the Government pumped money, the life-blood of commerce and industry, into many veins of business. Recovery was steady, the return of prosperity was in the air, the budget needed balancing, and business now seemed able to stand on its own feet. In March, however, reports showed the undistributed earnings tax was not yielding expected returns. The deficit was piling up. In January the Administration estimated a surplus of $37,000,000 for the fiscal year. In April a new estimate set the probable deficit at $418,-000,000. A third estimate made after the fiscal year began placed the deficit at $695,000,000. With the mounting debt, greater economy seemed urgent, especially since business was stronger.

A consistent downward trend in business curves during the summer and fall brought demands from all corners of the country that the Government do something—no one seemed to know quite what. Security markets were encouraged when the Federal Reserve Board cut margins from 55 to 40 per cent but this action alone was not enough to stop the downward trend of the stock market. Other concessions were demanded.

The undistributed profits tax seemed intolerable to corporations. A survey of 405 companies, conducted by the National Association of Manufacturers, made this tax appear a hindrance to re-employment. One fourth of the concerns claimed they would hire more

men and another fourth stated they "would probably"
hire more men if the tax were abolished.   Also in

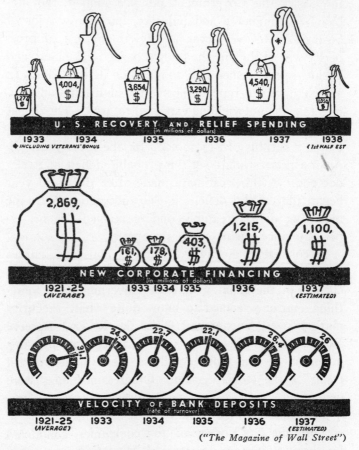

U. S. RECOVERY AND RELIEF SPENDING
(in millions of dollars)

1933   1934   1935   1936   1937   1938
✦ INCLUDING VETERANS' BONUS   (1st HALF EST

NEW CORPORATE FINANCING
(in millions of dollars)

1921-25   1933 1934 1935   1936   1937
(AVERAGE)   (ESTIMATED)

VELOCITY OF BANK DEPOSITS
(rate of turnover)

1921-25   1933   1934   1935   1936   1937
(AVERAGE)   (ESTIMATED)

("The Magazine of Wall Street")

other quarters the Government's "punitive policy" toward the power corporations was cited as being largely
responsible for the lag in utilities constructions, esti-

mated to require an expenditure of $2,600,000,000.
Executives blamed Administrative measures for
"frightening" the capital needed to finance construction. Investors were said to be in need of relief from
the capital-gains tax. The railroads were placed in
a disadvantageous position because the Interstate Commerce Commission failed to give them a decent living.
Finally, it was urged that Congress and the President
do something about the other obstacles that prevented
money from being invested—such as high wages, high
interest rates, and high material costs. But the Government was not inclined to shoulder the blame for
the business recession—nor was it pessimistic about the
future.

On the other hand business believed that the period
of the decline, which started in August, would be determined by Administrative policy. Two courses were
open: (1) efforts to balance the budget could be abandoned and the Government might return to "pump
priming," (2) the Government could encourage private
enterprise by constructive changes in legislation and in
general attitude. Either policy might be effective.
On the whole, business believed strongly in the latter
course. "Let business alone" was the slogan of the
hour. But business cannot and will not be left alone.
Government regulations are essential if the exploitation of previous generations is to be avoided. The
government is in business to stay. The questions that
still need to be worked out are those of degree.

Utilities. The effect of the government upon industry is well illustrated in the field of utilities. At

the beginning of the year plans for new construction and maintenance were made by electric light and power companies and by steam generating concerns. Their budgets were the biggest since 1931—being from half again as big to twice as big. In spite of plans for expansion and unprecedented demands for power from industrial and commercial plants and from domestic consumers the attitude of the utilities was one of caution. Plans were made only for the immediate pressing needs.

In the first half of 1937 the output of electric energy established a new high record—being about fourteen per cent above the same period in 1936. The rate of gain narrowed in the closing months of the year. Since industrial activity began to decline in August the fact that power production did not drop lower was due to the lower rates, forced in part by the government, which stepped-up consumption. In some cases even, earnings increased with rate reductions. Normally, power companies keep their capacity two years ahead of demand but in recent years the fear of government interference inhibited normal expansion until the safety margin became extremely narrow. At the end of the year reports indicated that a construction deficit of $2,600,000,000 had piled up in the last five years.

Most hated by power companies are the Government-aided enterprises such as the Tennessee Valley Authority and the Bonneville Dam—the so-called "yard-stick projects." During the year utilities leaders insisted upon the abolition of the Utility Act, cessation of direct government competition, abandonment of grants to communities for power plants, abandonment of the accounting practices by which rates are determined by the "yard-stick projects," and freedom from the three per cent tax levied on gross revenues.

Late in the year President Roosevelt suggested that the Government would not compete with private companies if they would accept his plan for determining fair rates for electricity. Power companies were encouraged, feeling they had the President on the run. Nevertheless they would not release capital until after some definite and final action were taken or official statement announced.

Automobiles. The automobile industry, being geared closely to public demand, can be taken as one good index of business conditions. At the beginning of 1937 car makers were looking forward to a good year—this in spite of labor troubles at the Fisher plants and the expectations of those who know the automotive labor situation that the winter season would be one of sporadic strikes. There were strikes and yet the year was a good one. Labor troubles continued in glass factories and other part-producing plants. The motor plants themselves were tied up with sit-downs. Still automobile production was above the 1936 level for similar months, except for two short periods—once in January and once in July and August. At other times the trend of production exceeded that for 1936 by as much as 40,000 cars per month. For the first nine months of 1937 the increase over the previous year was 500,000 units, a gain of sixteen per cent. Late in November labor troubles again reduced activity in the automobile plants.

A cheerful editorial in the *Iron Age* reflected upon the gains made by the automobile manufacturers:

> . . . and speaking of automobiles, no one ever saw a depression in this country when the automobile industry was good. Who buys automobiles? People with income. Then reflect on this: Farmers will average this year $24,000,000 more income per week than they did last year. Factory workers will average $50,000,000 per week more this year than last in wages. Stock-holders will average $10,000,000 per week more this year in dividends than last year. (Statistics from Babson Statistical Organization.) This means more automobiles bought, more steel required, more of most everything.

Truck registrations, too, were ahead of 1936 levels. For the first eight months 460,000 units were produced compared with the previous high of 439,442 units in the same period a year earlier. At this rate the production of trucks for the year will surpass the all time high of 1929.

Managers of automobile plants took the greater demand for cars as a signal to expand. Buick spent $10,000,000 for expansion. Packard, late in September, announced a $13,000,000 construction program. In October the Cadillac-LaSalle division of General Motors awarded a contract for a new plant to cost $6,500,000. Ford alone, upon resuming activity in

October, announced a $40,000,000 expansion program. A spreading out in one of the basic industries of this sort lends confidence in the future and brightens the picture for the key industry of construction.

The trend of business recovery is reflected in the price of automobiles. Prices started upward in the

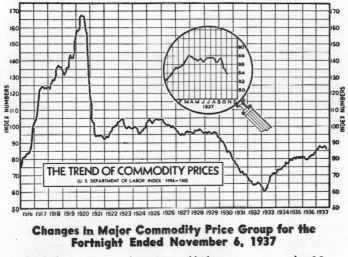

Changes in Major Commodity Price Group for the Fortnight Ended November 6, 1937

Farm Products...........down 3.0	Metals................down 0.5
Foods..................down 0.7	Building material..........down 1.0
Hides and leather........down 2.7	Chemicals...............down 0.5
Textiles.................down 1.2	Housefurnishings..........down 0.5
Fuel and lighting.........down 0.2	Miscellaneous............down 1.1

("*The Magazine of Wall Street*")

summer and continued to climb with the appearance of the 1938 models. Compared with the same models for 1937 the prices of cars are up from seven to sixteen per cent with most changes averaging less than ten per cent. One manufacturer of more expensive cars boosted the price twenty-five per cent. The car makers insist that higher prices are not out-and-out raises since accessories, previously calling for an extra charge, are now included in the standard delivered price. Moreover, buyers are getting a better car than they got in 1936, especially in the matter of comforts and refinements. As anticipated, higher prices have tightened the market and near the end of the year there was already talk of cuts to stimulate buying. However, prices reflect not only the attitude of the public but also conditions which have characterized all business activity; that is, the confidence of labor shown in strikes and conferences, the rise in the cost of raw materials and continued plant expansion.

Freight Carloadings and Railroads. Forecasters taking the pulse of business look to the carloading index for concise information on production, exchange and distribution of goods. In spite of higher freight rates and the demands from employees for higher wages the index of carloadings was consistently above that of 1936 for the first eight months. In September and again in October the line for carloadings dipped below the 1936 marks. Over a number of years, however, carloadings indicate that production and distribution are better than at any time since 1932.

During the year, the Interstate Commerce Commission permitted railroads to increase their rates. These increases were effective, for the most part, on non-competitive products like petroleum, bituminous coal, and steel. On November 1, southeastern roads raised passenger fares in coaches from one and one-half to two cents a mile. Although these rate boosts upped income by $47,000,000, the gain was only one-third of the recent wage increases. At the year's end the railroads still sought higher rates. A November petition to the Interstate Commerce Commission asked for increases ranging from ten to fifteen per cent and amounting to a total of $400,000,000. This boost if put into effect would bring the return on railroad investments up to five and three-quarters per cent. To prevent freight from being hauled by trucks the railroads asked further that truck rates be increased proportionately.

Construction. Construction—a "crucial factor" in recovery—is a third of the way up from the low of 1932 to the high of 1928. But in spite of its slow and steady rise, it still lags behind general industry. Much confidence was shown in the early months of the year and activity was almost feverish in residential building. January marked an increase of 109 per cent over January, 1936. Since then there has been a steady lag which in the last few months of the year became more decided. By March the increase had fallen to sixty-three per cent and by August had skidded to a minus twenty-seven per cent. Total residential construction up to the end of October amounted to $802,401,300 as compared to $667,695,800 for the same period in 1936—an increase of twenty per cent. The decline during the latter part of the year took place in spite of big gaps in housing that needed to be filled. The total for all types of construction, however, yields steadier trends. An increase of thirteen per cent in January (over January, 1936) slipped to a minus eleven per cent by October. Where $2,269,-

027,200 had been expended in all construction in 1936, the total for the same period in 1937 was $2,510,-930,300, a plus eleven per cent.

The confidence of January was lacking in the latter part of the year. The hoped-for building boom had bogged down, temporarily at least. Experts assigned many causes. The decline of the stock market had necessarily restricted building expansion. The widely proclaimed "business recession" dulled enthusiasm for building, this being, in turn, both a cause and a result of curtailed construction. The decline was hastened by rising costs both for building materials and labor —the same cause of the increase in the price of automobiles. Finally and according to business tycoons, the attitude of the Administration toward industry in general and toward the public utilities in particular, caused curtailment of construction—especially in the industrial field. All this happened when business was "jittery" and private income was uncertain. Whenever there is a slump, housing needs can readily be postponed—the family waits another year for a new house or before they decide definitely to add the extra room. Slums continue to provide bad housing for the underprivileged. Industry becomes frightened and stops most of its building programs. 1938 will be a crucial year in the building trades. Will there be an upturn and if so will it chart the way to complete recovery? Late in November President Roosevelt asked Congress to take note of the drag in building, suggested increasing FHA guarantees to 90% of loans on small homes, reduce interest rates from 6¼ per cent to 5¼ per cent, and take other steps calculated to revive the industry while solving the problem of a poorly housed, underbuilt America.

Steel. The steel industry fought a courageous but uphill battle from the beginning of the year. In 1936 steel production gained slowly but steadily, rising from slightly less than fifty per cent capacity in January to almost eighty per cent capacity at the end of December. By April, 1937, it reached ninety-three per cent of capacity. January floods in the Ohio Valley did not check the climb. In May floods rose again in the area of Pittsburgh, Wheeling and other communities bordering on the Ohio River and its tributaries. Production in Pittsburgh was cut off only slightly; but, in Wheeling shut-downs pushed steel operations from ninety-nine to seventy-five per cent capacity. Even this slowing up was looked upon as of minor concern. But a more serious blow was felt at the same time. In four independent steel companies Inland, Youngstown, Republic, and Bethlehem—there were C.I.O. walkouts. Floods and strikes were too much—the nation's steel production plunged from ninety-one per cent of capacity to seventy-seven per cent in a week. The Pittsburgh plant of Carnegie-Illinois, like others not hit by strike and flood, continued to run close to its capacity, but was unable to uphold the country's average.

Despite these set-backs, the steel industries produced more tonnage in the first nine months of 1937 than in the same period a year ago. By so doing, they pushed their customers with excess inventories—build-

ing construction had been slower than had been anticipated—and prices fell. A third heavy blow had
been struck at the steel industries.

By the end of October steel was staggering. The
drop in production to fifty-five per cent of capacity,
compared to seventy-four per cent in October, 1936,
represented, according to *Business Week* ". . . a far
more drastic decline than anyone in the trade anticipated a few weeks ago, and there is no sign of improvement for next week. November, however, is expected
to rise somewhat above the October level." Expectations fell short of realization. Far, far short. By the
middle of December production was down to twenty-
six per cent of capacity—the lowest point since 1934.
The floods, strikes, falling prices, huge reserves, uncertain futures for railroads and utilities, and general
"business recession" were more than the staunch steel
industry could absorb in its uphill fight. Further ad-
justments needed to be made. Business was still asking, "Will there be more or less government control?"

Stocks and Bonds. The pulse of business watched
daily by the public is registered in the activities and
prices of stocks and bonds.

Stocks were fairly steady for the first four months.
Railroads slowly improved, utilities declined slightly,
commercial and industrial stocks rose slightly and then
fell from January to the end of March. From April to
June a steady decline in all stocks took them to the
levels of October, 1936. July and early August showed
marked gains but not enough to bring them to the highs
of March. From late August until late in November

the decline in all stocks was sharp and steady. During
the first two weeks in December the market slowly
improved although the rise was slight.

The trend in bonds was not much different from that
in stocks. After a slight loss in March, United States
Government Bonds were steady throughout the year.

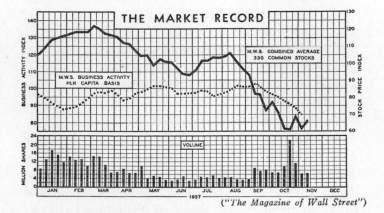

("*The Magazine of Wall Street*")

Utility, industrial, and railroad bonds also dipped in
March, were steady until the end of August, and then
dropped decisively. Railroad bonds, weak throughout
the year, suffered most, going from $90 on a $100 bond
in August to below $75 in November.

In the many explanations for the sharp break since
mid-August some of the numerous complications are
apparent. *Business Week* lists the following:

    1. The spectacular rise and fall in commodity
       prices which led, first, to forward buying and

accumulation of inventory; later, to a lapse of buying.

2. Declining profit margins due to higher labor costs and higher prices of raw materials.
3. Consumer resistance which prevented marking up finished goods to compensate for materially higher costs.
4. War scares in Europe and the Orient.
5. Credit contraction due to increased bank reserve requirements, gold sterilization, and declining deposits.
6. Government interference with business, past and prospective.
7. The undistributed earnings tax.
8. High estimates of installment selling, imposing a considerable lien on future income.
9. Failure of construction to come up to expectations because (a) high costs cut residential building, and (b) declining business activity delayed industrial expansion.
10. Fears that England's building boom is topping off.
11. The break in stock and bond prices (a cause and result) which curtails spending, particularly in the luxury lines.
12. The new financing log-jam, caused by the fall in stocks and bonds.
13. Deterrents to stock purchases such as capital-gains tax, high margin requirements, and restrictions on "inside" buying.
14. Labor troubles.

Admitting that all these factors have some influence the barometer becomes less reliable. The trend is

BUSINESS ACTIVITY

M.W.S. INDEX (PER CAPITA BASIS)

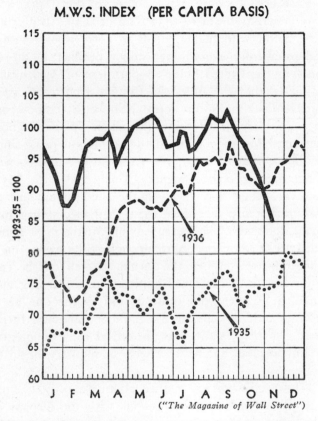

("The Magazine of Wall Street")

plain but the relative importance of various causes is not made clear. Most frequently, Government interference is cited by business as the factor of greatest influence. But the true explanations are probably not that simple. It is altogether likely that more Government regulation and control would result in less fluctuation.

Farmers' Income Up. Prices of farm products were generally lower in 1937 than in 1936. But crops were better with higher yields of corn, wheat, cotton and practically every other major product. Late in the year the United States Department of Agriculture estimated that the American farmers received in cash for live stock and crops approximately $8,500,000,000. In 1936, their cash receipts ran about $7,920,000,000. The total for 1937 climbed to the highest peak since the boom year of 1929, when the farmer income was about $2,000,000,000 higher. Compared with 1932, however, when they received the smallest amount of cash during any year since 1924, their income had just about doubled. The increase is one of the most hopeful signs of recovery. Agriculture is still a basic American industry. When the farmer is well off, he can buy more seed, improved implements, a washing machine, a used car not quite as old as the one he is driving, and, perhaps, even a radio or some new furniture. In turn, this increase in orders calls for greater production and again the wheels of industry begin to spin.

Wheat growers will realize about $666,549,000 on this past year's crop compared with an income of $408,000,000 of a year ago. Cotton growers, in addition to a higher income, established five new records which are not likely to be duplicated in the near future: (1) highest total production on record, (2) greatest yield per acre, (3) top ginnings up to December 13, (4) peak Southern consumption, and (5) record spot sales for one week. On December 8, the Department of Agriculture estimated the total yield at 18,746,000 bales which exceeds by 768,626 bales the previous high set in 1926. For 1938, acreage will probably be cut drastically to curb the mounting surplus. As a result the current record is not likely to be equaled for some years to come.

Not all farmers shared in the higher total income. Corn producers, for example, harvested a billion bushels more than in 1936 but received less cash because of lower prices. However, the income from corn cannot be taken as an adequate index of general conditions. In normal years about 90 per cent of the crop is used in the county where it is grown and is not available commercially. Albeit the farmer who had corn to sell did not fare as well as his neighbor with other produce.

Even with the higher general income, the farm problem is by no means solved. At the close of the special Congressional session, disagreements between the Senate and House caused the crop control bills to be sent to a conference committee (see Chapter III). Final action and a more permanent solution of the farmers' plight await developments of 1938.

Foreign Trade Improves. In the early months of 1937 the United States imported more goods than it sent out. It appeared for a time that the year would end with an import balance. But during the last four months of the year, exports of farm products jumped up and imports of raw materials for manufacturers dropped. The Department of Commerce estimated the total imports and exports at $6,400,000,000 or 31 per cent above 1936 and 118 per cent above 1932—the low point of the depression. Exports exceeded imports by about $100,000,000 whereas the 1936 balance was approximately one-third that amount. The general picture of foreign trade appears promising but below the surface trend may be found conditions not so hopeful. A business slump at home and wars abroad have been basic influences—no one knows their full effect.

Michigan Helps the Buyer Get His Money's Worth. A new consumers' bureau has just been set up by the State of Michigan. The first of its kind, it will function beginning January 1, 1938, as a Division of the State Department of Agriculture. Through its offices in Detroit, it will answer the buyers' inquiries by sending proper specifications for any article they may wish to purchase. Using its broad police powers, the bureau may bar questionable products from Michigan markets. But above all, its aim is to educate the consumer so that he will demand his money's worth. What Michigan has done in 1937 to accomplish this result, other states are likely to do in 1938, 1939, 1940 or beyond.

At Year's End. There was no getting around it—even the chief of the optimists had to admit that United States business had a major set-back in 1937. In three months the stock market drop was 40 per cent. Not since 1907 had the business curve shot down so precipitous a toboggan slide as it did in August. But the aggregate volume of business and income for the year was still above 1936. The major question at the year's end was: will the depression continue into 1938?

By mid-December, the outlook for 1938 appeared brighter. The *New York Times* index recorded an advance in business activity for the first week since August 14, when it had reached a high for the year and for recovery. For the week ending December 11, the index stood at 85.0 compared with 84.8 for the previous week, and 107.5 for the corresponding week of 1936. The major gains were in electric power and carloadings.

Regarding the same week, *Barron's, The National Financial Weekly* commented as follows: "Decline in business has halted for the longest period since September. Steel operations held last week at the previous week's level for the first time in three months; steel scrap prices have advanced. Cotton goods markets are more active with prices firmer. Some western shoe plants are resuming operations following several months of drastic curtailment. Retail trade is enjoying a relatively good business as holiday buying and colder weather act as stimulants, with merchandiser's estimates now placing December sales 5 per cent behind last year. The general level of commodity prices gives indication of growing stability."

All signs reveal that the present business recession will not follow in severity that which began in 1929. Then, money rates were high; today, money is cheap and means are at hand for making it still cheaper if necessary. Then, swollen inventories gave evidence of overproduction; today, inventories are at an exceedingly low point and any business stimulation will call immediately for greater production. Then, the depression was world-wide; today, practically no recession is apparent in other countries. In view of these facts the trend is likely to be upward early in 1938.

The Business Outlook. The prospects for 1938 are not so clearly defined as they were at the beginning of 1937. A year ago business magnates did not differ much in their statements concerning the direction of recovery.

Near the end of 1937 the Bureau of Agricultural Economics forecasts did not strike up enthusiasm. They predict that,

> the current recession would continue well into 1938; that national income would fall below the $69,000,000,000 (revised downward) estimate of 1937; that wholesale prices would continue downward into 1938; that farm income would fall somewhat under 1937; that the automobile industry would meet with a smaller replacement demand next year, due to the higher prices asked, and to the more stringent terms of financing; that textile production would fall considerable under 1937, especially in the first half of the year; and that steel production also would slip below its 1937 total.

The one bright spot is a probable increase in building construction under the impetus of new federal aid.

However, this stark pessimism is not shared by individual leaders in the business field.

Says Walter Lichtenstein, Vice-president of the First National Bank of Chicago,

> I am not looking for a very sharp recession comparable to the one we had in 1930-32, but I am expecting one of those gradual declines with which we are also familiar. . . . After all, the collapse which began in 1929 was probably the final liquidation of the economic ruin caused by the war, and it is unlikely that without another great war we shall have in the near future a recession of similar magnitude and severity.

Says Leonard P. Ayres, Vice-president of the Cleveland Trust Company,

> The optimistic hope is that as business recovers we shall once more have the old volumes of commercial loans. . . . The pessimistic fear . . . is that we may have another banking crisis like that of five years ago. . . . Now this pessimistic fear is even less warranted than the optimistic hope. There does not now exist any set of conditions that could result in a credit collapse like that of the great depression. . . . No collapse of general price levels on a similar scale is now possible for the simple reason that we had the collapse several years ago.

And Charles R. Gay, President of the New York Stock Exchange,

> It seems clear that the recovery has not pro-

ceeded to the point where it has become desirable for industry to give serious consideration to the enlargement of productive facilities, to increasing its absorption of unemployed workers, to the training of skilled labor, and thus to the contribution of a more abundant life.

Mr. A. W. Stelmok, Economist of the International Statistical Bureau, Incorporated, predicted an extention of the present recession in general business during a large part of the first half of next year and a substantial upturn in the last half. "While the present recession may continue for several months, it does not mark the beginning of a major depression."

Says Mr. Ernest G. Draper, Assistant Secretary of Commerce,

Today the outlook is encouraging. We have just emerged successfully from a period of severe strain. The future holds a still greater promise which will be realized if statesmanship and unselfish vision are exercised by those who are responsible for developing our major policies in both industry and government.

At the convention in New York City of the National Association of Manufacturers, Lammot Du Pont expressed doubt regarding the future because of the lack of confidence on the part of business: "Are taxes to go higher, lower, or stay where they are? We don't know. Is labor to be union or non-union, is the A. F. of L. or the C.I.O. to dominate it, and in any event what will be expected of the employer? It is impossible even to guess at the answers. Are we to have inflation or deflation, more government spending or less? Industry is without a scrap of knowledge on either subject. Are new restrictions to be placed on capital, new limits on profits? Industry doesn't know. The whole future is a gigantic question mark."

Optimism was expressed by Glenn Griswold, publisher of *Business Week:* "Developments of the next twelve months should prove that the business man who does not plan his program in preparation for a substantial increase in the volume and activity of business in 1938 will be responding to fear impulses rather than translating sound thinking into action. Favorable factors include the strongest credit and banking situation in our history, an increase of nearly 1,000,000 in the list of employed in the last year, a gain of $7,000,-000,000 in national income, cash farm income close to the record high, and, finally, a tremendous total of unfilled wants that have been accumulating for seven years. The negative factors are almost entirely summarized in the word "fear."

But behind all this optimism there is a basic question regarding a final solution to our economic difficulties. What of the future? Not merely of 1938 but of the next hundred years or so? Can depressions be conquered under the present economic structure? Events of 1937 provide the answer less clearly than did those of 1936.

CHAPTER V

SCIENCE ADVANCES

That science moves along impelled by infrequent sparks of genius, flashes of sudden and startling discoveries, magic touches to inert matter, inspiration —not hard work and persistent drive—is a common belief. The public generally looks upon the end result. They see that some new formula has been devised for saving and prolonging life. They watch pop-eyed the first public demonstration of a new gadget, a novel mechanical contraption designed to save time, effort and energy. They hear about the discovery of a new star a prodigious number of light years off in the heavens. They are amazed at the complexity of the universe. What they seldom awake to is the enormous amount of steady and painstaking work that goes on, year in and year out, day and night, in the research laboratories of giant corporations, tiny industrial plants, colleges, universities, private homes and shops. Many a menial worker whose name has never glared from headlines or even been slipped into lists of contributors to science has laid the groundwork, has discovered principles upon which a notable invention has been based. Without reward, without even being noticed, he works on—sometimes in irritating drudgery, more often in the joy of creation. Thus

148

thousands of workers each year assist in breaking down the barriers against scientific progress and act as midwives at the birth of new creations. Even among the great—an Edison, a Steinmetz, a Marconi—each discovery grows out of years of hard work not merely out of sudden thought without effort.

The year 1937 was no exception. New discoveries, inventions, were announced from time to time, but the steady labor of searching that has been going on in laboratories which will lead to the notable contributions of five, ten or fifty years from now will never reach the public eye. Some day articles and books will be written to reveal fully the men and women, the patient labor, the problems of the rank and file of science. They cannot be reviewed here; they can only be assumed.

To Stave Off Death. Man, impelled by his deepest instincts, has always fought to preserve himself, to ward off disease and pestilence, to prolong his life. In primitive times when he did not understand the nature of diseases, or epidemics, he blamed them on the wrath of the gods—nothing could be done about them except by prayer and sacrifice. They were dreaded but accepted. Civilized man, however, has seen the ravages of one disease after another checked, its fangs drawn, its venom made harmless. He has seen a smaller and smaller proportion of babies die, has seen life lengthened. Still unsatisfied, he is eager to push further forward all efforts to ward off diseases and stave off death. He supports, therefore, medical research of all kinds. He builds great research centers, gleaming laboratories, and hungers for results. Lengthened life brings new problems in its wake. As disease after disease that preyed on childhood and youth has been partially or completely conquered, as more and more people have lived to middle or old age, medicine and science have had to shift their forces to battle against diseases peculiar to later life. Surgeons, X-ray specialists, biochemists have launched a wide attack on cancer, sometimes called "the accident that takes five years." Internists and bacteriologists have fought, are fighting year in, year out to type and control pneumonia which has been cynically branded "the old man's friend" since it permits him to die without too much pain or struggle. But curiously the scientists have not yet made much progress in checking the varieties of ways in which tired old hearts grind to a final stop. As a matter of fact, about one third of all deaths in the United States result from some type of heart disease —more deaths than occur from cancer, Bright's disease, pneumonia, and tuberculosis combined. A few scattered efforts here and there go on but the amount of money invested in permanent research funds to find out more about the heart is pitifully small—probably no more than about a million dollars.

The automobile has become in fact the chief of the "grim reapers"—killing about 40,000 in 1937 as against 37,800 in 1936—but little is now being done to dull its devastating claws.

Thus 1937 brought scant progress in curbing the number of deaths by heart disease or the automobile. In other directions research has been more fruitful.

Dr. Charles G. Heyd, who during the year retired as
president of the Association of Medicine, said in a talk
at Atlantic City, "Medicine is to be rated well in
advance of any of the physical sciences." And why
should it not be, for research in medicine results, after
all, from man's most fundamental urge—the will to
live.

The battle against cancer made tangible gains
through bigger support for research. One might wish
that acknowledged gains in treating the disease were
as tangible. During the year, Congress passed a bill
introduced by their own ever-persistent doctor, Senator Royal S. Copeland of New York, and Representative Alfred Lee Bulwinkle of North Carolina, authorizing a grant of $750,000 for a research center, The Na-
tional Cancer Institute, and $700,000 to support the
center "for the purpose of conducting research, investigation, experiments and studies relating to cause,
diagnosis and treatment of cancer. . . ." A much
larger fund—$10,000,000—came as a gift to Yale Uni-
versity from Starling W. Childs and his sister, Alice
S. Coffin, for cancer research. With these two gifts,
the end of 1937 found cancer research funds more than
double their total at the beginning of the year. The
positive results of these researches, however impatient
the public, may not be felt for some years to come.
The usual annual flare-ups of hope that a "cure" had
been found and disappointment that it had not, occurred in 1937. Experimenters tried freezing the can-
cerous tissue where it could be reached with a freezing
machine. Other researchers tried different dye injec-

tions. But as the year ended medicine was still warning the public that no universal "cure" had been found. In early diagnosis, X-rays, and surgery still lay the best hope.

The anti-syphilis campaign that got under way in 1936 grew more widespread and significant in 1937. The "hush-hush" policy of former years is outmoded. And well that it should be. The quack venereal doctors who flourished at the expense of the victims of the disease are finding it more and more difficult to survive. Early in 1937, Dr. Thomas N. Parran, Surgeon General of the United States Public Health Service, called a National Conference of physicians and health officers to discuss the program to wipe out venereal diseases. A number of states already require pre-marriage medical certificates for both bride and groom, indicating that they are free from syphilis. In the Chicago area, particularly, the drive to stamp out syphilis is intense. Blanks were sent out widely asking the question: "In strict confidence, and at no expense to you, would you like to be given by your own physician a blood test for syphilis?" The tenor of the whole campaign is to find syphilis, to treat syphilis, and to teach anti-syphilis.

Also during the year a book was issued under the authorship of Dr. Parran with the title, *Shadow on the Land*. It stresses for physicians and laymen alike a platform for action in the fight against syphilis. To wit: (1) locate syphilis, (2) get public funds to assure adequate treatment of all infected persons, (3) educate the private physician and the general public about syphilis. A major battle it is and, if present trends persist, one that is likely to be fought until the new rapidly spreading plague is not only checked but wiped out.

The fight against disease goes on at other fronts. During the year, Dr. James F. Kelly of Creighton University's Medical School reported that X-ray treatment of gas gangrene cut the mortality rate to eight per cent. Before X-rays were used, patients with gas gangrene had only one chance in two for survival even after the affected part was amputated.

A more effective treatment of whooping cough has been developed. A substance similar to that coughed up by a patient is now available and may be used to soften the spasms and protect against death in the worst stages of the disease. Forward-looking and progressive Denmark has begun to vaccinate its children against whooping cough and has met with marked success. Only six out of 3,900 vaccinated children who had the disease died, whereas for 26 out of 1,000 unvaccinated children whooping cough proved fatal. Vaccination, it seems, is another good way to keep the mortality rate down.

Another novel medical experiment has been carried on in connection with the war in Spain. How strange that wars, designed principally to kill, should also result in means of saving lives. In the Spanish situation, blood taken from recently killed soldiers and private donors has been sealed in bottles after being treated scientifically, refrigerated, and sent to war hospitals where it is used to save lives of critically wounded soldiers. Estimates place the number of lives saved thus far at more than four hundred.

From the Physician-in-chief of the St. Stanislaus Hospital in Warsaw comes the report that insulin is effective in relieving allergic asthma patients. By giving just enough insulin to produce shock, the shortness of breath is quickly relieved in most cases. After a number of insulin shocks, the asthmatic attacks change, become less severe, occur less often, or, perhaps, disappear altogether. A welcome omen, this, for allergic asthmatic patients who up to now have found relief only by seeking far climates or by living in thoroughly air-conditioned rooms. Doctors warned, however, that this treatment had no effect upon asthma that often accompanies some forms of heart disease.

Insulin made still greater contribution to medical science with the sometimes successful treatment of certain forms of insanity such as schizophrenia, including dementia praecox, which is characterized by a "cracking-up" of the personality or a detachment of the person from his surroundings. In this method of treatment, introduced first by Dr. Manfred Sakel of Austria, heavy doses of insulin, producing coma or "insulin shock," are injected into the body. About one-third to one-half of the cases so treated show improvement; the percentage is even higher when the disease is treated soon after its onset. This discovery is a decided step forward as these types of insanity attack mainly young people and have up to now been thought almost incurable.

Another bright spot in medical annals is found in the

report of Dr. O. P. Kimball of Cleveland on a goiter-prevention program started in 1924. When observation began, in Midland County, Michigan, part of a "goiter belt," one-third of all the children in school had a well-developed goiter. Almost every child showed a questionable enlargement of the thyroid. Since 1924, children in the county have been taking iodized salt to make up for the deficiency in food iodine in that area. A recent survey of the same county revealed normal thyroids in ninety per cent of the children. Just such follow-up studies as these show what can be done with painstaking scientific research carried on over a long period of time.

The most publicized and perhaps the most significant advance in medicine throughout the year was the successful use of sulfanilamide. It appears particularly effective in the treatment of meningitis caused by hemolytic streptococci which heretofore has usually proved fatal, in some bladder and kidney diseases, in gonorrhea, in malaria and in other types of bacterial infections.

To Move Faster and Safer. Americans characteristically cry for greater and greater speed. Scientists and research workers aim to make the world move faster, but to attain safety with speed. One of the greatest boons for speeding up transportation in modern times is the airplane. In 1937, the airplane was made safer—speedier as well. "Flight analyzers" which automatically make a record of almost everything going on between taking off and landing, were installed on planes of the United Air Lines. From the records, pilots can reconstruct the story of the flight. The efficiency of operation should improve as a result, particularly of the "automatic pilot" which is now used between eighty-five and ninety per cent of the time the plane is in the air. The "flight analyzer" will check airway traffic controls. It will aid also in determining causes of increasingly rare accidents when neither pilot remains to tell the story.

Ice forming on the wings of the airplane has always been an enemy of safe flying. Two methods are used to combat this danger. The first, improved by the U. S. Bureau of Air Commerce and approved this year, consists of rubber overshoes placed on the leading edge of the plane's wing and tail surface. The overshoes can be expanded and contracted, thus breaking up the ice formations so that the wind whistling over the wings will whip the cracked ice off, blow it away. The main defect in this device is that a hole in the rubber will make the whole mechanism useless. The second device, produced by Dr. Theodore Theodorsen of Hampton and William Clay of Buchroe, Virginia, uses waste heat from the exhaust pipe of the plane's engine to produce vapor heat which is projected against the inside of the leading edges of the wings to prevent the formation of ice. The condensed vapor flows into pockets and from there back to the boiler around the exhaust pipe to be used again.

From the head of Columbia's division of electrochemistry, Professor Colin G. Fink, comes the word that he has succeeded in coating steel with aluminum. This new process will be a boon to automobiles, buildings, railroads, house furnishings and industrial machinery as well as to the speed and endurance of airplanes, since it combines aluminum's rust resistance with the enormous strength of steel. In bridge construction, steel wires with a tensile strength of 460,000 pounds per square inch may be protected by aluminum which when used alone has a tensile strength of only 3,000 pounds per square inch.

Curiously enough, mechanical inventions have even been devised to speed up the work of the teacher, the student, and the research worker. Small photographs of documents and books, called "micro-films," are being made on ordinary motion picture films. They can be read by the use of a machine that enlarges the pages to more than their original size. By this new method, duplicates of valuable records, manuscripts, books and illustrations become more readily accessible to the student and research worker because of easy duplication.

A machine which grades examination papers at the rate of 600 to 900 per hour has come from the laboratories of the International Tabulating Machine Company. It works on the principle that graphite, of which pencil lead is in part made, conducts electricity. So-called objective tests, where the right answer is picked from several given, are used with answer sheets. For each question the student crosses out the number of what he thinks is the right answer. The answer sheets are then passed through the machine. If the answer is checked in the right space, electrical contact is made. The dial shows the total number of right answers. It is now, therefore, very simple for the teacher to grade certain kinds of tests.

To Make More and Better Things with Less Effort. The textile field has come forward in 1937 with several inventions which will make better materials more easily. It was when Robert M. Greenleaf, a Los Angeles mechanic, upset some "dry ice" on a woolen blanket that he discovered a process to remove the burrs and foreign material from wool. He has found that by passing the wool through a boxlike refrigerator which has a temperature of forty degrees below zero, Fahrenheit, the burrs literally drop out.

A process which makes wool unshrinkable without adversely affecting its quality, softness, fluffiness, color or ability to take dye, was patented by A. J. Hall, an English textile chemist. His method consists of immersing the wool one hour in a one-and-one-half to two per cent solution of the chemical, sulphuryl chloride.

There has been during the last few years an attempt to standardize textile measurements. Up to now many of the measurements, such as stiffness, thickness, and texture, have been measured by "rule of thumb." Recently a textile stiffness tester was invented by Dr. Irving J. Saxl of Rhode Island. In this tester a small piece of cloth is clamped by one edge on a shaft which can be turned by a knob and which carries a finger that sweeps over a scale. Turn the knob and both the sample and pan are pressed down. The stiffer the sample, the harder must be the pressure. No more

need for variation in stiffness of blankets supposedly
of the same quality.

A rivet which literally rivets itself when minute
charges of explosive placed inside of it go off, has been
patented by Karl and Otto Butler of Germany. It
will be particularly useful in joining the framework
of airplanes and dirigibles where small rivets and rivets
of softer metals are used.

A new efficiency-raising tungsten filament that re-
duces heat wastage and gives ten per cent more light
in electric light bulbs has been produced by J. E. Kew-
ley of General Electric. He took a standard 3.4 inch
filament coil of hair-fine tungsten wire and recoiled it
to the length of five-eighths of an inch. As a result the
"average American family will get eighty cents worth
of free light with its annual fifteen dollars worth of il-
lumination."

To Grow More and Better Products. From
abroad come reports of new uses of old products as
well as new and better products themselves. South
Africa reports that alfalfa makes an excellent and
palatable vegetable for human beings. It may be eaten
raw, or cooked like spinach. Russia's All-Union Institute of Plant Cultivation has been studying potatoes
in South America where many wild varieties are found.
It has found a wild variety, "acaule," capable of resisting frost of 17 degrees Fahrenheit, and several
other varieties which resist phytophthora, the most
dreaded disease of potatoes. The Institute is now com-
pleting its work of creating new hybrids from these
wild and native varieties which promise high yields

and resistance to disease and cold. From Hungary comes the report of the discovery of a new vitamin, designated P, which is closely related to vitamin C and found in lemons and paprika. It is a natural companion of vitamin C which is found mostly in fruits. Lack of it causes scurvy.

The U. S. Department of Agriculture has patented a device to overcome one of the difficulties in growing fruit, that is, heavy production one year followed by light production the next. This difficulty is brought about by the fact that often when winter conditions are unfavorable many trees do not flower and bear fruit. To overcome this condition, Daniel G. Sarber and Marston H. Kimball have devised a gas tight cover in which fruit trees are each enclosed for two hours two weeks before the normal time for the start of their cycle of growth. Butylene gas is released inside the tents and the temperature is kept between sixty and one hundred degrees.

Better fruit is the object of another development of 1937. Peaches free from fuzz, with smooth waxy skins like plums, can now be grown as the result of long patient breeding work of Dr. Fred W. Holmann, research horticulturist of Virginia Agricultural Experiment Station. The flesh is yellowish around the pit, the stone is free and small, and the flavor and texture are superior.

To Combine Elements and Materials in New Ways. Every days scientists are attempting to find new uses for waste materials. This year Japan, which is already among the world leaders in the production of rayon yarn as well as of pure silk, is promoting the production of rayon-making pulp from rice husks, of which a practically unlimited supply is assured. The political and economic question of boycotting rayon as well as silk must now be faced.

Several years ago Germany reported manufacture of sugar and the probability of producing several other food products from sawdust. Now a plastic has been made from this same waste material. Lignin, the substance which cements together the tree and plant cells and reinforces the cellulose within the cell, is the basis for this plastic. Simple decomposing of sawdust with dilute acid at the proper temperature and pressure is sufficient to produce a powder which will mold to a hard, black, dense material not very different from other well-known molding materials but at only a fraction of their cost.

Parts for automobile interiors, such as the instrument board, window moldings and ash trays, are being made from plastics. An experimental interior door panel is being developed in which even the fasteners are stamped out of plastic and the complete panel simply is snapped onto the door. A plastic substitute for glass, "Plexiglas," manufactured by Röhn and Haas, is being used for windshields and complete cockpit enclosures for pilots in airplanes. Optical lenses have been pressed out of synthetic resin plastic by Peter Kock de Gooreynd of the British Imperial Chemical Institute. Such lenses are much cheaper than those now in use since no grinding or polishing is necessary. So far as is now known their only disadvantage is that they are softer, more easily scratched than the optical glass. At this rate many things will no longer be what they seem.

But all the new materials are not plastics. A glass fabric suitable for blankets, filters, and insulators against heat and electricity has been made by John H. Thomas of Owen-Illinois Glass Company. A piece of glass cloth is not indestructible but it can be handled much like canvas. The tensile strength of the individual fibers is 250,000 pounds per square inch. This fabric is especially good for filter cloth because of its durability but it cannot be used for alkalis. It is expected that glass tapestries and theater curtains will soon be on the market.

To See More and Farther. Because science has enabled us to see more and farther every year we are now able to keep a careful watch on the heavens. Things of size and intensity which are incomprehensible to one not acquainted with stellar dimensions, are found there. Harvard astronomers have discovered on a photograph taken of the sky near the North Pole, the biggest of known galaxies. This huge galaxy is 50,-000,000 light years long, 20,000,000 light years wide and 1,000,000,000 light years away. And a light year is almost six trillion miles.

Two super-novae have been found by Dr. Fritz Zwicky of the California Institute of Technology within a fortnight. The first "new star," 3,000,000 light years from the earth, is situated roughly midway between the Big Dipper and the bright star Arcturus, in the northern sky. It was discovered August 29.

The second super-nova, which was discovered September 10, is 7,000,000 light years from the earth in the constellation of Perseus. Neither can be seen by the unaided eye although they are said to produce 500,-000,000 times as much light as the sun. If such a stellar explosion happened near the earth and sun and its planets, it would undoubtedly wipe them out, and H. G. Wells' *Things to Come* would not be so fantastic.

On June 8 of this year one of the longest eclipses on record was observed at a spot in the open ocean 1,500 miles from the nearest land. It was seen from a freighter by Professor John Q. Stewart of Princeton and James Stokely of Franklin Institute. The eclipse lasted seven minutes and four seconds at this remote spot. It was studied at Peru where it lasted over three minutes. Important discoveries were made from pictures taken by Major Albert W. Stevens who viewed the eclipse from an airplane. They confirmed the inference of von Klueber that the corona, a mystery on which astrophysicists have always speculated, is really a huge globe of highly tenuous matter about a million miles deep, a globe in which the sun and its glowing atmosphere is encased.

To Make the World a Better Place to Live In. The movies are attempting to make themselves more realistic than ever by devices demonstrated before the Society of Motion Picture Engineers, New York. These devices make pictures three-dimensional in both sight and sound. The sound device consists of two independent systems that feed two loud speakers so arranged that the sound from the screen is given direction and depth. Two sound tracks are equalized within the usual space on the film. Theaters must have two sound systems instead of one to give this effect. Polarized light is used to produce the effect of three-dimensions in sight. The audience wears glasses with lens of Polaroid, a synthetic substance which cuts out all light except that which vibrates in one direction. One lens is blind to the light that can enter the other lens. Two cameras are used and two movies are flashed on the screen simultaneously.

In order to make voices more pleasing to the ear in the "talkies" and radio, John Hays Hammond, Jr., has invented an electric voice editor. The main works of this machine are a number of parallel electrical paths between the microphone and the recording instrument. Each path has a filter which filters out unpleasant qualities in the particular type of voice for which it is designed. It records only the more pleasing qualities of the artist's voice and suppresses the unpleasant. Telephone companies might find use in that discovery.

In this age of air transportation and attempted crop control, accurate weather prediction is more important than ever before. The United States Weather Bureau is trying out a new method of weather forecasting which consists of a vertical examination of the atmospheric conditions rather than a horizontal survey of the earth's surface. Small sounding balloons are sent up into the air with radio-meteorographs. They contain a thermometer, hygrometer, a barometer, short-wave radio transmitter and batteries, enclosed in a streamlined aluminum shell, the whole weighing only two pounds. No statistics as to its accuracy in comparison with the old methods have been reported as yet. But perhaps in the future, newspaper and radio weather reports may be more accurate.

Russia has sent P. P. Shirskov, I. D. Papanin, E. N. Fedoror, and E. T. Krekel to make a year's scientific study of the Arctic, one of the objectives of which is to send periodic reports of polar weather conditions to Moscow. These weather observations will be of benefit not only to aviators but to the whole world. Most of the weather of the United States is made in the North. Another question this expedition is attempting to answer is the depth of the ocean's basin at the pole. They are also studying a powerful sea current flowing from the Atlantic into the Arctic.

There are new developments in atom-smashing to be reported. The physics department of the University of Wisconsin reports a new 2,700,000-volt electrostatic generator which is the "highest steady operating potential" ever used in atom bombardment research. This new "atom smasher" which excels all other machines of its type in exactness of data, has already in preliminary form aided in the discovery of gamma radiation even more powerful than radium rays. This gamma radiation is freed when fluorine gas is bombarded in the new apparatus. A promising field of research in treatment of cancer, tumors, and other diseases is expected from this development.

Still Unexplored. In the latter part of September one of the few remaining "blank spots" of America

was explored by a party sent out by the American
Museum of Natural History and led by Dr. Harold
E. Anthony and George B. Andrews. The spot explored was Shiva Temple of Arizona's Grand Canyon.
The Temple is a plateau 4,000 feet above the canyon
floor almost level with the rim, some 300 acres in extent, which is believed to have been carved out by
erosion in the Ice Age. Before exploration it was
believed to be a "biological island" where animals
would have been isolated from those of the mainland
for thousands of years. The expedition spent ten days
on the island trapping animals such as mice, woodrats,
chipmunks and cotton-tail rabbits. Primitive tools and
ornaments found showed the explorers that they were
not the first human beings to have climbed to the top
of this plateau. The expedition was disappointing as
"not a single new species, let alone a new genus or a
new family" was discovered. Dr. Anthony thought
he observed "pale characteristics" in the animals.
Thus year after year man continues to explore the
earth and its inhabitants, sometimes, as here, finding
nothing but the old and familiar, again the new and
the strange.

Scientific Progress and Social Justice. The
United States Government is realizing that it has a
part to play in the development of inventions. The
National Resources Committee made a report this year
on the relationship of government to science and technology. The committee is particularly interested in
the type of new invention which may affect living and
working conditions in America in the future. The

suggestion of the committee was that national effort be used to assist in adjustment to these changing situations so that they "would result in the least possible social suffering and loss." Perhaps, in time, we shall not only continue to invent, but we will know how to use the power of these inventions for social good.

Nobel Prize Winners. Vitamin research was granted major recognition with the 1937 Nobel Prizes for Medicine and Chemistry going to three distinguished scientists all of whom had carried on extensive studies of Vitamin C. The $40,000 award for Medicine went to biochemist Albert Szent-Györgyi of the Hungarian University of Szeged. He found during the course of his studies that the adrenal glands secrete a substance, ascorbic acid, which is identical chemically with Vitamin C—the scurvy-preventing vitamin. In following up his early discoveries he traveled to a number of European universities and later to the Mayo Clinic in Rochester, Minnesota, where he was provided with a large stock of adrenal glands from the South St. Paul stockyards. Not able to get enough to conduct the research he wanted to do, he returned to Hungary. There, sometime later, while being served a heavily spiced dish prepared by his wife, the odor led him to make a chemical analysis of paprika which he found was the best source of Vitamin C that had yet been tried. Later he identified, along with Vitamin C in fruit juices and adrenal glands, a new substance which he calls Vitamin P.

The Nobel Prize in Chemistry was divided equally between Dr. Walter N. Haworth, biochemist at England's Birmingham University, and Dr. Paul Karrer, biochemist at Switzerland's University of Zurich, for, respectively, analyzing the chemical structures of Vitamin C and ascorbic acid and for producing Vitamin C artificially.

Similarly, the Nobel Prize in Physics was divided between Dr. Clinton J. Davisson of Manhattan's Bell Telephone Laboratories and Dr. George P. Thomson of Aberdeen for their independent researches on the nature of electrons. With these awards, two additional names were added to the list of distinguished scientists whose investigations of the atom have attracted world-wide attention.

CHAPTER VI

EDUCATION IN A DEMOCRACY

The schools of America reflect the democracy in which they function. No one point of view dominates. Educational leaders are not content to consider the schools right and perfect, to let them rest on set patterns. Trial and experimentation are part of the picture in every section of the country. To an outsider, such diversity, such apparent conflict as to the nature of education, spells confusion. But to an American, born and reared on a geographical and social frontier, experimentation in the schools is essential to progress. In some schools—perhaps most of them—a traditional course of study consisting of the three R's is followed rigidly and smacks of older generations, of stodgy tradition. In other schools all reading, writing and arithmetic *as such* has been discarded. Instead these schools provide pupils with a wide range of experiences approximating those of actual life. They read to learn about themselves and the life about them, not just to read. They write to persuade people to do things for them, or to communicate interesting or important information, or to express an idea or feeling in a bit of verse or story. Their arithmetic problems are real ones to them. Pupils work on individual, social, economic, artistic, human problems. They develop skills

169

such as reading, writing or calculating incidentally. As they need knowledge they find it. In the grown-up phrase, they "live and learn." They grow in and for family and social living. They are active human beings in the learning process, not "storage batteries" charged with the memory of the multiplication tables, dates of major events in history, or a junk heap of isolated facts. Between these extremes of tradition and experiment the American schools represent every conceivable variation. But in 1937, they moved consistently and definitely in the direction of providing broader, more real social experiences for moppets. The concept of education for social living, of education for living in a democracy, is taking hold as never before.

This trend is significant. When other nations such as Italy, Germany and Russia are using the schools to perpetuate a dictatorship, when Mussolini, Hitler and Stalin see in education one of their major hopes for continuing their political dominance, it is highly important that the American schools should move in the reverse direction, that of educating for freedom in expression and action. Fascist forces in the United States want nothing more than to gain control of the schools. Should they succeed, the country will readily overthrow its democratic tradition. On the other hand, if the current trend continues and gains momentum, future generations will be prepared for living in a democracy and for extending their freedom to a degree never yet achieved by their ancestors.

Fewer in Lower Grades. The number of empty seats in the elementary grades continued to grow in

1937. When in the fall, high school and college enrollments broke all records, there were about 1,000,000 fewer pupils in the elementary schools than eight years ago. And the trend will continue. From 1930 to 1936 the U. S. birth rate decreased steadily from 18.9 per 1,000 of the population to 16.6. Soon this decrease will begin to show itself in the high schools and still later in the colleges. Communities laying plans for the future cannot well afford to ignore these trends.

Schools—a Big Business. From the standpoint of the number of individuals involved, the educational system of the United States is the nation's biggest business. Estimates show that about 22,500,000 pupils were enrolled in elementary schools, another 6,500,000 in high schools, about 1,250,000 in college and almost 3,000,000 in other schools. The total of more than thirty-three million includes one person out of every four in the country. This gigantic enterprise required more than a million adults to carry on instruction. Herein lies the potential power of the nation. These are the human resources of future America. With this in mind, no citizen interested in the welfare of society can treat the problems of the schools with either ignorance or indifference. It is a big business and one of the most vital America has to manage.

Although still very low, the salaries of teachers mounted slowly in 1937 along with the recovery of business. Not yet, however, have they reached the pre-depression level. For the school year of 1936-37 the per pupil cost was still under that of 1931-32 by 9.1 per cent. New buildings scattered here and there rose with the aid of federal funds. Forecasts indicated that for the year, the contracts let for school buildings amounted to about $200,000,000. Obviously, America believes in its schools and in their potential power for the health and growth of Democracy.

Movies and Radio in Education. A number of years ago schools and churches were practically the only educational agencies in a community. Of the two, children spent much more time in the schools, which were the chief centers for the education of youth. Today the picture is changed. Other organizations have sprung up by the hundreds and thousands, each commanding the attention of youth in one direction or another. Inventions, mechanical devices, have also appeared to detract from or add to educational facilities, depending upon how they are used. The printing presses are running faster and faster, turning out newspapers, magazines and books well printed, fascinatingly illustrated, and cheap, in almost a bewildering quantity. Anyone to whom these appeal can secure through his own initiative an education that would extend far beyond that provided by the schools. In a very real sense these books and magazines are rivals of the schools. The automobile, another rival, has increasingly lured youth into wider and faster travel experience, and in many cases to the point of dulling his classroom drives, his interest in books and teachers. The movie industry, a third competitor for children's attention, attracts about 88,000,000 paid admissions to its shows weekly. The radio, a fourth rival, is being used so extensively that it is difficult to ever guess the millions who listen daily to its output. But in no sense have the educational possibilities of these devices been fully realized.

Not until recently have the schools become concerned with the educational value of movies, of meeting these rivals on their own ground. The 280,000 public and private schools are poorly equipped for the use of sound or silent films or even slides. Gradually such equipment is being added and trained technicians appointed to assist in using visual aids as effective learning procedures. The results of a survey reported during the year indicated that 97 cities already have full-time visual education directors.

Perhaps the most striking advance in the use of motion pictures came through the first large scale attempt to bring about a union between the schools and the movie industry. The Motion Picture Producers and Distributors of America formed a committee of educators who were to select from the vaults of Hollywood, films that might be used in the schools. Although the committee intends to review 15,000 sound films, a good guess would place the number of films in these vaults that have educational value at about 2,000. Viewing about 30 films a day, the panels select those that can be used with profit. In addition several member companies of the Hays organization are prepared to produce new educational films as soon as the committee is ready with its recommendations. It is wholly conceivable that the results of this effort will lead to much more dynamic visual instruction in United States classrooms.

Likewise the possibilities of the radio are just beginning to be sensed. With commercial broadcasting companies finding it necessary to make part of their programs educational, they want help. Up to now most of the broadcasting conducted by educational institutions has not had a broad appeal. Naturally enough, a large proportion of these programs were merely classroom lectures, sometimes dull, sent out over the air. Educators need to learn from commercial broadcasters the effective methods for the use of so vital a tool. They have not as yet done so.

To make the radio more useful educationally, the National Broadcasting Company appointed Dr. James R. Angell, retiring president of Yale University, as its educational counselor. The U. S. Office of Education has named an active co-operating national committee on Radio in Education. Together they and other agencies are exploring the field to find out what educational broadcasting is and how and when to do it. Their efforts for 1937 climaxed in a Chicago conference the last of November at which university and college presidents and professors, secondary and elementary schoolmen, and commercial broadcasters presented and discussed their ideas for two days.

In September a unique experiment in education by air was tried in the City of Chicago. Because of a mild epidemic of infantile paralysis, the schools were closed. To keep the children off the streets and busy, the radio stations and the newspapers offered their facilities to the Board of Education for a co-operative experiment. Committees consisting of members of the school staff were formed to arrange for the programs. They decided to offer instruction by air in English, mathematics, science and social studies for grades 3B to 8A inclusive. Each day a brief digest of the lessons to be broadcast together with questions, directions and assignments appeared in the newspapers. These articles served as guides to study. Pupils were directed to prepare their lessons from day to day and to turn in their work when school opened. During each broadcast a special committee of principals listened in and later made suggestions for improving the service. With more than 300,000 pupils going to school by turning on the radio, the experiment was a novel one. The educational results of this first trial are difficult to estimate, probably not great. Nevertheless, the more extensive such experiments become the more educators will discover how the radio can be used. Only the future can tell whether educators will be wise enough to use this new instrument effectively to turn it from a powerful rival into a resourceful ally.

The U. S. Office of Education is also experimenting with radio. On Sunday afternoons a series of broadcasts on "The World Is Yours" presents Smithsonian Institution dramatizations. On Monday evenings, the "Brave New World" series dramatizes Latin American life and culture. "Education in the News," presenting highlights of educational developments of the week, was on the air over the NBC-Red Network on Friday afternoons during part of 1937. Beginning in the fall also, the National Education Association sponsored a current events program, "Exits and Entrances" on

Monday afternoons, and two series on "Our American Schools" on Wednesday evenings and Saturday mornings. There can be little doubt, these programs are merely a beginning in educational broadcasting which in the years ahead will extend far beyond any current hopes or dreams.

Uncle Sam Aids Education. On July first the George-Deen Act became a law of the land. It stepped-up by about 500 per cent the amount of money the Federal Government makes available to the schools, particularly for the extension of vocational and agricultural education. Through its provisions, the Government will distribute $12,000,000 annually to stimulate training for jobs. In addition, it authorizes an annual appropriation of $1,200,000 for job training in distributive occupations such as retailing, wholesaling, jobbing, commission buying and selling and other merchandising occupations, of $1,000,000 for teacher education in the special fields covered by the bill and of smaller amounts to guarantee minimum allotments to states and territories. The law differs from the George-Ellzey Act which it replaces in that it makes almost five times as much money available; it requires the states and territories to match only 50 per cent of these grants during the first five years instead of dollar for dollar; it provides for training in the distributive functions; and it extends the benefits of vocational education to Washington, D. C. It is still too early to predict the effect of this bill.

In November, the Superintendent of Schools in the City of Chicago announced a new plan to make eighty per cent of the work in high schools vocational. At the same time he expressed his intention to derive large federal grants for this purpose. At once strenuous opposition developed. The chances are small that he will succeed in carrying out this plan or that other communities will get enough aid from the George-Deen Act to change their high school courses of study so radically. Educators themselves will object, for the move runs counter to a strong and growing demand for general education during adolescent years.

A second major bill to increase federal appropriations for the schools was temporarily blocked in the House Committee by the secret ballot. This Harrison-Black-Fletcher Bill was to make available ultimately $300,000,000 annually for educational purposes. It is definitely an effort to equalize educational opportunities by transferring some of the school tax money where wealth has been concentrated to poorer sections. Such a distribution of funds would enable the forty-odd thousand schools which for lack of funds have not been able to stay open for full school years, to lengthen their terms. With the current demand to balance the budget, it is unlikely that the bill will even come before the current session of Congress, and thousands of school children scattered throughout the land will continue to be denied the educational advantages of moppets in more fortunate centers. Nevertheless, in time—it may take another depression —the United States will actually put democracy into effect in the schools and provide an equal chance to learn for all its citizens.

Aid to Youth. The National Youth Administration which for several years past has distributed Federal aid to needy college and school youths, had its new allotment of funds for 1937-38 cut by one-third. This year the amount parceled out to states will not exceed $20,000,000 whereas last year it was more than $28,000,000. The total amount available for the NYA was cut from $75,000,000 to $50,000,000. The result will be a reduction from 310,000 to 220,000 youths who will receive aid while in school or college. The new quotas are based upon 8 per cent of the college population instead of 12 per cent as previously. Furthermore, no special allotment was made this year for graduate students who in 1936 drew monthly payments of $25.00 to $40.00. They are not cut off from aid entirely, but their number is greatly reduced, since colleges granting aid to them must now take the funds from their total allotments.

In all probability there is no feature of the New Deal that has been regarded with greater favor than the activities of the National Youth Administration. The funds are used not to give students outright grants but to pay them for services rendered. Undergraduates on the average can earn $15.00 a month—a very small amount but enough to keep many in high school and college who could not otherwise attend. Since by far the majority do creditable work, it is generally conceded that the investment is one of the best that the country can make. It is an investment in youth and none could be of greater import for future America. On the basis of 300 questionnaires from its members, the Association of American Colleges concluded: "Unquestionably no fund has ever been appropriated by Congress where so large a proportion has been applied to the individuals for whom the fund was created and so small a percentage to essential administrative control."

When the reduction in total appropriation for NYA was announced, organized youth all over the nation protested. The cut, however, was sustained. As yet, there has been no report on the number of youths who are actually being deprived of schooling because they are not within the quota of those receiving federal aid.

The CCC.   In the fall of 1937, the Civilian Conservation Corps was better equipped and prepared than ever before to meet the educational and job-training needs of 300,000 enrollees for whom it is responsible. Last June, Congress passed new legislation in regard to the CCC. Education is now a major function. The new act provides: "That at least ten hours each week may be devoted to general educational and vocational training." Additional funds were appropriated, making possible improved educational facilities. With a student body a fourth as large as that in all colleges of the country combined, the CCC offers technical training in about forty occupations. It provides, too, academic instruction on all levels—illiteracy, elementary, high school and college. Robert Fechner, director of the CCC, stated in the New York *Times* that "the underlying purpose of the new educational program is to improve each boy's employability and civic effectiveness."

Some notion concerning the vitality of the educational program can be had from the report of Dr. Howard W. Oxley, Director of CCC Education. He writes, in part:

On an average, there are about twenty-six courses and eighteen instructors in each company assisting in the educational program. The average enrollee spends the greatest amount of time in job training, eight hours per month per man; vocational courses are next with seven hours per month per man; academic courses, 6.8 hours; informal activities, 6.7 hours; professional courses, 3.7 hours; and miscellaneous instruction, 3.7 hours.

More than a thousand teachers in local school systems are volunteering their teaching services in the camps. Hundreds of companies have been invited by neighboring schools and colleges to use their facilities. State departments of education have shown a willingness to help improve and accredit instructional work carried on in the corps.

This readiness to co-operate with the camps has resulted in the attendance of more than 7,500 enrollees each month at elementary, high school and college classes. During the past year, 6,706 enrollees received elementary school certificates, 2,057 high school diplomas and 44 college diplomas.

Correspondence course materials are being supplied at reduced rates to enrollees from forty colleges and universities and from four state departments of education. More than 20,000 men are enrolled in these courses. Fifty colleges and universities have granted CCC men financial assistance or self-help positions this Fall to enable them to continue their higher education.

Although the average age of CCC enrollees is 20, half of them are not beyond the elementary school level and must therefore be trained in common school subjects. This situation has led to the preparation of many valuable texts designed to meet the needs of those enrollees on the elementary level. Special materials have been developed on vocational subjects, arts and crafts, and personal manners.

As indicative of the accomplishments of the CCC educational program, the records show that since 1933, 50,000 enrollees have been taught to read and write, 500,000 have been better grounded in elementary school subjects, 200,000 have pursued high school subjects and 40,000 have continued their college education. Almost a million enrollees have received systematic job instruction.

With many youths still unemployed it is not surprising that the American public has viewed with satisfaction the results of the CCC program. As a matter of fact CCC can now be considered as a permanent feature of the United States social structure. Probably in the future, citizens will look back and wonder how we ever got along without it just as we now are curious as to why it took the country so long to develop an extensive program of free public education.

President Roosevelt's Advisory Committee. Lay and educational leaders throughout the country are members of the President's Advisory Committee on Education under the Chairmanship of Professor Floyd W. Reeves of the University of Chicago. At first the Committee was to study the problems relating to current federal support of vocational education, its relation to general education and social conditions, and the need for an extended program. Later the scope of its responsibilities was much enlarged to include the study of all relationships of the Federal Government to state and local education. In writing of his committee's work, Dr. Reeves reviews the conditions out of which it arose, as follows:

Federal aid to keep schools open in many rural areas was provided during the depression, implying for the first time that the Federal Government has an obligation to maintain at least a low minimum of educational opportunity throughout the nation. Funds have also been made available in recent years, as part of the public works program, to assist in financing the construction and repair of thousands of school buildings. Several hundred thousand needy students in high schools and colleges have received financial aid under the program of the National Youth Administration. Thousands of unemployed teachers have been employed under the emergency education program of the Works Progress Administration to instruct over 2,000,000 persons who availed themselves of these new educational opportunities. Approximately a million and a half young men have already passed through the ranks of the Civilian Conservation Corps, which was first established as a form of work relief but has acquired educational objectives of increasing breadth and of great public interest.

Meanwhile, the Federal Government has continued and expanded the older and more familiar types of aid to vocational education in the high schools, to agricultural extension work for men, women, and children of rural areas, and to the land-grant colleges.

We are now coming out of the depression that produced so many of the developments just noted. Public attention is rapidly shifting from the existing emergency program to proposed permanent programs. The present Congress has before it a great many bills relating to education. . . . These various developments indicate the present necessity for re study of the problem of federal relations to education and have supplied the background for the work undertaken by the Advisory Committee on Education.

Throughout the summer and fall months the Committee conducted comprehensive studies of "the financing of education, educational research, educational administration as a major phase of state government, quality of existing educational programs in the states, the new and emergency federal education programs, education in special federal jurisdictions, and the social, economic and governmental factors basic to a consideration of federal relations to education." In the collection of facts many agencies are co-operating. The NYA, the CCC, the U. S. Office of Education, the National Resources Committee, the American Youth Commission, the heads of departments of education in the forty-eight states are only a few of the groups whose resources are open to the Committee. As the work proceeds it is increasingly clear that 1937 marks the beginning of a new era in the relation of the Federal Government to education. At the year's end, reports are not yet available. The educational world as well as the Government will look to them, when they appear, for guidance. It is clear this early, however, that major changes will result.

Grown-ups Go to School. Dr. Studebaker's public forums got well under way in 1936 and continued in 1937. Over a fifteen-month period, more than 10,000 meetings were held in nineteen centers. Over 1,000,-000 individuals attended. At each meeting serious consideration was given to problems of citizenship. No subject was tabu. The insight into common United States problems gained is hard to estimate; a more enlightened citizenry must result.

According to C. S. Williams, Assistant Administrator of the federal forum project, the broader program for the current year faces in these two directions: "It seeks to assist local school systems in developing community-wide forum plans for adults." "It undertakes to promote more vital considerations of public affairs by young people in schools and colleges."

But forums are only a small part of the vast adult educational program that has become effective since the depression. The CCC camps make up another part also small. Everywhere under local school boards, under state leadership, under the WPA-Adult Education Program, classes are conducted daily in almost any subject one might think of. Adults go to these classes hungry for more knowledge, greater skill, and a broadened understanding. Only a tiny group of them want the usual school marks and credits. Some are looking for advancement on their jobs and others want to shift occupations. A large proportion take courses surveying political conflicts here and abroad; economic problems of debts, labor, strikes, co-operatives; social patterns in falling birth rates, crime, family crackups; and science and new knowledge of psychology, all in the search for clearer interpretations of society and human relationships. Many want training so they can be better spectators and listeners during weary hours. Still others take courses in stamp collecting, photography, music, sports, and dancing to become more apt in their leisure time activities. They form a motley crowd. Unknown laborers, tired housewives, illiterates and Ph.D.'s are all registered. Each year this mass of learners increases in size so that now it appears that public education will extend from the cradle to the grave, from infancy to senility.

In New York City alone, over 100,000 adults registered in classes conducted by the WPA-Adult Education Program. More than 500 courses in commercial, cultural and social subjects are offered. And such programs are being duplicated on a smaller scale in practically every town and hamlet. America believes in education not alone for its young but for all. Clear evidence again that its democracy is becoming more dynamic. Yet this is only a beginning. Adult education is sure to expand.

Colleges Grow. College enrollments mounted higher in 1937 although the rate of growth has slowed up somewhat. Representative colleges in the East, West, and South showed an average 1937 gain of 3.9 per cent over the 1936 figures whereas the enrollments in the fall of 1936 were 6.5 per cent above those of the year before. In the last ten years the number of college students has doubled; in the past thirty years, it has multiplied ten times. At the present time, one-seventh of the youth of college age are in college. As a matter of fact, going to college today is more common than was attending high school twenty-five years ago.

And in that twenty-five-year period colleges have changed. A study of 200 catalogues made by two members of the staff of the Florida State College for Women indicates a shift from the classics, from science and from psychology to an emphasis upon social studies, upon man's relation to his fellow-men.

President Hutchins of the University of Chicago persisted during the year to decry the modern trend in higher education. He wants students to return in a mass to study the classics. Professor Gideonse of his staff, however, published a book, *The Higher Learning in a Democracy*, to tell the world that the University of Chicago does not follow the educational ideas of its youthful president. Apparently the president experienced difficulty in putting his notions into practice at his own University. He turned, therefore, to St. John's College in Maryland, of which he is a trustee, and there succeeded in setting up a curriculum consisting of the study of classics. Succeed he might in this small institution but his views apparently will have little influence upon the total college world. Present day American colleges and universities have grown out of the society of which they are a part. That society now demands thorough training in social studies in an effort to save the coming generations from the political and social mess in which we have found ourselves in recent years. Without some major change in society itself, President Hutchins' expressions will continue to fall upon unreceptive ears and colleges will go on providing a general education with emphasis upon social studies for an ever-expanding proportion of the population.

New College Presidents. An unusually large number of new college presidents were inaugurated in 1937. Among the larger and better-known institutions with new heads are Cornell (Dr. Edmund Ezra Day), Yale (Dr. Charles Seymour), and the University of Wisconsin (Dr. Clarence Dykstra). These new administrators together with some sixty others will chart the course of the institutions of higher learning in 1938-39 and the years ahead. They cannot wholly determine the nature of higher education for they are constantly confronted with pressures of one kind or another. They can, however, exert a leadership that may change not only the college courses but the future of society. As educational statesmen they bear watching, study, and support.

An Educational Newspaper. As schools opened in the fall there came an announcement from Minneapolis of the publication of *Education News* with a sub-caption, "America's Only Educational Newspaper." Published once a week it attempts to review what is new in education. Undoubtedly it will serve to keep schoolmen better informed concerning educational activities hither and yon.

A Magazine for Juniors. Having succeeded with *Scholastic*, a weekly magazine for high school students, Scholastic Corporation in the fall of 1937 launched *Junior Scholastic*, a "weekly for the Upper Elementary Grades and Junior High School." Eased in content and scope to the level of the average twelve-year-old, this new periodical is kept on the same high level as *Scholastic* and is already reaching the kids who until now had limited their "outside reading" to comics.

New London, Texas. On Thursday afternoon, March 18 at 3:05 o'clock a terrific explosion occurred in New London, Texas. Before that time the community had barely been heard of outside the state. Within a few minutes, radio flashes, and later that afternoon and evening, newspaper headlines in every city of the land glared with news of the disaster. The high school wing of the consolidated school—the finest rural educational plant in America—was blown to bits.

As the superintendent of schools sadly related afterwards: "The roof just lifted up. Then the walls fell
out and the roof fell in." Tragically, 690 boys and
girls and 40 teachers who in ten minutes would have
left the building were scattered in all directions by the
blast—most of them torn to death.

Fathers hurried frantically from their posts at the
oil derricks surrounding the school plant and mothers
rushed hysterically to the scene. Hour after hour, all
through the night and into the next day, they worked
pulling the broken, lifeless bodies from the debris.
On Sunday a great mass funeral was held for almost
all the high school population in the community.

Causes of so major a calamity were sought at once.
On the day of the explosion, W. C. Shaw, superintendent of schools, told how a "wet" gas line had been
tapped on his orders. On the third day of the investigation he admitted that the line was tapped without
permission and that he had been warned of the danger.
Later a report of Dr. David J. Price of the U. S.
Bureau of Chemistry and Soils stated that the explosion resulted from the ignition by an electrical flash
of combustible gases that had accumulated in an open
space under the first floor. All schools in oil areas were
immediately checked for similar gas pockets. But no
amount of checking could wipe out the greatest school
disaster in years.

Schools Closed. Near the end of the year the
schools in two major cities were forced to close for an
extended Christmas vacation because of lack of funds.
Minneapolis lengthened its holiday from two to three

weeks. The Cincinnati schools also found it necessary to prolong their Christmas vacation in spite of many days already lost during the year because voters failed to pass a special tax levy. These were exceptions. General conditions throughout the country were better for the schools in 1937 than they had been in 1936.

CHAPTER VII

RELIGION IN 1937

At first glance, religion in 1937 presents a confused picture. A Mohammedan mosque was dedicated in London. Fundamentalists launched a new crusade against evolution in Indiana. Brahmin temples were opened to outcastes in India. Roman Catholic bishops objected to faddish halo hats and the child labor amendment. Methodists voted themselves into union of all Methodist bodies in the United States. Spanish Loyalists now refuse to say "Adios." And Japanese and Chinese Christians held a retreat together.

Key to the Picture Is the New Paganism. Enlisting armies of world discontents and youth under the banners of national and class deities, worshiping organized human power, it appeared last year as the single rival religion against all other world theistic faiths. Suddenly involved in conflict with it, established religions on many fronts suffered disintegration and defeat. Elsewhere, jarred away from parochial selfishness to concern for a world headed to secular confusion and decay, religion underwent resurrection and revival.

Germany. Most dramatic of all 1937 pagan-religious struggles was the German. Nazis sought to subjugate Jews, Roman Catholics and Protestants to the new religion of the Nazi state. In general, state (Lutheran) churches acquiesced, obeyed the Reich-bishop, refused baptism to converted Jews, capitalized Jew hatred to be found in the Gospel of St. John, used deleted Bibles and hung pictures of Hitler above their altars. Jew-baiting continued as in previous years. Jews were persecuted, driven into ghettos and mur-dered. Even 178 B'nai B'rith lodges, though they had favored a policy of silence and passive acceptance, were padlocked, had property confiscated. Roman Catholics, opposing the Nazi youth program, met new Hitler insistence that all youth be solely government-trained. But priesthood and laity, strengthened by a secret papal encyclical to German Catholics, courage-ously resisted Nazi threats and new accusations of immorality among priests and nuns.

Most strengthened by Nazi pagan persecutions has been the Confessional Synod, comprising Protestants in non-state churches. Pastors and people, steadily refusing compromise and fearlessly proclaiming sov-ereignty of the Christian God as above sovereignty of the state, were often barred from pulpit and church, frequently sent to concentration camps and sometimes killed. Leader of them all was athletic Martin Nie-möller, world-war submarine hero and pastor to many a high Nazi official in Jesus Christus Kirche in Dah-lem, aristocratic and wealthy suburb of Berlin. Last summer, defying the government, Niemöller preached a sermon—since heard around the world—saying, "Here stand I. We must obey God rather than men." When police surrounded his pulpit to arrest him, his congregation arose as one man, singing, "A mighty fortress is our God." The following week, Niemöller's members, disdaining all risk, held the first organized public demonstration against an amazed government, forced his temporary release and led Hitler indefinitely to postpone a proposed church election. Thus, while the close of 1937 finds over 125,000 Jews and 20,000 German Christians fled to penniless exile, Niemöller's courage and the cumulative power of an aroused Christian conscience present the first real threat to totalitarian claims of the German state.

Spain. Although an English church commission reported Spanish Loyalists conduct no anti-religious campaign, and later the Loyalists have even opened churches for believers, profoundly significant is the Loyalist refusal to continue the use of the traditional farewell, "Adios" (God be with you!). Behind this change of custom lies Loyalist bitterness at Roman Catholic clericalism which they allege betrayed both people and state and led to confiscation of church property. Hence, the Catholic Church has an important stake in the Spanish civil war and sides with Franco Fascist forces.

Chief result in 1937 was a papal encyclical launching a world anti-Communism campaign. While some observers hastened to point out that Communist revolt has made greatest gains in countries where the Roman Church has been strong, Catholic leaders organized such a campaign against Communism as speedily became a campaign for Fascism. In Manila, pilgrims attending the 33rd International Eucharistic Congress fought Communism by celebrating world Fascist gains. In Quebec, a hastily passed law and sympathetic enforcement officers throttled free speech by banning all meetings called to aid Spanish Loyalists. And in New York, Catholics crowded into Madison Square Garden to hear appeals for "the sick and wounded on both sides of the contending lines"; but the meeting was distinctly pro-Franco, and one wonders how much of the money raised went to Loyalist needy.

Africa. Amid pretentious military display in Libya, the new paganism as embodied in Mussolini pledged itself "protector of Islam," and banned all Protestant missionaries from Ethiopia. At the same time, elsewhere in Africa, Protestant leaders hurried publication and distribution of the Bible in the new 850-word Basic English Vocabulary to counteract breakdown of tribal mores due to influence of modern Western culture brought to Africa by trade, factories, mines. In Egypt, Coptic monks went on a sit-down strike.

India. Under new paganism's threat, all great religions in India last year girded themselves to battle against the world sweep of their rival. Alarmed by rising outcaste power and fearing loss of the masses from Hinduism to secularism, leaders in Travancore, soon to be followed by others, last year threw open ancient Brahmin temples to multitudes formerly kept out by caste. A leader in the movement, Gandhi instructed outcaste crowds in the use of their new shrines and told them to revere shrine images as visible reminders of the presence of God. Christian forces, though German missions were crippled by Nazi gold export interdict, took cognizance of "the present ferment among many classes," saw "the Spirit of God moving on the face of many waters" and set up money and machinery for a mass movement survey.

China and Japan. While war occupied the stage of these nations in late 1937, religion provided the stage lighting. Japan, with a student population by 1937 become 90% atheist, having freely imbibed the new paganism of Western "Christian" nations, melted down its Temple of Humanity into munitions and had no moral scruples against waging undeclared imperialist war on China, bombing defenseless cities, killing noncombatants, women and children. Previous to this, Communist missionaries from Russia had preached their doctrines of humanist redemption to discontented Chinese and threatened the Empire from the West. To unify his people against these enemies, Chiang Kai-shek, the Chinese leader, aided by his wife, a member of the powerful Soong dynasty, a Wellesley graduate and a Christian, launched the Chinese "New Life" movement; last year sought aid from the National Christian Council. Fearing Japanese imperialism and seeing Christianity a better answer than Communism to needs of his suffering people, Chiang Kai-shek sought reforms having Christian inspiration, rejoiced in "plans Sun Yat-sen got from Jesus for freeing weak peoples and for bringing happiness to the poor and oppressed," and on Good Friday confessed that for ten years "I have been a follower of Jesus . . . and make a daily practice of reading the Scriptures for the cultivation of the religious life." Thus, in the closing days of 1937, while news dispatches told of defeat for Shanghai and Nanking, Christianity also suffered defeat before Japan's new paganism.

Yet more potent than guns in Sino-Japanese relations may be the 1937-proved determination of Chinese and Japanese Christians to bridge barriers of national hatred and jointly seek peace. Sensing conflict and also sensing a Christian Community with loyalty to humanity instead of to warring states, Japanese Christians early in the year proposed a conference in China for Christian Chinese and Japanese. Jumping at the chance, the National Christian Council in China arranged the conference, sent delegates. Thus, while Japanese warriors unlimbered big guns before Shanghai, other Japanese, holding their Chinese hosts not enemies but brothers, deplored their nations' war, sought solution apart from armed force and together pledged allegiance to a higher sovereignty in their "peace-Lord, Jesus Christ." Later years will prove whether guns or such new technique for Christian "enemies" will at last win in Sino-Japanese affairs.

America. Superficially, United States religious statistics would seem to indicate abundant strength for stemming new paganism's tide. Last year there were 212 United States denominations and 232,000 churches with an annual budget of $817,000,000 and $4,000,-000,000 worth of property. 1937-released figures for 1936 reveal 63,493,036 church members with 20,831,-139 Roman Catholics, 10,332,005 Baptists, 9,109,359 Methodists and 4,589,660 Lutherans in largest groups. Characterizing its statistics as "a direct contradiction to pessimists who claim the churches have lost ground," the *Christian Herald* noted a year's increase of 837,404 new members, a 1.33% gain as compared to .71% for population growth. Denominations of more than 50,000 members gained 1.1% while, oddly enough, smaller groups gained 29.49%! Moreover, 49.43% of United States population had some religious affiliation, gaining 2.83% over ten years ago.

In spite of gains, however, United States religion last year appeared by no means wholly triumphant over new pagan ideologies involving worship of organized human power. Many a church pastor and council, zealous for resurrection of a now ghostly faith, but blind to real revival requirements, turned up the volume of meeting-house chit-chat. Led by one Verdi Allen, Fundamentalists in Indianapolis started a new anti-evolution crusade. Roman Catholic bishops forbade the appearance in churches of women wearing halo hats. A ministerial association in Middletown, N. Y., urged funeral reform. And, while the Southern Presbyterian General Assembly gagged a young preacher who spoke out for Negroes and tenant farmers, marking him a man never to be called to influential churches, a study of 18,434 Virginia high school students revealed inability of some 16,000 to name 3 Old Testament prophets, of 12,000 to name the four gospels and of 10,000 to name 3 of Christ's disciples.

Hence, many saw as tragically true Rollo Walter Brown's warning that the Church today is "an empty topheavy organization that hinders the direct appli-

cation of the philosophy of Jesus" and that "I could
tell in advance what kind of gospel I should hear
preached in a given church just by studying the length
of the wheel-base of the automobiles parked out in
front." Published last year, the Lynds' *Middletown
in Transition* gave a factual basis for such conclusions.
In spite of ten transition years bristling with challenge
and change for vital religion, this study of the average
American town reveals for that period churches as
little more than "emotionally stabilizing agents," turning a negative face to the community and "relinquish-
ing to other agencies leadership in the defining of
values" and "in every adventurous enterprise on the
frontiers of social progress."

Nevertheless, though many churches were content
to dawdle in dales of holy debauchery, many another
so girt up its loins for adventurous enterprise in defining new Christian human values on life frontiers that
in them religion showed beginnings of what may prove
the mighty revival for which its prophets have prayed.
Strongest 1937 gains against secularism and greatest
revival have come where churches, rediscovering the
Christian Community (Kingdom of God) and Jesus'
belief in the sacredness of human personality, have
labored for man's salvation at the cutting edge of vital
daily concerns.

Thus, last year, labored many a Roman Catholic
leader and group. To be sure, Catholics urged defeat
of child labor amendment ratification and birth control efforts; and Father Coughlin, radio crusader, was
rebuked by his superiors for speaking too freely

and irresponsibly over the air. On the other hand, young priests continued organization of the Catholic Radical Alliance, pledged to a labor front for realization of papal Christian social order aims outlined in recent encyclicals. And at Washington, Catholic University added a new department of social science, and Msgr. John A. Ryan continued vital leadership as National Catholic Welfare head.

Protestant churches, too, long asleep under blanket of "brand from the burning" religion, woke up to religious implications and opportunities in every social situation. Hence, many supported Sherwood Eddy's Delta co-operative farm experiment for ousted, murder-threatened tenant farmers. With gusto and zeal, they whipped up attendance, signed resolutions to Congress for the Emergency Peace Campaign's no-foreign-war crusade, headed by Admiral Byrd.

In fact, aside from Christian and Jewish religious differences, practical efforts of both Catholic and Protestant awakened groups were similar to those for Judaism outlined in 1937 by the Central Conference of American Rabbis. "Judaism seeks the attainment of a just society by the application of its teachings to the economic order, to industry and commerce, and to national and international affairs. It aims at the elimination of man-made misery and suffering, of poverty and degradation, of tyranny and slavery, of social inequality and prejudice, of ill-will and strife. It advocates the promotion of harmonious relations between warring classes on the basis of equity and justice, and the creation of conditions under which personality can flourish." Thus did United States leaders of three great faiths last year do battle with paganism.

Facing opposition to all religion, they did many things together. At Williamstown Institute, Catholics, Jews and Protestants sought solution for national problems of public opinion created by radio, motion pictures, press. Sensible leadership in all faiths prevented news of Justice-elect Black's former Ku Klux Klan membership from inaugurating a new era of religious bigotry and persecution. Realizing with Bishop McConnell that in the next ten years there will be a drive against free speech "far more deadly than any person listening to me can remember," 50,000 Roman Catholic, Protestant and Jewish clergymen jointly signed a statement reaffirming American principles of civil and religious freedom. Supporting the Federal Council of Churches, leaders of all three faiths made an appeal on June 24 for steel strike settlement. And, Jews and Protestants, continuing support of Catholics' Legion of Decency for better motion pictures, joined other groups in a new organization to encourage the production of anti-war films and those bettering understanding between racial and religious groups.

Moreover, Protestants answered 1937 secular currents with important new gains in denominational co-operation. Chief among co-operative efforts was the Preaching Mission. Begun in 1936, it held four-day discussion groups and mass meetings in over 100 United States large cities and smaller towns before its conclusion in spring of 1937. Hoping for a revival of religion to answer the new paganism, Preaching Mis-

sion leaders made history by staging Protestantism's first united evangelistic campaign and by their
first-time evangelistic use of a basic social emphasis.
Justifying such shift of emphasis was Missioner E.
Stanley Jones' observation that on Mission tours oldtime appeals to repent of individual sin brought little
response, while appeals from social sins back to individual implication in them brought great response.

Here it is that Christian theology in 1937, reflecting
Paul Hutchinson's statement, "It is either on to Moscow, or back to sin!" swung further right away from
purely humanistic, or pagan, doctrines of social sin.
In these, followers, judging others on basis of themselves, see evil as incarnate in other people, classes and
races but as external to self. Sensing weakness here,
Protestant theology last year took a new position, holding all of life to be under judgment not of man but
of God, and thus requiring individual repentance for
implication in social evil, prayer for divine forgiveness
and realignment of one's life with the will of God for
self and society. Hence the observation that in 1937
religion, in Protestantism at least, was moving socially
to the left but theologically to the right.

But greatest Protestant answer to secularism last
year was rediscovery of the Christian Church. Cradled
in isolated meeting houses and chapels, Protestantism
has never sensed the Church as the super-class, super-
national Christian World Community. Last year, however, cursed by senseless divisions inadequate for
world-front onslaughts, Protestantism saw the Christian Church in a new light, took steps for greater par-

ticipation in it. Negotiations for church union continued. Episcopalians at General Conference voted further study of proposals for uniting with Presbyterians. Presbyterians U.S.A. awaited a favorable moment to renew negotiations for union with United Presbyterians, Presbyterians U.S. and other Reformed Church bodies. But red-letter union event of the year was a final vote assuring a united Methodist Church from three smaller Methodist groups.

Important for the new conception of the Church as these gains are, even more important were the ecumenical conferences held at Oxford and Edinburgh in the summer of 1937.

Oxford and Edinburgh. Though separate and distinct, these two conferences supplemented one another to make one total impact on the mind of Christendom. Concerned with thorny problems of the task of the Church as it impinges upon the economic order, and upon community, state and world, the Oxford Conference on Church, Community and State vitalized and made more urgent Edinburgh Faith and Order delegates' search for a common Christian faith of such catholicity as would promote a united world Christian Church.

No chance meetings, years of conference, prayer and publication had gone into their preparation. On no summer holiday, delegates, barring Roman Catholics, German Confessional Synod representatives to whom Nazis refused passports and German State Church people who failed to come, were official representatives of every Christian church body in the world. In fact,

so representative of all Christendom were these conferences that when the Archbishop of Canterbury addressed Oxford delegates and said, "We stand at a
moment in history as crucial and decisive for mankind
as the period when Rome fell, or the period of the
Renaissance and the Reformation," Christian world
opinion united in holding Oxford and Edinburgh in
1937 to have momentous significance for the Church
akin to the Reformation.

Aiding new conceptions of the Church as the world-
wide Christian Community were: the representative
character of the two delegated bodies; the pageantry
of Russian Orthodox, Greek Catholic, Chinese, Japanese, Indian and other distinctive dress; the historic
celebration of the Holy Communion, from which not
one delegate was barred, by the Archbishop of Canterbury in famous St. Mary's Church, Oxford. But
greatest aid of all to new ecumenical Christianity was
realization of the threat of paganism everywhere to
all economic, community, state and international affairs.

Meeting this challenge, dramatized by absence of
German Confessional delegates, Oxford affirmed the
sovereignty of God over every human life and institution. Condemning war in every form, pledging itself
to a Christian economic order and denying state jurisdiction over individual conscience and religion, this
conference concluded that only by "being the Church,"
as the super-class, super-national Christian Community,
transcending all human divisions and institutions, can
the God of Christ be assured of sovereignty over every
department of life. To triumph over the new pagan-

ism, the Christian Church must be "a revelation of the true community . . . a sacramental anticipation of the community which God wills for all mankind. . . . Its witness is to be borne by the realization of the divine community within its own life and by carrying of this witness into the social order through the multifarious relationships in which they [Christians] stand."

At Edinburgh a few weeks later the same delegates crowned the work begun at Oxford. Seeking a common faith for an ecumenical Church of Christ with surprising unanimity, considering their real theological differences, these men who "loathed to differ and determined to understand," wrought out a comprehensive statement of the Christian faith. Contrary to secular faiths worshiping organized human power, the fundamental Edinburgh note was, "the grace of our Lord Jesus Christ," a phrase further explained by the statement, "Man's salvation and welfare have their source in God alone, who is moved to his gracious activity towards man not by any merit on man's part, but solely by his free, out-going love."

World Council of Churches. But of all things done by all religious groups in the world in 1937, most significant by far was action of Edinburgh delegates from all Christian communions, except Roman Catholics and Germans, forthwith to organize a World Council of Churches. The final report stated that "the churches should come together on the basis of the doctrine of the Incarnation," and that "the largest success of the plan depends upon securing adequate representation of every communion."

Thus, save for Roman Catholics and Germans, did a united Church of Jesus Christ accept paganism's challenge for control of human life and society. Wherever else in 1937 religion may have suffered defeat, here it underwent resurrection and new life.

CHAPTER VIII

THE WAR AGAINST CRIME

Four days after the kidnaping of 10-year-old Charles Mattson in Tacoma, Washington, the nation greeted the New Year dazed by the crime and wondering if the boy was still alive. While Charles was playing in his home with a brother, a sister and her chum, a masked man smashed the window, walked into the living room, picked up the boy and carried him off. The other children, stunned and frightened, saw a dirty printed note on the floor with the broken bits of glass. They picked it up and read:

The price is 28,000   10000 in fives and 10s   18000 50 and 100s. Old bills please no new ones. Put ad in Seattle *Times* personal colum read Mable—What's your new address Tim   Put this ad *Times* no other paper   If no answer from you within week price goes up double and double that each week after. Don't fail and I won't. The boy is safe. Tim.

An exchange of notes followed between kidnaper and parents. G-men came and worked cautiously under the direction of Harold Nathan, chief assistant to J. Edgar Hoover, director of the Federal Bureau of Investigation. But the boy was dead. The middle of January his naked body was found fifty miles north of Tacoma. By the year's end the Mattson case was still the most shocking unsolved crime of 1937.

As in previous years, other cases of kidnaping followed and kept G-men busy. Early in the fall, Charles S. Ross, a Chicago business man, dined out one evening with his former secretary. While on the way home, his car was forced to the side of the road, the real estate dealer was transferred to another car which sped away. Ransom notes followed. By the year's end there was still no trace of Ross. G-men were hot on the trail, had few clues. It was everybody's guess that Ross was no longer alive.

Although such crimes continue, the drive by G-men under the direction of J. Edgar Hoover has made kidnaping for ransom a hazardous racket.

Lynching. In April the U. S. House of Representatives debated the pros and cons of a federal anti-lynching bill as two Negroes, Roosevelt Townes and Bootjack McDaniels, were being tried in Winona, Mississippi, for the murder of a country grocer. In the courtroom they pleaded "not guilty." Handcuffed they were led to the side door of the courthouse. An angry mob surged up, took the law in its own hands, threw the Negroes into a school bus and with forty automobiles sped off to a spot near the scene of the murder. Here the two blackamoors were fastened to trees. With the flame of a plumber's blow torch burning his flesh, McDaniels was forced to confess. A stream of bullets brought a quick and certain death. The ugly scene was repeated with Townes as the central figure except that a huge bonfire touched off by gasoline burned his body to a crisp. With this the curtain dropped on 1937's lynching victims No. 2 and 3. At least six others were dealt with in a similar way before the end of the year. And yet when an anti-lynching bill was put to a vote in the House of Representatives only 17 of the 123 Southern Representatives voted for it. Nevertheless the bill was passed by the House. If it became a law it would make officers who gave up prisoners to mobs liable to stiff federal prosecution.

Each time the House has passed a federal anti-lynching bill in the past, Southern Senators have killed it. Although a recent survey by the Institute of Public Opinion showed that 57 per cent of Southerners now favor such legislation, and although a larger and larger number of Southern newspapers urged passage of a federal anti-lynching bill in 1937, when the special session of the 75th Congress met November 15, Southern Senators again filibustered for a full week to prevent consideration of the bill. Perhaps 1938 will see a federal law with teeth in it that will help to put a stop to lynch rule which has no place in a democratic society. With more severe penalties, lynching is sure to decline, for, as James H. Chadbourn pointed out in regard to the South Carolina law, "the average number of lynchings per year in the state has declined sharply after the infliction of each penalty."

Sex Crimes. Following the trend of the past few years sex crimes continued to increase during 1937. From city to city have come grisly reports of seduction, rape and attempted rape. One of the most ghastly was reported from Inglewood, California, near Los Angeles early in July. Madeline Everett, Jeanette Stephens, and Melba Everett, ages 7, 8 and 9, respectively, started off one Saturday afternoon for a picnic in the park. When they failed to return, the anxious parents notified the police. Over the week-end a network of searchers combed the countryside. Then, early Monday afternoon, four Boy Scouts found themselves in a deep gully in Baldwin Hills. Continuing their search, they found the lifeless body of one of the girls. The other two bodies were close by. All three had been raped, strangled and murdered.

Suspect after suspect was rounded up. Finally clues led to the identification of Albert Dyer, who with his wife had collected newspaper clippings about the crime. Public sentiment ran high. To protect Dyer from lynching he was placed in the Los Angeles skyscraper jail. There he told his story with all its gruesome details.

As each such story of a sex crime comes from the press men and women everywhere become indignant. No other type of crime so arouses public ire. They demand that something be done. And unless something is done, then they, like the Southerners, begin to take the law into their own hands. Police are fully aware of this pressure. Almost every large city is now on a constant and close search for suspects. Councils of citizens, lawmakers, psychiatrists are busy shaping legislation to control what seems to be a growing menace. Criminal perverts will not much longer be left at large.

Easter Murder.   Early Easter Sunday morning, a beautiful artists' model, Veronica Gedeon, her mother and a male lodger were murdered in their apartment. Robert Irwin, a former insane asylum inmate, had committed the crime.   The motive was not wholly clear, but later details made it evident that it, too, was sex. Irwin, at large, became the most hunted murderer in the United States.   On April 12, he telephoned the Chicago *Tribune,* said he would give himself up for a price.   Skeptical, that newspaper turned him down. He made the same offer to Hearst's *Herald and Examiner* which believed him and printed extra after extra telling all the gory details, then turned him over to the police.

A Review.   But all crimes of 1937 cannot be reviewed here.   The newspaper headlines calling attention to them would more than fill a volume.   Not a day passes without criminal reports from all sections of the country making headlines.   In the first 9 months of 1937 police departments of 1,759 cities with a total population of almost 60,000,000 reported more than a half million crimes to the Federal Bureau of Investigation.   In round numbers this represents an average of 2,000 a day among less than half the population of the country.

As to type of crime the aggregate is distributed by percentage of total as follows: larceny 53.6, burglary 22.7, auto theft 15.1, robbery 3.8, aggravated assaults 3.4, rape .6, murder .4 and manslaughter .4.   Over a period of years there has been a sharp decline in the number of robberies and auto thefts and a marked increase in rape cases. How long will the nation continue to tolerate crime on so large a scale?

A New Hero. The support given to the G-men is clear evidence that the public is tired of so large a crime bill and of the constant fear of crime striking at individual homes. Before the dawn of 1937, J. Edgar Hoover was already a national hero. During the year a new hero emerged in the person of Thomas Edmund Dewey. Prosecutor Dewey of New York City became the biggest racketeer-smasher in the United States. First he cracked down on the loan sharks—the modern Shylocks who were demanding and getting up to 1,000 per cent interest on small loans to ignorant folk. Then he crushed "Lucky" Luciano the "big boss" of prostitution in New York City. One after another the racketeers fell—racketeers in contracting, baking, union organizing and restaurants. And he kept his record perfect. Every one of the 52 loan sharks and prostitution racketeers he brought to trial was sent to prison. He refused to strike until his evidence was enough to convict. It is his unswerving belief that crime thrives through rackets. It does little good to strike at the small fellow—to pinch a penny ante game here and another there, to shut down an occasional brothel. Instead the district attorney struck at the bosses. They are the ones who perpetuate crime in all its forms. And the public liked the way he struck. In November he was elected District Attorney by an overwhelming margin. As small boys play they are G-men, now they are beginning to play the part of

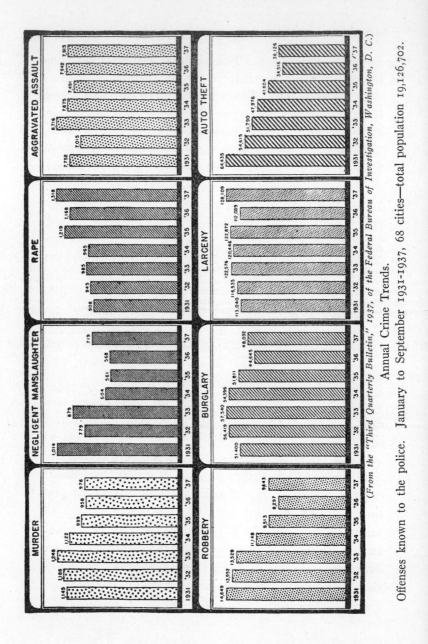

(From the "Third Quarterly Bulletin," 1937, of the Federal Bureau of Investigation, Washington, D. C.)

Annual Crime Trends.

Offenses known to the police. January to September 1931-1937, 68 cities—total population 19,126,702.

Thomas Dewey. A terror to crime, he stands a national figure.

100 **Young Delinquents—Why?** Each year come reports of studies on the causes of crime. 1937 was no exception. The Council of Social Agencies of Jacksonville, Florida, conducted a thorough study of 100 delinquents who were committed to a state training school in 1936 and during the latter part of 1935. Like reports of other studies, this investigation revealed that the young delinquent comes from so low an economic status that it is small wonder he takes part in crime. Of the 100, 59 came from families who were trying to live on incomes below the minimum as set by the FERA's Weekly Budget on Restricted Diet. They lacked clothes and other essentials. Many of them were kept out of school. Of 92 mothers of whom information was available, 65 were employed over long periods. They had no time to care for their children. Over and over again they said: "If I could only have been with him more this would not have happened." In only 14 families did parents live together, and in but five of these was there no evidence of "family disharmony." All of the remaining homes were broken. For 47 of these families there were previous criminal records. Most of the houses were not fit for dogs. The children lived in squalor and filth. Is it any wonder there were 28 cases of syphilis, 3 of gonorrhea, 11 of undernourishment and anemia, 6 of severe cardiac disorders, 5 of tuberculosis in 100 cases? Such is the environment that breeds crime. One can't help raising the question as to what would happen if society put as

much of its resources into clearing up these conditions and into sound education as it now puts into war and preparations for war. The huge dividends from such a policy can not now be fathomed.

J. Edgar Hoover in an address before the Round Table Forum under the Auspices of the New York *Herald Tribune* at New York City on October 4, made a striking reference to the enemy on our soil.

But we should not for a moment lose sight of the fact that even while we fear war, we are engaged in war; while we hope for isolation, we are already engulfed in the penalties of invasion; while we pray for peace, we are without peace.

No nation can call itself free from turmoil when it is beset by more than 4,300,000 active enemies, many of them armed, and all of them enlisted in predacious warfare against society. This is the extent of the criminal army which ceaselessly carries on its aggression against the possessions, the safety and even the life of the American family. There is no other way to regard its activities than those of warfare, a campaign of plunder which never ceases.

Day and night, in every hour and in every minute, this invasion of our peace and our security continues. My statement is not mere bombast, but a matter of grim facts and figures. When any nation is assaulted to the extent that a major crime occurs every twenty-four seconds, that every forty minutes someone dies by the violence of homicide, then, indeed, are we a nation besieged. And to this picture, which

WORLD'S LARGEST AIRSHIP COMES TO TRAGIC END

Top: The *Hindenburg* at moment of explosion (Life Magazine).
Bottom: Survivor (lower right) flees from twisted wreckage (Life Magazine).

HAVOCS OF NATURE

Top Left: Swollen waters sweep away temporary dam in Gene-see River (Life Magazine). *Top Right:* Ice jam crushes factory in Athol, Mass. (Life Magazine). *Bottom:* Pittsburgh under flood (Life Magazine).

portrays only the more desperate of the forays against our security, confining itself to the shock troops, as it were, of robbery, aggravated assault, rape, burglary, murder, extortion, and kidnaping, we must add the ravages practiced upon us by the secondary line of assault, the snipers, the looters, the rookies and recruits and training squads of crime, those lesser evils which annually roll up a total of more than fourteen million assaults against our statutes, or one every two seconds.

This is the true picture of crime; the exact story of what is going on to destroy our peace, our happiness and our hope of safety, even while we deplore war and while we give thanks that ours is a land of quietude, free from the danger of the invader. And during this period of self-hypnosis, while we are being plundered; while over thirteen thousand homes each year are being shadowed by death, brought about by the actions of a roving army of potential murderers greater even than our standing forces of self-defense; while a condition exists in which three out of every four persons are potential victims of serious crimes, we are paying a national crime bill of fifteen billions of dollars a year in tribute. Every person must pay this tribute; the forces which demand it exempt nobody, not even the baby in the cradle, rich or poor, young or old; in one way or another, every single member of our population is assessed ten dollars a month in crime taxes. If this sum is not forthcoming in money, then it shall be collected in robbery, in suffering and in bloodshed.

Later in the same address, he adds:

> No greater thing can anyone do than to aid a young human being upon the straight path. No more important accomplishment lies before the citizen or the organization to which he belongs than to hamstring crime before crime hamstrings society. Youth is the recruiting ground of crime. Youth is the training school of the vast army of over 4,300,-000 vicious beings who threaten our well-being. May we band together in concerted and never-ceasing vigilance to outwit crime on its own proving grounds, and by straightening the course of youth, point the way to a clear path ahead to our goal of a happier, a safer and a more peaceful America.

G-Men and Crime. Before the Convention of the International Association of Chiefs of Police at Baltimore, the aggressive director of the Bureau of Investigation delivered another address in which he summarized the federal war against crime.

> . . . During the past four years, the Federal Bureau of Investigation has brought about the convictions of 15,777 violators of Federal laws, convictions having been secured of over 94 of each 100 persons brought to trial. During this period, sentences imposed in our cases have totaled 7 death sentences, 41 life sentences, and 43,733 years of imprisonment. Within the same four years, 25,063 fugitives from justice have been located, of which 20,713 were located through the fingerprint files of the Bureau on

behalf of law-enforcement agencies, without cost to them. These more than twenty thousand wanted criminals probably would be at large, committing more crimes, had it not been for the existence of the Identification Division of the Bureau, which was established with your aid. Of the over four thousand Federal fugitives apprehended by the Special Agents of the FBI during the past four years, it has been necessary to shoot and kill only ten criminals, and this was done only in defense of the lives of our agents after the criminals had resisted arrest by use of weapons.

The cost of operating the Federal Bureau of Investigation during the past four years amounted to $18,354,580. During the same period, we were able to return in savings, in fines, and in recoveries of stolen goods, a total of $135,110,342 to the taxpayers of America, or more than one hundred and sixteen million dollars in excess of expenditures. This represents a return of $7.36 for each dollar spent. The same profitable record can be made by any other law-enforcement agency of America which is allowed to concentrate upon crime, aided by every known practical and scientific method, plus freedom from influence. The Federal Bureau of Investigation is not a mere law-enforcement body—it is an institution entrusted with the task of giving aid to crime prevention, to detection and apprehension everywhere. Every growth of investigative, identification and training methods conceived by the Bureau is yours for the asking.

Increase in Crimes. In spite of the sharp battle being waged by the Federal Bureau of Investigation, the number of crimes committed in a year is still climbing. Figures for 1937 reveal a definite increase over the 1,333,526 major crimes of 1936. The number of robberies, burglaries, larcenies and auto thefts is greater. More persons were murdered and the number of sex crimes moved up at an alarming rate.

A study made by the Federal Bureau of Investigation of the Public Enemy File of 1937, containing complete criminal records of 13,519 criminals, revealed that 30 per cent received clemency not only once but in some cases as many as ten times. Furthermore, more than 22 per cent of 22,737 fugitives from justice who were being actively sought by one or another of the various law-enforcing agencies throughout the country were parole violators. Such figures make it clear that if crime is to be curbed in the United States, the parole system must be modified.

How to Fight Crime. In the interests of a "crime-free-America" *This Week* magazine waged a campaign against the growing menace. Through its pages articles prepared by J. Edgar Hoover are distributed by many of the leading newspapers of America to more than 5,000,000 homes. As part of this campaign a booklet on *How to Fight Crime* has circulated widely. It points out clearly that crime can be reduced by quick conviction. The certainty of some sentence carries far more weight with the criminal than the remote possibility of a severe sentence.

It points out further that the causes for a low conviction ratio and a time-lag between the offense and disposition of a case are numerous. But in all probability low conviction ratios and delays can be laid at the feet of police departments that are handicapped by the following conditions:

1. Lack of man power, equipment or facilities.
2. Lack of expert leadership or training.
3. Pay too low to attract dependable men of satisfactory "young blood."
4. Political entanglements.
5. Local conditions beyond police control.
6. Public prosecutor incompetent, inferior to criminal attorneys or involved in political affiliations.
7. Jury system inefficient.
8. A bar association that is passive or impotent or dominated by criminal lawyers.
9. Courts overworked, undermanned or run by politically-minded judges.
10. Parole system weak, unintelligent or corrupt.
11. Bail bond racket grown to vicious proportions.
12. Lack of community policy for the restraint of perverts.

A remedy lies in the education of the public to the seriousness of these conditions which breed crime and the adoption of a social policy which will better the environment out of which the youthful delinquent comes.

PART II

THE INTERNATIONAL SCENE

CHAPTER IX

ERUPTION IN THE FAR EAST

Background of Conquest. The Asiatic tinderbox burst into crackling explosion in 1937. Long predicted as inevitable, for years seen as the only possible result of an aggressive policy of conquest by a nation dominated more and more by one-track military minds, the undeclared war between Japan and China which flared up early in July was nonetheless a shock to a world grown accustomed to viewing a weak, disorganized, and poorly equipped Chinese government turn the other cheek to the bold territorial robbery of a Nippon fiercely determined to take its place among the great imperial nations of the world.

The modern conquest of China began back in the last quarter of the nineteenth century, just a few years after an isolated Japan had been forcibly opened to the world by western powers demanding the right to sell their goods to the islanders. When her doors were finally opened, Japan, with an unsuspected genius for ape-like imitation, adopted the techniques of westernization over night, changed from a slow-moving agrarian to a highly industrialized civilization with a speed that left no time for the development of a philosophy of living, a sense of international co-operation, a willingness to conform to the amenities of "civilized" warfare, suited to the new machine age. She entered a period of adolescence when the nations she sought to emulate were approaching maturity. And she discovered, as had the other great powers before her, that a machine civilization necessitated two all-important things: markets and sources of raw material.

Fortunately for Japan, perhaps for China, the virus industrialization had not infected the blood stream of her Oriental cousins on the mainland. The Chinese, proud of their ancient civilization which had been in full flower when the forbears of the peoples who now tried to teach them new methods were living in caves and ditches, resented and resisted the impact from the Occident. Fortunately also for the little dark islanders, westernization brought with it European military advisers who quickly shaped a modern army and navy.

With this new-found power Japan began satisfying her lust for imperial power at the expense of the huge blob of mainland loosely held together as the nation of China. Before the end of the century she had obtained the island of Formosa and planted a foothold in Korea. With the victory over Russia in 1905 came the sharing with Russia of concessions in the Chinese province of Manchuria. Then Korea was annexed outright a few years before the World War. The World War itself provided the opportunity for Japanese troops to take over German concessions in the Chinese province of Shantung. And only strongest pressure by Great Britain and the United States at the Washington Conference of 1922 forced the relinquishment of Shantung.

The great drive to establish what the Japanese liked

slyly to term a "Monroe Doctrine" for the Far East, began in 1931 with the conquest of Manchuria and establishment in its place of the new Japanese puppet state of Manchukuo in 1932. Now with a buffer state between China and Siberia, the Japanese militarists were in position to drive their wedge deeper inland and southward. Claiming that Jehol was geographically part of Manchukuo, Japanese troops occupied and annexed this province for Manchukuo in 1933.

On the pretext that Chinese "Communist" irregular soldiers were menacing the lives of Japanese and Manchukuoan citizens along the Manchukuo border, Tokyo next set out to control five more northern provinces— Shantung, Hopei, Chahar, Suiyuan and Shansi. In the fall of 1935 an ultimatum was sent to the Nanking government demanding that these five provinces be permitted to form an autonomous government of their own, which presumably would become another Japanese puppet state. But now for the first time the Nanking government began to exhibit spunk. A young Chinese named Yin Ju-keng set himself up as dictator of East Hopei and welcomed Japanese advisers in this small area bordering on the Gulf of Chihli, with the result that East Hopei became an important base for Japanese smuggling in the ensuing months. And a General Sung Cheh-yuan formed the Hopei-Chahar Political Council which purported to rule these two provinces more or less under Japanese supervision. But efforts to carve another puppet state from these five northern provinces were meeting with disappointing success down to the beginning of 1937, although all during 1936 Japanese gold flowed freely into the hands of Mongol armies fighting for Japan in the provinces of Chahar and Suiyuan, two strategic areas bordering on Soviet-controlled Outer Mongolia. Since the World War a strong new Soviet Russia had become a formidable rival for control of the Far East. And Russian resistance to Japanese domination 'in North China was taking the form of money and supplies seeping down through Outer Mongolia to Chinese irregular armies.

Chinese Communists. Since 1931 thousands of these irregular troops had banded together and styled themselves Chinese Communists. With able Chinese Generals, and propagandists and administrators furnished from Moscow, they set up a provisional government of their own. When they grew too presumptuous in their claims to independence, China's Dictator Chiang Kai-shek, whose rise to power could be attributed in large part to the aid Russia had given him between 1921 and 1927, sent his armies against them in 1934, gradually drove them inland. By the close of 1936 they were concentrated in an area roughly comprising about 80,000 square miles of the provinces of Suiyuan, Shensi and Shansi.

Kidnaping of Chiang Kai-shek. In charge of a large army of Chiang's Anti-Communist Bandit Suppression Forces engaged in a desultory and half-hearted pursuit of the Communist forces near the city of Sian in Shensi province was the former warlord of Manchuria, the "Young Marshal" Chang Hsueh-liang. When Chiang Kai-shek, in December, 1936, came out

from Nanking to check up on rumors that the Young
Marshal was not doing his job with the desired verve,

("*The New York Times*")

Communist Strength in China, Early 1937.

Chang Hsueh-liang and a General Yang Fu-cheng kidnaped the Dictator and sent an ultimatum to Nanking
and the world that the price of his release must be
a reversal in the policy of the Nanking government.

China must stand up to the Japanese aggressors and, instead of fighting the Chinese Communists, accept their co-operation and work with them to drive Japan completely off the Asiatic mainland.

"The Deal." Days passed during which negotiators sped between Sian and Nanking, with the government loudly denying any intention to bargain with the traitorous Chang, and making a great show of starting troops toward Sian. But in a typical Chinese denouement Marshal Chang suddenly announced he had seen the error of his ways, released the Dictator without a struggle, and came back to Nanking to stand trial for his heinous offense. When a Chinese court sentenced him to ten years in jail and loss of his civil rights for five years, the Young Marshal was not at all worried. Sure enough, a few days after sentence was passed the Chinese government granted him a full pardon and restored his civil rights. Co-kidnaper General Yang Fu-cheng was not even tried. Instead the government presented him with $300,000, packed him off on a jaunt around the world to "investigate military and economic conditions in the United States and Europe."

The whole affair had so much of the comic opera about it that some cynics even suggested the kidnaping had actually been staged as a dramatic means of rallying all China for a war with Japan. In any case it had the effect of bringing to Nanking Chinese warlords who had been on the outs with Chiang Kai-shek for years, and who now offered their armies to do or die for the Dictator. Also, as events unfolded during 1937, it became clearly apparent that out of the kidnaping incident had come some sort of "deal" with the Chinese Communists. When the showdown with Japan came the following July, Red forces fought side by side with those of "Chiang's Own."

ARMY AND NAVY VERSUS CIVILIANS

Meanwhile as the year opened in Japan, there were strong indications that not all Japanese were in wholehearted sympathy with the program of the military faction in North China. Perhaps the very failure of the army to capture control of the five provinces was galling to Japanese pride. Certain it was that the cost of these operations on the mainland was a severe headache to civilian taxpayers. Ever-increasing demands for military and naval appropriations were depleting the Japanese gold supply, upping the government debt to an unprecedented peak.

The struggle between the civilian leaders in the Japanese Diet (Parliament) and the heads of the army and navy had been growing in bitterness since the militarists tasted victory in the conquest of Manchuria. A curious dualism in the Nipponese Constitution gave the army and the navy powers which in the final analysis could be limited only by the Emperor himself. Their only real concern with the Diet was to see to it that its members voted the money necessary for their aggressive tactics, and to keep the civilian liberals from arousing any concerted opposition to their program among the population which provided their cannon fodder. To win the peasantry to them, army and navy officers spouted the Fascist propaganda used so effectively in Germany and Italy. Damning with equal fervor the Communists and the moneyed interests, they pointed to the military as the savior of the middle and lower middle classes. Like the fascists also they harked back to the grandeur of an older Japan, talked glibly of the "Restoration" to the Emperor of the absolute power enjoyed by his hallowed ancestors.

The lives of those who dared oppose the army's program were in constant danger. In February, 1936, a fanatical band of young officers murdered the Finance Minister, the Inspector General of Military Education, and did their best to kill Premier Keisuke Okada because the cabinet had been too "liberal," and not sufficiently enthusiastic about the Chinese venture.

As a result of these assassinations the militarists had gained a greater measure of control over the government, though they were still in a minority among the members of the Diet. And when the signing of an Anti-Communist pact with Germany in the fall of 1936 almost resulted in a refusal by the Russian government to renew a lease permitting Japanese fishermen to fish in Russian waters, the civilians screamed out their denunciations of the cabinet of Koki Hirota, forced him to hand in his resignation early in January, 1937.

Hayashi Cabinet. But instead of producing a less military-minded cabinet the resignation of Hirota had precisely the opposite result. Called to the Premiership now by the Emperor was General Senjuro Hayashi, a onetime War Minister and staunch army man. His troops had been the first to cross the border from Korea into Manchuria in 1931. Hayashi took up where Hirota had left off. He bullied the Diet into passing the largest budget in the history of the nation, $802,-400,000, over half of which was earmarked for army and navy expenditures. But he struck a stone wall of civilian opposition when he tried to push through a law for the "preservation of military secrets." This proposal was a bald-faced attempt to give the army license to jail or murder anyone who dared oppose their program.

Elections. When the Diet stubbornly refused to pass the military secrets law, General Hayashi asked the emperor to dissolve the legislature and called for a new election on April 30. The military then went to the people with the demand that they elect a new Diet which would be more in sympathy with the enlightened program of Asiatic invasion which the army and navy were sponsoring. Surprisingly, however, the civilians gained by the elections designed to unseat them. They captured over 400 of the 466 seats, and the gains within the Left Wing parties were significant. Now, instead of resigning in accordance with Parliamentary procedure, General Hayashi refused, blustered that it was up to the new members of the Diet to "sacrifice personal interests and serve the higher interests of the nation." Finally, however, the Diet forced a showdown by voting no-confidence in his government, and the Premier handed the emperor his resignation late in April.

Coalition Cabinet. This time the Emperor selected a civilian to head the government. Prince Fumimaro Konoye, 45-year-old President of Japan's House of Peers, was called to the job. A liberal of sorts, even though an aristocrat of the aristocrats, Prince Konoye tried to put together a cabinet which would give representation to several political factions to form a "national," or coalition government. Eight civilians were given posts. But Lieutenant General Sugiyama, War Minister in the Hayashi cabinet, continued in the same position, as did Navy Minister Vice Admiral Mitsumasa Yonai. Worst of all, from China's point of view, Koki Hirota, the man who had started the year as Premier and who had been Foreign Minister during much of the two years when Japan was scheming and working to grab off the five northern provinces, was restored to the cabinet in his old spot as Foreign Minister. The new government took office early in June. A month later the war with China had begun.

Flareup with Russia. Near the end of June, however, war appeared much more likely to break out between Japan and Russia than between the two Oriental states. Another of those border flareups which had been occurring with monotonous regularity ever since Japan took over Manchuria, threatened this time to become serious. Two small islands in the Amur River, the stream forming much of the boundary between Manchukuo and Siberia, were claimed by both nations. Sharp fighting between rival border troops over possession of the islands resulted in several deaths on both sides and the sinking of a Soviet river gunboat. In spite of angry protests emanating from the foreign offices of both powers, the incident was settled by a pact under which both nations agreed to withdraw their troops from the disputed area.

UNDECLARED WAR!

Unperturbed by Cabinet changes and Parliamentary squabbles at home, the Japanese militarists in Manchukuo and North China continued to use every weapon at their command to break Chinese resistance and take over control of the five provinces they had announced their intention to dominate.

Mongukuo. By no means satisfied with the co-operation they were getting from the Hopei-Chahar Political Council which, as a matter of fact, stoutly disclaimed any intention of severing all connection with the Chinese central government, the Japanese now turned to financing a Mongol Prince Teh who was more amenable to their reasoning and gold. Late in March reports leaked out from the remote hinterlands of the province of Chahar that control of the northern part of the province had been captured by Prince Teh, and that a new state called "Mongukuo" had been proclaimed. Presumably, Japan was to bear the same relation to this state that she did toward Manchukuo.

Marco Polo Bridge Incident. Meanwhile Japan was concentrating more and more troops in the Peiping Tientsin area in the province of Hopei, treating the area as if it were already a part of Japan. To impress the local population with the strength of their military machines Japanese commanders announced maneuvers beginning July 7 just outside the city of Peiping. A certain understandable lack of enthusiasm for this display manifested itself among the Chinese troops in the vicinity. And on the evening of the 7th, as the maneuvering Japanese troops neared the "Marco Polo" bridge in a southwestern suburb of Peiping, someone fired a potshot. Japanese officers insisted their men had only blank cartridges in their guns when the firing began. Chinese on the spot asserted just as heatedly that Japanese troops had no business maneuvering in the area, and had done so to create an "incident" which would provide an excuse for establishing complete control of North China. In any case the "incident" touched off skirmishes which in the next few days spread all through the Peiping Tientsin area.

Japanese Demands. Lieutenant General Kiyoshi Kazuki, number one Japanese commander in the Peiping Tientsin area, quickly presented Chinese authorities with demands for (1) an official apology; (2) evacuation of Chinese troops from the Yungting River where the fighting broke out (This was later expanded into an ultimatum to withdraw the entire 37th Division of the Chinese Army from the Tientsin-Peiping area.); (3) punishment of Chinese officers responsible for the conflict; (4) suppression of anti-Japanese activities; (5) joint co-operation against Communism.

On the spot, General Sung Cheh-yuan, Chairman of the ambiguous Hopei-Chahar Political Council, had already caved in to these demands when he received a call from a member of the Chinese general staff at Nanking. Nanking was insisting that no "local settle-

ment" of the incident should be agreed to, refused to
accept any settlement which might be reached between
Sung and the Japanese. As they had already pointed
out in a memorandum to the powers which signed the

("*Glasgow Record*")

Just a Little Bit of Politeness.

Nine-Power Treaty guaranteeing Chinese independence, Nanking officials again insisted that "the national government of China is bound to control closely
the basis of settlement since it is a well-known tactic
of the Japanese military to promote disruption in North
China by insisting on overawing the local authorities.
The Japanese also aim to mislead world opinion by pre-
tending that such specious attempts at local negotia-

tions, intended to flout the national government, are directed toward minimizing the 'incidents' that they continually engineer."

Fighting in Earnest. Japanese airmen prodded the stubborn Chinese by bombing the Chinese barracks in the Peiping zone and the important railway center of Langfang, between Peiping and Tientsin. On the morning of July 29, the Chinese struck back by staging a surprise attack on Tientsin itself. And on the same afternoon 5,000 members of Yin Ju-keng's Peace Preservation Corps, a body organized and armed by the Japanese to maintain order in the puppet state of East Hopei, turned on their leader and his Japanese advisers, practically wiped out the small Japanese garrison at Tungchow, Yin's capital. Then Nipponese flyers loosed their bombs over the native section of Tientsin, reducing it to a smoking shambles by August 1.

"Fight Japan!" Now finally it was obvious to all that the Far Eastern showdown had at last arrived. Banners were popping out all over China exhorting the populace to "Fight Japan," and as he started troops north from Nanking to join the armies already in the field, Dictator Chiang Kai-shek exhorted them to "fight to the last man" . . . "we cannot surrender any territory or allow our sovereignty to be encroached upon. I call upon the Nation to mobilize our total resources and struggle hand-in-hand to save China."

China's Strength. When he talked about "mobilizing resources" Chiang Kai-shek well knew that only in manpower and the very raw materials the Japanese were seeking did he have an edge over his foes. He could put 400 planes of varying ages in the air. He could point with a good deal of pride to his 280,000 smartly trained and well-equipped troops known as "Chiang's Own." He could also muster another 2,000,-000 "irregulars" in varying degrees of raggedness who might be soldiers one day, bandits the next. But he could look to no reserve of trained civilians in a nation where for centuries the soldier had been looked down on as a member of a lower social order. Nor could he wax enthusiastic about his navy. Twelve cruisers and 18 destroyers made up the entire Chinese fleet—no battleships, no submarines. Even with the necessary raw materials, factories which could be relied on to turn out munitions, guns, and planes were scarce articles in China. And to get money with which to buy needed military supplies from foreign powers would become increasingly difficult in a country whose peasants had been taxed to death—some of them having been forced to pay as much as 30 years in advance.

China's principal strength, then, lay in two factors: (1) a population which had never been counted but which would probably comprise 450,000,000—a population which had been conquered before but which had always swallowed up its conquerors by sheer force of numbers and perhaps superiority of culture, giving rise to the old Chinese proverb, "It will all be the same in a hundred years"; (2) the economic interests of the western powers in China and in other Far Eastern territories which had in the past led them to check Japan's drive to dominate China. Great Britain and the

United States in particular were expected by Chiang to help him repel the invader.

Japan's Strength. Opposing Chiang Kai-shek was one of the world's finest military machines. An army of 300,000 was backed by a reserve of 7,000,000 trained Japanese civilians. Twelve hundred planes could devastate other Chinese cities as they had laid waste Tientsin. One of the world's top three navies boasted 10 battleships, 13 cruisers, 106 destroyers, and 62 submarines. Behind this impressive array of military strength stood a highly industrialized nation equipped to turn out shot and shell as fast as its army and navy might use them. True, Japan sadly lacked the three vital raw materials, coal, oil and iron, some of which she was after in the northern provinces of China. But she had ships to bring them from other countries. Thus far also she had been able to pay for these raw materials by selling her own goods abroad, though tariff barriers and quota restrictions against the articles produced under her starvation wage conditions had increased greatly during the Depression. And a constantly dwindling gold supply coupled with an ever increasing national debt was evidence that a long drawn out war would surely bankrupt her government.

It was an uneven fight from the outset, as events during the summer and fall of 1937 were to prove. Only a desperate China with its back to the wall would have dared accept the challenge of such a powerful adversary.

By the end of the first week in August the Japanese

military was in complete control of the entire Peiping-Tientsin area, had kicked Sung Cheh-yuan out in favor of his reputedly more pro-Japanese subordinate, Chang Tsu-chung, and it began to look as though the conquest of the five northern provinces would go ahead as smoothly as had the conquest of Manchuria. But two columns of Japanese troops advancing along the Tientsin-Pukow and Peiping-Hankow railways met unexpectedly strong opposition early in August from troops dispatched by Nanking, as did the forces crawling out along the Peiping-Kalgan-Suiyan railway. At Nankow Pass, twenty-five miles from Peiping on the railroad going to Kalgan, 30,000 Chinese troops engaged a similar number of Japanese along the fifteen-mile mountain defile in a battle which raged for more than two weeks. Only when a Japanese-Manchukuoan army, pushing westward north of the Great Wall, arrived on the scene August 29 and caught the defenders in the rear did the Chinese forces withdraw. The bitterness of the fighting in this area demonstrated the fierce desire of China to hold Kalgan. Gateway to the Northwest, it stood at the head of the ancient caravan trail into Outer Mongolia and thence Siberia. And it was over this trail that much-needed supplies from Russia might come. A few weeks later Kalgan fell before the combined forces of the Japanese and Manchukuoan armies.

Clash in Shanghai. All hope of confining the fighting to North China was ended by events which developed in the great and cosmopolitan city of Shanghai just as the battle at Nankow Pass was beginning. On

August 9 a Japanese Navy lieutenant and his sailor chauffeur were shot and killed by Chinese sentries while motoring near the Chinese military airdrome at Hungjao, outside Shanghai. Rejecting the Chinese story that the two men had attempted to force their way into the airdrome, Japan immediately brought several river gunboats down from upriver Yangtze stations, landed 1,000 marines. Two days later warships began steaming into the Shanghai harbor. By the end of the month a fleet of 50 battleships, cruisers, destroyers, and airplane carriers was patrolling the Shanghai harbor. And over 8,000 marines had been landed in the area.

When Chinese authorities refused to punish the sentries or to withdraw troops which had been sent into the Chinese section of the city in violation of the agreement reached following the fighting in Shanghai during the Manchurian conquest in 1932, fighting broke out on August 13.

International Settlement. Complicating the war which was to follow in the Shanghai area was the huge section of the city designated as the "International Settlement" and the "French Concession." Here the various nations had obtained concessions from early Chinese governments, and here Europeans, Americans and Japanese, living and working under laws of their own making, swelled the population to make Shanghai the world's sixth city. Treaty rights guaranteed the inviolability of these areas, and in the hostilities of 1932 residents had enjoyed comfortable and comparatively safe box seats at a war which was fought under their very noses.

The foreign concessions fared far worse in the war of 1937. Day after the first clash of troops in the native city of Shanghai, two Chinese flyers with more patriotism than skill loosed a couple of bombs intended for the *Idumo,* flagship of the Japanese fleet which was moored in the Whangpoo river just opposite the International Settlement. One fell in the Palace Hotel, the other a mile away in an amusement palace teeming with a Saturday crowd. More than 500 were killed in this tragic mistake which proved the signal also for a wild return from the Japanese warships and for a series of aerial bombardments of the native sections of the city by Nipponese airmen. And Chinese guns were now deliberately trained on that section of the Settlement where 30,000 Japanese lived and where the Japanese naval headquarters was located.

Evacuation of Foreigners. Special treaty rights gave nations with concessions in the International Settlement power to station warships in the Shanghai harbor and soldiers or marines on land to guard their citizens. Two days after fighting commenced these warships began the slow process of evacuating thousands of non-combatant foreigners.

Bombing of Civilians. At the same time thousands of terror-stricken Chinese civilians streamed into the International Settlement, hoping to find there protection against the wholesale aerial bombing now begun by Japan. Squadrons of bombers not only trained their sights on the native sections of Shanghai, but flew far inland to raid Hangchow, the capital at Nanking, and Hankow. Others sped down to drop their missiles of death on Canton, far to the south. Stories from the small towns and villages even reported Japanese bombing accompanied by deadly machine-gun fire upon the helpless inhabitants fleeing from the destruction of their homes. Bombing operations in the larger cities might have been partly justified from a military standpoint by the presence therein of airfields, army cantonments, and railway stations. But the attacks on the villages were obviously a part of a plan to terrorize the population and cause them to plead for peace at any price.

Attack on British Ambassador. While the press of the world was protesting these frightful invasions of the rights of non-combatants, an incident occurred which revealed in starkly bold outline the Japanese tactics. On August 26 the British ambassador to China and two members of his staff were motoring from Nanking to Shanghai. Forty miles out of Shanghai they were attacked by two Japanese navy planes which dropped down to close range with machine-guns spurting. Ambassador Sir Hughe Montgomery Knatchbull-Hugesson was seriously wounded. Instead of making a formal apology instantly, the Japanese rebuked the ambassador for not having a Union Jack spread on the roof of his car. The British foreign office retorted angrily in a sharp demand for an apology in which they pointed out that the matter of the flag was irrelevant as was the identity of the persons wounded. "The real issue is that they were non-combatants." More than a month later Japan issued a grudging apology.

Chinese Bomb "President Hoover." Meanwhile, four days after the attack on Sir Hughe, China offered Japan a lesson in international ethics. Chinese planes, mistaking the American passenger ship *President Hoover* for a Japanese gunboat, rained bombs on the decks of the steamer as it lay at anchor at the mouth of the Yangtze river awaiting a contingent of refugees. One member of the crew was killed and nine others were injured. Less than eight hours after the incident occurred the Chinese ambassador to the United States called on Secretary of State Cordell Hull to express regrets and say that his government "assumed full responsibility for the unfortunate occurrence and was prepared to make prompt indemnification."

"Pacific Blockade." To check Chinese importation of military supplies the Japanese naval authorities on August 25 gave notice that a "pacific blockade" was being established along the coast of China as far south as the port of Swatow. This was later extended to take in the entire coast line down to the boundary of French Indo-China. Assurance was given to the world, however, that the measure was not directed against foreign ships "engaged in peaceful trade" with China, and expressly excluded from the blockade were the ports of Tsingtao, Hongkong, Macao, and the French leased port of Kwang-chowwan. To have declared anything but this "pacific" blockade would have been tantamount to a declaration of war, which Japan wanted to avoid at all cost. Her conquest of Manchuria had been made without a declaration of war, as had the capture of Ethiopia by Italy. War had been outlawed as an instrument of national policy by the Kellogg-Briand Pact of 1927, and since that time it had become the fashion to fight but not to declare war. The fact that the President of the United States would be forced to invoke that nation's Neutrality Law bringing about a stoppage of arms shipments from America was also a strong factor in the refusal of either Japan or China to declare war. So with troops of both nations fighting in what gave every appearance of being a man-sized conflict diplomatic relations remained unsevered. The Japanese ambassador continued to dodge shells as he went about his duties in Shanghai, and the Chinese representative at Tokyo was ostensibly busy trying to obtain a peaceable settlement.

WOOING WORLD OPINION

With the war now in full swing both sides turned to the job of wooing the western powers—the Japanese to keep them out of the fracas; the Chinese to bring them in.

Japan's "Case." Japanese propaganda stressed the fact that Japan was one of the world's greatest "Have-nots." Forced to accept western civilization by concerted efforts of the western powers themselves in the middle of the last century, they had developed under German, American, British and other expert tutelage a highly industrialized civilization. With industrialization had come an enormously increased population. To feed both her population and the maws of her new machines she was forced to seek abroad the food and raw materials she so shockingly lacked. And to purchase these materials abroad she had to produce goods to exchange in available markets. Faced with the same problem at a much earlier date, so the Japanese apologists claimed, England, among other nations, had gone out to every corner of the globe to carve a great colonial empire with little regard for the feelings of the peoples she conquered. Japan, on the other hand, seeing on her very doorstep a vast disorganized country infested with bandits and making little or no attempt to exploit the abundant resources of the very materials Japan lacked, tried for years to "co-operate" with the Chinese in a spirit of neighborliness.

Only when the Chinese resisted this neighborliness too strongly had it been necessary for the Japanese army to take over Manchuria. And now, if the Chinese leaders would only recognize the advantages which would result to their nation from a scientific development of the rich coal veins in Shansi, the iron ore in Chahar, and the oil shale deposits in Shantung; and if they would buy the goods turned out by Japanese machine efficiency instead of boycotting the island's products, they might still live together as friends. In short, if China would recognize Japan's needs and desires and co-operate to fulfill them, it would not be necessary for Japan to control the five northern provinces. But because China refused this offer of collaboration with her sister nation in the Orient, refused also to keep her house in order so that orderly Japanese business in China might continue undisturbed, and finally, because China gave evidence of flirting with Japan's chief rival, Soviet Russia—witness the new united front between Chiang Kai-shek and the Chinese Communists coupled with the Sino-Soviet non-aggression treaty signed shortly before Shanghai hostilities began—Japan must now turn from persuasion to steel.

Furthermore, her past attempts at persuasion, almost always to be sure accompanied by an impressive array of steel, had uniformly led to treaties and truces agreed to and signed by Chinese leaders only to be violated later on some pretext or other. The very presence of Chinese troops in the Shanghai area was a flagrant violation of a treaty agreed to at the end of the hostilities there in 1932, so the Japanese contended. (The Chinese insisted that the Japanese had themselves first violated this agreement by landing marines.)

The gist of the Japanese case then was the cry "The Orient for Orientals"—a "Monroe Doctrine" for the Far East, with Japan playing the role occupied by the United States in the western hemisphere.

The Case for China. Chiang Kai-shek's best answer to all these arguments was to point a long yellow finger at Japanese soldiers and marines occupying Chinese soil, Japanese battleships pouring shells into Chinese ports. In the other hand he held aloft the Nine-power treaty signed by Japan at Washington, D. C., in 1922. At that conference Japan had joined with Great Britain, the United States, Belgium, France, the Netherlands, Portugal, and China herself to guarantee the Open Door in China, (the right of every nation to equal trading rights in China) and to guarantee

THE TIGER TAMED AT LAST?

Top: Thomas E. Dewey tells reporters about racketeering (Acme). *Right:* New York's mayor campaigns for second term (Life Magazine).

CHINA AND JAPAN IN UNDECLARED WAR

Top: Jap soldiers advancing (Life Magazine). *Center:* Japan's guns boom (Life Magazine). *Bottom:* Generalissimo and Madame Chiang Kai-shek (Life Magazine).

the territorial integrity of China. Japan had flouted this treaty in the Manchurian conquest and got away with it. Was she to be allowed to continue to trample on this treaty obligation until all China was swallowed up by her militarists?

British Interests. The answer to that question was to be found only in the state department of the United States and in the British foreign office. The League of Nations had tried its hand before. When it indicted Japan for grabbing Manchuria, demanded that the Maritime Provinces be returned to China, the Japanese had responded by withdrawing from the League. And though China appealed to the League again for help after the developments of July and August, she well knew that any aid forthcoming would emanate from Washington and London. Chinese leaders banked heavily on the fact that Britain had a billion dollars invested in China, had also extensive colonial and do- minion territories in Hongkong, the Malay peninsula, Australia, New Zealand and the East Indies whose ties to the Mother country might well be endangered by a Japanese Monroe Doctrine. Yet when the United States Secretary of State Henry L. Stimson in 1931 called Japan's attention to the fact that her Man- churian activities by no means jibed with her obliga- tions under the Nine-Power Pact, the British Foreign Office suddenly went stone deaf, dumb and blind, re- fused to endorse the U. S. warning, and left Secretary Stimson swinging freely out on one of the longest limbs in the history of modern diplomacy. That was in 1931, during the period when Great Britain was taking worldwide disarmament more or less seriously. Since then, so Chiang Kai-shek may have reasoned, the British had begun a 7½ billion dollar rearmament program. Perhaps now they were better prepared to face a showdown with Japan in the Far East.

But all during the fall and winter of 1937 events were to demonstrate that John Bull was much more anxious to have Uncle Sam take on the job of checking the swart islanders than to undertake the task himself.

Uncle Sam's Position. American investments in China were only about half those of Britain. Similarly her territorial holdings in the other side of the Pacific consisted only of Guam, Samoa, Wake, and the Philippine Islands, with the Hawaiian and one or two other relatively unimportant island possessions farther to the east. And the Philippines, the largest of these possessions, had already been given a measure of independence with the promise that they should be definitely on their own after 1946.

Also, complicating whatever interest the government at Washington might have in preserving the status quo in the Orient, was the inescapable fact that while the average American sympathized strongly with the Chinese, a peace-minded population bent on erecting safeguards against any possible seduction of the nation into foreign controversies had pushed through Congress a Neutrality Law to keep us out of war. (See Chapter III.)

American Neutrality Policy. Even as the fighting was getting hotter in Shanghai and in North China daily, so was the heat being put on the President of the United States by World Peaceways and other peace organizations to invoke the Neutrality Act. Principal effect of this act would be to stop immediately all shipments of arms, ammunition, or implements of war to both China and Japan. Knowing that to take this step would be to hurt a weak China far more than a powerful Japan, the President hesitated to put the Neutrality Law in effect. Under the law he was required to declare the embargo whenever he should decide that an actual state of war existed. Thus, in the Far East, he simply refused to recognize that a real war was being fought. Finally, however, on the 14th of September he forbade merchant vessels owned by the United States government to carry arms to China or Japan. Although he warned them they would do so at their own risk, private American shipping concerns might still continue to carry war supplies to either belligerent.

This partial embargo was interpreted by Chinese as a concession to Japan, but within three weeks they had reason to believe that the American government was moving toward something stronger than sympathy for their cause.

Nanking Air Raids. When Japanese air raids of September 20 drove U. S. Ambassador to China Nelson T. Johnson out of his embassy and onto a gunboat on the Yangtze river for a few hours, the U. S. state department sent its sharpest note of the war to Japan. The fact that Japan gave prior notice of the bombings, and warned foreigners to take shelter, in no way softened the effect of shells deliberately rained on non-

combatants and neutrals in non-military areas. And
two days later the American Admiral Harry Yarnell
was bluntly warning that he would employ U. S. Naval
forces under his command to protect American citizens
for the duration of hostilities.

But American protests, even though joined by similar
messages from Britain and Russia and by a condemnation from the League's Far Eastern Advisory Committee, brought no change in Japanese tactics.

The "Quarantine" Speech. Then came the remarkable "quarantine" speech made by President
Roosevelt at Chicago on October 5. In a scathing denunciation of "war makers" he pledged his administration to join with "peace-loving nations" to take "concerted action" against the lawless aggressor powers.
While reaffirming his devotion to the cause of peace and
his determination to keep the United States out of war,
he implied hearty dissatisfaction with restraints imposed on him by the Neutrality Laws. Isolation was
not enough, he declared. Yet he had no constructive
plan to offer the peace-loving nations beyond the vague
hint that when disease breaks out among civilized
people they co-operate to "quarantine" the sick members of the population. Did "quarantine" mean, for
example, boycott of Japanese goods such as the Labor
elements in the United States and Great Britain had
been agitating for since the outbreak of war in China?
The President did not elaborate.

Yet the speech was received with wildest enthusiasm
by the press of the "peace-loving nations." Naturally
its reception was very different in Germany, Italy, and

Japan, the nations obviously singled out by the address which named no names.

League Action. By a coincidence which seemed to indicate that Geneva had warning of the Roosevelt declaration of a new U. S. foreign policy even before it was released, the League of Nations Far Eastern Advisory Committee on the same day pronounced Japan an aggressor and treaty-breaker, invited the signers of the Nine-Power Pact to assemble and consider means of ending the Sino-Japanese war.

Two days later the United States endorsed the League's action wholeheartedly and indicated it would gladly accept an invitation to a conference of the Nine Powers. The stage was now set for another of those international get-togethers which had previously proved so futile in upholding the sanctity of treaties.

BRUSSELS CONFERENCE

On October 16 the Belgian government, "at the request of the British government and with the approval of the government of the United States," formally invited signatories of the Nine Power pact and other interested nations to a conference on the Far Eastern undeclared war. Those nations whose representatives arrived for the opening session November 3 included: the United States, Britain, France, Russia, Belgium herself, Portugal, The Netherlands, Mexico, Bolivia, Italy, Norway, Sweden, and France. Germany had refused the invitation, as had Japan, the culprit whose manners were intended to be mended by the conference.

Despite the promise contained in President Roosevelt's Chicago speech, it was apparent at the outset that the conference would accomplish nothing. Before sending Foreign Secretary Eden off to Brussels, Prime Minister Neville Chamberlain told members of the British House of Commons, "It is a mistake . . . to go to this conference talking about economic sanctions, pressure, and force." And when Norman Davis, America's representative, made the keynote address he proposed only that Japan and China be "urged" to resort to peaceful procedures.

"Illegal." The delegates finally went so far as to adopt a resolution branding the Japanese action as "illegal," Italy, which acted as the unofficial spokesman for Japan throughout the conference, voting "No." [1] Then a note was sent to Japan asking her whom she would be willing to have mediate the war. When Tokyo sent back a flat refusal, the meetings were suspended while delegates went back to find out from their respective governments what would be their next move. The conference met again on November 22, but the principal delegates from Britain, France, and Russia did not even deign to return. The pleas of China's delegate, Dr. Wellington Koo, to withhold supplies of war materials and credits from Japan, fell on deaf ears, and the conference adjourned. Only a harmless report praising the peaceful intentions of the Nine Powers, condemning treaty-breaking by force, and pleading for peace in the Far East was produced.

[1] On November 6, three days after the Brussels conference convened, Japan signed a three-way "anti-Communist pact" with Italy and Germany, leading to the well-founded suspicion that the Rome-Berlin axis had become a triangle with Tokyo at the point of the new angle.

JAPAN MOPS UP

Meanwhile the Japanese had not permitted the meddlings of international fussbudgets to hinder their methodical job of mopping up in China. Closing in on the mainland's biggest city from the north, south, and east, they completed the conquest of the Shanghai peninsula on November 9, after an 89-day siege which cost the lives of an estimated 100,000 Chinese. As thousands of Chinese civilians and some soldiers poured into the overtaxed International settlement, bringing with them cholera and typhus which killed off hundreds more before the epidemics could be checked, most of Chiang's troops retreated in good order back along the Yangtze River toward Nanking. They left behind them one "Lost Battalion" of 500 troops pledged to hold until death the warehouse in which they were quartered. But after 123 of the 500 had been killed by Japanese artillery and machine-guns, the rest changed their minds, ran a 20-yard gauntlet of fire to gain safety in a British outpost.

Chiang's troops next dug in at their famed "Hindenburg Line," a row of thousands of pillbox concrete forts built on hummocks in the swampy terrain extending from Fushan to Soochow to Kashing. Less than two weeks after the fall of Shanghai the Japanese had cracked the Hindenburg line wide open, and were rushing on toward Nanking, with the Chinese fleeing ahead of them burning and laying waste the entire countryside.

Fall of Nanking. Chiang Kai-shek, unable to check the Japanese tide approaching closer and closer to his capital, moved the government from Nanking in mid-November. Part of it went 1,000 miles up the Yangtze to Chungking, the rest to Hankow and Wuchang, 400 miles away. Chiang himself stayed on until the last. But he too was soon in flight as General Iwane Matsui, Japanese commander in charge of the Shanghai-Nanking campaign, blasted his way into the capital city on December 10. Scores of bombers, tanks, warships in the Yangtze, and an estimated 100,000 troops made a ruin of the great city. Reports told of wild-eyed Japanese troops looting the city, and lining citizens up against walls to be shot by the hundreds.

As the year ended Nipponese troops were pushing on up the Yangtze River toward Hankow, and were also launching the long-postponed drive on China's southern metropolis, Canton.

Northern Campaign. In the North too the campaign to dominate the five northern provinces, had by mid-December been highly successful. Though Japanese troops continued to be harassed by guerilla tactics effectively practiced by the Communist forces, they had brought practically all of north China down to the Yellow River under their control. Chahar and Suiyuan had been completely conquered and organized into "The Inner Mongolian Nation," another puppet state under the Mongol Prince Teh. The capital of Shansi, Taiyuan, also fell in mid-November. And though some resistance still existed in Southern Hopei, Shansi, and Shantung, Japanese commanders in the field anticipated little difficulty in wiping it out in short

order either by bribery or bullets. Bribery enabled
them to establish a new puppet government in Peiping
late in the year. Willing Chinese in charge promised
to do what Japan wanted; namely, eradicate Communism, and oppose both the Chinese government of
Chiang, and the Chinese Kuomintang, or National
Party. And the name of Peiping (Northern Peace)
was changed back to the original Peking (Northern
Capital).

Thus, including Manchuria, Japan by the close of
1937 had wrested roughly 700,000 square miles of
territory from China—an area greater than Texas,
California, Montana, and New Mexico combined.

PANAY INCIDENT

Japan had good reason to believe, even before the
Brussels conference, that the other two powers with
big stakes in China—the United States and Great
Britain—were not seriously determined to curb her
aggression. The British foreign office had been thoroughly annoyed by the tardiness of Japanese apologies
after the shooting of the British ambassador to China,
after the attempted murder of a British consul, and
after the killing of four British Tommies by Japanese
airmen who claimed to have mistaken them for Chinese. And both Britain and the United States had
been worried by the Japanese seizure of Chinese customs in Shanghai because of the threat to their interests. But they had accepted Japanese assurances that
control of the customs did not mean closing the Open
Door in China, and that loans made to China by the

United States, for which the customs receipts had been pledged, would be paid. The year was almost over, and Japanese militarists were getting ready to congratulate each other on the fact that the conquest of China had been accomplished without any break or near-break in relations with the United States and Britain.

Then a foolhardy attack on British and U. S. gunboats brought bristling notes of protest and demands of redress from Washington and London which not only gravely strained relations between the two Democracies and Japan, but indicated also a possibility, however remote, of harmonious joint action against the aggressors.

A treaty of 1858 gave the United States the right to protect its citizens in China, led to patrolling of Chinese waters by specially-constructed river gunboats. One of these, the *Panay*, had been stationed on the Yangtze helping with the work of evacuating Americans from Nanking when the siege of the capital began. When the fighting grew too hot it moved 27 miles upstream where it acted as a protector of three Standard Oil ships. Plenty of American flags were flying from masthead, prow, and poop on the *Panay*, and the awnings, which had U. S. flags painted on them, were spread out. Suddenly, at mid-day on Sunday, December 12, a squadron of Japanese bombing planes swooped down out of the clouds dropping bombs which sank not only the *Panay*, but the three Standard Oil ships nearby. As the ships were sinking Japanese launches began machine-gunning the survivors in lifeboats. Three were killed—two Americans and an Italian correspondent—and more than 50 were injured. Survivors insisted that the planes had flown so low that they could not have mistaken the nationality of the vessels, and that therefore the attack must have been deliberate. On the same day British gunboats, on the Yangtze by terms of a treaty similar to that between the United States and China, were also raked by Japanese fire. Planes and field guns bombed, shelled, and machine-sprayed the *Ladybird, Bee, Scarab,* and *Cricket.* One British seaman was killed, several wounded.

Immediately President Roosevelt, working closely with Secretary of State Hull, issued orders that a note be dispatched to Tokyo asking for an immediate expression of Japanese regret, full indemnities, and guarantees against repetition. He also indicated that he was perfectly aware of the dualism under the Japanese constitution which made the military and naval forces independent of the civilian government and responsible only to the Emperor, by "requesting" that the incident be brought to the attention of His Imperial Highness, Hirohito. The Japanese government sent a formal note of apology to Washington even before they received the protest from the United States state department. The government expressed deep regret over the incident. Rear Admiral Mitsuzawa, commander of naval forces in China whose bombers had sunk the *Panay,* was relieved of his post. The Japanese navy declared a formal salute would be fired in honor of the Americans lost, and a fund was started in Japan for the victims. Japanese ambassador to the United States Hiroshi Saito even went to the radio to apologize profusely for the "terrible blunder."

But the United States did not consider this sufficient. When survivors' stories of the attack from Japanese launches were corroborated by a naval inquiry, another note of protest was sent, demanding redress. The Japanese government began an investigation of this angle of the affair. Col. Shingoro Hashimoto, commanding the Japanese troops along the upper Yangtze, denied the launch attacks.

Meanwhile, as no formal reply to the American demand for redress came from the Japanese government, President Roosevelt conferred with naval officials. Mysterious maneuvers were reported on the Pacific coast. England too had sent sharp notes to Japan after the shelling of her ships, had received an apology in return which she had accepted while pointing out acidly that previous promises to halt Japanese attacks on British subjects and property had been ineffectual.

Although Premier Konoye reported the sinking of the *Panay* to Emperor Hirohito on December 18, for almost a week no reply was forthcoming from the exalted "Sun of Heaven." To prod him into action Mr. Roosevelt on December 21 made public a reply to a letter written him by Alf Landon, G.O.P. candidate for the Presidency in 1936. Mr. Landon had commended the President on his able handling of foreign affairs, and had denounced those Congressmen who were signing the Ludlow petition for a referendum before war could be declared, and insisting that Ameri-

can gunboats be withdrawn from China. In his reply
to Landon the President declared that while the American people want peace they have "rejected every suggestion that ultimate security can be secured by closing
our eyes to the fact that whether we like it or not we
are a part of a large world of other nations and peoples.

"As such we owe some measure of co-operation and
even leadership in maintaining standards of conduct
helpful to the ultimate goal of general peace."

By a coincidence too well-timed to be completely
a coincidence, Britain's Prime Minister told the House
of Commons on the same day (December 21) that, "It
is time now for the Japanese government to show it is
not unmindful of the rights and interests of foreigners."
Finally, the day before Christmas, Foreign Minister
Hirota personally handed U. S. Ambassador Joseph C.
Grew a note officially approved by the "Sun of
Heaven," in which the Japanese government acknowledged full responsibility for the sinking of the *Panay*,
said that the flying squadron, commander, and "all
others responsible," had been punished, and assured
the American government "definite and specific steps"
had been taken to prevent a recurrence, and promised
full indemnities.

Although rejecting the note's contention that the
attack was entirely unintentional and a mistake, Secretary of State Hull and President Roosevelt accepted
the apology on Christmas Day, and the incident appeared to be closed. But the Far East continued in
eruption, and it was still a tinderbox from which might
flare worldwide war.

CHAPTER X

LITTLE WORLD WAR IN SPAIN

Spaniards surveying their shell-torn land in 1937 might have been excused for inquiring somewhat querulously, "Who owns this war, anyway?" For not only were whole divisions of Italians blasting away at French and Belgian in opposing trenches, and German scout planes engaging Russian bombers in the air above Spain, but also the big noise of the conflict in press and radio came as often from the capitals of Britain, France, Germany, Italy, and Russia as it did from the Iberian peninsula. And although somewhat less deadly than the hostilities along, say, the Cordoba front, the wranglings of diplomatic longbeards around the green baize table often made bigger world headlines.

All Things to All Men. A mess of apparently inextricably conflicting interests, the war which descended on sunny Spain in July, 1936, was all things to all men. To millions of the uninformed it was simply a war of law and order (represented by the Insurgents or Rebels) against Communism and Anarchy (the Loyalists or Government forces). To other millions of onlookers it was a clearly defined defense of democracy against the murderous tactics of disgruntled warlords and other reactionary elements. But the intelligent Spaniard knew that the complex and involved issues present in the sad state of affairs he saw around him could not be described in such unstudied terms.

Centuries of conflict not alone in Spain but throughout the world had gone into making the Spanish civil war.   Among basic conflicts involved were those between peasant and grandee over the use and ownership of the arable land controlled for centuries by the nation's religious and lay nobility.   Deep-seated differences over the part the Catholic church should play in government and education were also at the core of the conflict.   The fanatical desire of Basque, Catalan and other separatist groups within Spain for regional autonomy played its part.   And more recently the growing world conflict between capital and labor had in Spain, as in other countries, fed the distended bellies of the antagonistic philosophies of Fascism and Communism—two socio-economic theories equally incompatible with liberty and democracy.

These were the issues which divided the Spanish people, sent brother against brother, and father out to kill son.   And because they were so complex, Monarchist and Fascist fought at the side of mild Republican on one side against Anarchist, Communist, Socialist, Republican and Centrist, who had been forced to join hands against what appeared to them to be a common danger.

Genesis of a War.   The monarchy of Hapsburg Alfonso XIII had been overthrown in the Republican revolution of 1931.   Efforts of Republicans and their more radical supporters to put into effect social, economic and religious reform in the succeeding two years resulted in their going too fast for their slower-moving electorate. The Parliamentary elections of 1933 brought a swing back toward the Right, and the reversal of what reforms had been accomplished. This caused Leftists to man the barricades again in 1934, but the revolt was confined to a few provinces only, and was put down by the army with much bloodshed, particularly in the province of Asturias. But a United Front of Left Republicans, together with the Socialists and Anarchists who had previously spurned the ballot, returned the Left Wing to majority power in the February elections of 1936. And again the job of dividing up the landholdings of the grandees, reducing the power of the church, and raising the living standards of the lower classes was resumed—resumed with the inevitable violence which was sure to follow in the wake of such sweeping change. A series of attacks on churches, priests and nuns, by the Left Wingers, accompanied by rioting, strikes and political murders, caused defenders of the old order to resort finally to civil war against the government. With nine-tenths of the army and navy on their side, they quickly seized control of the western half of Spain within a few days after the first clash broke out in Spanish Morocco July 17, 1936. On the other hand, the revolts of army garrisons in Spain's Mediterranean ports were put down by hastily organized militia groups and sections of the Civil Guard which remained loyal. Most important of all, the capital of Spain at Madrid was retained in the firm control of the government.

High among modern military marvels ranked the fact that, eighteen months after the civil war broke out, Spain's capital, defended during most of that period by raw untrained recruits with inferior equipment, stood off repeated offensives by a well-disciplined soldiery including thousands of fierce North African Moors and the finest military equipment the money of grandees could buy. Day after day of merciless aerial bombing of her civilian population killed thousands, reduced a quarter of the city to a shambles, forced the government itself to flee to Valencia, but failed to bring the city's surrender. And as days stretched into weeks and weeks into months, the siege-ridden capital evinced a growing resistance which made increasingly ridiculous the early boasts of the Rebel leader General Francisco Franco that he would occupy the city before Christmas of 1936.

"NON-INTERVENTION"

Franco's boasts were based on his belief in the superiority of the guns, tanks, planes and troops he had been receiving ever since war broke out from the Fascist powers of Italy, Germany and Portugal; while the fact that he failed to make good his boast was in no small part due to the active interest in the Loyalist cause displayed by Russia and France.

Europe had taken sides in the Spanish civil war immediately. Benito Mussolini and Adolf Hitler fell all over each other tendering material assistance to General Franco, whom they loudly hailed as a bulwark against Communism. Léon Blum in Paris and Joseph

Stalin in Moscow evinced the opposite belief that Democracy was making a valiant stand against an un-
lawful effort to saddle the Spaniards with hated
Fascism, and backed up their beliefs with munitions
shipments to Madrid.

What was even more dangerous to the peace of the
world was the fact that as the propagandists hammered
home the cliché that the civil war was a last ditch stand
of Left against Right, came a great surge of "foreign
volunteers" into the Iberian peninsula fired with a zeal
to die in this Holy War. Far from discouraging the
desire of their nationals to "give their all" for this
cause, the governments of Italy and Germany on one
side and at least Russia on the other, lent such able assistance in organizing, transporting and commanding
these zealots as to make the word "volunteer" the rank-
est of euphemisms. Spain became thus a rehearsal
stage for troops and maneuvers, a proving ground for
new war machines of all kinds.

Viewing with real alarm this tendency of the powers
to make Spain the battleground for a "Little World
War," which might easily extend its operations over a
larger field as it had in 1914, Great Britain and France
hastily contrived a Non-Intervention Pact to which 27
European states, most of them with their fingers crossed
and their tongues bulging cheeks, finally agreed about
a month after war broke out. Prime provision of the
agreement was an embargo on shipments of munitions,
arms and men to either side in the civil war. And a
committee was formed, with Britain's Lord Plymouth
at its head, charged with enforcing the pact.

Escape Valve. By the opening of 1937 it was obvious to all that the principal function of the non-intervention committee was to act as an escape valve for international steam. In that sense it worked admirably. The Russian delegate to the committee meetings in London might and did damn the Fascist powers for continuing to give assistance of all kinds to Franco, while Soviet planes and tanks arrived at Valencia in ever-increasing number. And the bristling German and Italian representatives might and did hurl accusations of Russian and French disregard for international agreement, while Nazi and Black Shirt brigades poured into Insurgent ports to bolster the Rebel cause.

But the committee as a whole played the game by keeping its eyes tightly closed against any and all of these fast-flying charges. The purpose of the non-intervention agreement, as British statesmen liked to point out in their testiest manner, was to prevent the war from spreading. By the end of 1937 it had not spread beyond the Iberian peninsula, though few ventured to predict that the same thing would be true at the close of 1938. But if the non-intervention agreement had had anything to do with confining the Little World War to Spain, not even its stoutest champions cared to assert it had done its avowed job of stopping intervention in Spain.

Fighting for Stakes. The simple fact was that each of Europe's great powers had or thought it had too big a stake in the outcome of the Spanish war to be willing to sit quietly on the sidelines and let the conflict run a normal homegrown course.

Britain's Interests. Great Britain, as the greatest of the satisfied powers, was interested chiefly in maintaining the status quo. Her policy in this crisis was the same as it had been for centuries—power politics designed to prevent any one nation or group of nations from growing strong enough to upset the European balance. Thus she wished above all to see Spain preserved for the Spaniards and not for the increasingly powerful Fascist bloc. Italy's frank espousal of the Rebel cause, and the presence of thousands of Italian troops in Spain and in the Spanish-owned Balearic islands, raised the threat of an Italian protectorate over Spain following Insurgent triumph, or at least a Fascist Spain in which Germany and Italy would receive preferred treatment in matters of international commerce. Furthermore, a foundation stone of British foreign policy was the protection of the "lifeline" to its eastern colonies and dominions. Gibraltar had been established for that purpose, as had been the domination of the Suez Canal, the Malta naval base. The well-known desire of the new Caesar in Rome to make the Mediterranean an Italian lake was closely linked to Il Duce's campaign in Spain and a constant threat to British interests.

At the same time, Britain's attitude toward the civil war was vastly complicated by the personal sympathy of her Tory government for the conservative followers of General Franco who were distinctly more "their sort of people" than the Left Wingers at the helm in Valencia. Going hand in hand with this fraternal attitude was the more compelling belief that Britain's huge investments in Spain would be safer under a Fascism committed to Capitalism than under a radicalism bent on nationalizing raw materials and large industry. And coloring the whole picture of British policy was London's conviction that until her $7,500,000,000 rearmament program, begun the year before, was further along she must continue to play a stalling game.

France. France also could be classed among the satisfied powers. At the same time, however, her Leftish government was definitely sympathetic toward the Popular Front government in Spain and opposed to the rise of another Fascist state to supplement those already pinching her from the east and southeast. But the French were also eager not to permit the civil war to spread. History was proof of the fact that European wars too often found "la belle France" the most convenient battlefield. And Paris also had its "lifeline," extending from Marseilles across the Mediterranean to her North African colonies whence came the black soldiers so necessary in time of war. All this added up to a policy under which France felt it absolutely necessary to keep a firm grip on the apron strings of Mother Britain across the channel.

Soviet Russia. Russia certainly had more territory and raw materials than she had thus far been able to put to good use. There seemed to be little reason to doubt that Moscow's interest in Spain rested in the Marxian concept of spreading world revolution. The Soviet prophet Lenin had designated Spain as the locale for the next great uprising of the proletariat, and agents of the Comintern had found fertile soil for their indoctrination among Spain's dissatisfied workers. Russian advisers, particularly the Soviet ambassador, Marcel Rosenberg, were in high favor in the period before the civil war broke out and for months after fighting

("*Glasgow Record*")
The Great European Pantomime Season.

began. Closely bound up with the desire to spread Communism was, of course, the negative zeal to combat the growth of Fascism in Spain. And as the war dragged along the Soviets were louder in their championing of democracy than in advocating Communism for the Spaniards.

Germany and Italy. Most glibly expressed reason given by Germany and Italy for their intervention in Spain was the determination to check the spread of

world Communism. Mussolini's known desire to make
the Mediterranean "Mare Nostrum" and establish a
great empire also were factors in keeping Italian interest in Spain keen. There was good reason to suspect, too, that Hitler saw in the Spanish crisis an opportunity to increase his nuisance value to the point
where Britain and France might be more willing to
bargain for the return of Germany's lost colonies. But
more obvious to the student of modern economics was
the fact that the civil war in Spain was essentially an
extension of the worldwide struggle for raw materials,
with two mineral-poor dictators forcing a little war in
Spain to provide themselves with the sinews of a big
war to come.

Spain's Ores. Iron, the very guts of any war machine, was notoriously scarce in both Germany and
Italy, but abounded in the part of north Spain skirting
the Bay of Biscay. The best copper mine in Europe
was at Huelva (firmly controlled, you may be sure,
by the ubiquitous British). Rich mercury mines were
to be found at Almaden, southwest of Madrid in an
area which also contained much valuable lead. The
peninsula also contained great deposits of tin, tungsten,
zinc, silver, molybdenum, salt, phosphates, sulphur,
pyrites, coal and graphite. And across the Straits of
Gibraltar in Spanish Morocco were important lead,
iron and manganese mines in which Germany had been
acquiring huge interests for 30 years. Paris newspapers early in the year were full of stories, angrily
denied from the Wilhelmstrasse, that German troops
were arriving daily at Ceuta in Spanish Morocco—14

miles across the Straits from Britain's Gibraltar, and within easy cannonading range.   Charles Reber, writing in *L'Oeuvre* for February 11, 1937, offered proof that Germany and Italy had joined in a consortium to exploit Spanish minerals as early as 1934, with the avowed purpose of rendering the two dictatorships absolutely independent of Britain, France and Sweden for all minerals, especially iron.   After Franco seized control of the Spanish Morocco iron mines, ship after ship full of iron ore went to Germany in payment for munitions loans to the Insurgent forces.

Anglo-Italian Mediterranean Pact.   These, then, were the international factors which threatened to blow the civil war in Spain up into a general European conflagration as 1937 opened and which were still starkly in evidence as the year closed.   Even so the year started on a happy note with the signing of the Anglo-Italian pact guaranteeing the status quo in the Mediterranean area.   The Italian foreign minister, Mussolini's son-in-law, Count Ciano, on January 2 scratched his name to a treaty specifically guaranteeing the territorial integrity of Spain.   Pundits were still freely predicting that this pact meant a change in the direction of Italian policy away from Germany and toward Britain and France when reports out of the Insurgent port of Cadiz told of the landing of 10,000 Italian "volunteers" before the ink on the agreement was hardly dry.

Proposal to Withdraw Volunteers.   This was so definitely not "cricket" that Britain joined France in sending prompt and sharp notes to Italy, Germany, and Portugal, demanding specific answers by January 9 to proposals to withdraw all volunteers from Spain. Frightened Portugal immediately agreed to do whatever the other powers thought best in this regard, but Italy and Germany flatly refused to have anything to do with the plan unless it provided also for the withdrawal of "political agitators and propagandists" —a slap at the Comintern. Britain and France then made a great show of united action by dispatching their fleets to the Mediterranean for the purpose of impressing the dictators who had already demonstrated what past masters they were at this sort of bluffing.

"Observation Blockade." But the British had been prodded to action, and they were again ready to make another show of reviving efforts to localize the Spanish war. Spurred on by the visit of Germany's Air Minister General Goering to Mussolini, at which meeting the two dictatorships renewed pledges to continue their support of Franco, Britain summoned the non-intervention committee in February to force adoption of a definite ban on foreign volunteers. The ban was to take effect at midnight February 21. To put teeth in it Britain and France now sponsored an "observation blockade," under which a patrol of British, French, Italian and German warships would be stationed around the coastline of Spain. Land approaches to Spain, from Portugal and France, were to be similarly guarded against volunteers by foreigners delegated by the non-intervention committee.

After much fanfare and weeks of delay the "blockade" finally went into operation April 19, but with no more teeth than a leghorn. Before agreeing either to the ban on volunteers or the naval and land patrol Germany and Italy had made sure to render the whole procedure thoroughly innocuous. Patrol vessels were empowered only to report offending ships, could not seize nor fire upon them. Most important of all, the agreement made no mention of air control.

DRAWN BATTLE LINES

Meanwhile, away from the sound and fury of the committee room, the workaday war went ahead in Spain along a battle line which had changed surprisingly little since hostilities began. Christmas of 1936 had come and gone with the Rebels still knocking at the door of Madrid, but without any better chance of gaining admission than they had had early in November.

As the new year opened, General Francisco Franco, ably assisted by his two chief aides, Generals Emilio Mola and Queipo de Llano, was directing his forces along a front which extended southward from a point in the Pyrenees about 75 miles east of Irun (Bay of Biscay port near the Franco-Spanish border captured by Insurgents early in the war) down to the Guadalajara hills northeast of Madrid; thence around the capital city in a half-moon, with Rebel troops strongly entrenched in Madrid's University City, south again in a wider semi-circle to Granada, then west along the Sierra Nevadas to the Mediterranean about forty miles east of the British fortress at Gibraltar. A 200-mile "island" strip of land including the Basque and Asturias provinces along the Bay of Biscay also remained in Loyalist hands though completely cut off from land connection with the rest of government-held territory. All told the Insurgents controlled about two-thirds of Spain.

Since early in November fighting had been bitterest around the capital city itself. Failing to take Madrid after repeated onslaughts, Franco had determined to surround it, cut it off from its sources of supplies on the Mediterranean, and starve the population into submission. Beginning an offensive shortly after the new year from west of Madrid, he drove the defenders back to within three miles of the capital and strengthened his position at University City. About the same time he captured several strategic positions north of Madrid near Guadalajara. Then in the first week of February came a smashing, bitterly-contested drive into the Loyalist lines along the Jarama river, about 15 miles southeast of the capital. Focus of this attack was the "Loyalist lifeline," Madrid-Valencia highway, this road being the only direct communication between Madrid and the sea. Result of this thrust was to bring an important sector of the highway directly under Insurgent machine-gun fire and greatly increase the hazards of using it as an artery for food and munitions.

Fall of Malaga. The same week in February found the Rebels smashing their way eastward along the Mediterranean in a plan to strangle the Loyalists by capturing seaports through which poured their much needed military and other supplies. The war picture

was a dark one indeed for the Loyalists when General
Queipo de Llano led a large Insurgent force into Malaga, important Government port on the south coast,
on February 8.

The General's promise to execute all Marxists in
the town resulted in a wholesale evacuation of the
population up the coast toward Almeria, Cartagena,
and Valencia.   Wrote Dr. Norman Bethune of Mon-
treal, head of the Spanish-American Transfusion Institute: "Imagine 150,000 men, women, and children setting out for safety to a town situated more than 100
miles away with only one road. . . . They staggered
and stumbled with cut and bruised feet along the white
flint road, while the Fascists bombed them from the
air and the sea."

Battle of Brihuega.   For a month after the fall
of Malaga the war bogged down under weather conditions which were almost as disheartening as bullets
to the Latin temperament.   Then, in an enormously
important battle, beginning on the Guadalajara front
March 11 and lasting for a week, the Loyalist forces
won their first great victory.   And sweetest of all music
to the ears of the government at Valencia was the
news that of the 40,000 Insurgent troops engaged in
the offensive, at least three-fourths had been Italians.

The Rebels had begun an offensive south of the
town of Siguenza, northeast of Madrid.   Within a few
days they had advanced 20 miles and on March 10
they were 15 miles from Guadalajara and only 45
miles from Madrid.   As they drove on toward Alcala
it began to look as though the half-moon around the

capital city might become full, and the Madrid-Valencia lifeline severed. But either the Insurgents advanced too fast or the Italian troops lost their stomach for the fight. Many of these so-called volunteers had left Naples thinking they were on their way to Ethiopia, and had wound up one cold gray dawn fighting a bewildered battle for a cause they understood little and cared less about.

The Loyalists were occupying strongly entrenched positions around the town of Brihuega. Beating back the attackers, the Loyalists then took the offensive themselves. By March 20 they had won a decisive victory and for almost a week thereafter the Italians were thrown back continuously. Capture of great quantities of Mussolini's war material, including millions of cartridges left behind by the fleeing Black Shirts, large quantities of gasoline, and nearly a hundred trucks, added significance to the triumph.

But far more significant was the effect of the achievement on the morale of Government forces throughout Spain. Here was the first proof that the raw untrained militia which the Loyalists had thrown into a purely defensive war had now been whipped into a fighting machine capable not only of holding its own against the Spanish army but of planning and carrying out a co-ordinated offensive. More than 150,000 new recruits flocked to the Loyalist banners in the month of March.

"Little Caporetto." The news of the Italian defeat found Benito Mussolini on a triumphal tour of Libya where he had been posing as the "Protector of Islam," vacationing as it were from his job as protector of Roman Catholicism. Cutting short his tour, the Italian dictator hurried back to Rome in raging temper made more violent by the accounts of the Italian defeat in British and French newspapers. Journalists of both countries had gleefully likened the Brihuega rout to the disastrous Italian retreat from Caporetto in the early days of the World War, about which all Italy is abnormally sensitive. About this same time also the British press began carrying stories of atrocities being practiced on the Ethiopians by their Italian conquerors, causing the outspoken Dean of Winchester to publicly liken Mussolini to the Assyrian emperor Antiochus, "surnamed the brilliant, nicknamed the madman." And to cap injury with insult the consistent British, who refused to recognize Italian conquest of Ethiopia by force, invited the deposed and exiled Ethiopian emperor Haile Selassie to attend the coronation of George VI as his country's official representative.

Coronation Boycott. Sounding off bitterly against "illiterate journalists" and stupid clergy in a speech immediately after his return from Libya, the Italian dictator reaffirmed his intention to support Franco. A few days later he recalled all Italian newspaper correspondents from England, amused Britons by clamping on the Italian press a boycott of British news, and refused to permit Italian official representatives to attend the coronation. What was more to the point, he dispatched, according to neutral observers, 50 planes from Turin to aid the Rebels. And in London his ambassador and delegate to the non-intervention committee, Dino Grandi, flatly refused to entertain the suggestion now being raised by Britain that all volunteers already in Spain be withdrawn.

Loyalists Take the Offensive. The defeat at Brihuega had seriously impaired Italian prestige, just as it had raised the flagging hopes of the Loyalist forces. New troops were dispatched to the Cordoba front where a well-planned drive resulted in another victory at Pozoblanco on March 30. Chief significance of this gain lay in the fact that it strengthened Loyalist hold on the vital lead and mercury mines at Almaden nearby. With new planes, tanks, and machine-guns arriving daily from Russia (also from the United States via Mexico), General Miaja on April 9 began a heavy attack on the University City sector just outside Madrid, which caused Rebel bombers to rain more death on the city's civilians but accomplished little else.

DEFEAT OF THE BASQUES

Effect of this new evidence of Loyalist strength and determination was to convince the Rebel high command of the necessity for carrying through the clean-up campaign against the Basque provinces (Alava, Guipuzcoa, and Viscaya), Asturias, and Santander which formed the Loyalist "island" along the Bay of Biscay. If resistance could be broken in the north, thousands of troops from that area could be diverted for a final push on Madrid and Valencia. Also the mines and heavy industries in the area would be extremely valuable to the Rebel cause.

But the proud Basques had a centuries-old tradition

of never having been conquered, while the Asturian miners had been making life thoroughly miserable for the Insurgents with their dynamiting tactics since the war began, particularly around the city of Oviedo, which housed a besieged Insurgent garrison.

Burning of Guernica. Late in April General Mola singled out the Basque capital at Bilbao for a concerted attack. More Italian troops were poured into the area, and a fleet of German bombers began operating with deadly effect. One of the strange paradoxes of this war was the fact that the Basques, a deeply religious Catholic people, were fighting staunchly on the side of the Loyalists, accused of persecuting the church and its clergy. In the drive on Bilbao German flyers utterly destroyed the ancient Basque capital of Guernica with incendiary bombs. The wanton burning of this most revered religious and patriotic shrine brought stirring protests from religious leaders all over the world.

Bilbao's lack of adequate air base facilities, coupled with its distance from Valencia and the fact that the Insurgents had by this time gained mastery of the sea in the north and were capturing Loyalist supply ships right and left, made the fall of the city inevitable. Sources of food and other supplies were soon cut off by land and sea. The prospect of thousands of civilians starving caused British ships taking part in the non-intervention blockade to escort to the three-mile limit outside the port merchant vessels carrying food to the besieged population. Franco's threats of reprisals against these tactics were met with a show

SPAIN'S CIVIL WAR CONTINUES

Top Left: Señor Negrin, loyalist premier. *Top Right:* Franco receives German ambassador (Wide World). *Bottom:* Franco's Italian troops first to enter Santander (Wide World).

FASCISM ON THE MARCH

Top: Der Führer und Il Duce meet in Munich (Life Magazine).
Center: The Windsors in Berlin as guests of Nazis (Acme). *Right:*
Hjalmar Schacht resigns, but is not out (Acme).

of naval strength; warships rushed to the scene soon caused the Insurgent leader to change his mind.

Under the goading of British Laborites and Liberals, the wartime Premier David Lloyd George being in the front ranks, Britain also joined France in evacuating thousands of wild-eyed Bilbao women and children to Bordeaux and southern England.

Sinking of the "España." Only bright spot in the Bilbao siege for the Loyalists was the sinking of the Insurgent warship *España*. Despite Insurgent contentions that the ship had gone to the bottom after ramming a submerged mine, Government reports insisted that a well-aimed bomb dropped by a Loyalist airman had done the trick. Never before had a warship of this size been sunk by a plane, and the fact that the claim made by the Loyalists might be true, and there were neutral reports to support it, caused easily discernible shudders in the admiralties of the great naval powers. One new weapon had demonstrated its effect under war test conditions and they didn't like the result.

Fall of Bilbao. Driving in on Bilbao from the south and east, General Mola took in stride the bitterly contested outposts of Durango and Eibra. By May 9 his forces were in position to make the final thrust at the "ring of steel," the city's famed defense system. On that day he issued a proclamation offering to respect the traditional rights of the Basques and urging them to surrender to prevent further bloodshed. When the offer was spurned 50,000 troops, strongly supported by several hundred planes, heavy siege guns,

and tanks, were loosed on the city. Ten days later the
city was in Rebel hands, the Basque government accompanied by the remnants of the city's defenders
and thousands of civilians having fled up the coast
to Santander.

LOYALIST CABINET SWINGS TO THE RIGHT

One reason why Loyalists in the south were unable
to offer more aid to their Basque allies was to be found
in a resurgence of squabbling among the various shades
of Red represented in the Government color wheel.
Anarcho-Syndicalists, contemptuous of all government
but that of local trade unions, were the prima donnas
who kept the Valencia government in a constant state
of jitters. The Catalonian provinces were their stronghold. Here they had combined forces with other Left
Wing factions to produce a Socialist state in which
railroads, public utilities, industries, land, commerce
and finance, theaters, places of amusement, and educational institutions had all been taken over by the
provincial government.

Civil War Within a Civil War. But these accomplishments had not come without much jealousy and
internal bickering among the various political and labor
union groups. Each had organized and maintained its
own defense militia in the early days of the fighting,
and the Anarchists in particular often failed to display
much capacity for teamwork when good sense dictated
co-operation among the various units. On April 3
Catalonia's President Luis Companys announced the
formation of a new ministry with a view to strength-

ening the government's control over the contesting
factions while granting representation to Republican
Left, Socialist, Communist, and Anarcho-Syndicalist.
When the new cabinet attempted to merge the Anarcho-Syndicalist's militia with the military units of the
regular government, street fighting broke out in the
capital at Barcelona. A temporary truce was patched
up under which the Anarchists were given four representatives in the cabinet. Even this did not satisfy
them, and they revolted again. Meanwhile hundreds
of their members who had been on duty on the Sara-
gossa front left their posts to return to Barcelona and
fight in the civil war within a civil war. Insurgents
took advantage of this move by sinking the long Sara-
gossa-Teruel salient much deeper into Loyalist territory and very nearly cutting the line of communication
between Catalonia and Valencia.

To quell the rebellion Valencia sent 4,000 heavily
armed troops to Catalonia. They arrived in Barcelona
May 8 and promptly restored order.

Caballero Out. In lesser degree the quarreling
which ripened into open rebellion in Barcelona was
going on all over Loyalist Spain. The hatred of the
military which stood just as much as a symbol of past
repression as did the Church and Nobility in the minds
of the Left Wingers led to the formation of numerous
"people's armies" composed of political and labor
union groups. The concept of rule from below rather
than from above extended into these militias, led to
no discipline at all in many instances. With the lowest
private able to question and criticize the plans of the

commander, the few military experts who had remained loyal to Madrid found it difficult at times to keep from throwing up their hands in despair. And private vendettas between Communist and Anarcho-Syndicalist units, all of which must be fused into a united front for efficient military operations, gave both Government and high command gray hairs.

The fact that as Premier, Francisco Largo Caballero, himself a trade union leader with strong Communist views, had failed to bring about this fusion made him the target for much criticism at Valencia. The Barcelona uprising was held up by his opponents as further evidence of his weakness, and on May 15 he resigned after having held office continuously since September of 1936.

Negrin In. Spain's President Manuel Azana came out of his Barcelona hibernation long enough to call Dr. Juan Negrin to the premiership. A distinguished Liberal Socialist professor of medicine, Dr. Negrin opposed a policy of conciliating the extreme Left, insisted that winning the war was the paramount issue. In an interview with *The Nation's* correspondent, Louis Fischer, he admitted that he favored nationalization of Spain's heavy industries—metallurgical, chemical, electrical, mining, etc. He also advocated Government ownership of all plants employing more than 50 workers. But he favored compensation in Government bonds for properties appropriated except, of course, those of the Fascists. And he felt that the social revolution might well wait until after the war had been won.

For efficiency he reduced his cabinet to nine, combined the war and navy jobs under a single Minister of National Defense, the fiery Indalecio Prieto, and refused to appoint to the ministry any members of the Anarcho-Syndicalist groups. Caballero had included two Anarchists in his cabinet. The new Premier also restored complete control of Madrid to General Miaja who had recently been forced to play second fiddle to a civil government appointed by Caballero.

The Negrin cabinet was definitely a more moderate one. For that reason it found much more favor among the world Democracies, particularly in England, than had its predecessor. Because it was moderate, however, Caballero and some of his followers loudly accused it of abandoning the revolution. Perhaps the best indication of Dr. Negrin's strength was to be found in the fact that for months he made no effort to stop Caballero's attacks on his government, and that most of the former Premier's own followers gradually were won over to the new cabinet and its policies. When on August 7 the Negrin government decreed that religious services might be resumed in its territory and granted 14,000 licenses to nuns and priests permitting them to officiate at private services, many of the more conservative republicans were pleased as were good Catholics in other parts of the world who learned that there were many servants of the Church alive in Loyalist territory, that the early reports of universal slaughter were, like all war propaganda, grossly exaggerated.

Insurgents Adopt Fascism. Before the fall of the Caballero cabinet Insurgent Spain had already begun to set up a Fascist government modeled after that of its principal supporter, Italy. The original capital was at Burgos in the north, but early in 1937 most of the government was shifted to Salamanca. A decree of unification issued April 19 dissolved all political parties except the Fascist "Phalanxists" and the Royalist "Requetes." A Junta of 20, resembling Mussolini's Fascist Grand Council, was set up and given the task of developing a Fascist state under General Franco's dictatorship. The Fascist salute was prescribed for all. After the manner of his Italian and German counterparts, General Franco gave himself the title "El Caudillo," the chief. By the end of the year this new totalitarian state had been given official recognition by eight governments—Italy, Germany, Switzerland, El Salvador, Nicaragua, Guatemala, and Japan. The Vatican also had extended "de facto" recognition.

THE "DEUTSCHLAND" INCIDENT

Just 9 days after the land and sea blockade of Spain went into effect the whole flimsy structure of non-intervention was shattered to bits by an incident which came closer to bringing general war in Europe than any previous development of the civil war. Loyalist fliers, reconnoitering over the Rebel air bases in the Balearics, bombed the German pocket battleship *Deutschland* as it lay in the harbor at Iviza. Twenty-three sailors were killed, many others wounded, and the ship, which had been a part of the blockading patrol, was put out of kilter. Loyalists claimed their planes were shot at by anti-aircraft guns on the deck of the battleship. Germans denied this, and stated that the sailors were off duty and in their quarters directly below the part of the deck where the bomb lit, which was why so many of them were killed.

Shelling of Almeria. Two days later, without diplomatic protest of any kind, and apparently against the counsel of his foreign office, Hitler dispatched the *Deutschland's* sister ship, *Admiral Scheer,* to the Mediterranean coast of Spain where it lined up its guns off the port of Almeria and poured shells into the city during a period of several hours. Thirty civilians were killed and several hundred wounded.

With European chancelleries in a panic at what seemed to be evidence that the "mad dog of Europe" had finally gone on the long expected rampage, Berlin suddenly announced that the Almeria shelling closed the incident and that there would be no further reprisals. Now, however, both Germany and Italy formally withdrew from the international patrol, Italy giving as her reason the attack on her ship, the *Barletta,* a few days before the *Deutschland* incident. Both nations, suspecting Soviet airmen and planes in the service of Valencia of responsibility for the accurate bombing, talked darkly of seizing ships suspected of carrying Russian war materials to the Loyalists.

Another Agreement. Again Britain jumped in to piece together the shattered non-intervention structure. After two weeks of almost continuous conferences Foreign Secretary Anthony Eden obtained an agreement under which everyone would agree to respect certain safety zones in the area around the Spanish peninsula, and Germany promised not to act independently in case of another attack on a ship of hers. Germany and Italy then came back into the naval patrol.

Germany and Italy Quit Naval Patrol. British and French sighs of relief over the Eden agreement were cut short late in the same month by a second German flareup. This time the two Fascist powers withdrew from the naval patrol and no amount of wheedling could bring them back in. Officers aboard the German cruiser *Leipzig* charged that a Loyalist submarine had discharged torpedoes at the ship, another unit in the international sea patrol. Under the agreement to consult with the other powers formulated after the *Deutschland* and Almeria incidents, the Berlin foreign office now demanded that Britain, France and Italy join the Nazis in a naval demonstration to overawe the Loyalists. The fact that nobody was hurt, and that the presence of the torpedoes near the *Leipzig* had been detected by a sound-detecting device aboard the ship, made the whole thing sound a bit fishy to the French and British. They refused to join in the demonstration. Whereupon Italy and Germany again withdrew from the sea patrol, explaining that they were "unwilling to expose their naval forces . . . to further target practice off Red Spain."

Instead of withdrawing their ships, however, Germany and Italy hastened even more of their fleet to the area and gave notice that they would be used to protect their shipping against Loyalist attack. At the same time the German and Italian delegates to the non-intervention committee were insisting that withdrawal from the patrol did not mean withdrawal from the committee. The value of the non-intervention structure as a means to further the sort of delay tactics which had been so useful in preventing the Democracies from doing anything to stop Fascist intervention in Spain was too great to be cast lightly aside.

Belligerent Rights versus Withdrawal of Volunteers. All through the summer Germany and Italy threw sand in the eyes of the non-intervention committee by pressing demands that the powers represented grant to General Franco the rights of a belligerent. Principal gain which this move would bring about for the Rebels would be the right, under international law, to erect a blockade around Loyalist Spain which neutral nations would have to respect or have their cargoes confiscated and ships captured.

Patiently the British and French kept maintaining their original thesis: foreign volunteers should be stopped from entering Spain; volunteers already there should be withdrawn. With less patience the Russians refused to listen to any proposals to grant belligerent rights to Franco. All attempts at compromise having failed for the time being, the non-intervention committee adjourned August 6 for an indefinite time.

END OF BASQUE OPPOSITION

As July marked the beginning of the second year of the war, the Loyalists began a new offensive on the front west of Madrid. By now General Miaja and his aides had welded the militia units into a seasoned army of 520,000 men. Snappy new uniforms had re-

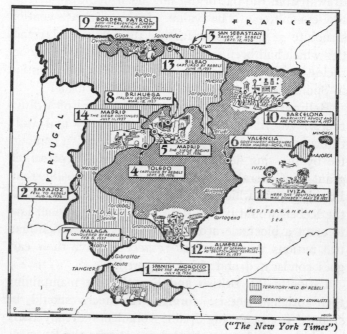

("*The New York Times*")

Spain, July 1937, After One Year of War.

placed the proletarian overalls of the early fighting. And a confidence, born of months of successfully defending the capital, led the Government forces to attempt to smash the Insurgent lines along a twelve-mile front. Bloodiest fighting of the war developed out of this drive in which Miaja was successful for only a short time. More than 200,000 troops were engaged, witnesses reported more than 100 planes in the air at one time, and during the twelve days when the battle was at its height (July 6 to 18) Loyalists admitted losses of 5,000 to 6,000 daily on this "Brunete drive."

After Miaja had driven the Insurgents back 14 miles they stiffened and launched a counteroffensive which regained all they had lost. By the end of the month the Loyalists had been driven back to their original positions and the siege of Madrid was again at deadlock.

Capture of Santander. More concrete results marked the fighting in the north. Since the fall of Bilbao the Insurgents had been closing in on Santander, the only remaining big port in the Bay of Biscay region, and mopping up the smaller inland towns as they forged ahead. Here the Basque government had been fighting a hopeless battle. With members of the Italian Black Arrow division very much in evidence, the Insurgents finally marched into the city on August 25 under the leadership of General Jose Fidel Davia, who had succeeded to the northern command when General Mola was killed in an air crash late in June. The President of the Basque republic fled with his ministers to France. Thirty-five thousand Loyalist troops left behind were reported as having surrendered.

Only the mountainous province of Asturias with its small harbor at Gijon remained outside Insurgent control in the north now. The Asturians managed to hold out until mid-October, but the resistance in the north had been broken with the capture of Santander, and the Insurgents were now free to divert troops to the Madrid and other fronts.

"Italian Victory." In Rome the Santander triumph was hailed by the controlled press as "typically and essentially an Italian victory." And Mussolini wrote congratulations to Franco referring in tender terms to the "intimate fraternity of our arms as a guarantee of final victory." All this while Italy was still pledged to non-intervention.

MEDITERRANEAN "PIRACY"

The fact that Italy had about decided to throw overboard the whole fiction of non-intervention was brought forcibly home to the Democracies and Soviet Russia by a series of mysterious submarine attacks on neutral shipping in the Mediterranean, which began shortly after the naval patrol was deserted by Germany and Italy. During July and August scores of ships carrying supplies to Loyalist Spain, including British, French and Russian tankers, were attacked by submarines in an area extending from the Dardanelles to the coast of Tunis. More than a dozen were sunk, including the British tanker *Woodford,* and one of the undersea boats even launched a couple of torpedoes at a British destroyer. When it became apparent that these attacks were not cases of mistaken identity, the British admiralty, looking squarely at Benito Mussolini, notified General Franco in August that any future attacks would be treated as piracy. Orders were issued to captains to fire on all attacking craft, and additional destroyers were sent to the Mediterranean.

Nyons Conference. Simple arithmetic was enough to convince the British and French that the Spanish Rebels' extremely limited supply of submarines could not have accounted for the widespread attacks in the Mediterranean. And the obvious conclusion was that the subs were from the great underseas fleet of Italy. To convince the Italians that this kind of outlawry would not be condoned, Britain and France summoned a conference of all Mediterranean powers at Nyons, Switzerland, September 10.

Italy was invited with the rest, but while Mussolini was debating whether or not to accept the invitation, the Russian government, whose ships had been particularly unfortunate in this Mediterranean game of hide and seek, sent a note to Rome laying the blame for the attacks squarely at the Black Shirts' door. Mussolini then flew off the handle, answered the Russian note in terms which cast aspersions on the ancestry of all Soviets, and announced his refusal to send a delegate to the conference.

Without either of the big Fascist powers present to interject their delay tactics, the Nyons conference, attended by England, France, Russia, Yugoslavia, Greece, Turkey, Egypt, Bulgaria, and Rumania, formulated a program in 36 hours which brought an immediate cessation of the piratical practices.

Sinking Subs on Sight. A new patrol system was established and charged with the duty of protecting neutral shipping in certain designated traffic lanes through the Mediterranean. Members of the patrol were authorized to sink on sight any submarine attacking neutral ships contrary to international law, or any submarine discovered in an area in which a neutral ship had been attacked.

Britain and France took over the patrol duties, moving their warships from the area where they had still been carrying on the original observation blockade despite German and Italian desertion. But they informed Mussolini that if he wished to join the new patrol system the door was open. They even suggested that Italian warships might do good work chasing their own submarines in the Tyrrhenian Sea, the part of the Mediterranean between Sardinia and Corsica, Sicily, and the Italian mainland.

Refusing to be downed by this Franco-British sarcasm, Il Duce admitted his desire to enter the patrol, but protested vehemently against bottling up his ships in the Tyrrhenian Sea. Having had their little joke, Britain and France then extended Italy rights of full participation in the patrol in other parts of the Mediterranean. Despite farcical aspects of the system, and a marked absence of reports of Italian patrol vessels sinking any of their own subs, attacks on neutral shipping ceased.

Threats Fail Against Il Duce. Perhaps unduly encouraged by the success of the Nyons conference, the French and British governments now brought forth a suggestion for a three-power conference, including their representatives and those of Italy, for the purpose of arranging withdrawal of volunteers. To add force to the "invitation" sent Il Duce, the French foreign office allowed it to be generally understood that failure on Italy's part to accept this conference bid would be followed by opening of the Franco-Spanish border to permit men and munitions to enter Loyalist Spain.

But Mussolini accepted the dare, refused the invitation, and to give point to his refusal sent his own son Bruno at the head of a squadron of Italian bombing planes to the Spanish island of Majorca, one of the Balearics. Here the Italians had long since established a naval and air base, and Bruno was soon reported joining bombing expeditions to Valencia. Insurgents soon found, however, that the presence of the Dictator's son in their midst was not an unmixed blessing. Loyalist flyers learning of his whereabouts made air raids on Majorca with such annoying frequency that he was ordered back to Rome only a few weeks after he arrived.

When the Italian leader refused to attend the proposed three-power conference, he advanced as the perfectly logical reason for so doing the contention that the place to discuss a matter of this sort was at a session of the non-intervention committee. Rightly suspecting that the three-power conference plan was a move to drive a wedge between Italy and her ally, Germany, the new Caesar declined to walk into the Franco-British parlor. France immediately found a dozen reasons why it would be unwise to carry out the threat of opening the Franco-Spanish frontier, the conference plan was abandoned, and in mid-October the tiresome job, that of trying to make the non-intervention committee function as its name suggested it should, began all over again.

THE "DEAL"

When the Non-intervention Committee met again in mid-October there did not appear to be a chance in the world that it would deviate a whit from its prior routine of failure. The Italian press was screaming that reports of Italian troops in Spain were grossly exaggerated, that there were no more than 40,000 in the peninsula at the outside. (Estimates by neutral observers had placed the Italian "volunteers" at between 80,000 and 100,000.) At the same time, Italy was asserting that the number of foreigners fighting for the Loyalists far outnumbered Italians on the Rebel side. (The International Column fighting with the Government had never numbered more than 25,000, according to correspondents on the scene.)

Then, unexpectedly, late in the month, Anthony Eden went before the reconvened British House of Commons to announce in pleased tones that the Italians had consented to a British compromise plan to withdraw volunteers. The plan, which British Laborites immediately termed a "deal" as odorous as the one under which Britain and France had tried to buy off Mussolini two years before with an offer to permit him to grab about half of Ethiopia if he would leave the other half to Haile Selassie, embodied the following points: (1) "Token" withdrawals of volunteers by both

Loyalists and Rebels—that is, a certain number of soldiers would be recalled from both factions in order to bind the bargain; (2) Following the token withdrawals commissioners would be sent to Spain by the Non-Intervention Committee to ascertain the number of foreigners fighting on both sides, following which all foreigners would be withdrawn; (3) After a "substantial" number of volunteers had been withdrawn, the Great Powers would grant full belligerent rights to both Rebel and Loyalist governments, thus enabling the Rebels, who had mastery of the seas, to blockade the Loyalist ports.

An obvious reason why Mussolini was willing to accept this compromise was the fact that the complicated nature of the withdrawal plan made it apparent that the Spanish civil war might well be over long before the commissioners could do their job of counting and submit a report covering the number of foreigners to be withdrawn. In other words, it was simply another delay tactic. Also, Il Duce was undoubtedly doing the British government a good turn by permitting Eden to appear before the Commons in the role of one who had gained a great victory in European diplomacy. What Laborites suspected, however, was that there was more behind the agreement than appeared on the surface. Russia, too, thought the plan smelled very strongly, and for a time refused to accept it, finally giving in early in November when Germany backed up Italy by threatening that it was either this plan or nothing. While the details of the plan were being worked out, the British Labor press discovered that their government had begun negotiations with the Duke of Alba, wealthy Spanish grandee with important British connections, to arrange for an exchange of commercial representatives with Rebel Spain. In short, Britain had probably obtained the withdrawal agreement in return for not only the promise of eventual extension of belligerent rights to the Rebels, but also in return for an immediate commercial relationship which amounted to a form of *de facto* recognition of the Rebel government.

When the newspapers finally flushed him out, Prime Minister Chamberlain admitted before the House of Commons that, "We are bound to take into account our responsibility for the protection of British . . . commercial interests throughout Spain . . . as well as the Spanish zone of Morocco, where General Franco's forces now have effective occupation. . . . Accordingly the Government has entered into negotiations for the appointment of agents. . . . These agents will not be given any diplomatic status. . . . His Majesty's Government has kept the French government fully informed."

Simply stated, this meant that the British rearmament program needed the mercury, iron, copper, and other raw materials under Franco's control, and was not going to permit idealism to stand in the way of getting them. There were rumors that the pro-British Duke of Alba had arranged such a good deal with England that, even though the Rebels won the war, England might be in a preferred position better than that of Italy or Germany with regard to access to these raw materials. In any case, Franco was so pleased that he released to their British owners seven ships captured while running food and supplies to the Loyalists the previous July.

The close of the year found the Non-Intervention Committee still making a show of working out the details of the plan to withdraw the volunteers, with no reports of any foreigners having actually been recalled from the peninsular war.

WAITING FOR THE BIG PUSH

Meanwhile the whole world waited all fall for news that the "Big Push" by the Rebels had begun. Stories told of thousands of troops being moved down from Asturias after the fall of Gijon, of the concentration of hundreds of tanks, bombers, and heavy artillery along the 300-mile Aragon front, and on the Guadarrama front north of Madrid. The Rebel fleet also moved around from the Bay of Biscay region into the Mediterranean also after Gijon was taken. There were numerous false alarms to the effect that General Queipo de Llano in the southeast was beginning the drive up along the Mediterranean coast to take Almeria.

On October 16 the Rebels dropped more than 1,500 shells into Madrid, killing a few hundred more civilians, but otherwise not seriously interfering with the lives and work of the hardened *Madrileños*. Then the shelling became desultory until Thanksgiving eve, when another terrific barrage was loosed. Abortive drives were made on the Jarama river front, south of Madrid, and on the Cordoba front. Barcelona and

Valencia were also bombed at intervals. And General de Llano nipped off another section near Penarroya containing valuable deposits of lead, copper, iron and coal. But still the threatened major offensive failed to develop.

Franco Courts the Catalans. Very probably an important reason why the big push kept being postponed week after week was the fact that Rebel agents in Catalonia were doing their utmost to increase dissatisfaction with the Loyalist cause in that area to the point where the Catalans would force the provincial government to accept the separate peace terms being offered them by Franco. They were promised complete autonomy if they would defect to the Rebel side. To attract some of these dissatisfied elements General Franco made a new statement, obviously cribbed from Loyalist dogma, of the Rebel aims: "We are going to divide up the land with proper payment to the owners, establish more schools, and keep the church out of politics." Thus the already mixed issues in this conflict were rendered more confused than ever.

Loyalist Government Moves Again. To forestall any such defection on the part of the Catalans, many of whom had been extremely bitter against the Loyalists since the uprising of the previous May, and also to avoid being separated from their wealthiest and most highly industrialized area in case the Rebels made good on their promise to cut Loyalist territory in two by sinking the long Teruel salient down through to the Mediterranean, the Loyalist Government moved from Valencia to Barcelona on October 20.

Rebel Ultimatum.   Finally, late in November, Franco broadcast an ultimatum to the Loyalists to surrender by December 5, or suffer the consequences of the long postponed major offensive. The day came and went with no sign of weakening on the part of the Loyalists, and the Big Push seemed about to begin. The fact that the Rebels were collecting all the manpower they could scrape up for the drive was evidenced by the report from the port of Algeciras that 500 Moorish boys, none of whom appeared to correspondents to be more than 13 years old, were landed and rushed to the front.

Loyalists Steal the Show. Meanwhile the weather, which had earlier been an important factor in delaying the Rebels, because of extremely bad flood conditions all through Aragon, became so bitterly cold early in December that troop movements were undertaken only with the greatest difficulty. It seemed an even bet that the war would bog down until spring when suddenly a flabbergasted world was awakened to the fact that the Government itself had started the Big Push.

All the while that they had apparently been lying low, strengthening their defenses against the expected Rebel assault on all fronts, the Loyalists were carefully planning the most difficult, daring, and complicated operation of the war. On December 17, in the face of what correspondents termed the "worst weather imaginable," 50,000 Government troops were thrown against the tip of the Rebel salient at Teruel. Four days later they had won their greatest victory of the war with the capture of the immensely important city of Teruel

—the city which had been so strategically situated, and so well fortified that Franco had kept only a small garrison there.

The well-executed Loyalist plan was designed to clip off the end of this salient which had been a constant threat to the communications between Madrid, Valencia, and Barcelona, and in so doing force a diversion of Rebel troops and a counter-offensive which would relieve the pressure on the Madrid and other fronts.

A half dozen counter-attacks by Franco were thrown back. And while the end of the year found the Rebel leader massing his troops on the snow-covered plains north of the city, preparing for a powerful drive to regain the city, there could be no doubt that the Loyalists had stolen the Big Push right from under his nose. Loyalists were encouraged as they had not been since "Little Caporetto," and the war in Spain was far from over.

CHAPTER XI

FASCISM ON THE MARCH

"Democracy is finished! Democracies today are simply the centers of infection—the tools of Bolshevism. That is one group. We are the other group."

Thus Benito Mussolini in an interview with a German press correspondent early in January dismissed with contempt the concept of political freedom, sounded the advance for a world march toward a sterner, more vigorous, non-humanitarian ideal—an ideal against which groping, disunited Democracy had found no effective check as 1937 ended.

The year found Fascism of the Blackshirt, Brownshirt, and tatterdemalion varieties locking horns with Liberalism and Radicalism. The "shirts" were in dictatorial control of about two-thirds of war-torn Spain. (See Chapter X.) In Austria, birthplace of the German Fascist dictator, Brownshirts harried the semi-dictatorship of Chancellor Kurt von Schussnigg as they had that of his predecessor, Engelbert Dollfuss, whom they murdered in the summer of 1934. In Czechoslovakia 3,000,000 Germans made life miserable for the other four-fifths of the nation's population by their Berlin-financed agitation for union with Germany under Nazi Fascism. All through the Balkans Nazi agents formed Fascist parties, struggled to win governments to Germany. National Socialists in Danzig finally gained absolute control of the city which had been set aside by the Treaty of Versailles as a "free city" under the supervision of the League, boasted openly that the restoration to German rule would come soon. In France the Communist-turned-Fascist Jacques Doriot aped Nazi method with his Popular Party, was accused openly of accepting funds from the Brown House at Munich. Another Frenchman, Col. François de la Roque, with a somewhat more anemic brand of Fascism, attracted the dictator-minded to his Social Party, successor to the Croix de Feu which had been outlawed by Léon Blum. Young Léon Degrelle in Belgium studied *Mein Kampf*, and tried to enlist enough members of his Rexist party to put him in as dictator. Sir Oswald Mosley, in Democratic England, used the freedom of speech which would be denied him under a dictatorship to bellow for a Fascist Britain, though his followers had been unshirted by law, and he was not always successful in his lively efforts to dodge rocks and bottles heaved at him by Communist and anti-Fascist. Native uprisings in British and French colonies were laid to Italian or German money bribes. South Americans awakened to find an authoritarianism somewhat different from their usual brand of dictatorship invading the continent when Brazil adopted a new constitution patterned after the Italian model. Even in the United States brown-uniformed German-Americans drilled smartly under the swastika, led by their "Führer," a Detroiter named Fritz Kuhn. And across the Pacific the last vestiges of Democracy withered on the branch as an Asiatic war brought absolute military control to Japan, brought also a three-way compact among Italy, Germany, and the Nipponese.

These, then, were all evidences of a surging powerful new dogma which, even if its claims that Democracy was "finished" were premature or permanently false, could nonetheless assert without fear of contradiction that it was scaring the daylights out of Democracy in Europe, and getting the wind up on this side of the water. Furthermore, and most important, the two foremost exponents of Fascism had pretty well convinced the rest of the world by the end of 1937 that they were committed to a common policy, would stand united against any attempt to stand in the way of their joint ambitions.

Rome-Berlin Axis. For years the Italian dictator had watched with a jealous eye the efforts of Adolf Hitler to bludgeon his way to power by adopting the political methods which had proved so successful in Rome. The expatriate Austrian's dreams of a German empire extending through southeastern Europe had come into conflict with Mussolini's own ideas of territorial expansion. And when Hitler's agents staged a coup to take over Austria in the summer of 1934 as the first step toward realizing this empire, it had been a roar from the "Tarzan of Europe" and the presence of Italian troops along the Austro-Italian border which had caused the Führer to drop the Austrian plan like a hot potato. But two years later, after the European Democracies had alienated Italy by an unsuccessful attempt to keep her out of Ethiopia, and Britain and France had resisted the attempt to install a totalitarian state in Spain, the two Dictators flew to each other's arms. The fall of 1936 saw them signing a formal pact agreeing to co-operate against "the spread of world Communism," there being absolutely no danger of a Communist uprising in either nation. In 1937 Air Minister General Hermann Göring began making official and unofficial trips to Rome. In July the German Labor Front Leader, Dr. Robert Ley, traveled to the Italian capital to shape with Tullio Cianetti, president of the Italian Confederation of Industrial Workers, what appeared to be a Fascist Labor International in opposition to the great international labor organizations which were so strongly critical of Fascism.[1] Under the terms of the joint labor agreement arrangements were made to begin immediate exchange of workmen, labor leaders, and foremen between the two countries to study each other's methods.

Wedding of the Dictators. But the grand finale to these diplomatic love feasts came with the mid-October visit of Mussolini to Germany for the obvious purpose of demonstrating to the world that the Rome-Berlin axis had firmly united Fascism against whichever nation or nations might dare stand in its path. Here in Germany the two dictators plighted their troth amid scenes of military display which made Mussolini's declaration that "my visit is a demonstration for a common policy of strong peace" seem strangely out

[1] In November the 23,000,000 members of the Soviet Trade Unions formally joined the Democratic "International Federation of Trade Unions" in a move to present a solid anti-fascist Labor front.

of place.   Arriving in Munich, Il Duce was met by the Führer and a 21 gun salute.   Moving over to the Baltic province of Mecklenburg, the good companions watched a display of war games, then sped to the great Krupp munitions works at Essen.   In Berlin the two Strong Men spoke to a rain-drenched crowd with the customary blasts at Democracy and Communism.

When he returned to Italy Il Duce reported to his followers, "The   objectives   of . . . Italo-German friendship, consecrated by the Rome-Berlin axis . . . are close solidarity of the two revolutions and a re-birth of Europe among the peoples of peace."

End of the Era of Surprises.   Always in his most bombastic utterances the Italian dictator wound up on a note of belligerent peace.   His German counter-part had also learned the appeal of this technique. When the Reichstag was convened January 30 to hear Hitler's speech commemorating the fourth anniversary of Naziism in power in Germany, they listened to what was one of the most pacific pronouncements of German policy Der Führer had ever made.   The 741 deputies in the Reichstag (according to one wit the best paid male chorus in the world, since each member receives $240 a month and free transportation to Berlin for the sole purpose of singing the national anthem and shouting himself hoarse in approbation of everything Adolf Hitler says) were solemnly told that their leader was withdrawing Germany's signature from the dec-laration of the Treaty of Versailles to the effect that Germany was guilty of starting the World War.   They were told also that Germany must regain her colonies

lost in the War. And they were informed that no
German might in the future accept a Nobel prize.[1]
At the same time, however, their Führer promised that
the "era of so-called surprises [the series of lightning
strokes by which he had remilitarized the Rhineland,
restored military conscription, wiped out other restrictions imposed by the Versailles Treaty on Germany]
has been concluded. Germany with the fullest loyalty
will henceforth do her share in solving such problems
as may concern not only ourselves, but other nations."
He declared also that Germany was prepared at any
time to guarantee the permanent neutrality of Belgium
and Holland.[2] And toward the close of his speech
Hitler was even suggesting the possibility of better
economic understanding between France and Germany
—the same France he referred to constantly throughout
his autobiography, *Mein Kampf,* as "Germany's
deathly enemy" who must be "annihilated." Antici-
pating Hitler's speech a week before it was given,
France's Premier Léon Blum had warned that "There
is a necessary and unavoidable liaison between eco-

[1] Nobel peace prize for 1936 had been awarded to the German
pacifist Carl Von Ossietzky, who had been thrown into a concentration camp by the Nazis when they came to power, and was under
close guard even at the time the award was made. An aroused
German nationalism had no place for pacifists within the Reich, and
the Hitler government considered the award a direct slap, which
indeed it was. Von Ossietzky was interviewed in the summer of 1937
in a sanatorium where he was confined with tuberculosis. He insisted the German government had permitted him to accept the
$40,000 prize, said he had promised the government not to engage in
pacifist activities and seemed anxious to be forgotten.

[2] A treaty between Belgium and Germany the following October
guaranteed Belgian neutrality, which had also been guaranteed by
Germany at the time her troops marched into it in 1914.

nomic co-operation on the one side and the organization
of peace with the limitation of armaments on the
other." And in London Foreign Secretary Anthony
Eden had also indicated Britain's skeptical attitude
when he said: "We cannot cure the world by pacts and
treaties. We cannot cure it by political creeds, no
matter what they may be. We cannot cure it by
speeches, however lofty and peace-breathing they may
be. There must be a will to co-operate which is un-
mistakable."

Four Year Plan in Operation. When the German
leader spoke of economic co-operation he was touching on the sorest spot in his regime. Economists everywhere were in agreement that had Germany not had
the genius of its Minister of Economics and Reichsbank President, Dr. Hjalmar Horace Greeley Schacht,
the Nazi concentration on rearmament, best summed
up in Air Minister Hermann Göring's declaration that
the Reich must have guns before it could afford to
buy butter, would have piled the Hitler government up
on the financial rocks long before. Under Schacht
every bit of foreign exchange had been strictly controlled. Exporters and hoarders of capital were threatened with death. So far as possible Germany's needed
raw materials were bought from those countries which
would agree to take German products in exchange. A
half dozen different kinds of marks had been devised
for the purpose of inducing trade in German products
and to lure tourists within the German borders to bring
the Reich essential foreign currency.

Yet each winter brought suffering among German

families deprived of pork, butter, lard, oranges, white flour, and other food products which Germany did not produce in sufficient volume to fill the needs of her population, and which she refused to allow to be imported because all foreign exchange was needed to buy the pig-iron, nickel, manganese, tin, etc., which went to make bigger and better guns.

In September of 1936 a "Four Year Plan" had been inaugurated, under the guidance of General Göring, for the purpose of regimenting German industry and agriculture towards self-sufficiency for the Reich. Late in March of 1937 came the announcement of the Four Year Plan's drive to increase agriculture's efficiency. A decree from Göring promised Reich farmers $400,-000,000 over a four year period ($80,000,000 to be given them in 1937) in return for their co-operation in increasing farm production 30 per cent. To make it easier for the farmers to accept the money proffered, the Economics Ministry warned them that they would have to grow the kind of crops they were told to, or lose their land. And farmers who tried to leave their land would be treated as deserters. Kindergartens were set up to permit farm women freedom to work with the men in the fields. University students were notified that they would be mobilized as a special "land service" corps to help with the crops during the summer and a crew of sleuths was put to work combing the banks, business houses, stores, etc., to discover all white-collar workers "not fitted for commercial employment," and ship them out to work as laborers in the fields.

When the crops began to come in, a new decree was announced under which all wheat and rye crops were requisitioned by the Government. State police were sent out to supervise the harvesting, transporting, and storage activities. Farmers were permitted to retain only enough for seed and for the appetites of themselves, families, and hired help. Fines up to $40,000 and penitentiary sentences were decreed for violators. By this means the Reich aimed to save 2,000,000 tons of rye and 500,000 tons of wheat, previously fed livestock, for food. But a cold winter and a late dry spring damaged the wheat and rye harvest so that it fell 15 per cent below that of 1936 which had also been under average. Despite his elaborate measures then, Göring was forced to import 1,500,000 tons of foreign grain. And figures for June showed that food imports as a whole had increased 16 per cent, all of which had to be paid for out of Dr. Schacht's hard won foreign exchange reserves.

To counteract this discouraging news the German government released statistics late in August showing that the nation's July exports had set a new high for the Hitler regime, 34 per cent better than in 1936. Iron products, machines, chemicals, textiles, automobiles and other finished goods had been exported to the amount of $213,219,000 during the month, while only $210,029,310 had been spent for imports. Yet economists in other countries were quick to point out that this trade balance of $12,189,690 had been dearly bought. Germany had sold her finished goods abroad at less than cost of production prices in order to get currency to buy the raw materials she needed. The plight of Germany's financial condition was revealed by the fact that, at the same time these trade statistics were being released, the Government was floating its third loan of the year, and the tenth since Schacht took over his tough job. The loan asked was $281,610,000, which, added to previous touches on the German pocketbook, indicated that the Reich had borrowed the huge sum of $2,622,191,400 during the past two years. Some indication of the fact that these figures were beginning to worry even Hitler himself were to be found in his speech at the Nuremberg party congress in September, when he bluntly warned German industrialists that if they could not speed up production to make the Reich economically self-sufficient, state capitalism would follow.

Out Again, in Again, Schacht Again. This policy of buying raw materials for arms while the population went without essential foods and the Government continually skirted the abyss of bankruptcy finally drove Dr. Schacht, whose job it was to keep the German economic ship on an even keel, to the verge of distraction. Rumors of sharp disagreement between him and Four Year Plan Chief Göring over the continual drain for armament cropped up with increasing frequency during the summer and fall of 1937. The report that he had handed Hitler his resignation early in September made German industrialists who had counted on him to curb the Nazi's wildest schemes, jumpy with fright. Despite Hitler's repeated denunciations of the "Marxists" who had plunged the German currency into the

KING AND COMMONERS OF ENGLAND

Left: Official photograph of King George VI and Queen Elizabeth (Life Magazine). *Right:* Soldiers and civilians try on gas masks (Newsphotos).

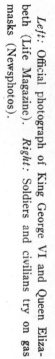

POLITICAL LEADERS: ENGLAND AND FRANCE

Top Left: Neville Chamberlain, new English premier, with Sir John Simon (Acme). *Top Right:* Stanley Baldwin retires (Wide World). *Bottom:* Léon Blum, obviously tired (Wide World).

headlong inflation of the immediate post-war period, some among the Nazi bigwigs were urging "controlled inflation" as a means of financing rearmament. Dr. Schacht had always recoiled at this idea with all the revulsion of a "sound currency" banker. While objecting to the size of the expenditures for arms, he had insisted on financing them through more loans and higher taxes.

From August on, correspondents visiting the Ministry of Economics offices could find no one but Göring henchmen on the premises. Then, late in October, Schacht himself told correspondents he had resigned, that he had not been at the Ministry since August 11. At the same time he indicated that he had "not yet" resigned his office as President of the Reichsbank. But for almost a month afterwards there was no announcement of his resignation having been accepted by Chancellor Hitler. And when the Führer did get around to acting on the matter he left German industrialists as high up in the air as ever. The resignation of Schacht as Minister of Economics was accepted, but he was retained as Reichsbank President. Moreover, Der Führer reappointed him to full cabinet rank with the title of Personal Counselor. Göring took over as Acting Minister of Economics until January 15, when he is to be succeeded by Walther Funk, a state secretary in Joseph Goebbels' Propaganda Ministry who is in sympathy with Göring's rearmament ideas. Thus the cabinet will apparently still have the benefit of Schacht's high-powered brain, but no one can say whether or not his financial wizardry will be used.

CLASH OF CREEDS

The Jews. The problem of the Jews in Germany was no longer a frontal issue in 1937. The Nuremberg decrees of September, 1936, had accomplished the Nazi's goal of reducing them to the status of alien guests on German soil who were denied all rights of citizens, permitted to remain in the country only so long as they toed a well-defined line. Though thousands had fled the country, forfeiting 25 per cent of their wealth to the Government in order to be able to leave, more than 300,000 remained under laws pushing them nearer and nearer the ghetto of the Middle Ages. Typical of their treatment in 1937 was the seizure by the Government of all properties and funds belonging to the B'nai B'rith lodge. Orphanages, schools, sanatoriums, and homes for the aged had been maintained by this philanthropic organization. All were seized and evacuated on the pretext that one of the lodge's 14,000 members had engaged in Communist activities.

One significant development of the Rome-Berlin axis was the beginning of attempts by Mussolini to stir up anti-semitism in Italy. Il Duce's personal news organ, the *Popolo d'Italia* of Milan, declared editorially late in May: "Jews in Italy must either publicly declare themselves enemies—we mean enemies—of all anti-Fascist Hebrewism . . . or renounce their Italian citizenship. . . . They must abandon all participation in the Zionist movement for a national Jewish state in Palestine . . . which would tend to create in the Mediterranean another zone of expansion under British political and economic control, definitely contrary to the Italian Mediterranean spirit."

Catholic and Protestant. As in every year since the Third Reich was established in 1933, the only effective opposition to the Nazi regime came from embattled Catholic and Protestant clergymen fighting every step of the way against Director of Culture Alfred Rosenberg's campaign to supplant Christianity with a newer more militant paganism. Mass trials of German monks on immorality charges during the spring of the year, the closing of every Catholic school in Bavaria, and the jailing of popular ex-submarine commander Reverend Martin Niemoller, served only to intensify the opposition of religious leaders against the Nazi encroachment in things spiritual.[1]

Germans were told by Rosenberg that Hitler had

[1] During the mass trials of German monks charged with immorality, staged by the Government in the spring for the purpose of discrediting Catholic schools, Chicago's Cardinal George W. Mundelein created a minor international incident by lashing out at Hitler as an "alien Austrian paperhanger, and a poor one at that." The Cardinal not only brought down a flood of abuse on his own head and those of Americans in general in the German press, but he also was faced by the indignant wrath of the Chicago paperhanger's union, which objected strenuously to the comparison. An earlier tirade against the United States in the German press resulted from the suggestion of New York's part Jewish Mayor Fiorello H. La Guardia that a statue of Hitler be exhibited in a "chamber of horrors" at the forthcoming New York World's Fair. German editors had plastered their front pages with pictures of lynchings in the South and other examples of American depravity. A formal protest to the U. S. state department by the German foreign office brought an explanation from Secretary Hull that in a Democracy the government did not have the same kind of control over the statements of its local officials as was enjoyed by the Dictator nations, and that whereas the American press was similarly free from censorship, the German government had notoriously effective power over its newspapers which were printing so many unpleasant things about the United States.

as good a claim as anyone to being the Son of God. "We need a son of God. . . . Today there stands among us one blessed by the Creator. No one has the right to find fault with those of our people who have found their Son of God and have thus regained their Eternal Father." And the Cologne Court of Appeals upheld a decision of the lower court which had held that scoffing at the salute "Heil Hitler" was a gross misdemeanor "like spitting on the cross," while German newspapers continued to receive death notices containing the formula that the deceased "died in the faith of Adolf Hitler."

But there was startling evidence of the manner in which the religious question was splitting the nation in the bold petition sent Adolf Hitler himself late in the year by united Chaplains of the German army. Mincing no words, these religious militarists told the Führer that the armed strength of the nation was being threatened by the religious controversy. Branding Jesus as a "swine" or "Jewish tramp" was creating a revulsion against the regime itself. Smearing Catholic priests with immorality charges while condoning the same practices among party leaders was making national heroes of religious leaders. And the fact that most intelligent Germans had no confidence in the truth of what they could read in the controlled press was conducive to a spirit of suspicion which would make it difficult indeed to enlist enthusiastic co-operation in time of war.[1] Coming not from Communist,

[1] The iron hand of censorship and State supervision had already brought all art, literature, education, the press, and the theater under

Jew, or atrocity manufacturer, but from the mighty German army itself, this cold criticism of a regime which depended for its existence on the backing of the military must have been a jolt to the Führer. And the world waited to see whether heads would come off as they had in 1934 when Captain Ernst Roehm and others dared challenge the policies of the dictator, or whether a more moderate attitude toward religion would result. (See Chapter VII.)

WHAT PRICE PEACE?

Worrying Europe in 1937, as it had in every year since Hitler came to power, was the question: Where will the German dictator strike next in his rush toward his avowed goal of an empire of 250,000,000 Germans on the continent of Europe. Like most politicians in their campaigns to win public acclaim and support, Adolf Hitler had made extravagant promises of what he would do when once he gained power. But unlike the average politician he had not forgotten his promises —at least not all of them. In his autobiographical blue print of the Third Reich, *Mein Kampf,* he had given the German people his solemn word that the limitations saddled on them by the Treaty of Versailles following their World War defeat would be wiped out. And no one could deny five years later that he had kept

the control of the Propaganda Ministry when in May Minister of Propaganda Joseph Goebbels forced Alfred Hugenberg to resign as director of the great German motion picture company, UFA, hand-picked an entire new board of directors. This gave Goebbels control of the German film producing world. "The German film has reached the point where it must fulfill its duty to the state, nation and culture," he declared.

his word. An army, which had been limited by the
treaty to 100,000, had grown to a grandiose 800,000
by the close of 1937. An air force, which had been absolutely forbidden, was now one of the most formidable
in the world. Told she could have only a petty skele-
ton patrol navy, Germany under Hitler had boldly
launched a program of battleship and submarine construction which finally forced Great Britain to recognize her right to build a navy more than a third as
large as that of England. The Rhineland, demilitarized
by the Treaty and subsequently guaranteed neutral
by Britain, France, Germany, Italy, and Belgium in
the Treaty of Locarno, had been occupied and reforti-
fied by German troops in March of 1936 in another of
Hitler's "surprises."

These had all been promised and all had been accomplished. But Hitler had included other plans in
his program for the new Reich, and it was the fear that
at any moment he might plow on to carry out these
plans, despite his assurances that the "era of surprises"
had ended, which kept the temperatures of Britain,
France, Russia, and the nations of Middle Europe at
fever pitch.

On page 1 of *Mein Kampf* he insisted that Austria
must be united with Germany. A little later in the
volume he outlined his dream to sweep through eastern
Europe until the Russian Ukraine and all of "Mittel
Europa," whose population was largely of Germanic
origin, had been brought within his empire. "Today
when we talk about new land in Europe, we think
first of all of Russia and of the border states subject

to it." Without doubt this boundless ambition also included the acquisition of the "border states" of Latvia, Lithuania, and Estonia, together with the Polish Corridor and the Free City of Danzig—all along the Baltic Sea. The final result for Germany was hoped to be an empire extending from the Baltic to the Adriatic.

Since he had never repudiated anything written in *Mein Kampf,* never denied his intention to carry out to the letter the program outlined, Europe had good cause to worry that now, after he had blasted away all but the territorial humiliations of the Treaty of Versailles, had raised Germany again to the ranks of a Class A power in doing so, the next move of a dictator grown used to doing big things in a dramatic way would be a land grab.

The Colonies. Perhaps the fact that the German leader remained as quiet as he did concerning the question of Mittel Europa during the year increased European apprehension. The German press concentrated its demands on the return of the colonies taken from the Reich after the World War. In his January speech to the Reichstag and again at the Nazi Party Congress at Nuremberg in September the Führer demanded that these lost lands be given back to Germany. Yet in *Mein Kampf* Hitler had advised his people to forget the colonies. "Take care," he said, "that the power of our people is not based on colonies, but on land in Europe." And the French, in particular, remembered well that while the German army was preparing to march into the Rhineland in March of 1936, the German press was laying down a heavy smoke screen of colonial demands.

The German colonial empire had been won and lost in a single generation before the World War. It had comprised an area of more than a million square miles (five times as big as Germany), and held a population of 14,000,000, only 24,000 of whom were whites. When the War blockade made it impossible for Germany to protect the colonies they were seized by the Allied powers, and divided up among them under a system of League of Nations mandates by the Treaty of Versailles. Most of the colonial territories had been in Africa. Of these France and Great Britain split Togoland and the Cameroons. Britain, Belgium, and Portugal divided up German East Africa, and Southwest Africa was allotted to Britain's dominion, the Union of South Africa. Small island holdings in the Pacific area were divided among Japan and the British dominions of New Zealand and Australia, with all north of the equator going to Japan. Japan also seized the Kaiochow peninsula which had been leased to Germany by China, but returned it to China, together with other German concessions she had seized, at the Washington conference of 1921.

Probably the best reason why Hitler could not get very enthusiastic about these colonies was the simple fact that they contained few if any of the essential raw materials Germany lacked. In the year preceding the World War German imports from her colonies had amounted to less than ½ of 1 per cent of her total imports. Nor had the colonies provided an important outlet for German goods. Again, in 1913 Germany's exports to them had amounted to only seven-tenths of 1 per cent of her total exports. And the argument that they would provide an outlet for an ever-growing population at home had been fairly well answered by the fact that few Germans had been willing to brave the torrid climate in the years before the colonies were lost.

But to most Germans the colonial question was not one of dollars and cents; it was one of prestige. The land had been taken away from Germany by the hated Treaty of Versailles, and a revived nation was determined to remove all of that document's restrictions upon them. Moreover, and with a deal of justification, Germany contended that secret agreements between the Allies had divided up the colonies prior to the end of the war, in direct violation of President Woodrow Wilson's Fourteen Points which had formed the basis of Germany's surrender. One of these points had declared that secret international understandings made before the peace treaty ending the war would not be recognized.

Obstacles. Principal obstacles to the return of the colonies were (1) the fact that the Tory imperialists dominating the British government had never made a practice of giving up any land grabbed by Britain; and snorted at the thought of what would have happened to their great empire had Germany won the war; (2) the fact that even though Great Britain might be willing to give up her share of the colonies it might be extremely difficult to persuade her Dominions, who had probably been brought into the World War under some promise of territorial spoils, to do the same; (3) and the belief prevalent in both France and Britain that if the colonies were returned Hitler would have another victory under his belt to enhance his prestige at home and increase his power for the ultimate drive toward Eastern Europe.

Lord Halifax Visit. The Democracies, therefore, had a dual fear: on the one hand that the German furore over the colonial issue might be simply a smoke screen to blind the Democracies to designs in Europe; and on the other that even though Hitler had changed his mind and was now actually in favor of a strong drive to get back the colonies, it was still a secondary issue with him and its solution would give no assurance of peace in Europe. These fears had led Britain's Foreign Secretary Anthony Eden to send a carefully worded questionnaire to the German dictator late in 1936. The Führer did not deign to reply at that time. Then in November, 1937, the British tried again. This time they dispatched the pro-German cabinet minister Lord Halifax personally to interview Herr Hitler.

The ostensible reason for the Halifax visit to Berlin was to attend an exhibition of big game trophies. But the Lord President of the Council was after bigger game than was represented by any of the elephant or tiger heads he was asked to view. He was after Adolf Hitler's minimum terms for a guarantee of European peace. Those with long memories recalled that another British Lord, Haldane, had made a similar visit to Germany just 25 years before. Lord Haldane had tried to settle Anglo-German differences with the German Kaiser in 1912. But two years later the general European war was proof this earlier diplomat had failed.

On Halifax's return, the British summoned French Premier Camille Chautemps and Foreign Minister Yvon Delbos to London to discus these minimum terms. The French statesmen arrived in England on November 29. As the discussions got under way, Britons were led to believe that the undisclosed minimum terms of Hitler were substantially as follows: (1) Germany wanted immediate recognition of her right to her lost colonies, but was willing to wait a half dozen years before actually recovering them. At Augsburg, shortly after the visit of Lord Halifax, Hitler told a German audience that the Reich must regain her lost colonies with the next five or six years. (2) The Reich regards Austria and Czechoslovakia as her sphere of influence and demands that Britain and France stand aside and permit her to establish whatever form of domination she deems necessary over these two nations. (3) Germany will not participate in any general European settlement, and will not return to the League of Nations until her aims are satisfied.

Anglo-French Views. Whether or not these were actually Hitler's terms, they probably closely approximated his views. At the end of the Anglo-French conversations a typically complicated communiqué was issued from London from which observers were able to weed out the following significant points: (1) Britain and France wanted it to be understood that there was a perfect community of interest between them. (2) "Preliminary examination was made of the colonial question in all its aspects. It was recognized that this question was not one that could be considered in isolation and, moreover, would involve a number of other countries." (3) The two governments were in agreement on the necessity of maintaining "peaceful conditions in central and eastern Europe."

To all outward appearances then, nothing was settled at the London meetings. Both Britain and France were anxious to give the impression that they were doing nothing before consulting other European nations. Even before the London conversations ended, France announced that her foreign minister, Yvon Delbos, would make a tour of Eastern European capitals to sound out opinion on the German views. At the same time, however, Germany could congratulate herself on the fact that the two principal national bulwarks of the Treaty of Versailles were actually discussing what to do about returning Germany's lost colonies.

Sounding Out Eastern Europe. Early in December Delbos started out on his two weeks' jaunt to the capitals of Poland, Rumania, Yugoslavia, and Czechoslovakia—all nations with which France had military alliances. France had made a point of publicizing the fact that she would make no move before consulting these allies. Delbos' job was essentially one of finding out what would be the reaction of these eastern allies if France said *no* to Germany's demands, and also one of discovering how strong were these alliances formed in the immediate post-war period when French loans had been freely extended to Germany's eastern neighbors in an effort to erect a "ring of steel" around the Reich.

Poland. First stop of Delbos was at Warsaw. The Polish Corridor was a constant area of rough friction between Poland and Germany, as was the Nazi domination of the supposedly Free City of Danzig at the top of this corridor. At the same time the ring of militarists dominating the Polish government had much more political sympathy with Fascist Germany than they had with Democratic France. And millions of Poles were just as violently anti-semitic as even the Nazi's champion Jew-baiter, Julius Streicher. Furthermore, one of Hitler's first diplomatic acts had been to arrange a treaty of non-aggression with Poland.

Yet after Delbos' visit to Warsaw the official report released by the Polish government spoke enthusiastically of the Poles' devotion to their alliance "for the sake of their own interests as well as the sake of peaceful relations of all nations."

Rumania. Next the French foreign minister traveled to Bucharest. Here he was heartily welcomed by King Carol, who was having a bitter fight to keep the Nazi-financed Iron Guard organization from overthrowing his government. Carol had even had to exile his own brother, Prince Nicholas, when the Prince got too intimate with the Iron Guard faction. However, less than three weeks after Carol had sealed Delbos' visit with the statement that "Rumania's path will never separate from that of France," he yielded to the fascistic Octavian Goga by appointing him Premier of his new cabinet.

Yugoslavia. In Belgrade, however, the sledding was tougher. The previous March Yugoslavia had signed a five-year treaty with Italy which was intended to bring to an end the period of hostility. The treaty included a non-aggression pact; an agreement to consult together in case of "international complications threatening their common interests" (such as, for example, a Hapsburg restoration in Austria); an agreement not to harbor subversive movements aimed at each other's territory or political regime; improved trade relations, with better possibilities for increased export of Yugoslavian cattle, timber, and agricultural products to Italy; a guarantee of the independence of Albania; and a guarantee of the rights of minorities in each country.

Even as Delbos started out on his eastern tour Yugoslavia's Premier Milan Stoyadinovitch was in Rome conferring with Mussolini and buying Italian armaments. He dashed back to Belgrade just in time to welcome the Frenchman. Conversations led to the signing of a commercial treaty between France and Yugoslavia, and Stoyadinovitch announced publicly that his nation ardently desired the friendship of France, and was willing to renew the alliance with Paris for "five years more." Violent pro-French demonstrations among Yugoslavian citizens during the Delbos visit were proof that their government's recent pro-Italian attitude was not universally popular. But the French foreign minister came away from Belgrade knowing that Yugoslavia was very definitely dividing her affections.

Italy Leaves the League. In a roaring speech before 100,000 dutifully assembled Black Shirts who congregated in the Piazza Venezia on December 11, Il Duce announced that he was withdrawing the Italian nation from the League. Long expected, the withdrawal was neither as dramatic nor as impressive as Il Duce undoubtedly intended it to be. The constant sabotage of League activities by Italian delegates made many pro-League nations suspect that of the two evils —Italy's membership or Italy's withdrawal—perhaps the latter was the lesser. The resignation did, however, mark another milestone in the shaping of the Fascist entente which now found Germany, Japan, and Italy all outside the League.

Czechoslovakia. Only in Prague did the French minister receive the hearty welcome of a government and people thoroughly in sympathy with Democratic anti-Fascist ideals. President Eduard Benes welcomed Delbos to Czechoslovakia with open arms, and countless Czech officials emphasized in speeches their devotion to France and the cause of Democracy.

By the end of 1937 it was still too early to know what had been the real results of this eastern tour. The recently-renewed diplomatic game was still in a state of highly mobile flux. To show that there were still many loose ends to be sewed together in the patchwork quilt of European politics, Delbos announced late

in December that two months hence he would travel
to the capitals of Greece, Turkey, and Bulgaria.[1]
Perhaps 1938 would reveal a program suitable to
check the apparently inexorable march of Fascism.

[1] Early in November Turkey, Afghanistan, Iran, and Iraq signed a
non-aggression treaty which was proudly hailed by Turkish Dictator
Kemal Ataturk as a "further contribution to world tranquillity."

CHAPTER XII

BRITAIN REARMS

Britons awoke on the first day of 1937 still more than a little stunned by the rapid-fire sequence of events attending the constitutional crisis in the last hectic weeks in 1936. The shock of hearing their popular Prince Charming, Edward VIII, tell them "at long last" that he "found it impossible to carry on the heavy burden and responsibility and to discharge the heavy duties of king . . . without the help and support of the woman I love" had made millions of them wonder. Many wondered if this indication that an English king, for the first time in the empire's long history, now voluntarily surrendered his throne, was not a telling sign of national decay. And others, casting a wary look at the increasingly troubled state of world affairs, worried lest upstart Fascist and Nazi powers seize on the crisis as perhaps unwarranted evidence of more of the sort of disunion which had enabled them to bluff Britain out of countenance for the past two or three years.

Yet the speed and smoothness with which Baldwin and his advisers eased Edward out of the picture, eased his brother George in, was startling evidence of just how perfectly equipped the British constitution was to deal with crises of this kind. Thirty-six hours after

he abdicated the throne on December 10, the now
"Duke of Windsor" was already out of England, speeding across the Continent into exile at Castle Enzesfeld
near Vienna, home of his friend Baron Eugene Daniel
Rothschild. The end of 1937 found him married to the
former Mrs. Simpson, still an exile, and very much
the Tory Government's "forgotten man." That he and
his bride continued to make headlines at all was no
fault of that Government. With hardly so much as a
backward glance in his direction, they pushed forward
to build up the 40-year-old George VI, his gracious
Scottish Queen Elizabeth, and their two attractive children, Princess Elizabeth and Princess Margaret Rose,
as the symbols of British respectability desired above
all things of the occupants of the throne; the sort of
aura of solid gentility which surrounded George V, late
father of the new king, and endeared him to millions
during the 25-year reign which had ended less than a
year before the second of his two sons to succeed him
now ascended the throne. George VI's willingness to
do as he was told, and the fact that he did not share
his older brother's penchant for buzzing about in Britain's "depressed areas" to promise down-and-out subjects assistance in a manner excessively irritating to the
Tory Government, made the task of restoring the dignity of the monarchy an easier one.

37th Coronation. Chief domestic concerns of the
Government all winter and spring were the elaborate
coronation ceremonies which tradition demanded be
staged with all the requisite pomp and circumstance before all Britons would be satisfied that their new mon-

arch was indeed the inheritor of the divine right of kings. What was even more important, thousands of gadget-makers, hotelkeepers, and business men of all descriptions, were counting on these ceremonies to swell their profits by bringing to London thousands of empire subjects together with other thousands of curious foreigners. The abdication of Edward had made these business gentlemen go deathly pale. And their color was only restored when the Government hastened to assure them that coronation ceremonies would go ahead as scheduled. After all, it made little difference *who* was crowned, so long as there was some distinguished symbolic figurehead around to hold the center of the stage and bring on the visitors.

Royal Succession. Before the Coronation, however, George VI insisted that some provision be made for his successor in event of his death or serious incapacitation. Since he had no male heir, George was worried lest, under the law governing descent on ordinary peerages, the throne descend equally to both his daughters. But Home Secretary Sir John Simon called on his vast knowledge of the British common law to convince the king and Parliament alike that Princess Elizabeth, the older daughter, would become queen by right of succession. Parliament then passed a Regency bill early in February declaring that the king's next younger brother, the Duke of Gloucester, would become Regent for Elizabeth if she came to the throne before she was of age.

Westminster Pageantry. With a strike of 25,000 London busmen barely settled in time to handle the terrific traffic problem, the Coronation took place May 12 in historic old Westminster Abbey. Here the Right Honorable and Most Reverend Cosmo Gordon Lang, Lord Archbishop of Canterbury, and Primate of All England, administered the oaths to the new King and Queen. Before Peers and Peeresses, Government officials, diplomats and representatives of all nations save only Italy accredited to the British empire, George VI promised to "maintain and preserve inviolably the settlement of the Church of England, and the doctrine, worship, discipline and government thereof, as by law established in England." And to "preserve unto the Bishops and Clergy of England, and to the Churches there committed to their charge, all such rights and privileges as by Law do or shall appertain to them." [1]

After this solemn promise, followed by a full communion service, the king seated himself in the ancient high-backed Coronation throne under which rested the Stone of Scone, upon which all British kings have been crowned since Edward I. Then the Archbishop anointed him with holy oil, saying: "As Solomon was anointed King by Zadok the priest and Nathan the

---

[1] Two "British insults" had so angered Mussolini that he ordered an Italian boycott of the Coronation, recalled from London all Italian newspaper correspondents, and carried only the briefest accounts of the ceremony in the press of Italy. Britain's Coronation invitation to the deposed Haile Selassie, emperor of Ethiopia which had been conquered by Italy's army and attached to the Italian colonial empire, had been interpreted by Il Duce as a direct slap. And the gloating British press accounts of the Italian rout at Brihuega, in Spain, had made Il Duce roaring mad. (See Chapter on Spain's Civil War.) American representatives at the function, besides Ambassador Bingham clad in satin knee-breeches, included the President's special delegation, consisting of Admiral Hugh Rodman, James W. Gerard, and General John J. Pershing.

prophet, so be you anointed, blessed and consecrated King over the peoples, whom the Lord hath given you to rule and govern." George then received in turn the various symbols of his office until finally the Dean of Winchester handed Canterbury the heavy golden crown of St. Edward. Raising it high in the air, the Archbishop placed it firmly on the monarch's head. As he did so, everyone in the Abbey shouted "GOD SAVE THE KING." A moment later 103 guns began booming from the Tower of London, and all the world knew that George was King by the Grace of God.

Queen Elizabeth then came forward to be anointed and crowned. The ride in the gold coach back to Buckingham Palace followed, and the 37th Coronation since William the Conqueror and the beginning of modern Britain became history.

That evening the King delighted millions of his followers by revealing in a world broadcast that he had got under effective control the embarrassing speech defect which had made him abnormally sensitive and shy all his life. With scarcely a sign of his old stutter other than a pleasant slowness of speech he wished health and happiness to all his subjects, thanked them for their "love and loyalty." Visitors in London to attend the ceremonies and the rounds of revelry that followed in homes and night spots numbered about 1,-500,000. They came from the Dominions, the Colonies, from the United States, from every country in Europe, Asia, and South America, and even included wide-eyed dignitaries from the tribes in British Africa. Financially, the show was a success, and Britain could now turn to other pressing concerns, chiefly the Rearmament Drive.

REARMAMENT

The British naval review at Spithead during Coronation week was impressive warning to assembled representatives of world powers that England's goal in 1937, as it had been in 1936, was to restore her world prestige by building up a naval and military force no other nation would dare challenge. (See Chapter XVI.)

"Two Years Behind." But Britain had indicated months before with what drive and determination she was preparing for war. The year had opened with sharp criticism from all sides directed against Government's lagging defense program. *The Aeroplane,* British aeronautic journal, led off with an attack on Air Minister Viscount Swinton.

> "The year 1936 was a disappointing one when you consider the millions in money that has been flung about by the British Air Ministry in obedience to scared politicians who have ordered them to produce airplanes like rabbits out of a conjurer's hat regardless of whether these airplanes could be of slightest use in a real war.
>
> "The key to the whole political lunacy lies in a delightful expression used by a very junior officer of the air force when he said that if Britain wanted to go to war with Germany we would have to arrange with the German air force to allow us to use advanced landing grounds in Germany and supply us with fuel when we got there. . . . The great

majority of the airplanes which we had in the Royal
Air Force . . . during the last year, ostensibly as
bombers, could not carry themselves, let alone a load
of bombs, 300 miles out and 300 miles home."

In Parliament, too, M.P.'s were hurling charges that
"Rearmament is two years behind."   Butt of these
charges was Minister for the Co-ordination of Defense,
Sir Thomas Inskip, appointed for the job by Prime
Minister Baldwin early in 1936.   Scornful opponents
of Inskip contended that his only recommendation for
the job had been his deep religious piety which had
greatly impressed Mrs. Baldwin.   Sir Thomas admitted
to the Commons in January that the rearmament program was officially three months behind schedule.

$5,000,000 **Every Week Day.**   But most Britons
were satisfied that the Government was spending
enough money on rearmament, even though they might
criticize the value received.   In February Chancellor
of the Exchequer Neville Chamberlain, later to be
Prime Minister, told the House of Commons that even
though the Government was committed to spending
$1,500,000,000 on armaments each year for the next
five years ($5,000,000 each week day), "it may be
that in the end we shall find that even this has not
represented the total amount this country has been
compelled to spend."

Reason for these frank figures from Chamberlain
was that he was asking the Commons to authorize a
$2,000,000,000 defense loan.   Crown ministers repre-
senting the fighting services had meanwhile asked for

$410,000,000 for the army, $525,000,000 for the navy, and had revealed that the Government was setting up

("*New York World-Telegram*")

A New Heir-Apparent!

14 new munitions factories. Later Admiralty head Sir Samuel Hoare revealed that by the end of the year Britain would have under construction 148 new battleships, including 26 of the most formidable battle power

and size. Britons, told by Sir Samuel that the United
States navy was building at the same furious rate, were
jubilant rather than worried over the competition. In
the minds of most of them an eventual Anglo-Ameri-
can naval and military alliance was assured, unpaid
war debts to the contrary.

British Liberal's Dilemma. British Labor party
leaders, faced with the dilemma of either supporting
the rearmament drive or going on record as opposed
to the comparative prosperity coming to the workers
they represented because of the arms boom which was
opening mines, mills, and factories, didn't know which
way to turn.[1] Major Clement Attlee mustered practically the full strength of his Labor party followers
behind a motion to censure the Baldwin Government
for: (1) Dealing a death blow at the League of Nations; (2) Raising the cost of living; (3) Preparing
the way for a new depression worse than the last.
But when the motion was overwhelmingly defeated by
the conservative members, the $2,000,000,000 Rearma-
ment bill was passed early in March without even the
formality of a count of votes. Attlee could have forced
this count if he had wanted to have his party members
on record as opposed to Rearmament. Fact was, of
course, that while the workers were for peace, they
were also opposed to Fascism. And the conservative

[1] A "White Paper" sent to Commons by Prime Minister while the
debate on the rearmament bill was in progress showed how effective
the arms boom had been in the depressed areas of Britain. For the
year ending January 1, 1937, unemployment had been reduced 30 per
cent in Scotland, the Tyneside and Durham areas; 20 per cent in
South Wales and Monmouthshire; 10 per cent in West Cumberland.

Government was cleverly playing up the Fascist ogre as the reason why the huge arms expenditures were needed, just as they had played on the fears of the populace to end short-lived Labor administrations in the past.

No one paid the slightest attention to what Left Wing Laborite, Sir Stafford Cripps, said: "We are witnessing the most magnificent subscription to a world suicide pact ever publicized by any country in the world." Shares on armament and allied firms had risen on the London Exchange 20 per cent. Though the Foreign Secretary might rap Germany's Four Year Plan under which General Göring was telling Germans they would have to tighten their belts until the rearmament program was completed; though Eden might, as he did early in the year, tell Britishers "We definitely prefer butter to guns," the facts seemed to be that they were going to take guns, and like 'em.

State Capitalism. While Hitler was warning German industry that unless it speeded up production the Government would take over its plants, and the Popular Front of France was nationalizing the arms and railway industries, so also in England the Tory Government was keeping a jump ahead of its Labor opposition by going into business.

In March came an announcement that $10,000,000, given the Government by Motor Manufacturer Lord Nuffield as a personal tribute to Prime Minister Baldwin, was being used in a scheme to give the Government a 25 per cent interest in the capital stock of new munitions factories to be built in Britain's depressed areas, particularly in the South Wales districts where Edward VIII had found conditions among unemployed workers so deplorable.

And with little fuss or furore the cabinet late in the year was introducing a bill to force all owners of coal mines in the United Kingdom to sell them to the Government by July 1, 1942, and at the Government's own price of $330,000,000. Though the mine owners were asking $750,000,000 as their price, there was little doubt that the Commons would pass the bill substantially as demanded by the Ministry, since even the Laborites included state ownership of key industries in their party platform.

When King George opened Parliament late in October, his Cabinet-composed speech from the throne declared that Rearmament was still the number one item in a program for the coming year. It included also promises to inaugurate penal law reforms; regulate the coal mining, and electric power industries; combat stock frauds; add judges to relieve pressure on divorce courts; expand housing; regulate working conditions; increase the efficiency of the United Kingdom's fire brigades.[1]

Who's Looney Now? Small wonder then, that the sight of an entire Government concentrating on

[1] In July a bill sponsored by famed British humorist, A. P. Herbert, finally liberalized Britain's antiquated laws which had permitted divorce only on grounds of adultery. New grounds provided by the bill are (1) Desertion without cause for 3 years or more; (2) Cruelty; (3) Incurable insanity if under treatment for at least 5 years. To prevent too hasty marriages, the law also provides that couples must remain married for at least 3 years before either can sue for divorce except in cases of "exceptional hardship" or "exceptional depravity."

bigger and better guns to the tune of bigger and better billions of pounds, caused a quizzical "Who's-looney-now?" expression to spread over the faces of some Britons when the man who so harshly interrupted the Armistice Day ceremonies at London's Cenotaph with the wild scream, "Stop all this hypocrisy! You are deliberately preparing for war!" was announced to be one Stanley Storey, escaped inmate of the Cane Hill Insane Asylum.

Dragooning Them In. Major worry of England's two War Secretaries (Alfred Duff Cooper before the Cabinet shuffle in June; Leslie Hore-Belisha the rest of the year) was the fact that apparently the cannon fodder "limey" Briton preferred the dole to joining the army or navy. All year long the War Department issued one sugary inducement after another to wheedle lower-class youth into agreeing to die for his country. "Sitting rooms" were introduced in barracks where men might read, write, or listen to radio. Soldiers were relieved of Kitchen Police duty, this "dirty" work being consigned to hired civilians. Four meals a day were offered with a ration of milk for younger soldiers. Extra dress uniforms were issued free to provide the "sex appeal" which plays so vital a part in dragooning men into an army, and the extra issue of "a spot of grog" was added. Life pensions of $8.50 a week were stipulated for men who had been in the service 21 years.

All these offerings were intended by the Government to offset the fact that Democratic Britain would not stand for universal military conscription used by Fascist powers to build their military machines. Because Britons were not forced to enter this period of military training, the Government feared they were not fit enough for the coming war. In October $12,500,000 was set up as a special fund to provide more playing fields throughout the Kingdom and more physical instructors.

Meeting the Cost. Major worry of England's two Chancellors of the Exchequer (Neville Chamberlain until June; Sir John Simon thereafter) was how to pay for these huge expenditures. On "Budget Day" in April, Chamberlain appeared before the Commons with his financing proposals.

After casually announcing that the Government would spend a total of $4,315,500,000 in 1937, an increase of $324,755,000 over 1936, he proposed two tax changes: (1) A raise in the basic tax on net incomes to five shillings in the pound (25 per cent). This meant that Englishmen would pay seven times as much tax as Americans in the same income bracket. (2) A "growth-of-profits" tax on all firms making an annual profit of more than $10,000, which was drawn so as to bear directly on the arms manufacturers who, after all, were the principal beneficiaries of the rearmament boom. Average earnings during 1933, '34, and '35 were to be the yardstick. Earnings in 1937 were to be compared with this average, and a tax levied on the percentage of growth of profits. This tax might be as high as thirty-three and one-third per cent, depending on how swiftly profits had risen. Thus, companies whose profits had been swelled by the rearmament boom would be hit hardest.

The growth-of-profits tax proposal came as such a shock to financial Britain that the securities market slumped badly. Opposition on the part of conservatives to this evidence of treachery on the part of their own men in office was so violent that the Government was finally forced to back water. In the first Parliamentary debate after he became Prime Minister, Chamberlain made as graceful a retreat as possible, declaring contritely, "I do not think I have ever been inclined to show a pig-headed obstinacy." A substitute tax was worked out under Sir John Simon and passed by the Commons late in June. Irrespective of the speed with which a firm's profits are increasing, the Simon tax was designed to bear on all British firms and individuals with net profits of more than $10,000 annually, and was in the nature of a super-tax to raise the already enacted 25 per cent income levy. On partnerships the income tax was thus raised to 29 per cent; on corporations to 30 per cent. Salaried employees, doctors, lawyers, accountants, and professional people generally, few of whom earned $10,000 annually, are exempt from the super-tax. Net effect of the Simon tax was to place on prospering firms as a whole the burden which Chamberlain had hoped to inflict most heavily on Rearmament profiteers.

CABINET SHUFFLE

Stanley Baldwin announced in the fall of 1936 that he would resign office following the Coronation of

George VI, curiously enough for the same reason—
"burden of office"—that had made Edward VIII abdi-
cate. But unlike Edward, his reason was age and
fatigue, not romance. Fifteen days after the new
King had been safely crowned, and 14 years after he
formed his first cabinet, the 69-year-old Prime Minister
handed in his resignation. His parting words to the
House of Commons assured him of the shattering ap-
plause he received. For he told M.P.'s their salaries
were being raised from $2,000 to $3,000 a year.

According to his standards and those of his party
he had served his country well. Believing firmly that
anything but conservative rule for Britain was bound
to be disastrous, he had first forced the Labor government in power to compromise its principles, or at least
those of its leaders in 1931. By doing so they formed
with his party and a few members of the unimportant
Liberal party a so-called National Government, made
up of a coalition of Tories, Laborites, and Liberals.
But it was obvious from the start that the National
Government was a Tory Government. Baldwin had
assumed formal leadership of this coalition, which he
had pretty well dominated behind the scenes from its
inception, the spring after the elections in the fall of
1935. These elections had been called to take advantage of the Italo-Ethiopian war scare and the old
adage that a frightened England is a conservative England. And to win the votes of a peace-minded Britain
which had mustered 11,000,000 signatures to a petition
advocating support of the League of Nations, the National Government had made a great show of backing

the League to the hilt in the attempt to keep Mussolini out of Ethiopia. This had served only to infuriate Mussolini who had half-believed the British Government meant it. And the same policy of playing the middle against both ends was well under way in the sessions of the Spanish Non-Intervention Committee in 1937. (See Chapter X.)

Yet Baldwin could point to the fact that, like America's Woodrow Wilson, he had kept his nation out of war—even though he was furiously preparing England for the next war when he stepped out of the role of Prime Minister, and into that of a member of the House of Lords. George VI conferred on him an earldom and a knighthood in the order of the Garter, making him henceforth the Earl of Bewdley. To millions of Britons, however, his familiar stocky figure would be the personification of John Bull until his death. Few of them paid any heed to the political epitaph recited by his own estranged son, Laborite Oliver Baldwin, that: "He has been lucky. His patience and inborn laziness have been among his greatest assets."

End of the Trail. It was the end of the trail also for another of Britain's famed elder statesmen. The one-time leader of the Labor party, Ramsay MacDonald, who had been Prime Minister at the time the National Government was formed and continued in office under the domination of Conservatives until 1936, also stepped down into retirement. He, who had been one of the founders of the Labor party and had made himself one of England's most cordially hated men by his outspoken opposition to participation in the World

War, had become, like most old men, as staunch a Tory as the rest by the end of his career. Only reason he refused a proffered peerage was because it would have forced his son Malcolm "upstairs" into the House of Lords and cost him his Cabinet post as Secretary for the Dominions. In November, while aboard a British liner on a vacation cruise to South America, he died of a heart attack.

New Ministry. Baldwin's successor was the 68-year-old Arthur Neville Chamberlain, third of a line of Chamberlains who had aspired to the Prime Ministry and the first to achieve the goal. His father, Joseph Chamberlain, had founded the family fortune and gunned unsuccessfully for his nation's highest post. His older half brother Sir Austen had been Britain's Foreign Secretary, but had climbed no higher. Sir Austen died a few weeks before Neville took office.

The new Premier entered Parliament at the age of 47 after a career as merchant and mayor of Birmingham. His genius for finance had been recognized by the elevation to the tough job of Chancellor of the Exchequer during depression years. And his readiness to soak the rich to keep the nation in the black, witness the proposed growth-of-profits tax, was indication that he had inherited his father's belief in social reform as "ransom" owed by capitalism for the security of its property. But there was little sentiment in his makeup. Political prophets foresaw that Britain under his ministership might be slightly more liberal at home, while harder, cooler, less idealistic abroad.

The Chamberlain cabinet included 15 Conservatives,

4 National Liberals, and 2 National Laborites. And the only infusions of new blood were the appointments of Edward L. Burgin as Minister of Transport, and Lord De La Warr as Lord Privy Seal. Otherwise it was the same group as under Baldwin, somewhat reshuffled, and with Ramsay MacDonald and President of the Board of Trade Walter Runciman left out. The complete lineup follows:

New Cabinet:

Prime Minister and First Lord of the Treasury—Neville Chamberlain

Chancellor of the Exchequer—Sir John Simon

Secretary of State for Home Affairs—Sir Samuel Hoare

Secretary of State for Foreign Affairs—Anthony Eden

First Lord of the Admiralty—Alfred Duff Cooper

Lord President of the Council—Viscount Halifax

Secretary of State for War—Leslie Hore-Belisha

Minister of Transport—Edward Leslie Burgin

President of the Board of Trade—Oliver Stanley

Lord Privy Seal—Earl De La Warr

Lord Chancellor—Viscount Hailsham

Secretary of State for the Dominions—Malcolm MacDonald

Secretary of State for India—Marquess of Zetland

Secretary of State for the Colonies—William George Arthur Ormsby-Gore

Minister for the Co-ordination of Defense—Sir Thomas Inskip

Secretary of State for Air—Viscount Swinton

Secretary of State for Scotland—Walter Elliot Elliot

Minister of Agriculture and Fisheries—William Shepherd Morrison

President of the Board of Education—Earl Stanhope

Minister of Health—Sir Kingsley Wood

Minister of Labor—Ernest Brown

In the Event of War. As the year closed this new cabinet was still feverishly at work preparing England for war. Early in December the new War Minister, Leslie Hore-Belisha, "purged" the army. Four older heads of the Imperial General Staff stepped out to make room for a new and younger crew headed by the 51-year-old holder of the Victoria Cross, Viscount Gort. About the same time, Sir Kingsley Wood, Minister of Health alarmed Britons with the news that the United Kingdom was ceasing at such an alarming rate to bear children that its population will have dropped from 44,000,000 to 5,000,000 in 100 years. A suggestion that Britain, too, might begin soon to try to accelerate the birth rate lag by large family subsidy in Hitler and Mussolini fashion, was to be found in the bill passed by the Commons calling for a special census of birth statistics—a census which, according to Sir Kingsley, was too urgent to await the regular census of 1941.

The Commons Christmas present to the British population was a bill authorizing the removal in wartime of some 7,000,000 people from crowded areas that might be endangered by air raids in the coming war. Thus the population of London would be moved out to camp grounds in the open country where the government would have set up facilities for food, water, and sanitation. Even the problem of transporting the people to these camps was provided for in the act. If Britons had doubted they were preparing for war, this law left little room for such doubts.

THE WINDSORS

Baltimore-born, 40-year-old Wallis Warfield Spencer Simpson was the cause of Edward VIII's abdication. Her first divorce from an American naval lieutenant, together with the fact that she had not yet received the final decree from her second husband, Ships Broker Ernest Simpson, at the time her romance with Edward was in full flower, made her unfit, in the eyes of those who ran the British government, to sit beside Edward on Britain's throne. Several days before the abdication she fled to the villa of American friends at Cannes, France, where she remained hidden from the curious.

In sleepy rural Ipswich Sir Boyd Nerriman granted a grudging final decree, after an unknown Britisher named Francis Stephenson withdrew his right of "intervention" possessed by every subject when a decree nisi is granted in the Kingdom, and after the usual letters and other evidence indicating Husband Ernest's unfaithfulness had been duly listened to.

When she had legally regained her maiden name of

("*The Milwaukee Journal*")

Some First-hand Experience.

Wallis Warfield, she and the Duke were reunited early in May at the Chateau de Cande near Paris, one of the several European castles belonging to millionaire French-American Friend Charles Bedaux. Here they listened to the broadcast of Brother George's corona-

tion, then, after protracted haggling with the Royal
Family and Government of England, announced their
wedding date for June 3.[1]   Earlier in the year, while
still at the Rothschild castle and after he left there
for a small *pension* on Austria's Lake St. Wolfgang
after reputedly falling out with the Rothschilds, Edward had wrangled with his family over money. The
Government had refused to include him longer in the
royal lists, and informed the Royal Family they would
have to provide for him out of their own funds. Best
guess, since the Family did not divulge the settlement,
was that the Duke was given $500,000 outright, with
a promise of $200,000 annually for himself and the
future Duchess.

But most of the haggling immediately before the
wedding concerned not money but the refusal of the
Government to permit any member of the Royal Family to attend the ceremony, the question of the social
status of the future Duchess, and the refusal of the
Church of England, whose primates had been responsible with Baldwin for the refusal to permit Edward to
marry Mrs. Simpson and remain on the throne, to
allow one of its clergymen to officiate at the ceremony.
Again the Government won out. No member of the
Royal Family was present. By reducing Edward to a
rank of Fourth among members of the Royal Family,

[1] Royal wedding of the year united Crown Princess Juliana, daughter of Holland's Queen Wilhelmina, with Prince Bernhard zu Lippe-
Biesterfeld.   The amiable young German prince proved popular
among the Dutch burghers.   And when Juliana revealed over the
radio in June that she was pregnant, Dutchmen were pleased.   There
would be great rejoicing in the Netherlands if Consort "Benno"
fathered the first male heir to the Dutch Crown in 52 years.

his wife was given no chance of taking precedence over her sisters-in-law. But the Church lost out when Rev. Robert Anderson Jardine, an obscure clergyman from Darlington, England, defied his superiors to run over to France and marry the two.

From the Chateau de Cande the Duke and Duchess dashed to the honeymoon castle, Wasserloenburg in Austria. Later they went into Hungary, and made a short appearance in the Lido society of Venice.

By fall the Duke had apparently had enough of obscurity. He and the Duchess came to Paris and announced that they would begin an intensive investigation of workers' housing and working conditions, starting in Germany, France, and the United States. Early in October they traveled to Berlin, where the German Labor Front Leader, Dr. Robert Ley, took them in tow for two weeks proudly to show off model Nazi factories and housing developments. Here also they visited Hitler in his Bavarian chateau. Returning to Paris, they made plans for a trip to the United States. With all arrangements completed and bags packed the Duke suddenly canceled the trip early in November when it became apparent that his welcome among American laborers might not be the same as it had been in regimented Germany. Chief objection of American Labor was the fact that arrangements for the trip were largely in the hands of the friend in whose chateau the Duke and Duchess had been married. Charles Bedaux had come to the United States as a young engineer. He had devised an efficiency system under which a given job is divided into units, with each worker on the job allotted a required number of units of work to be accomplished in a certain period of time. Labor contended that the result was a "speed-up" and "stretch-out" system, under which the last ounce of effort was ground out of the worker. The branch of the American Federation of Labor in Baltimore, Maryland, home town of the Duchess, voted a resolution condemning the proposed housing tour as a "threat to Labor," and called attention to the fact that neither Bedaux nor the Duchess, while she was a resident of the United States, had given the slightest heed to the sufferings of the poor. A. F. of L. and C.I.O. groups the country over endorsed the Baltimore resolution.

Bedaux offered to withdraw completely from the tour, but the damage had already been done. Whether or not, as was contended in London, the British Government brought strong pressure to bear on the Duke to cancel the trip, it was called off. The squelched and bewildered Lord and Lady Bountiful unpacked their bags, and talked vaguely of coming to the United States early in 1938 . . . but in a strictly private, non-housing-inspecting capacity.

It was an even bet that the United States Government was just as relieved as were British officials by the cancellation of the trip. Members of the Washington official family had by no means tripped over each other offering to assist with the projected visit. And Mrs. Roosevelt had already made the convenient discovery that a lecture tour would take her away from the capital when the Duke and Duchess were due to arrive, making it impossible for her to entertain the Baltimore Duchess.

Although British Laborite Sir Josiah Wedgwood was storming about in Parliament as the year closed, criticizing as the height of stupidity the policy of forcing Windsor to live in exile while he might be doing useful things for the empire, such as serving as Governor General of one of the Dominions, the Government was more convinced than ever, after the American incident, that England was too small for the impetuous ex-monarch.

One morsel of comfort for the Duke, who by this time had doubtless convinced himself that the whole world was down on him, was the settlement of the libel suit his solicitors had brought against the London publishers of Geoffrey Dennis' *Coronation Commentary*. The book, which had been the May selection of the Book Society of England, made insinuating comments about the pre-marital relations between the Duke and Duchess, spoke of the Duchess as "shop-soiled," and spoke slightingly of the Duke's mental powers. Although the book was withdrawn from sale in England immediately after the suit was threatened, and both author and publishers sent humble apologies to the exile, it was published in America by Dodd, Mead & Co., and widely sold. Windsor refused to drop the suit even after the apologies and withdrawal of the book in England, and the publishers were forced to pay through the nose a reported $50,000.

Neither Duke nor Duchess could obtain much cheer, however, from the latest edition of *Burke's Peerage*,

which came out late in December with Wally ranked
as the 33rd Lady of the Land. *Debrett's Peerage,* an
equally standard work, placed the Duchess 8th. But
as the Royal College of Arms declared when queried
on the discrepancy, only King George could say for
sure what the lady's position in British royal society
would be if she ever returned to resume her place in
that society which both she and the Duke loved so
well.

THE EMPIRE

Two days after the coronation ceremonies at Westminster spokesmen for Canada, Australia, New Zealand, and the Union of South Africa assembled with
England's officials. Purpose of the conference was to
survey common problems of trade, defense, foreign
policy; and to establish, if possible, a framework for
joint action in the future. England's solicitude for
the co-operation of the Dominions was so apparent
because of the Statute of Westminster, which in 1931
had given each of them the position of equal partner-
ship with the Mother country. They were no longer
subservient to the Parliament at London as they had
been in matters of foreign policy at the outbreak of
the World War in 1914.

Principal announced result of the conference was a
plan to pool supplies in event of war. But if there
was any agreement on the part of the Dominions to
join the Mother country in a *European* war, it was
not revealed to the rest of the world.

Ireland's New Constitution. Conspicuously ab-
sent from the Dominion conference were representa-

tives from Ireland. Republican Ireland was in the midst of a campaign to adopt a new Constitution which would sever all but the tiniest thread connecting the Free State with the British empire.

When Edward VIII abdicated in December 1936, President Eamon de Valera had seized that strategic time to get the Free State lower house to pass an act abolishing the British office of Governor General. Then, early in 1937, De Valera presented his people with a new constitution which was remarkable for the fact that in all its 63 articles there was not a single mention of England or the English king.[1] As ratified by a national referendum the first week in July (686,-042 to 528,296), the new constitution invested a President with authority comparable to that of the President of the United States. He will be elected by the people for seven years and ineligible for a second term. He will appoint the Prime Minister, who in actual practice will perform most of the executive duties, the cabinet, the judiciary. He will be the head of the defense forces, and must sign all bills passed by the legislature before they become law.

"Eire," as the state is called in the new constitution, will have a two-house legislature—the Dail, lower house, and the Senate. The corporative state of Mussolini is followed in the provision that more than two-thirds of the 60 Senators will be elected to represent arts, agriculture, commerce, and industry.

[1] When the new king and queen visited Belfast in northern Ireland (no part of the Irish Free State) republicans threw a bomb which exploded in the midst of the welcoming address. The rulers were told that a leaking gas main had accidentally exploded.

Another slap at the British was contained in the article declaring Gaelic as the official language, with English as an alternate. The constitution permits no divorces, and although the Roman Catholic Church will be recognized as "the guardian of the faith," there will be religious freedom guaranteed to other denominations.

Although the new constitution designates "Eire" as the entire island, the six Ulster counties in the north refused to come in under the new constitution just as they had refused to join the Free State in all earlier efforts to break the ties with England.

The new charter was scheduled to go into effect on January 1, 1938, but before it did President De Valera could not resist one parting crack at Britain. Late in December the Dail voted *de facto* recognition of Italy's conquest of Ethiopia—pointedly unrecognized by Britain. This amounted to an unprecedented open break with the mother country—something no dominion had ever tried before. The recognition took the form of an appointment of an Irish Free State minister at Rome accredited to "Victor Emmanuel III, King of Italy and *Emperor of Ethiopia*." Under the British constitution the appointment would have to be approved by George VI, but also under that constitution the British king is supposed always to act as advised by one of His Majesty's governments. Thus at the close of the year the British cabinet was scratching its collective head trying to find some loophole by which King George could avoid placing himself in the inconsistent position of recognizing Victor Emmanuel

as "Emperor" at the Irish legation in Rome and refusing to do so at the British embassy there.

Partition of Palestine. A new scheme to remove
the age-old friction between Jew and Arab in the Holy
Land was devised by Britain in 1937, but by year's
end with ugly street fighting breaking out on Christmas day, it was extremely doubtful whether the scheme
had helped matters, or had aggravated them beyond all
hope of reconciliation.

In return for Jewish aid in the World War, Britain
promised that Palestine should be set aside after the
war as a national home to which persecuted Jews from
all over the world might return. The trouble was that
Britain failed to take full account of a vigorous Arab
population already on the ground who resented the
influx of Jews, particularly after the Nazi program in
Germany drove thousands from the Reich to the Holy
Land. Both Arab and Jew claimed Palestine as their
ancient homeland, and each had countless religious
ties to the territory. Although outnumbering the Jews
2-to-1, Arabs feared that the Jewish immigration would
soon relegate them to a secondary position. They also
resented the fact that the Jews, arriving with money
from abroad, were able to buy up the choicest land.
Jews contended, on the other hand, that they were
bringing wealth, prosperity, and improved health and
sanitation to the land, that they had a right to come
to some haven from the persecution which was being
directed against them in Europe.

British efforts failed to work out a legislature which
would give representation to both groups. And in 1936

such serious rioting broke out between the rival religious groups that thousands of British troops were rushed to the area to keep order.

Finally British Prime Minister Chamberlain determined that the way to end the 17 years of bickering was to divide the territory into separate countries. The scheme finally adopted called for a Jewish state in north Palestine, mostly along the Mediterranean; an Arab state in the south, mainly inland; and a corridor running inland from the port of Jaffa to the holy places of Jerusalem and Bethlehem to be retained by His Majesty's Government.

Although the Jewish state was to contain nearly all the best and most fruitful land in Palestine and would have the country's only deep-sea harbor, Haifa, the relatively small area apportioned them was a blow to the Jews who had come to look on all of Palestine as their national home. Arabs in turn cried out not only against the allotment of coastline and productive land to Jews, but also against British imperialism's retention of the corridor, and reservation of rights permitting British forces to operate by land, sea, and air in Palestine.

Nearly 30,000 Jews met in the World Zionist congress at Zurich in mid-August and voted in favor of the plan with reservations. But Arabs resorted to their familiar raiding and terrorist methods to show their anger. The Grand Mufti of Jerusalem, spiritual leader of the Arabs, escaped into French-mandated Syria, from where he continued to exhort his followers to resist the partition. British troops then seized Moslem religious funds, and the infuriated Arabs retaliated by burning airport buildings and equipment valued at $100,000, and stealing the rifles, pistols, and munitions of Christian police at Daharieh.

Britain then brought over soldiers of the kilted Scotch Black Watch, the "Ladies from Hell" of War fame, who began a systematic policy of dynamiting Arab houses after Moslems refused to return the stolen rifles. When the arms were still retained a $10,000 fine was levied on the whole village of Daharieh. And British colonial strong-arm methods continued until Benito Mussolini, remembering well the tirades launched by Britain's press against his methods in the Ethiopian conquest, righteously printed in his personal newspaper, *Il Popolo d'Italia:* "No one ever entrusted anyone with a mandate to sow destruction and massacre in the Holy Land. . . . Whole streets are razed as punishment for acts whose perpetrators the British authorities are unable to detect and do not wish to investigate. Laws which for thousands of years have guaranteed Justice to civilized mankind, are openly trampled on and innocent citizens are punished for deeds for which they bear no responsibility. . . . The news from Palestine cannot but rouse a sense of horror throughout the civilized world."

Realist Mussolini well knew that Britain's interest in Palestine was imperialistic rather than altruistic. As an air and naval base the Holy Land formed an important link in British domination of the Mediterranean area. The partition of Palestine had not been put into effect by the end of 1937, and Britain was still uncertain whether this solution of the Arab-Jew conflict presented the best method of keeping the peace so essential if the territory was to retain its value in the British scheme of empire.

CHAPTER XIII

FRANCE—A PENDULUM

Like its American counterpart, the French New Deal bumped smack into the complex job of combining reform with recovery in 1937. And like its model in the United States the Popular Front government wound up the year taking at least two steps toward recovery on the Right for every three it had moved Reformwards under the direction of its first Socialist Premier, the Jewish bibliophile, litterateur, and brilliant statesman, Léon Blum.

Blum took over the Premiership of France in June, 1936, after a huge popular vote had given a united front of Radical Socialists, Socialist, and Communist parties a crushing majority in the French Parliament. He rushed through a series of reform measures which called to arms the revolutionary spirit of 1789, long dormant under the crushing weight of France's ruling oligarchy of "200 families." From June, 1936, until January, 1937, the Popular Front majority whipped through Parliament some 70 laws designed to satisfy the revolutionary demands of France's proletariat and lower middle class. Foremost among these reforms were (1) the 40-hour week, (2) compulsory annual paid vacations for workers, (3) compulsory collective bargaining, (4) higher wages, (5) reduction of taxes paid by war veterans, (6) nationalization of the arms industry, and (7) revision of the Bank of France to bring this powerful private institution, which issued the nation's currency and held the enormous gold supply of the treasury, more directly under the control of the Government and bank stockholders, less under the domination of these same 200 families which had ruled the Bank and with it French finance for more than 100 years.

Under such governmental beneficence trade unionism thrived. The French Federation of Labor jumped its membership from one to five million. Such gains for the Left were not attained without a fight. In the spring and all through the summer of 1936 France was harried by an epidemic of sitdown strikes which at one time found 1,000,000 workers occupying factories, hotels, and other places of business. Employers shrieked to high heaven, cursed the radical Popular Front fervidly, had no recourse but to give in to workers' demands when backed by the Government of France. Yet French sitdowns, lasting over a far longer period than the American epidemic of 1937, were proof that they could be settled without bloodshed. Only one shot was fired; only one man injured.

Nor were these gains achieved without the expenditure of vast sums of government money. And increased labor costs from the paid vacations and shorter work week reduced employer's profits, cut tax payments sharply, encouraged tax evasion. Three months after Léon Blum took the Premiership it was apparent that the treasury drain called for forceful measures.

French gold in private hands, supplies of which had long been drifting out of the country as the depression increased strain on successive governments, now fled out of the country by the boatload with the accession of a "spend-your-way-to-prosperity" New Deal. And the franc, which had reflected this flight of capital, fluttered on world exchanges like a broken-winged bird.

A large part of France's financial difficulties could be laid to the fact that, unlike the other great powers, including Britain and the United States, France had not devalued its currency. Pressure from the financial interests, together with the host of thrifty middle class Frenchmen who had tucked away a part of their earnings in the banks each month, and who wanted to get back a franc worth the same as the one they deposited, was enough to satisfy each Premier between 1932 and 1936 that in devaluation lay political suicide.

Devaluation. In September, with a comforting majority in the Popular Front to back him up, Blum cut the value of the franc from 15 to about 21 to the dollar, decreed that its gold content should be controlled between 43 and 49 milligrams. At the same time he arranged for agreement with Great Britain and the United States under which each nation was to set up a stablization fund to prevent wide fluctuation in the value of the franc, pound, and dollar. Devaluation brought the government a neat profit of 17,000,000,000 francs, 10,-000,000,000 of which went into the stablization fund.

Trouble with profit-taking of this kind was that it inevitably led to higher prices. In an attempt to prevent prices from climbing too steeply, Parliament, after confirming the devaluation, voted to reduce French tariffs 15 to 20 per cent. The lag, always present in price rises due to currency manipulation, kept the workers fairly contented through 1936, and the profit permitted the government to meet its obligations for a time.

But by the end of January 1937 a great deal of grumbling was heard again. Workers who had earlier sent Blum 30,000 postcards expressing their satisfaction with his New Deal for them, were now complaining that higher wages had been more than offset by higher prices, were demanding still higher wage increases. Employers were tearing their hair at these demands, insisting that the excessive prices were a product of the Government's labor and reform policies, complaining also that the rigidity of the 40-hour week law prevented them from increasing production sufficiently to offset these factors. Their principal complaint was that trade unions refused to permit a system of labor shifts to be put into operation. Employees would work their five-day week, leave their jobs for a two-day holiday, but refuse to permit other workers to work a different shift under which expensive machinery and production lines could be kept steadily operating. And the Right Wing opposition to the Blum government was screaming that his financial policies were ruining the country.

Thus the financial outlook did look bad again. The ordinary budget for 1937 would be only from 3 to 5 billion francs out of balance. But the same sort of double entry bookkeeping used by the American New

Dealers showed a forthcoming deficit in the "extra budget" for such things as national defense, civil works, and pension funds of from 16 to 23 billion francs. At the same time the tax returns at the close of 1936 had indicated a shortage of nearly a billion francs.

Socialist Finance Minister Vincent Auriol had already turned to Britain to obtain a $250,000,000 loan, pledging the French railroads as security, when on February 5 he announced that the Treasury needed 35,000,000,000 francs. This announcement came the day after the Chamber had voted a vast rearmament program to cost 19,000,000,000 francs, neglecting to indicate how the money was to be raised.

In the midst of furious denunciations of his Government's financial heresy from the Right opposition led in the Chamber by Paul Reynaud, Blum again took a page from the American New Deal book by declaring "La Pause"—a breathing spell for business from further reform measures. At the same time he appealed to the workers not to press their reform demands for the time being, and to work together for increased production. Léon Jouhaux, extreme Leftist leader of the French Labor Federation, had meanwhile been loudly demanding that the Government spend billions for a huge new public works program.

Communists, accusing the cabinet of throwing overboard the social revolution, threatened now to withdraw from the Popular Front, revealing the weakness of this combine, which in essence was simply a defensive alliance against the Right. But by this time both Blum and Auriol had been convinced that the time had come

to take one step away from Reform and toward Recovery.

On March 5 the Government announced the floating
of a huge new loan of 8,000,000,000 francs for national
defense. To woo French capital into returning to the
country and into subscribing to the loan, the Cabinet
promised to take immediate steps to balance the budget,
ordered all government departments to make drastic
economy cuts, promised to stop large government
spending, reduced the Treasury's needs by 6,000,000,-
000 francs, promised gold hoarders, who had previously
been threatened with severe penalties if discovered,
that they might cash in their hoards at the Bank of
France and receive full value, and held out a hand to
the conservative opposition by appointing a committee
to manage the currency exchange control fund headed
by the hard-shelled conservative regent of the Bank
of France, Professor Charles Rist.

The loan was oversubscribed in a very few hours,
the Communists changed their minds about deserting
the Popular Front, and practically the entire Chamber
of Deputies voted to authorize the concessions promised
by Blum and Auriol.

Communist Gadflies. Communists, who supported
the Popular Front while refusing to participate in the
cabinet itself, were the gadflies who made the life of the
members of the other two Popular Front parties miserable. Without their votes in the Chamber Blum could
not count on a majority. Their worst gripe against the
Blum Government was its failure to give open support
to the Spanish Loyalists, Blum having sponsored the

non-intervention policy from the outset of the Civil
War. (See Chapter X.) Yet the Communists knew
that if they deserted the Popular Front at this time
it would be supplanted by a Government farther to
the Right and consequently less to their liking. That
they proved as tractable as they did then was because
of their desire for the lesser of two evils, and perhaps
also because of the bad name the Moscow trials were
giving Communism all over the world. Even some of
the French Communists themselves thought they detected a strong odor of frame-up coming from the direction of Judge Ulrich's court room, and it made the
time less opportune for them to become too fractious.

Clichy Riots. Tests of their willingness to stick by
the Popular Front came in March after a bloody riot in
the Paris suburb of Clichy. The French Social Party,
successor to Col. François de la Roque's Croix de Feu
Fascist organization which had been outlawed by Blum
early in his administration, hired a movie hall in Clichy
for the showing of a film of theirs titled *The Battle*.
Selection of Clichy, a workers' suburb and hotbed of
Communism, was a direct incitement to violence. The
Communist mayor demanded that the meeting be
stopped. Failing in this, and after the Social Party
members had already assembled in the theater, he demanded from police at the scene the right of Clichy
citizens to stage a demonstration in front of the theater.
Knowing full well that this demonstration would lead
to broken pates, the police refused. Meanwhile thousands of citizens had gathered around the movie hall.
Someone threw a brick. Bottles followed. Police

struggled desperately to evacuate the Social Party members who, when they emerged into the street, joined the scrap with flying fists and feet. A citizen from a rooftop fired into the crowd, killing a policeman. Two bullets nicked Premier Blum's secretary who had dashed to the scene to restore order. Hours later, after 3,000 police had been rushed in, the riot was quelled. Five were dead, 100 police injured, and 200 citizens had been rushed to hospitals.

The next morning Communist leaders were up in arms over Blum's use of the police against their party members. Communist chief Maurice Thorez tried to exact a pledge from Blum that the Government would never again use the police against the workers. When the Premier refused, Thorez called a strike of union workers. But when Blum warned he might resign at any such display of lack of unity in the Popular Front, the strike was limited to a half day, and called simply as a "demonstration of Labor's solidarity." The Communists were still standing by the Popular Front.

The Exposition. One reason why Blum had made concessions calculated to bring about a truce between capital and labor was the fact that the great Paris exposition, scheduled to open May 1, was being sadly retarded by strike troubles. The exposition had been looked to as a financial savior. Tourists would bring millions into the country, business would improve, tempers would grow longer, and Government income would increase. But the opening of the fair had to be postponed twice. Building unions were threatening a strike unless Blum set aside $265,800,000 for increased public works. When it finally opened its gates on May 29 only the pavilions of the dictator countries, Germany, Italy, and Russia, and that of Belgium were finished. There weren't even gates at most of the entrances, so thousand of Frenchmen and visitors got in free that first day. Now French pride was definitely wounded. Labor was blamed on all sides until it got under the hides of the workers. They stopped nagging and soldiering, went to work with a vengeance, and within a few days the work had been rushed to completion. By the first week of August it was apparent that the fair was a huge success. One hundred and sixty pavilions representing virtually every nation in the world were receiving a flood of visitors.

Paris hotels were all more nearly full than at any time since 1929. The Parliament had even passed a law abolishing tipping. Prices had been kept reasonable. By the first week in October the amazing number of 20,000,000 persons had passed through the fair's turnstiles.

Fall of Blum. But before the success of the fair had been assured the Blum government had gone down to defeat. Despite all promises of "La Pause," French capital was still fleeing, the franc was still shaky, and the Government was again running short of cash. Government economists were declaring that another 20,-000,000,000 francs would have to be unearthed somewhere to run the nation through the year. The Bank of France upped the discount rate from 4 to 9 per cent as the gold drain became more and more pronounced. The Right was pointing out that when the Popular

Front took office there were 3,636 tons of gold in the
Bank, that by the end of June this had been reduced
to 2,504, with only 20,000,000 paper francs left in the
Treasury.

Summoning his Cabinet in emergency session late in
June, Blum determined to ask Parliament to grant him
the very powers to deal with the crisis which he had
damned with all his oratorical might when preceding
premiers had made the same requests.   Dictatorial
powers over French economy and finance for six weeks,
during which time the Cabinet, unhindered by the explosive Parliament, might decide in a more tranquil
mood what had to be done.

Communists tried to bargain for their favorable vote
on this request, asking a pledge of French support for
the Spanish Loyalists.   But they finally caved in on this
demand, voted with the rest of the Popular Front in
the Chamber 346 to 247 to grant the decree powers.
The story was different in the Senate.   All over 40 years
of age, elected for nine-year terms, Senators were far
more conservative as a group than the Chamber.   Although Blum, realizing how slim were his chances in
the Senate, was careful not to make the vote in the
upper chamber one of confidence in his administration,
he decided to resign after the Senate had voted 188 to
72 against giving him the powers of a financial dictator.
Late in June he handed President Lebrun the resignation of his cabinet, and the President called Camille
Chautemps to the office.

Swing to the Right.   Although the new cabinet was
simply a shuffle of the old one, with Blum remaining

as Vice Premier, and Yvon Delbos retaining his post
of Foreign Minister, it was apparent from the start
that it was determined to woo French capital and
steady the shaky franc by going farther than Blum
had under "La Pause" in the direction of satisfying
business and financial interests of the nation. Restoration of confidence was the problem confronting Chautemps, and his first smart step was to recall from
Washington the hardheaded Georges Bonnet, who had
been sent as ambassador to the United States to try and
wring loans from the American government. Bonnet
was of the old balance-the-budget school, and his appointment as Minister of Finance undoubtedly did
much to restore confidence within France. Both he
and Chautemps were members of the Radical Socialist
party, which was neither radical nor socialist, but the
Leftish party of the small French business man and the
peasant. It stood on the Right hand among the three
Popular Front parties, and the fact that two of its
members were now holding the top posts in the Cabinet
was welcomed by moderate conservatives even though
most of the members of the Blum Government were
still holding seats in the Cabinet, and even though, as
events soon developed, Léon Blum was still very much
a power in the coalition Cabinet.

Bonnet prepared an emergency bill calling for a
"strictly balanced budget . . . to be obtained through
. . . an important reduction in the Treasury's burden."
He asked for the same powers refused Blum by the
Senate, "To take by decree adopted in Ministerial
Council all measures tending to assure repression of

injuries to the credit of the State and to the reserves
of the Bank of France."

After stormy sessions in the Parliament during which
former Finance Minister Auriol, now Minister of Justice in the new Cabinet, was called all sorts of names,
the Chautemps Government was given a vote of confidence and the decree powers in both houses. Bonnet
then set to work to cut French expenditures 6,000,000,-
000 francs while increasing taxes 10,500,000,000. He
arranged a new contract with the Bank of France
under which the Bank's gold stocks were revalued more
nearly to correspond to the depreciated value of the
franc (down to 27 to the dollar by this time, August),
thus effecting a profit for the Government of 6,000,-
000,000 francs which was immediately earmarked for
defense. At the same time he quieted the Left by
agreeing to leave alone a fund of about 4,000,000,000
francs already earmarked for public works. And the
news that the French railways, badly in debt to the
Government, would be taken over by the Government
September 1 was another sop to the Socialistic theories
of the Socialist and Communist members of the Popular Front.

Early in October the new Cabinet had a chance to
gauge the general popularity of its moderate program.
The Canton elections for local offices throughout
France showed a gain for the Radical Socialists at the
expense chiefly of the Communist and Socialist forces.
The Right and Center parties held their own.

On the eve of the elections, Chautemps had gone before the nation with a program sounding strangely like

those being put forward by the Dictators across the Alps and the Rhine. The nation must "defend its prosperity by great efforts of work, discipline, and union," he told the population. At the same time he announced a new program which appeared to be such an about-face from the policies of the Popular Front that French Leftists could only gasp at the fact that Blum and his Socialist cohorts remained in the cabinet. The 40-hour week was to be modified by decree to increase factory production. The Government went on record as determined not to let sitdown strikes recur. "Foreign agitators were to be suppressed wherever found." And there was to be "absolute opposition to all further measures of exchange control."

Exhibiting this program the new Government won a vote of confidence in the chamber 299 to 160 when Parliament reconvened late in November.

"Royalist Plot." The vote of confidence came under dramatic circumstances as Premier Chautemps revealed to a shocked Chamber details of a "Royalist plot" which had just been uncovered by the state secret police. A hooded band, like America's Ku Klux Klan, and called by police *Les Cagoulards* ("The Hooded Men"), had been all set to overthrow the government, so the Premier announced. In 450 homes and shops in the country police had discovered 120,000 rifle and pistol cartridges, 500 machine guns, 65 sub-machine guns, and other stores of anti-tank, and anti-aircraft guns and shells.

According to Minister of the Interior Marx Dormoy, a secret para-military organization modeled on army lines, with general staff, intelligence departments, divisions, brigades, regiments, even a sanitation service had been scotched before leaders were able to carry out their plan to "replace the republican form of government by a dictatorial regime that was meant to precede restoration of the monarchy." Plotters even had photostats of cabinet ministers' signatures, had also an exact plan of the Paris sewers with passages leading to the Chamber, plans of buildings occupied by Leftist newspapers.

Among 26 Frenchmen arrested and charged with complicity in the plot, the only well-known names were General Edouard Duseigneur, former French air staff chief, Banker Eugene Deloncle, and Count Hubert Pastré. These denied vehemently all knowledge of the threatened coup.

Bourbon pretender to the throne, the Duc de Guise, manifested from his Belgian exile, "We have decided to reconquer the throne of our fathers." But most Frenchmen took the news of the plot calmly, some even suspecting that the Government was making a political mountain out of a molehill by building the affair up far beyond its real proportions to scare the Chamber into supporting Chautemps as the last bulwark against reaction.

It was significant that none of France's would-be Führers were implicated in this plot. Colonel François de la Roque had been trying to build a powerful fascist movement for several years, but with indifferent success. Blum had outlawed his Croix de Feu, whereupon he had come out in the open as head of a new "Social Party," which was legal and no more effective than the other legal Right Wing parties.

Early in 1937 the Right thought they had found a more powerful leader in the person of Jacques Doriot, a sort of French Huey Long, who had been a communist until he differed with Moscow and was ex-communicated in 1935. A man of the people, with the required bull voice and demagogic tricks, Doriot went violently Right Wing in 1936, admitted his admiration for Hitler, and founded the French Popular Party on which he planned to ride to dictatorial power. With money from the cognac king, Hennessy, and others, he bought the Paris newspaper *La Liberti*. But he was removed by the government from his job as mayor of St. Denis, Paris suburb, charged with corruption and when he resigned his seat in the Chamber, to run in a by-election as a "challenge to the Popular Front," he was defeated. By the close of 1937 he was not the power he had hoped to be, and Rightists were still searching for a "man on horseback." Meanwhile, the apparent success of Chautemps' more moderate program made it seem unlikely that the passionately individualistic middle class Frenchmen would be lured into support of any scheme to saddle them with dictatorship.

Year's-End Strikes. During the last days in December the public utility workers of Paris went out on strike—tying up not only the subways and buses but also gas and garbage services. After prolonged negotiations between union leaders and Marx Dormoy,

Minister of the Interior, the strike was called off on New Year's Eve—with both sides claiming victory. Meantime a thousand coal miners went out on strike at Anzin, near Valenciennes, in protest against the discharge of three workers.

CHAPTER XIV

RUSSIANS AND RUSSIA ON TRIAL
TWENTY YEARS AFTER

BLOOD PURGE

When Soviet Russia completed its Second Five Year Plan nine months ahead of schedule on April 1, 1937, many an observer of the Russian Dictatorship in action frankly wondered whether the Third Five Year Plan would be dedicated to eradicating the cream of its entire population. For the blood purge of Old Bolsheviks begun in the summer of 1936 with the trial and execution of such famous Revolutionary figures as Grigory Zinoviev and Leo Kamenev had continued with increased fanaticism all during 1937, showed no signs of abating as 1938 opened.

Correspondents, keeping a daily box score of only those executions which were reported in the Soviet official press itself, chalked up the deaths of 700 Russians during the thirteen month period between September, 1936, and October, 1937. At the number unreported they could only guess—conservatively or wildly, according to the range of their imaginations or their regard for the world's sole Communist dictatorship. To have counted those jailed during the manhunt for all of the enemies or potential enemies of the state would

have left Moscow correspondents time to do little else.
The Soviet's own press told of "tens of thousands" of
Communists being kicked out of the party, and it was a
good guess that many of these had landed in jail. Best
estimates of the government shuffle which accompanied
the purge figured that at least 60 per cent of all local
Communist officials had been either dismissed or de-
moted. And in many instances dismissal was accompanied by at least a prison term.

Only a few of those who faced firing squads were
given the benefit of a public trial for their offenses,
which ranged from high treason to the vague and all-
inclusive "deviation from the party line." But the
names of those who were privileged to receive one of
the widely-publicized state trials were so high and
mighty in Soviet officialdom as to shock the outside
world into a state of complete bewilderment as to what
was actually going on under the dictatorship of Mr.
Joseph Stalin.

Trial of Radek. One so privileged was Karl Radek,
until his arrest in the fall of 1936, Russia's foremost
writer on foreign affairs, and one of the "Old Bolsheviks" who had played an important part in bringing
the Communist Revolution into being in 1917. In
January he was brought to trial with 16 others, charged
with being a party to a hair-raising plot which included
everything from the projected assassination of Stalin
to the giving away of Russian territory to Fascist
Germany.

On trial with him were such prominent Red figures
as Grigoriy Piatakov, until his arrest Vice Commissar

for Heavy Industy; Leonid P. Serebriakov, a potent
Old Bolshevik who had for two years (1919-1921)
held down the job of Secretary General of the Communist Party, the post which makes Joseph Stalin Russia's dictator today; Grigoriy Sokolnikov, former Vice
Commissar for Foreign Affairs; N. I. Murdlov, for
years the commandant of the Moscow military garrison; and Vladimir Romm, who had been the able and
well-liked Washington correspondent for the Soviet
newspaper, *Izvestia*.

The story of these men's treason as pieced together
by Russia's most famed Prosecutor, Andrei Vishinsky
in the court room presided over by the even more famous Judge Vasily Ulrich, was that, under the master-
minding of the Soviet's greatest exile, Leon Trotsky,
they had all been tools in a plan which aimed at the
sudden and violent overthrow of the Stalin government. Piatakov was supposed to have made a secret
flight to Oslo, Norway, to meet Trotsky. Hardest part
of the alleged plot for the world to swallow was the
charge that present at this same meeting in Oslo had
been Adolf Hitler's Nazi party handyman, Rudolf Hess.
And that all the defendants had acquiesced eagerly to
give Nazi Germany the rich Soviet breadbasket, the
Ukraine, in return for their support in the coup to upset Joseph Stalin. To make the wild tale complete,
Japan was to get Eastern Siberia and the part of the
Pacific island of Sakhalin which she did not already
own—"from which she might get oil to make war on
America."

Ready Confessions. A strange aspect of these state trials was the zeal with which the defendants confessed everything. The same thing had been true of the Zinoviev and Kamenev trials the previous August, and it continued to be the outstanding feature of the court room scenes all during 1937. But in the case of Radek the confessional reached an all-time high. With an impish grin the irrepressible journalist declared, "I am guilty of all the charges . . . even those I didn't know about."

To many of those familiar with the backgrounds of the Old Bolsheviks on trial, these confessions reeked of fakery and falsehood. However, official Soviet Russia explained that the defendants fell all over each other trying to make the most lurid admissions of guilt because they had seen the error of their ways, had been reborn in the cause, and were anxious to atone for their sins. Among those who expressed willingness to accept the confessions at face value were the newly-arrived U. S. Ambassador, Joseph W. Davies, and able New York *Times* correspondent Walter Duranty. Other explanations for the wholesale admissions advanced by the skeptical were: (1) by "telling all," and possibly a good deal more than all, the defendants were assured that their wives and families would not be persecuted after their deaths; (2) if they could make their story good enough their lives might be spared even though the public would be told they had been executed; (3) some even offered the fantastic opinion that the Soviets had perfected and were using a "confession gas" or "truth serum" to make the defendants cough up all their secrets.

Sentence. Strange too, in the case of the January trials, was the fact that while the Moscow press had outdone itself in screaming at Karl Radek as the vilest offender among the 17 charged with treason, the court spared his life. He, Sokolnikov, and two others were given ten year prison terms, while the rest faced the firing squad.

International Bogeyman. But stranger even than the confessions and the inconsistent sentences was the fact that the bogeyman throughout the August and January trials, and in the subsequent purge which was to force out 250,000 Communist party members and shake up an estimated 60 per cent of all local Communist officials throughout the Union, was a mild-looking little professorial Russian Jew who was arriving in Mexico City just as the Radek trial opened. Until 1927 when he split with Joseph Stalin on the issue of whether the Communist International should rest on its oars and concentrate its endeavors on building a Socialist state in Russia, or spread the revolution of the masses all over the face of the earth, Leon Trotsky had been one of the most powerful figures in the Soviet bureaucracy. It had been Lenin the Leader and Trotsky the War Minister whose names and faces were emblazoned in the minds of the Russian people in the early days of the revolution. And at the death of Lenin it had been generally expected that Trotsky would rise to the number one post. But a shrewder, stronger, better politician named Joseph Stalin had somehow forged ahead until by 1927 he was able to veto Trotsky's drive for world revolution, carry on his own plan to build a strong internal Russia. Two years later he was able to banish the former War Minister. And swiftly Stalin's efficient Soviet propaganda service had done its best to transform the Russian picture of Trotsky into a symbol of all that was vilest among the enemies of the state. Not because of his race and religion, but because his views differed from those of Stalin and the men whom he kept in power, Trotsky was intended to become to the Russian what the Jew is to the Nazi.

That, then, was the concept which the state spent eight years trying to create in the minds of its people. Was the purge of 1937 evidence that the propaganda machine had failed, that there actually existed in Russia a big share of the population who still revered and followed the old hero? That was exactly what Stalin admitted in the spring of 1937. In a speech transcribed and broadcast to the nation he answered his critics abroad who were contending that there was a more fundamental reason for his devil hunt by declaring, "It is a rotten theory to say the Trotskyists do not have reserves in the Soviet Union among the remnants of the exploiting classes."

Trotsky's Denial. From the home of the famous Mexican artist, Diego Rivera, where he had finally found refuge after being shunted about as a dangerous radical by one European government after another, Leon Trotsky issued bristling denials of all the Moscow charges. He ridiculed the story of the Oslo meeting, calling attention of the world to the fact that his hosts, the Norwegian government, had been so solicitous of his welfare during his short sojourn there that he had been under the strictest surveillance by their secret service every hour of the day. He demanded that the letters he was charged with having written to the Soviet defendants be produced. And he dared the Stalin bureaucracy to extradite him and give him a chance to take the witness stand in his own behalf. Finally he asked that a committee of Liberals of all shades constitute itself a court to hear the charges against him and examine what evidence they could uncover. This was done during the spring of 1937 under the sponsorship of members of his own world organization for spreading Socialism, the Fourth International. Columbia University's famed Liberal philosopher, John Dewey, headed a group which went to Mexico City and held 13 hearings during March and April. Although Author Carleton Beals, accusing the committee of being unduly influenced in Trotsky's favor, resigned from it in a huff, the majority of the Liberals could find no evidence of Trotsky's connection with the plots supposedly being uncovered in Moscow.

Jitters in the Party. Meanwhile the purge was taking on the appearance of a snowball headed down a steep hill. Like the sit-down in America it developed into a sort of mass hysteria. Managers of industrial plants who were behind in their quotas, officials of farm collectives who were behind in their spring planting were accused of being Trotskyists, or anyway "wreckers" of the state. Many of them were jailed without warning. Hundreds of others, jittery at the prospect of finding their names next on the government's list, hastened to resign their offices of responsibility, confessing their political unfitness, and expressing their intention to devote their future efforts to "learning more about Bolshevism."

In June President Alexander G. Chervyakov of the White Russian Republic, one of the seven making up the Soviet union, and his Railway commissar, killed themselves as two others in the White Russian cabinet were jailed and 1,000 ranking members expelled from the Communist party in that republic. A short time later the Premier of Uzbek, another of the union republics, was thrown out of his office. The President of the Ukrainian Socialist Soviet Republic shot himself early in September. The Premier of the Republic of Azerbaidzhan was ousted in October. The "heat" continued until by the end of the year Stalin had either broken or killed a premier or a president of every one of the seven Soviet Republics which comprised the union.

Higher up in government and party circles, the heads also continued to fall. In April Genrikh G. Yagoda, dreaded for 10 years as the head of the Ogpu, secret police, and later Commissar for Internal Affairs, was dismissed from office.

The Commissar for Heavy Industry, Stalin's good friend Grigoriy K. Ordzhonikidze, apparently died a natural death late in February. "Paralysis of the heart" was the official medical report. That he was not under a cloud when he died was proved by the fact that his funeral was the biggest Moscow had seen since the death of Lenin, Stalin himself being a pallbearer.

But there were rumors that he had been killed by the friends of his former Vice Commissar Piatakov, who had been executed after the January trials.

Ordzhonikidze's successor, Valery I. Mezhlauk, lasted only a few weeks in this tough assignment. The Moscow press was soon flaying him because of the backwardness of the automobile industry, and he was ousted in favor of another of Stalin's close friends, Lazar Kaganovich.

Another world famous Communist arrested in August as a "Trotskyist" was Bela Kun, erstwhile Communist dictator of Hungary, who had been a minor party official in Moscow since he was chased out of Hungary in 1919.

More Executions. Run-of-the-mill arrests and executions were occurring with such frequency by spring that foreign correspondents were kept humping to keep track even of those reported in official newspapers. In May 66 were shot in the Far East alone. A single batch of 64 was mowed down in July for "Trotskyism." By this time there was some indication that the party zealots were going too far even for their chief. In a broadcast to the nation Stalin warned that "because a man was once a Trotskyist . . . it does not mean that he cannot be a responsible Communist."

Purge of the Military. Worst shocker of the whole manhunt was the running to earth of the very cream of the Red Army. A foreboding of what was to come appeared in the news released late in May that Marshal Nikolaivich Tukhachevsky, youngest and generally considered most brilliant of the Soviet's five field marshals, had suddenly been stripped of his office of Vice Commissar for Defense, and sidetracked to an insignificant Volga military district. His name had been mentioned during the January trials, but he had been absolved at that time.

Early in June another Vice-Commissar for Defense, Jan Gamarnik, killed himself. Then, a few days later, came the announcement, breath-taking to the ordinary Soviet citizen, that eight top-ranking army men including Marshal Tukhachevsky and seven generals had been arrested. The seven were A. I. Kork, former commandant of the Frunze Military Academy (Soviet West Point); Vitovta K. Putna, military attaché at London, Berlin and Tokyo; Iona E. Yakir, commandant of the Ukraine; Robert P. Eideman, in charge of training army reservists in aviation and chemical warfare; Ieronim P. Uborevich, commander in the district of White Russia; and B. M. Feldman, chief of the Administrative board of the People's Commissariat for Defense.

With the speed of justice unhampered by the presence of defense attorneys, the eight military chiefs were tried on charges of being in the employ of the secret service of a foreign government (presumably Germany or Japan) who were unfriendly in policy toward the Soviet union. All pleaded guilty in the prescribed manner and were executed before most Russians knew they were even under suspicion. Closely guarded were the details of their treason. One theory given wide circulation was that German and Russian officers, recognizing the futility of throwing their strong military machines against each other, had been conspiring behind the backs of the Soviet civilian chiefs to pool their forces to establish domination over Europe and Asia. Another possible reason for the sudden execution of these bright stars in the Red Army was the fact that they were suspected of building a political machine to take control away from the party politicians. This has happened before in history, may happen again.

Counter Revolution? Among those stunned at this sudden downfall of the mighty may have been the Soviet censors. At any rate, New York *Times* Moscow Correspondent Harold Denny was able to cable from the Russian capital: "If one accepts only what is authoritatively published here and what has admittedly happened, two conclusions suggest themselves—either the Government and the Communist party leadership, which in reality are identical, have staged a frame-up on a gigantic scale, or there exists a situation of discontent, unrest and active disloyalty in the Stalin regime amounting almost, if not fully, to a counter-revolution.

"The Prestige of the Russian Communist party undoubtedly has suffered a severe blow in the eyes of the people of its own country. . . . 'These men, these great Bolsheviks, turn out to be crooks and traitors,' they say to themselves. And they wonder who will be the next of their heroes to be branded enemies of the people."

What the world at large wondered as these indications of wholesale mutiny within the Red ranks continued was how much the renovating process was affecting the strength of the Soviets. How strong was the world's only Communist state twenty years after the 1917 revolution which brought it into being? It was notable that Japan chose to invade China just a few days after the execution of Tukhachevsky and his fellow officers, at a time when disruption and fear were at their peak for the year in the Red Army. In France a feeling of coolness toward the Franco-Soviet mutual assistance pact was evident as the opinion became widespread that the Russian military was not working in perfect harmony with the civilian government. And the British, not very keen on the treaty between France and Russia, used the situation to pry the two nations a little farther apart. Naturally, each new story of disaffection among their hated Communist enemies was grist for the mill of the Fascist powers. With pious unctuousness the German press pointed out that their blood purge of 1934 had accounted for the lives of only 77—at least that was all Adolf Hitler was willing to accept responsibility for.

Military Strength. Yet there was little reason to doubt the power of the Soviet military machine during 1937. A well-disciplined army of 1,300,000 men could stand to lose a few generals and still have plenty of replacements. And an eye-opener to all the world in 1937 was the efficiency of the Soviet air force as revealed in the Spanish and Sino-Japanese wars. America's famed aviator, Bert Acosta, who fought for a time with the Loyalists in Spain, declared that the most impressive single observation he had brought back from Spain was the superiority of the Russian planes and airmen over those of any other European power.[1] And the two flights by Soviet aviators across the top of the world from Moscow to the United States testified in even more startling fashion the swift progress made by the Reds in taking wings.

In 1937, too, the Soviets began to build up their naval power. Three battleships, each 26 years old, formed the backbone of a badly out-dated fleet. In April they announced that two new 35,000-ton battleships would be built, each to carry 16-inch guns. Apparently one of these was to be built in the United States, then sailed to Leningrad where it would serve as a model for the building of the second ship. Moreover, stories were constantly popping out of Vladivostok in Siberia telling of trainloads of submarine parts which were being shipped out there to be assembled into a powerful underseas fleet.

The completion in July of the Volga-Moscow canal, product of convict labor like the Baltic-White Sea canal finished several years before, served notice of the Red Government's intention to facilitate water transportation to all parts of the union—an important military asset. When the Soviet canal system is finished, Russian goods, troops, and passengers can be transported

---

[1] For Russia in foreign affairs see Chapters on Spain, the Sino-Japanese War, and Germany-Italy.

by river steamer from Moscow to the Caspian, Black, Azov, White, and Baltic seas.

Industrial Production. According to League of Nations statistics the volume of industrial production in the U.S.S.R. at the close of 1936 was four times what it had been in 1929. The heavy industries, in particular, had forged steadily ahead under terrific pressure from the Kremlin. By August of 1937 pig iron was being produced at the rate of 15,000,000 tons a year. Stakhanovism, a Soviet speed-up technique invented two years before, was still increasing efficiency even though arousing resentment among some workers.

Yet critics of the Russian system who had lived close to its industries contended that figures of Russian industrial output meant nothing. Executives of plants, under pressure from above to fulfill quotas or be styled "wrecker" or "Trotskyist," often faked their reports. And the Moscow press itself was authority for the amazing statement that 48 per cent of the automobiles rolling off the assembly lines were "entirely inoperative."

Consumers' Goods. Russians freely admitted also the sad condition of their consumers' goods industries. Because of the great drive to build factories, machinery, means of transportation, and military equipment, there had been too little time and effort devoted to turning out the things calculated to make the life of the common man a more comfortable one. In his *Proletarian Journey,* published in 1937, Fred Beal, an American one-time Communist and labor organizer who spent years working for the Soviets, complained of having to eat "thin cabbage soup, black bread and tea, because the Government was exporting its food to buy capitalist machinery." The cheapest pair of shoes cost nearly a month's wages for the low-paid factory worker, while to buy a suit he must save his entire wages for four months. Even so millions of workers were better off than they or their fathers had been before the revolution. Their rents were low, and usually fixed at a proportion of the wage. Medical care and education were free, and vastly superior to pre-revolution facilities. And for many the social insurance funds provided free vacations, sanitorium treatment, care in the waning years of life.

ELECTIONS UNDER THE NEW CONSTITUTION

Russians were told during 1937, as they had been since their new constitution was handed them on June 12 of the year previous, that they were living in the world's greatest democracy. Already they had been guaranteed liberties and freedom which no other country in the world granted. And in the elections for village or borough, regional, provincial, republic or area, and national representatives which were set for December 12, 1937, they were finally to fashion their own government which would henceforth be responsible to them.

This fiction of democracy arose out of the constitutional provisions guaranteeing the right to vote, regardless of sex, race, class origin, or religious belief; the secret ballot; the right to work for a living (to be found in no other national constitution); the right to own and have protected personal property, including homes; and freedom of speech, press, assembly, and demonstration.

Yet the Russian press in 1937, as in every year under the dictatorship, was strictly a controlled press. Any criticism of the Government was pretty sure to land the critic in jail as a "wrecker." Anyone staging a meeting for the purpose of discussing a different form of government for Russia was still in imminent danger of winding up in a Siberian exile. And without a doubt the person foolhardy enough to venture to picket the Kremlin with a banner announcing the Government was "Unfair to World Socialism," stood a good chance of getting a bullet between the eyes.

Not surprising to anyone then were the results of this great Democratic election. While educating Russians in how to use the ballot, the Moscow press printed an "exposé" of polling corruption in the United States entitled "How I Was Elected Governor of New York." They neglected to mention that this piece had been written as humor by Mark Twain, who had been dead since 1910, and Soviets accepted the account as one of standard political procedure in the United States and other capitalist democracies.

Each citizen was asked to vote for at least five persons to fill the 2,000,000 brand new elective jobs under the constitution: his representative in the village, city, or metropolitan borough Soviet; his representative in the Soviet of the region; his delegate to the provincial Soviet; his choice for the Soviet of the area or republic; and his representative on the Supreme Soviet.

Although the ballot was to be secret, in practice the nominations took place at open meetings in factory or meeting hall by a showing of hands. Timid Russians who had been reading of the executions of those who dared to differ with Communists in power ran no chance of incurring this form of official displeasure by attempting to run a candidate in opposition to the one sponsored by the Communist higher-ups in their district. When such a candidate was nominated all hands went up. In almost no cases at all was there more than one candidate for the job.

Russians who concluded that since there was no opposition there was no good reason for voting, were warned by President Mikhail Kalinin on the eve of the elections that this was a "grave mistake" . . . "if an overwhelming majority of our electors go to the polls, many Fascist gang leaders will stop and think: 'Look . . . not only is their army strong, but even greater power stands behind the army!' " Kalinin also explained the lack of opposition candidates as "a sign of the impossibility of differences among the working masses, such as there are in bourgeois society."

Results. Election day and the day before were decreed holidays. Most of those who had considered not voting thought better of it and 90,000,000 votes, an estimated 96 per cent of the population, were counted —many of them contained such written in sentiments as "I would give my life for Stalin, let alone my vote."

New National Government. Russia's new Supreme Council, or Parliament, will have 1,143 mem-

bers, divided between two houses, the Council of the
Union, elected according to population, and the Council of Nationalities, elected according to the many races
and nationalities in the U.S.S.R. The Supreme Council will choose a praesidium of thirty-seven members,
of which Stalin may be elected President. When legislators are not in session, the praesidium, according
to the Constitution, will rule. In fact, whether or not
he is formally head of the praesidium, Stalin will continue to rule.

More Executions. That Stalin would continue to
govern as he saw fit, and without permitting sentiment
to interfere was evident as the year closed. On the
20th anniversary of the Soviet Secret Police, announcement was made of the execution of eight more prominent Old Bolsheviks. Best-known among the dead
were the following: Avel Yenukidze, former secretary
of the Central Executive Committee of the Communist
party, and recognized as one of Stalin's best friends;
Mamil D. Orakhelashviki, another old Stalin intimate
and former Vice Commissar for Education; Leo M.
Karakhan, Soviet ambassador to Turkey until recalled
a few weeks before his execution, and former Vice
Commissar of Foreign Affairs.

Thus while no one but Stalin himself knew precisely
what was going on in Russia, a careful count of political executions admitted in the Russian press revealed
the grisly fact that more than 1,300 former friends,
associates, and Communist party brothers of the Dictator had been put to death by him in 1937. Much
capital was made out of these killings, however, by

Stalin's enemies outside of Russia. Trotskyites everywhere were given much space in the world press; especially to the Trotsky "trial" and to such ex-Russian
diplomats as Alexander Barmine, who, when ordered
to return to Moscow from his post as secretary to the
Greek Legation, went to Paris instead and from there
sent his "exposé" articles on the Stalin regime.

CHAPTER XV

FASCISM BORES INTO LATIN AMERICA

Latin America, long used to dictatorships of one sort or another, had been the answer to the prayer of Fascism ever since Benito Mussolini first conceived the idea of surrounding an old scheme of one-man rule with a few modern trappings. Only in 1937, however, did the world become aware of the gains made by Black and Brown Shirts along the economic and cultural fronts of South and Central America.

The awakening came with a rude jolt in the new constitution foisted upon 40,000,000 Brazilians by their Dictator-President Getulio Vargas early in November. Here, in a charter chock-full of the same devices used by Mussolini and Adolf Hitler to control the Italian and German populations, was proof that Fascism had spanned the Atlantic.

Economic and Cultural Penetration. But for those who had been willing to ferret out the facts there had been plenty of prior indications of Fascist penetration of Hispaniola. Emigration of Italians, Germans, and Japanese to South American states, particularly Brazil, Argentina and Chile, had long been noted. But the Reich's bold demand made in 1937 that anyone of German blood any place in the world must regard himself a German forever, regardless of

394

the accident of citizenship under some other flag, gave point to this emigration. Brownshirted brigades began to appear in South American countries. In Brazil the Government was forced to intervene in certain of these German colonies to compel the teaching of the language of the country in the schools. German and Italian professors were provided free of charge to Brazilian schools and universities. And both Rome and Berlin sprayed daily shortwave broadcasts to South America which combined excellent entertainment features with much propaganda.

The Fascist invasion on the economic front had been annoyingly apparent to British and American exporters since the days when Germany's Dr. Hjalmar Schacht devised his scheme of subsidizing German exports by persuading South American exporters to accept payment for their products in ASKI marks which could only be used for the purchase of German goods, but which meant that German goods could be bought at a considerable discount over the same products Britain and the United States were trying to peddle. Result in Brazil and Chile was that the United States was pushed out of first place in imports by the Nazis. In other South American states also Fascist trade made great gains, as indicated by the fact that Germany's exports to South America during the first six months of 1937 were $149,000,000, as against $214,000,000 for all of 1936, and $108,000,000 in 1932. Mineral-poor Germany needed South American raw materials. Brazil's iron ore (said by some to be the richest in the world) was essential to the Reich's rearmament drive. To buy it, as well as the ferromanganese, nickel, and other raw materials she needed, necessitated exchanging her own goods for those of South America. Thus the subsidized exports.

These cold facts were brought out into the light by the publicity attending Brazil's new constitution. Since he had seized the presidency through a military revolt in 1930, Dr. Vargas had been entrenching his position. He suppressed what was branded a Communist uprising against his regime in November, 1935. Since then thousands of political offenders had been imprisoned, absolute censorship of the press applied, men responsible only to President Vargas placed in charge of Brazil's 21 states. All this despite a liberal constitution adopted in 1934.

Martial Law. After the 1935 uprising the nation had spent most of its days under virtual martial law. The latest of these "state of war" edicts came on October 2. A majority of the Vargas-dominated Chamber of Deputies voted to suspend all constitutional rights because of the "threat of a Communist coup." As in all Fascist states, Communism was the "whipping boy." To save the nation from this "Red Terror" it was necessary to take strong measures. "Regrettable failings," Dr. Vargas told the nation in announcing the new corporate authoritarian state November 10, had appeared in the republican regime. "The legislative branch of the government under the constitution of 1934 showed itself unworkable beyond hope of repair. The maintenance of that inadequate and expensive machinery of government has proved thoroughly inadvisable."

"Coincidence." By a queer coincidence Brazil's presidential elections were about to be held in January of 1938, and under the 1934 constitution no president could succeed himself. Another interesting commentary on this Fascist coup d'état was the fact that among those arrested as leaders of the planned "Communist uprising" were members of Brazil's oldest, most conservative, and wealthiest families, as well as ranking army officers who happened to be supporting the wrong candidate for president.

Constitution. The new constitution, lifted almost bodily from that of Portugal, aped Fascism in effecting the following: (1) It dissolved the federal congress, state assemblies, and municipal councils. To take their place new assemblies would be created under an indirect electoral system. But they would have power to pass only those laws approved by higherups; and members criticizing their government might be ousted by a two-thirds vote of the others. (2) Great power was concentrated in the hands of the president. All federal laws must be introduced by him. The constitution extended Vargas' term until a plebiscite could be held, for which no date was set. The president's term was defined as six years. This provision for a successor to the Brazilian "Führer" made it difficult to classify the new government as outright Fascism, but there were few Brazilians who believed the provision meant what it said. (3) A national economic Council was to be set up as a consultative body. Half of its members will be elected by workers' syndicates, and half by employer groups. This was a bow to Mussolini's corporate state. (4) Strikes and lockouts were declared to be anti-social and incompatible with the interests of production. (5) The press was forbidden to criticize the Government or acts of Government officials, and was ordered to publish in full all statements given out by the Government. Foreigners were barred from owning stock in newspapers. (6) State aid was provided for large families. (7) And with a nice gesture in the direction of the man in the White House of the big neighbor to the north, the constitution ordered Supreme Court judges to retire at 68, and provided that their veto on legislation might be overridden by a two-thirds vote of the national chamber.

The new charter also suspended all foreign debts, a matter of deep concern to the United States Government which was also concerned to know whether this pseudo-Fascism meant that Brazil was being drawn into the Italo-German-Japanese orbit. The three-way agreement of these powers to combat the spread of world Communism had been signed just a few days before the new constitution was announced by Vargas. If Brazil had been tied to an alliance of any sort with European and Asiatic nations, perhaps the Monroe Doctrine, which had been dying a lingering death under the Roosevelt good neighbor policy, might have to be revived.

There was good cause for suspecting that Brazil's adoption of some of the forms of Fascism might be the forerunner of a tieup with the Fascist powers.

But Vargas hastened to assure the United States and the rest of the world that the new government and its policies were strictly homegrown and would continue to be so. Specifically, he denied that his Government would join the anti-Communist pact. To add force to this denial he ordered the dissolution of the country's only real Fascist party, the Green-shirted Integral Democrats, or "Integralistas." President Vargas had not had to rely on this five-year-old private army, since his own military and political machine was powerful enough without the Integralistas. But the complacency with which Plinio Salgado, leader of the uniformed counterpart of the Nazi Brownshirts accepted the order to disband suggested a behind-the-scenes "deal."

U. S. Attitude. The attitude of the United States Government toward this political importation was one of watchful waiting coupled with more concern than it cared to admit as the year closed. There was reason to believe that when Franklin Roosevelt, on his good will trip to the Pan-American congress at Buenos Aires in the late fall of 1936, talked ostentatiously about the Americas as the stronghold of democracy he was doing so for the express purpose of bolstering up South American opposition to the influx of a European ideology. Whistling to keep up their courage, some state department officials contended that the pseudo-Fascism was but a temporary phase in Brazilian political life, that the innate desire of the people for freedom would soon force the return to Democracy. They were bolstered in this hope by the belief that even though the

South American states might borrow ideas of government from Europe, they would avoid any alliance designed to make them fight in defense of those ideas.

ELSEWHERE IN HISPANIOLA

Throughout all of Hispaniola the struggle between Right and Left went on during 1937. Accompanying Brazil in its leaning toward the Right were six other South American "republics": Argentina, Bolivia, Paraguay, Peru, Venezuela, and Uruguay. These nations were all under the control of ultra-conservative minorities who since 1930 had seized power from the masses.

Argentina. In Argentina the election of Dr. Robert M. Ortiz to the presidency in September assured the continuance of the conservative policies of the Justo government, though Ortiz himself was a self-made man who did not belong to one of the old families which had dominated Argentina's politics for more than 100 years.

Bolivia-Paraguay. The war between Bolivia and Paraguay for possession of a great area of jungle territory between the two states called the Gran Chaco brought military dictatorships to both countries. After three years of slaughter in the steaming fever-ridden jungle, the physically and financially bankrupt belligerents had stopped fighting in June of 1935. But two and one-half years later a peace conference of six neutral American nations, including the United States, had utterly failed to settle the boundary and other questions involved in the dispute. Diplomatic relations had not been renewed, and the newspapers of both nations were still spreading a campaign of hate.

War heroes Colonel David Toro in Bolivia and Colonel Rafael Franco in Paraguay had seized power by military coups early in 1936. Both of these leaders were ousted during the summer of 1937, but it was significant that it was the army again which caused their dismissal. Colonel Franco was given the boot because he co-operated with the Chaco peace conference by recalling troops from the front. The army put Professor Felix Paiva, Dean of the University of Asunçion, in his place. In Bolivia German Busch became the new president. Although the old democratic constitutions, replaced by a form of totalitarianism under the military dictators, were restored in both nations, and both presidents promised to call elections in the near future, observers found it hard to believe that the result would be real democracy in nations in which there was practically no middle class, where the wealth of the nations was either in foreign hands or owned by a tiny minority, and where the tradition of control by the wealthy minority was so ingrained.

Pink States. Chile and Ecuador continued during 1937 under the domination of Left Wing governments made up of coalitions of various liberal and radical groups. Only in these two states was Communism strong enough among the workers to warrant concern among the conservatives. And even so it was a home-grown variety of Communism, more rabidly Chilean and Ecuadorian than Russian.

One Lone Democracy. Students of South American politics found little to quarrel with in the contention of Colombians that their country was the only real democracy in Latin America. Here elections were on the level, and the will of the majority was permitted to prevail.

Central America. Fascist sympathies were even stronger if anything in Central than in South America. Guatemala, Nicaragua and El Salvador had joined Germany and Italy in giving official recognition to the Insurgent government of Spain early in the Spanish war. And when Italy joined the anti-Communist pact with Germany and Japan the news was given great prominence and editorial approval in the press of the three little states. Together with Honduras these nations had signed an anti-Communist pact of their own in the summer of 1937, which had for its unavowed purpose the retention of power by their dictators.

Because of close commercial relations with Italy, Guatemala was most sympathetic toward the Black Shirt rule. Editorials had even been published in Guatemalan newspapers advocating an outright alliance with Italy.

Tiny El Salvador was within the Hitler sphere. Germany was her biggest customer for the coffee crop which constituted 80 per cent of her exports. She had followed Germany in withdrawing from the League, as had Guatemala. And El Salvador was alone for years in its official recognition of the Japanese puppet state of Manchukuo.

Panama avoided any action which might displease its sponsor and benefactor, the United States, but the dominant state in Central America, Mexico, continued during 1937 to move directly away from Fascism in the direction of a Socialist state.[1]

MEXICO FOR THE MEXICANS

When Mexico's longtime political boss, General Plutarco Elias Calles, hand-picked and installed Lazaro Cardenas in the presidency of Mexico in 1934, he did so with perfect confidence in his ability to control the new executive. He soon found he was badly in error. Cardenas not only kicked him out of the country (April, 1936), but he began actually reading Mexico's radical constitution, and carrying out the policies outlined therein to restore Mexico to the Mexicans.

Soon after his election, President Cardenas announced a Six Year Plan calling for socialized education for the masses, improved housing and better living standards for workers, redistribution of land among the peasants who had existed for hundreds of years in a state of virtual serfdom on the great haciendas of the landed gentry, and the "Mexicanization" of all industries dominated by foreign capital.

By September, 1937, when he addressed Mexico's 37th Congress, Cardenas was able to declare that the Six-Year Plan was "30 per cent complete." He had expropriated 24,000,000 acres of land from the great hacienda owners, many of them foreigners, and distributed it among the peasantry. Former owners of the land were paid off in bonds which might or might not

[1] In the Caribbean Cuba continued under the iron hand of its dictator, Colonel Fulgencio Batista, who was careful to preserve the **forms of Democracy.**

be redeemed by the Government. Machinery and equipment on the estates was in most cases paid for in cash. When his Minister of Agriculture, the potent General Saturnino Cedillo, objected to his land distribution program he accepted his resignation, forced him to submit to his rule despite the General's private army of 7,000 men in the state of San Luis Potosi. He could also point to significant wage increases of 15 to 20 per cent for workers under his regime.

Early in the summer he ordered the nationalization of the railroads. About the same time he began setting up government-dominated national and state agricultural associations to allot production quotas, fix prices and market crops. He established an export-import bank to find markets, advise on production needs and restrictions of imports. And he gave notice that Mexico's large industries, most of which were dominated by foreigners, would soon be brought under Government control.

Mexicanization of the Oil Industry. Focus of the 1937 drive to return industries to Mexican ownership was the great petroleum industry, controlled largely by British, French, and American oil interests which had a half billion dollars invested. In March the Government established a National Petroleum Administration with the understanding that it would not only compete on a privileged basis with the foreign-owned oil companies, but would take them over as soon as it was equipped to do so. In June the 18,000 employees of the foreign oil companies went out on strike for higher wages. When the strike threatened to develop into a general strike of all Mexican workers, the Government stepped in with compulsory arbitration, stopped it, and, after making a survey of the companies' financial condition, ordered them to up wages to the amount of $7,200,000 a year. The oil companies had been prepared to grant a pay rise costing them $3,500,000 annually, but they refused to pay the larger increase, contending it would bankrupt them. They finally threatened to close down.

The Government responded early in November by decreeing the nationalization of 2,000,000 acres of oil lands held largely by foreign concerns. Three hundred and fifty thousand acres under lease to the Standard Oil of California was seized and turned over to the National Petroleum Administration, together with 500,000 acres leased to a French concern.

British Deal. This caused the British to run for cover with a separate deal which promised to become a model for future dealings between the Mexican government and those foreign concerns which were suffered to continue operating until Mexico could dig up enough capital and technicians to provide efficient home management. In return for concessions in a rich oil district, the Royal Dutch-owned Mexican Eagle Oil Company, granted record high royalties to the Government ranging from 15 to 35 per cent. There were also rumors of a $5,000,000 loan to the Mexican treasury from British sources. Britain thus protected herself against the heavy dependence for oil upon Iraq, lying inconveniently on the far end of the troubled Mediterranean.

American interests hoped for a similar deal. But Cardenas had again given startling notice of his intention to restore Mexico to the Mexicans. And the nation's mining industry, 90 per cent foreign-owned, shuddered at the thought that it might be next on the Mexicanization program.

NORTH AMERICAN STATESMEN

Top Left: President Cardenas of Mexico (Newsphotos). *Top Right:* Cordell Hull with Ambassador-at-large Norman H. Davis (Life Magazine). *Bottom:* Ontario's premier, Mitchell Hepburn, rejects C.I.O. (Life Magazine).

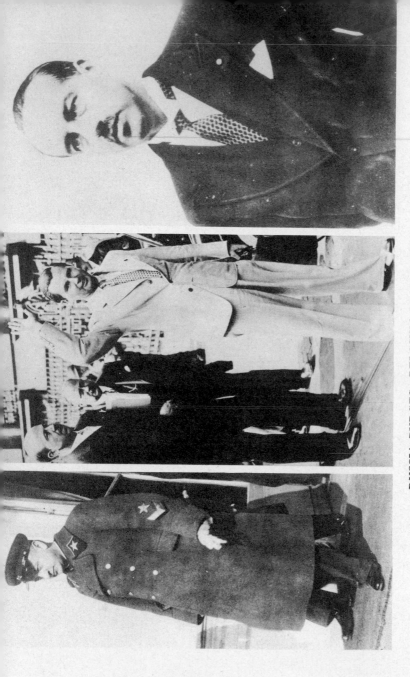

RUSSIA PURGES—BELGIUM REMAINS DEMOCRATIC

Left: Marshal Tukhachevsky executed for treason (International News). *Center*: Léon Degrelle, Belgium's would-be Führer, loses at polls (Acme). *Right*: Premier Paul van Zeeland forced out of office (Acme).

CHAPTER XVI

BELGIUM RETURNS TO 1914

Belgium's thoughtful intelligent young King Leopold III was keenly alive to the mad world arms race which threatened another European debacle in which his little nation would once more occupy a strategic and dangerous battleground position between conflicting armies. He struggled valiantly during 1937 to bring not only security to his own people, but peace to the world. By the end of the year he had brought Belgium to the best diplomatic position it had occupied since before the World War, and had struck at the very roots of modern warfare by sounding a call for international co-operation aimed at solving the economic problems facing the nations of the world.

War Preparations. In 1936 the great powers of the world spent the following sums either preparing for a war of aggression or building a defense system against expected attack:

Russia	$2,963,000,000	(one-fifth of entire Soviet budget)
Germany	2,600,000,000	
United States	964,000,000	
Italy	870,000,000	
Britain	846,000,000	
France	716,000,000	
Japan	307,000,000	

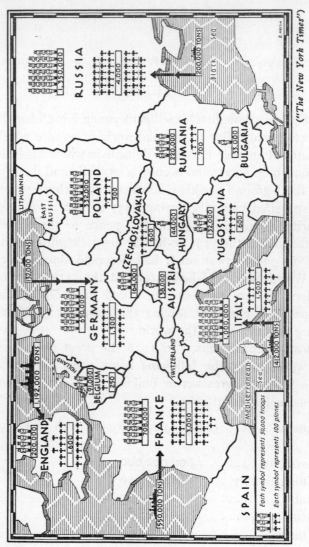

("The New York Times")

Comparative Military Strength of European Nations in 1937.

Adding to these astronomical figures the expenditures of lesser nations brought the total world armament bill to $10,730,000,000. Germany had spent more than the three greatest democracies, England, the United States, France, combined. Taken together, Russia and Germany had spent more than all the rest of the world. And in 1937 the figures for all nations were even greater, with England committed to a policy of spending $5,000,000 every week day for the next five years until $7,500,000,000 had been poured into guns, ships, and planes.[1] Every other power not already fighting was convinced that war was just around the corner, might course over the face of the globe from the civil war in Spain, the clash of arms in the Far East, or from some other now smoldering source.

These dreary facts, when placed alongside the miserable failures of the League of Nations, the Kellogg Pact to outlaw war, and all other attempts at solving the problem of war without taking into account its economic origins, led the Belgian monarch to set his house in order as best he could against a mighty military array with which his poor treasury could not hope to compete. Germany's march into the Rhineland in the spring of 1936 had borne home the danger of Belgium's position as a guarantor of the Locarno Treaty. And as soon as the crisis raised by this treaty violation had passed, Leopold gave warning, in the fall of that year, that his nation would henceforth "follow a policy strictly and exclusively Belgian."

"Political Bargain of the Century." He amplified

[1] Total world expenditures for arms in 1937 estimated at $12,000,000,000.

this statement the following spring at London when he conferred with British foreign office officials on the role of his nation in the next great war. Out of this conference and others with French officials came what one observer termed the "political bargain of the century." France and Britain formally acknowledged the new Belgian policy. Making a virtue of necessity, both France and Britain agreed to release Belgium from her Locarno promise to defend them from attack, but maintained their own pledge, from motives of self-interest, to fight if Belgium is invaded.

Turning next to Germany, Leopold, through his German ambassador Viscount Jacques Davignon, exacted a similar promise from Hitler in October. "The German Government," read the text of this treaty, "is ready, just as the British and French Governments, to grant assistance to Belgium in case she should become the object of aggression or invasion. . . . It confirms its determination under no circumstances to impair such inviolability . . . except, of course, in case of an armed conflict . . . in which Belgium should participate in military action . . . against Germany." Thus, aside from being bound by the cumbersome Covenant of the League of Nations to join with other members in resisting international aggression, Belgium was virtually as neutral as in 1914.

"For the Solution of Economic Problems." After the neutrality pledge had been granted by Britain and France, and after the January speech of Hitler at the opening of the Reichstag had made it obvious that Germany was prepared to do the same, Europe buzzed with rumors that Belgium would take the lead in a move to assure world peace through the medium of a world economic conference of some sort. From London came reports that Britain and France were using Belgium to front for them in a sincere peace move. When the Belgian Premier, Paul Van Zeeland, came to the United States in June to accept an honorary degree from Princeton University, there was much talk to the effect that President Roosevelt, on whom Van Zeeland called at the White House, was also involved in the scheme to promote a world organization to iron out economic inequalities.

Then late in July the Belgian plan was announced to the world in a letter from Leopold to his Premier, Van Zeeland. Widely hailed in the press of London and France, commended by U. S. Secretary Hull, the letter read:

"It is essential to create an organization for study, whose economic value would be marked by its triple characteristics—universality; permanence; independence. . . . It would have to be as independent as possible of nationalist influence. . . . Neither lowering of customs barriers, nor any other partial measure would put an end to the disorders which threaten peace. If we really are to avoid war and bring back humanity to more peaceful sentiments, we must have the courage to face economic questions in their broadest aspect and find a solution for such great problems threatening peace as these: (1) the distribution of raw materials; (2) apportionment of the

elements of monetary exchange; (3) distribution of
employment; (4) establishing an equilibrium between agricultural and industrial nations.

"I do not delude myself about the difficulties. At
the same time I am convinced that the moment is
favorable for the attempt. We would give humanity,
especially the Far Eastern Countries, not words, but
proofs that the Western countries have, above their
more immediate problems of material nature, a spiritual force emanating from the spirit of brotherhood." [1]

Even before the letter was published, however, the
"Far Eastern Countries" were already at war. And
the happenings in Spain cast a dubious light on the
question of any strong "spiritual force" in the Western
countries. (See Chapter on Religion.) Yet the peace-
minded peoples of the world saw in the Belgian suggestion a glimmer of hope for a more rational day
ahead. Most of them feared, however, that it might
take another great war to produce the kind of idealism
under which such a plan might blossom into effectiveness.

Van Zeeland Out. Before Premier Van Zeeland
had an opportunity to carry out his king's request, he
had himself been forced out of office. Heading a loose
coalition of Catholics, Liberals, Socialists, and Communists since 1935, Van Zeeland was credited with
having used his knowledge as a banker and economist

[1] Nobel peace prize for 1937 went not to Leopold but to Britain's
Viscount Cecil of Chelwood, President of the League of Nations
Union.

to avert a financial crisis in Belgium and restore a
measure of prosperity under a sort of New Deal similar to that of the United States. His arch-enemy was
the 30-year-old Léon Degrelle, leader of a Belgian
Fascist party called the Rexists. In April Degrelle
challenged the Premier to resign and compete against
him in a Parliamentary election from the Brussels
district. Van Zeeland accepted the challenge. Although Degrelle made a show of being a champion of
the Catholic Church, the Primate of Belgium, Cardinal van Roey, aware of the fate of the Church in
Germany whence came Degrelle's backing and ideas,
issued a public appeal to defeat the Rexist as "a
danger to country and Church." The Premier won
the contest 275,840 to 69,242 in what was widely
hailed as a "victory for democracy."

In September, Degrelle made sensational charges
against the Premier to the effect that he had been
accepting pay from the National Bank of Belgium
while serving as Premier. Van Zeeland had been vice-
governor of the Bank before taking the premiership,
and he denied having received any compensation since
leaving its employ except for work done previous to
his resignation from the bank. A vote of confidence
in the Belgian Parliament testified to his "integrity
and disinterestedness," but Degrelle kept hammering
away with his charges, indicating political influence in
the bank's affairs, until public suspicion grew great,
and Van Zeeland resigned.

Henri de Man, a mild Socialist who had been Finance Minister in the Van Zeeland cabinet, tried to

form a government but was unsuccessful. Then, because he was anxious to go to England to keep in touch with any Franco-British plan to dispose of the African colonies his nation had acquired from Germany after the World War, and hated to leave the government without a leader, Leopold persuaded Van Zeeland to stay on as premier until he returned early in December.

Finally, Paul Emile Janson, another statesman whose views coincided with those of Van Zeeland, mustered a majority in the Chamber behind him and became the first Liberal Premier of Belgium since 1884. His cabinet was simply a reshuffle of the Van Zeeland group, and he promised to continue the Van Zeeland policy of keep down prices and the cost of living. He promised also to carry forward Van Zeeland's extension of unemployment insurance, health insurance, and old age pensions—the principal elements in the New Deal Van Zeeland had brought the Belgians. And he indicated he would back up his king's newfound policy when he declared, "My new government will continue Belgium's policy of steering clear of foreign alliances."

But most Belgians believed that as soon as the state investigation of the Rexist charges cleared his skirts, Paul Van Zeeland would be back at the head of their government. Perhaps then Belgium might be able to push ahead with the plan to bring light into a world darkened by war clouds by obtaining international cooperation in the move to recognize and eliminate the economic causes of war.

But cynics would pooh pooh the Belgian king's plan, arms manufacturers would sabotage it as they had all previous similar attempts, and even those who believed Leopold on the right track would wonder whether this idealism had any chance in a world whose psychology was fast becoming one of "When," not "If" the universal war comes.

PART III
LITERATURE AND THE ARTS

CHAPTER XVII

SCREEN AND STAGE

Movie Business Best Since 1929. During the twelve months ending August 1, 1937, the flicker public flocked to the movies at the rate of 88,000,000 a week; paid an average daily admission of 22 cents. (Average weekly attendance in 1936 was only 80,000,-000.) Producers found that this year's public was more choosy about its entertainment and went shopping for pictures it wanted. Result was more "top flight" pictures. To the industry's apparent surprise, this resulted in unforeseen benefits. The pictures were good enough to step up the box office, to keep the censors from cracking down as much or as heavily as usual. And theater men were pleased because they resulted in longer runs. Air-conditioning in scores more theaters brought better summer business. It was a good year.

Double Feature Boycott. Women in Nutley, New Jersey, in October boldly started a boycott on the double feature—more evidence of the public's "choosiness" concerning entertainment. Nutley's boycotting women got swift and sympathetic response in every state. But Gilbert Seldes points out in *Scribner's Magazine* that attacking the exhibitor will not check the evil. He says the exhibitor is "victim of the pro-

416

ducer, and what the producer is making today the exhibitor is more or less compelled to show tomorrow." He feels that riddance of the double feature with its evils of riding a poor show on the back of a good one, its heavy strain on eyes and patience, can be gotten only if those who want change primarily go after the studios and not the exhibitors.

MOVIE AWARDS FOR 1936

Passing upon movies produced and released in the United States in 1936, the Academy of Motion Picture Arts and Sciences last March made the following awards:

Best picture—*The Story of Louis Pasteur*.

Best actress—Luise Rainer for her performance in *The Great Ziegfeld*.

Best actor—Paul Muni for his portrayal of Pasteur in *The Story of Louis Pasteur*.

Best direction—Frank Capra for his direction of *Mr. Deeds Goes to Town*.

The New York Film Critics, voting by closed ballot, made their second annual awards for pictures released during 1936:

Best picture—*Mr. Deeds Goes to Town*.

Best actress—Luise Rainer in *The Great Ziegfeld*.

Best actor—Walter Huston in *Dodsworth*.

Best direction—Rouben Mamoulian for his handling of *The Gay Desperado*.

Best foreign-language picture—*La Kermesse Heroique* (Carnival in Flanders).

Broadway Statistics. With super-night clubs, cabarets, unit-shows, movies to compete with, Broadway "legitimate" box offices showed about the same gross intake for 1936-37 as for 1935-36, but other records for the stage were less favorable. Hits—any show that runs 100 performances—were fewer, and the number of New York productions dwindled. *Billboard* listed only 24 hits against 34 the previous year. (During the 1925-26 season, number of hits went up to 74.) Productions numbered only 125, compared to 138 in 1935-36. The percentage of failures among all plays produced for the year ending June 1937 was up to 76 per cent; in June 1936 the figure stood at 68 per cent.

Revival of classics cheered those who think quality will save the show business. As proof, they point to such successes as *Hamlet, Richard II, The Country Wife, Candida*.

Musicals seemed on the downslide. There were only ten among the commercial premières, and never more than five running at a time. *Billboard* shows that 45 per cent of musicals were failures, against 18 per cent the previous season.

Many feel that only a cut in the number of plays, with emphasis on the best, will enable the stage to compete with other forms of entertainment.

TOP FLIGHT MOVIES

"Captains Courageous." Picture that made perhaps greatest impression upon audiences was one with social implications—*Captains Courageous* (MGM). Story was based on Kipling's novel of the same title. A young, wealthy, spoiled brat of a boy (Freddie Bartholomew) was accidentally forced to live and fish with fishermen in a cod schooner off the Grand Banks. Manuel (Spencer Tracy), most understanding tough guy on the boat, by friendship, beatings, and scorn, changed the brat into a stout normal little fellow. Other players in this salty story directed by Victor Fleming were Lionel Barrymore, Melvyn Douglass, Charles Grapewin. Pictured were some of the best nautical shots ever thrown on a screen. It is one of the unforgettable films of any season; Freddie Bartholomew did his best piece of acting and Mr. Tracy's performance may bring him the Academy Award.

"The Good Earth." Another of Metro-Goldwyn-Mayer's social dramas, dealing, however, with problems of the Chinese. The story was based on the novel by Pearl Buck, the play by Owen and Donald Davis. On his wedding day, Wang (Paul Muni) has mixed feelings as he goes to the Great House to meet his bride O-Lan (Luise Rainer) for the first time. Their wedding, birth of their sons, starvation during drouths, locust plagues, terror and revolution are amazingly and convincingly recorded. Luise Rainer gave a beautiful performance. Katharine Best of *Stage* felt that Director Sidney Franklin "made a masterpiece of a masterpiece."

"Topper." Topping the list of "light, dramatic compositions in which great latitude is allowed as to probability of happenings and naturalness of characters" is *Topper* (MGM). Thorne Smith's novel was basis of the cinematic version with direction by Norman Z.

McLeod. A young married couple (Constance Bennett and Cary Grant) are killed in a smashup. Their astral bodies rise, and together they decide to do their one good deed—free their hen-pecked banker friend, Topper (Roland Young), from his routine, humdrum life. Because they have unusual powers, they perform unusual tricks. Screamingly funny, they finally teach Topper to forget his inhibitions. Billie Burke was the domineering wife. *Topper* was the talk of dinner parties and "breaker-up" of bridge games. Mordaunt Hall commented: "It can boast of being pure cinematic entertainment, for such tricks are naturally beyond the possibilities of the stage."

"Day at the Races." In a class of its own is this racy film, seventh to be made by the Marx Brothers (MGM). Story: Maureen O'Sullivan operates a run-down sanitarium. Her fiancé lays out all his money on a race horse that looks like a total loss. The romance and their fortunes can be saved only if they locate a certain Doc Hackenbush to cater to the neurotic whims of a wealthy patient. The porter and a jockey import a horse doctor who takes care of the patient's needs. After many shocks and surprises it is discovered that the nag is a steeplechaser. Quote from *News-Week:* "At least 200 assaults on audience risibilities are included—along with a plot . . . which adequately serves as a setting for the Marx Brothers' zany brand of comedy."

"Elephant Boy." Katharine Best wrote: "If you remember *Man of Aran,* I need only mention that the man who made (it) has just completed *Elephant Boy,*

and you should already have your hat and coat on."
Robert H. Flaherty and Zolton Korda directed this
adventure film. The story came from a short tale of
Kipling's, "Toomai of the Elephants," and the filming
was done in Mysori, India, by an English company.
The boy, Toomai (Sabu), is descended from four generations of mahouts. His father is killed in a tiger hunt.
The elephant he had been riding, and which was rid-
den by his father and grandfather, is taken away and
given to another driver. Frank Nugent says *Elephant
Boy* "may be accounted one of the most likable of
the jungle pictures."

"Maytime." "[It is the] loudest, most lavish and
most lushly sentimental operetta of the season. . . .
Its singing is the best that Jeannette MacDonald and
Nelson Eddy have ever committed to a sound track."
Thus *Time* commented on MGM's *Maytime*, which no
one missed seeing. John Barrymore assisted the cast,
and responsible for the direction was Robert Z. Leonard; for the music, Sigmund Romberg. Plot of *Maytime* was told in flashback. It is May Day and an
elderly recluse tells her life story to a young girl who
has quarreled with her fiancé over pursuing an operatic career. The recluse had been a great prima donna,
and scenes move from her success at the court of Louis
Napoleon to other successes that followed.

"100 Men and a Girl." Universal's contribution to
the year's entertainment was this knockout musical
film. Charming Deanna Durbin portrays a singer who
organizes an orchestra of 100 unemployed men. They
are offered a radio contract if they can secure an out-

standing director, and after many difficulties, Miss
Durbin persuades Leopold Stokowski to be their leader.
Adolphe Menjou, Alice Brady, Eugene Pallette, Mischa
Auer, under the direction of Henry Koster, made *100
Men and a Girl* the success it was. Howard Barnes
commented: "As a straight photoplay [it] is far from
distinguished, but as a show about an epochal adolescent, set to great music, it is nothing short of triumphant."

"**Shall We Dance?**" Another musical, another
Fred Astaire-Ginger Rogers performance—another success was this RKO film. Decidedly a weak, overworked story, but box office receipts were more than
satisfactory.

"**Camille.**" This portrait of "the remorseful lady of
the boudoir" was considered by many critics as Miss
Garbo's greatest piece of acting. They also felt that
she made Robert Taylor (Armand) play far beyond
any talent he had previously shown. The final heart-
wrenching death scene accounted for more moist hand-
kerchiefs than any love story ever played. George
Cukor gave able direction to *Camille* (MGM).

"**A Star Is Born.**" Another tragedy, this time by
United Artists, with Adolphe Menjou, May Robson,
Andy Devine, Lionel Stander assisting Janet Gaynor
and Frederic March. *A Star Is Born* is the first modern story in Technicolor, and also the first Technicolor
to be as unselfconscious as black and white. The picture starts off as an amusing satire on Hollywood
mores, but soon settles down to portraying the downfall of a great film idol (Frederic March). He be-

comes a slave to drink, falls in love with a little screen-struck girl (Janet Gaynor), and commits suicide when he discovers he is in the way of her rising career. *Liberty's* critic thought that "March never has been better than as the skidding favorite. William Wellman's direction is shrewd and adroit."

"Stage Door." Most interesting movie of the year in one respect—it demonstrates the superiority of screen over stage as a medium for presentation of a stage play. Frank Nugent called it "a magnificently devastating reply on Hollywood's behalf to all the catty little remarks that George Kaufman and Edna Ferber had made about it in their play." It is their story of a group of girls living in an actor's boarding house; the ups and downs in the struggle to win fame on the stage. Katharine Hepburn and Ginger Rogers acted far above their usual heads. RKO produced *Stage Door* under Gregory La Cava's direction.

"Life of Emile Zola." Finest biographical movie of 1937 came from cinematic pioneers in that field—Warner Brothers. It is the story of Emile Zola—the man whose passion for truth and justice led him to fight a nation in his aim to free the exiled Captain Alfred Dreyfus. Paul Muni plays Zola with great dramatic strength—perhaps even greater than his *The Story of Louis Pasteur*. Surely the *Life of Emile Zola* will find a place among 1937's "Best Ten." To those keen about movie development, this picture was a landmark in that it successfully experimented with long sustained, uninterrupted speeches without any lapse of audience interest.

"Lost Horizon." This fantasy by Columbia Pictures, based on the novel of the same title by James Hilton, was another feather in Director Frank Capra's cap. It is the strange tale of a small group of travelers in China forced to flee because of an insurrection. They are kidnaped and taken by plane into an escapist's Utopia—a Tibetan lamasary. Ronald Colman, Jane Wyatt, Margo, and Edward Everett Horton head the cast. The picture has the best photography and sets of the year, and can easily take its place with the prestige pictures of the film industry.

Other Screen Events. *They Gave Him a Gun*— an attempt to deal with social problem. *Heidi*—Shirley Temple's best of 1937. *Double Wedding*—outright lunacy all the way. *Emperor's Candlesticks*—threadbare theme but fair entertainment. *Double or Nothing* —a Crosby-Raye combination with a couple of catchy tunes. *Thin Ice*—Sonja Henie's skating is extraordinarily effective. *Conquest*—a true but dull account of the romance between Napoleon and Countess Walewska. *Victoria*—kindly portrait of the widow of Windsor. *Easy Living*—wild farce about a poor stenographer, sable coats. *It's Love I'm After*—satiric comedy with Bette Davis and Leslie Howard as Shakespearian stars. *The Prisoner of Zenda*—a grand show. *Lancer Spy*—adventure film. *Hurricane*—an epic which glorifies man's pitiful struggle against the sea. *Damsel in Distress*—fine farce with Fred Astaire, Burns and Allen. *Nothing Sacred*—written by Ben Hecht and one of the best comedies of the year.

DOCUMENTARY FILMS

Paul Rotha, in an article on the British Documentary Film, makes this statement: "The documentary film has as its basis a simple set of beliefs: that the modern world turns on the fluctuations of industry; that each one of us must know more about its happenings; and that, if we are to be efficient citizens, we must get a closer understanding of the workings of the world in which we live. The film, with its power to "bring alive" modern event and modern experience, with its power to dramatize and report, is the most suitable medium to undertake this task."

America made a useful start in the documentary movement last year with *The Plow That Broke the Plains*. Second documentary film produced by our federal government was released this year—*The River*. It showed causes and effects of Mississippi floods, soil erosion, reforesting, dams, and power in the TVA.

The American Council on Education found that more than 48,000 reels of instructional motion pictures and 10,000 projectors are now owned by elementary and secondary schools in the United States. Over 400 new film subjects, produced by thirteen government bureaus, are available for free distribution to schools.

STAGE HITS

On the Road. Because of the perseverance of a few of the best actors in first class performances, "The Road" has again been revived. After a long famine, inland cities are seeing some of the best plays that Broadway offered last year.

Heading the list of past-season hits that are touring is *Victoria Regina*. Helen Hayes is taking last season's cast almost intact across the country. There is one major change—Werner Bateman has replaced Vincent Price in the role of Prince Albert.

Robert Henderson has a company playing *Tonite at 8:30*. *You Can't Take It with You* is being played by several companies, has even crossed the Atlantic to play in England. *Room Service, Brother Rat, Tovarich, The Women, Yes, My Darling Daughter*— all are enjoying extended runs in centers from Chicago to Seattle.

Holdovers in New York. There's always *Tobacco Road*, which opened December 4, 1933, and is still showing. Several plays that opened late last season, during February, March and even May, are still holding their own—with "absolutely no signs of gaiety diminishing": *Brother Rat*—all about young men in a military institute. *Having Wonderful Time*—a Bronx stenographer on vacation in the Berkshires meets a young lawyer who is acting as a waiter; it has the authentic Jewish-American sense of humor. *Room Service*—a shoestring producer and his actors cause loud laughter when they meet difficulties in paying their hotel bill. *The Women*—a vitriolic piece about Park Avenue ladies who "play with each other's hearts and husbands." *Yes, My Darling Daughter*—comedy, a contented matron objects when her daughter wants to have an affair similar to mother's early life in Greenwich Village. *You Can't Take It with You*—a charade about the Sycamore family, who go in for snake-collecting, making firecrackers and income-tax dodging. *Babes in Arms*—musical comedy with sure-fire songs.

NEW PLAYS ON BROADWAY

"Amphitryon 38." To be sure, this sumptuous 1937 legend of the loves of Gods and men is not strictly in accordance with facts. But M. Giraudoux and S. N. Behrman, according to Brooks Atkinson, have clothed "a bedroom farce and Restoration comedy in the dress of classical times. In this instance the result is a suave and crackling performance of a bawdy jest." Lee Simonson's dramatic settings, the superb acting of Alfred Lunt and Lynn Fontanne have made *Amphitryon 38* a beautiful, intellectually diverting production that lives up to all the hullabaloo.

"Susan and God." This portrait of a confused, ridiculous woman by Rachel Crothers seemed to be the first thoroughly enjoyable comedy of the 1937 season. There is no doubt that Gertrude Lawrence's portrayal of Susan helped make it so. Susan is a vain and indulgent woman of the world who by right of her interest in the Oxford movement meddles in other people's affairs. Finally her husband decides the creed may be just the thing to straighten out their own family. The sane humor of the play and Miss Lawrence's acting—her spontaneous, unexpected exaggerations of voice and manner—are well met.

"French Without Tears." This well-mannered light comedy, starring Penelope Dudley Ward and

Frank Lawton, was imported after a successful run in London. In it, a group of young Englishmen and an English girl are studying French on the Riviera. The young lady attempts to seduce all the young men, and when one of them (Lawton) attempts to save the honor of two others, he becomes involved himself.

"Blow Ye Winds." Some of the conversation in this play dealing with married life is stimulating, but some is boring. Henry Fonda likes to live on a sailboat; Doris Dalton likes her Ph.D. They marry; he goes to work in an office, but the work irritates him and he irritates Doris. A last-minute reunion prevents divorce.

"I'd Rather Be Right." Moss Hart and George Kaufman wrote this musical comedy, then gave it to George Cohan. It's his show! Ruth Sedgwick refers to the authors of this political satire as "two New Dealers in disguise . . . and they've practically insured Franklin D. the First his third term already." Mr. Roosevelt is a "perplexed and loveable gentleman, surrounded by a group of . . . people who spend an evening racking what is left of their brains and the country's resources trying to balance the budget." Mr. Cohan—America's greatest trouper—is in top form throughout this musical fandango of "good, clean fun" and honest sentiment.

"The Star Wagon." Another of Maxwell Anderson's works, with Burgess Meredith as a humble inventor and Lillian Gish as his drab and discontented wife. Not as great as Maxwell Anderson's other plays, yet

Ruth Sedgwick called it a "tender, nostalgic and humorous play."

Hopeful Plays. *George and Margaret*—a triumph from London about the dizzy Garth-Bander family. *The Fireman's Flame*—another Music Hall melodrama where everybody, including the audience, sings and drinks. *The Lady Has a Heart*—Elissa Landi and Vincent Price mixed up with politics and Parliament. *To Quito and Back*—Ben Hecht's wit and crackling dialogue somewhat spoiled by unfortunate casting. *Angel Island*—a murder mystery well done. *Golden Boy*—herewith Clifford Odets re-establishes the Group Theatre in a drama about a prizefighter who struggles for fame and money. *The Ghost of Yankee Doodle*—written by Sidney Howard especially for Ethel Barrymore. *Madame Bovary*—Theatre Guild version of Flaubert's novel with Constance Cummings in the lead. *Of Mice and Men*—John Steinbeck's dramatization of his own novel. *Virginia*—musical spectacle at Rockefeller Center about English actors who came over here during colonial times. *The Doll's House*—a Theatre Guild revival of Ibsen's controversy on marriage. *Father Malachy's Miracle*—a genial, refreshing presentation based on Bruce Marshall's book.

FEDERAL THEATRE

The most stupendous undertaking any manager ever faced—such is Hallie Flanagan's task. As Director of the Federal Theatre Project, she has made a distinguished record: over 100 new plays dealing with or relating to the American scene, other circuses, ballets,

musical comedies, children's plays, Gilbert and Sullivan. During June, July and August, summer caravans
brought a variety of theater to the city parks. The
winter circuit took out, to 36 locations, four plays
every month. Nationwide cycles of O'Neill, Shaw are
planned. An outstanding event is presentation of Paul
Green's new play *The Lost Colony,* with music by
Kurt Weill.

Mrs. Flanagan hopes that the words "Federal Theatre on a marquee shall come to be the same guarantee
of excellence afforded by the Government stamp affixed
by the Bureau of Standards."

MISCELLANY

Outstanding, too, are these films: *Dead End*—very
much like the stage version; *The Spanish Earth*—story
of the Spanish revolution; *Saratoga*—all about horse
racing, starring the late Jean Harlow; *King Solomon's
Mines*—provides opportunity for Paul Robeson's singing; *Merry-Go-Round of 1938*—a "skedaddling musi-
comedy"; *First Lady*—dealing with female Washington; *True Confession*—a skillfully played "dizzy hay-
wire skit"; *Snow White*—Walt Disney's first seven-reel
animated cartoon.

At the year's end, *Father Malachy's Miracle, Of
Mice and Men, Susan and God* were among the most
popular plays on Broadway. Well received, too, were
these dramas: *Julius Caesar*—Shakespeare's play at
the newly formed Mercury Theatre, done in modern
dress, no scenery; *Edna His Wife*—"a good trick,"
adaptation by Cornelia Otis Skinner of the Margaret

Ayer Barnes novel; *Many Mansions*—a young minister
has difficulties because he is more liberal than his
parishoners; *Hooray for What*—Ed Wynn in a musical
show; *Barchester Towers*—Ina Claire in a dramatization of the Trollope novel.

Dummy Becomes Star. Neither the movies nor
the stage are responsible for the biggest news event of
1937 in the entertainment world. Charlie McCarthy,
that saucy, impish "smart aleck" of the radio, captures
first prize for popularity. Edgar Bergen, ventriloquist
since his Northwestern University days, made Charlie
the star of their act.

CHAPTER XVIII

ART IN 1937

Art, as always, was in 1937 what artists and the public made it. The artist creates art and in so doing makes art history; the public creates appreciation by its buying art, looking at and talking about art in all its forms from ashtrays, to clothes, to paintings, sculptures, buildings. The feelings roused in the spectator and the reader by new things in art activity are influenced by the particular approach which has guided his judgment. To the average layman, gradually becoming art conscious, theories of art creation mean little; the intentions of artists and designers probably mean less. The work stands or falls on the feeling it creates in the one who sees it, buys, uses it; and the pleasure that each man is ready to receive from paintings, buildings, statues is in direct ratio to how much he has thought, learned, and felt about them in the past. Consequently art is what we make it—what we believe it to be.

This principle of artists and public together making art contributed largely to what happened in the art world in 1937. Art flourished with many exhibitions in public and private galleries, the growth of new schools of thought, the gifts to the public by wealthy patrons of several famous art collections, and the creation of

432

endowments which will enable artists to continue researching and experimenting into the problems of the expressive and the graphic arts. "Art for Art's sake," functionalism, Americana, the Classic and various "isms" all played a part this year. And a review of the twelve-month period reveals both the struggle by the artist for expression and recognition, and increasing efforts by the public to gain a sympathetic understanding of what its artists mean and what they are trying to do. On the theory that art is what we make it, the following artists and organizations made art in 1937.

The New Bauhaus (International Style Comes to America). In Germany before the reign of Hitler and his Nazi control over German life in all phases, there existed an important educational organization known as the Bauhaus (i.e., building house) located in Dessau. The school had been founded in 1925 by a few men headed by the German architect, Walter Gropius, to unify the architectural and industrial design problems of the twentieth century. Included on the faculty was Ladislaus Moholy-Nagy, Hungarian designer. Students were given thorough courses in the use of materials employed in building and manufacture, working under designers and technicians to develop new designs by experimenting with recently discovered materials such as steel, glass, new tiles, plastics, and textiles. Two of the most successful contributions given to the world were indirect lighting and tubular furniture. Closed by Hitler in 1935 because of suspected communistic activities and a Nazi dislike of

modern plastic principles, the generating forces of the
Bauhaus, the school was abandoned and the men who
had directed the young minds of the students left
Germany. In 1937 the founder, Walter Gropius, was
appointed Professor of Architecture at Harvard and
later in the same year his assistant, Ladislaus Moholy-
Nagy became Director of the New Bauhaus, founded
in Chicago by the Chicago Association of Arts and Industries. It was believed by many observers that this
New Bauhaus was destined to become the leading influence on American design, as it had begun to be on
German, and that the Reich's loss was America's great
gain. A limited number of students began a year of
preparatory training similar to that at the old Bauhaus
but taking advantage of many new U. S. plastics and
advances in scientific discovery of material. Following the preliminary training there will be three years
of technical and practical work leading to a diploma
which will get the student ready to go on for two years
more of study in architecture. The success of the
New Bauhaus seems assured.

Exhibitions. The Modern Museum in New York
City richly stimulated art appreciation by hanging, in
December 1936-January 1937, the largest exhibition
of Surrealistic art ever assembled. Noted for their unusually fine showings of modern works of art, particularly the Cubist and Abstract exhibitions of 1935-1936,
the Museum sponsored the Surrealism show to give the
public a comprehensive idea of this particular approach
to art. A room devoted to the works of Chirico, the
modern Italian who is in some measure the father of

the surrealistic movement, was an important feature of the exhibition, containing many of his early paintings with poetic and metaphysical content.

In February the exhibition was moved to Philadelphia and shown at the Pennsylvania Museum of Art. Here "the fur tea cups, disembodied heads and limp watches of surrealism with their stupefying and senseless titles" brought thousands to the galleries. From Philadelphia the exhibit went on tour to Chicago, Minneapolis, and other major cities creating comment and sometimes bitter discussion and much joking wherever it appeared.

At the same time the Philadelphia Art Alliance exhibited an important collection of 138 non-object water colors and oils, called abstractions. These paintings, diametrically opposed in thought to the surrealist work, gave Philadelphians and others an opportunity to view these projections of art. Included in the latter show were paintings by Vasily Kandinsky, Rudolph Bauer and Ladislaus Moholy-Nagy, of Bauhaus fame. The abstract paintings, as shown here, did not attempt to represent or suggest concrete objects; they are exercises in pure form and complete in themselves.

The Carnegie International Exhibitions. Thirteen nations were represented in the 1937 Carnegie International Exhibition of Paintings in Pittsburgh. The showing was aptly described in an Art Digest caption which read:—"School of Paris Sweeps 1937 Carnegie International Awards," and justly so, as European painters received most of the coveted cash prizes. France's George Bracque was awarded first prize for his painting "Yellow Cloth," a still life bordering on pure abstraction, which fact caused consternation and much discussion by the traditional critics. Second award went to the Italian painter, Fellice Casorati, for a semi-nude titled "Woman Near a Table." Germany's Joseph Pieper, exhibiting in the United States for the first time, took third prize for his oil "A Family Portrait." The only American to score was Robert Philipp of New York City, who won first honorable mention for his "Dust to Dust," a powerful, dramatic and slightly morbid picturing of a burial. Other honorable mentions went to Oskar Kokoschka, one of the founders of German expressionism, for his landscape "Karlsbruche, Prague"; Emilio Grau-Sala of Spain for his "Carnival"; and Marcel Gromaire, France, took fourth honors with his canvas "The Night Watchman." The Alleghany County prize was given to "Still Life with Flowers" by Vaclav Spala, of Czechoslovakia.

The annual exhibit of the National Academy of Design was held in April, prize awards totaling $4,735. While few of the paintings shown surprised the critics, the exhibit was important in its obvious attempt to instill new life into the conservative Academy. Nineteen new names were added to the Academy rolls as Associate Painter Members, including John Steuart Curry, Guy Pene du Bois, Reginald Marsh and Frank Mechau, Jr.

Paintings by twenty-seven American artists were shown in the United States Pavilion at the Paris Exposition. Among the better known were John Sloan, Thomas Benton, Gifford Beal, John Steuart Curry,

"CLASSICS" IN THE MOVIES

Top: Freddie Bartholomew and Spencer Tracy in *Captains Courageous* (Metro-Goldwyn-Mayer). *Right:* Greta Garbo and Robert Taylor in *Camille* (Metro-Goldwyn-Mayer).

"COMEDY TOPS" IN THE MOVIES

Top: Roland Young, Constance Bennett and Cary Grant in
Topper (Metro-Goldwyn-Mayer). *Bottom:* Chico and Groucho
Marx in *A Day at the Races* (Metro-Goldwyn-Mayer).

Walt Kuhn, Ernest Fiene and George Bellows. The exhibit of sculpture for the same showing was submitted only by American sculptors residing in Paris.

In May a collection of prehistoric rock pictures was shown at the Modern Museum in New York, one of the significant exhibitions of the year. These excellent full scale water colors and photographic reproductions gave a clear picture of man making art during the Fourth Ice Age, two hundred centuries past. Artists, in particular, were deeply impressed with the water color copy of a mural found in the Mtoko Cave in Southern Rhodesia. Containing elephants and humans always drawn in a frontal, wedge trunk position, quagga, antelope and symbolic representations of rain, roots and mountains, the whole was worked into a lively and interesting composition skillfully handled by the prehistoric artist.

Photography, which has been taking over the representational function which once belonged solely to the graphic and plastic arts, illustrated its importance in this field at a comprehensive exhibition of photographic art shown at the Modern Museum. All phases were shown there from the early daguerreotypes through to the modern dynamic photos, dramatic miniature snaps, and micro photos. Throughout the year the number of national and international photographic salons held in the U. S. showed marked increase as did the swelling number of contributors and exhibitors emerging from the ranks of box-camera snapshotters into those of advanced amateurs and professionals.

Gifts. Great artists of the past, Raphael, Titian, Holbein, Giotto and a host of others, made art by a close study of nature and then attempted to express on canvas their reactions and feelings. The resulting paintings made it possible for other men in later times to make an art of collecting these works after time had stamped them as masterpieces. In this field Andrew W. Mellon and Jules S. Bache have risen high. Early in January, 1937, came the announcement that Mr. Mellon would give to the United States his collection of paintings with sufficient funds to provide for the erection of a National Gallery in which to house them. The paintings, gathered together over a period of forty years, contain scores of old masters representing many countries and periods, and form the largest and finest group ever presented to the American public. Lord Duveen called it "the greatest classical collection ever put together by one man." The new National Gallery Building in Washington, D. C., included in Mr. Mellon's gift, will be a classic structure built on low, long lines to harmonize with the surrounding architecture. It was designed by John Russell Pope.

However, when news of the establishment of this new National Gallery was made known and while the bill authorizing its acceptance by the government was still before Congress, a storm of protests arose from artists, both individually and collectively. Principal objection was to the terms and limitations set forth by Mr. Mellon in making his gift to the nation, particularly the fact that control of the Gallery was to be vested in a board dominated by the donor, and a clause which limited the acquisition of additional paintings to recognized masterpieces. Artists throughout the country believed that provision should be made for contemporary art. The passage of the bill was shepherded through Congress by Senator Connally with the opposition being led by Senators LaFollette of Wisconsin, Black of Alabama, Norris of Nebraska and O'Mahoney of Wyoming. Before passage of the bill, an amendment was attached permitting contemporary American artists to exhibit their work in the National Gallery with the approval of the trustees. This was agreed to by the Mellon representatives and on March 15th the bill passed both houses of Congress and the nation obtained a National Gallery and Museum of Art.

Encouraged by this reasonable success, artists immediately began a campaign to secure greater recognition for contemporary art, and to insure true representation of all phases of present-day art in public galleries.

Of no less importance is the Jules S. Bache Collection, given to the State of New York. This collection of seventy-seven paintings from Flemish, Dutch, German, French and English schools contains only masterpieces, all excellent examples of the schools and periods which produced them. Unlike the Mellon gift, the Bache group of paintings will be retained in Mr. Bache's home, which has become a public museum.

Another man of wealth who is helping to make art in a vital way is Solomon Guggenheim. Probably the leading collector of abstract, non-figurative paintings, he created in 1937 an endowment for abstract art. The

purpose of the endowment is to educate the public
in understanding and liking the abstract, and to encourage the development of appreciation by means of
lectures, scholarships, exhibitions and publications.

Federal Art Projects. The United States Government made art with another year of federal art patronage. The Division of Painting and Sculpture and
Federal Art Project under the direction of Holger Ca-
hill continued to assist needy artists and steadfastly
continued the plan to forge an American School. Murals, easel paintings, sculpture and applied art were
produced during the year; some of the work was praise-
worthy, some not important.

The Index of American Design, a comprehensive
reference work of characteristic American design of
all kinds, progressed a step nearer completion.

The Treasury Department's Division of Painting
and Sculpture continued to award commissions through
competition. Important mural designs painted in 1937
under the supervision of the Treasury Division included panels executed for a low cost federal housing
project in Stamford, Conn., by James Dougherty, Connecticut artist. Early transportation methods are de-
picted in the main sections of the mural; the old-fash-
ioned steam engine, horseless carriages of an experimental period and the Model T Ford. Dynamic designs reveal the fright of the public at the appearance
of these now antiquated modes of conveyance; the
Model T panel showed the joys and heartaches of
early motoring. During the year, Rockwell Kent finished two murals for the Post Office building in Wash-

ington, picturing the arrival of the first air-mail planes in Alaska and Puerto Rico. A short-lived controversy arose over the wording of an Eskimo message to the Puerto Ricans ("Go ahead. Let us change chiefs") which appeared in the Puerto Rico panel, making Kent a minor hero among hot-blooded Nationalists of that country. In April twelve painters and three sculptors were given commissions to decorate the new Interior Department building in Washington, the most important commissions since the completion of the work in the new Justice Department and Post Office Department buildings. Designs are to portray the undertakings of the Interior Department's bureaus—Mines, Education, General Land Office, Conservation, Reclamation, National Park Service and Indian Affairs. Artists selected were John Steuart Curry, University of Wisconsin; Nicolai Cikovsky, Alexandria, Va.; Maynard Dixon, San Francisco; Ernest Fiene, Southbury, Conn.; David McCosh, Portland, Ore.; Henry Varnum Poor, William Gropper, James M. Newell, all of New York City; Millard Sheets, Los Angeles; Edward Buk Ulreich, Kansas City; Harold Von Schmidt, Westport, Conn.; and Edgar Britton, Chicago. The sculptors are Boris Gilbertson, Chicago; Ralph Stackpole, San Francisco; and Henry Warneke, New York City.

Among other projects open to competition during the year were murals for post offices in San Antonio, Texas; Phoenix, Arizona; Wilmington, Delaware; post office, court house and custom house at Miami, Fla., and the court house at El Paso, Texas.

Indicative of the number of art undertakings com-

pleted by the Federal Art Project is the report of the
New York City area. 207,620 allocations of fine and
commercial art were made to state and municipal institutions. Mural projects, with an average of six or
more panels, totaled 134. 2,950 easel paintings were
distributed to schools as well as 4,000 prints. Busts,
plaques, panels and figures, including one large fountain, amounted to 204 pieces. In another field, the
Art Gallery Tours, a free service for the public, conducted 420 museum trips and held 122 lectures. The
visual education department, conducting educational,
cultural, and amusement films for under-privileged
children and adults, had an average weekly attendance
of 5,000 persons. 275 lectures were given housewives
by the Creative Home Planning division. In the section of Art Education the project had an average
weekly enrollment of 30,000 children and 7,000 adults
in the art classes taught by WPA art teachers. 706
exhibitions of Federal art work were held in and around
New York.

Discovery. Of great importance to fresco mural
painters was the discovery in 1937 of a method whereby
the plaster on which the painting is executed may be
kept workable twice as long as formerly. Kudos went
to a New York artist, Elizabeth Ely deVescovi Whitman, and a Mexican chemist of the University of Mexico, Gonzalez de la Vega.

Squabbles. Thomas Benton made art history in
Missouri in 1937 by painting the social record of the
State on the walls of the Capitol at Jefferson City.
The mural begins with the early trail life of the eight-

eenth century, portrays the slave block days, baptism by immersion, the James brothers, Ozark farms, the brewing industry of St. Louis, and ends with the introduction of Boss Prendergast into the modern Kansas City political scene. Applauded by some as a faithful portrayal of life in the State, others rose in righteous wrath to denounce it as an insult to Benton's native Missouri. Replying to the later criticism, the artist said: "I am an ordinary American, painting the world in front of me, and I have no time for hocus-pocus. I painted in Jesse James because he inaugurated a rather important business in the United States." The murals remain as painted.

Again in Missouri, a battle of words arose over a work of art when Carl Milles, Swedish-American sculptor, was commissioned to create a fountain for the public plaza opposite the Union Station in St. Louis. His completed plan for the fountain showed nude figures of heroic size representing the marriage of the Mississippi and the Missouri rivers. Mississippi, a young god, advances to his "bride," the Missouri, riding a giant fish and bearing a water lily in his hand. Tritons attend him, while reveling maidens swim around the coy and charming bride. A controversy arose immediately as to the fitness of the proposed statue, with the Municipal committee divided in their opinions—two against and four in favor of the fountain as designed. Said the Director of the Municipal Art Commission: "The work is not appropriate to St. Louis. What will people think of two nude figures being mar-

ried? Why, we might as well have a nudist camp down
on the city plaza."

The dissenting members of the committee favor a
group of pioneers or Indians gathered around a tepee
as a suitable subject. Artists and earnest lovers of art
entered the dispute, temporarily dormant, but to be
active again in 1938 when the fountain is scheduled
for completion. The majority vote of the committee
directed Carl Milles to continue his work as planned.
So in Missouri art stands one for Milles's classic and
one for Benton's American scene.

Organizations. Federal Art Projects and the need
for economic security were two factors which influenced groups of artists to unite in their common interests and purposes. The Artists' Union, product primarily of the government's participation in art, was
organized in various centers throughout the country
to foster economic security for its members. The
first crucial test for the Union came in July when a
reduction in WPA personnel was announced by the
government. Joining with organized musicians, writers
and actors on WPA rolls, the artists fought to stop the
wholesale dismissals from projects. The government,
however, held firm in its decision to reduce personnel,
and the Union, defeated but not disheartened, immediately transferred its energies to working for the passage of a Federal Art Bill in 1938; a bill which will
provide for permanent government art patronage.

A second organization, The American Artists Congress, became definitely a part of the national art life
in 1937. Pledged to the promotion of art and freedom

MUSIC ON THE AIR

Top: CBS's Symphony Orchestra (Columbia Broadcasting System). *Center:* NBC's Symphony Orchestra (National Broadcasting Company). *Right:* NBC scoops Toscanini for ten symphony concerts (National Broadcasting Company).

"BEST-SELLER" AUTHORS

Left: Hendrik Willem Van Loon's *The Arts* makes Americans "art" conscious. *Right:* Ernest Hemingway's *To Have and Have Not* rouses heated controversy (Helen Breaker, Paris).

of artistic expression, the Congress held its first National Membership Exhibitions in seven cities during April. Representing their respective regions were New York, Philadelphia, Cleveland, Detroit, New Orleans, Los Angeles and Portland, Ore. The exhibit shown at Rockefeller Center was highly regarded by the critics, who recognized the function of the Congress. George Biddle's portrait of Margaret Zorach, wife of sculptor William Zorach, was purchased by the Metropolitan Museum. Other activities sponsored during the year included a circulating exhibit of prints, "America Today," a satirical portrait show and an exhibit "Against War and Fascism." The second meeting of the Congress held in New York in December became International in tone with the arrival of a group of foreign painters and sculptors and with the warm message from Pablo Picasso, famed Spanish artist.

While architecture was not a prominent factor in making art in 1937, the announcement made by the Modern Museum that plans for a new building had been completed raised cheers among modernists. Having become the leading American art institution during its eight years of existence, the Museum outgrew original quarters and this year begins erection of the first functional museum building in the United States. Built of concrete, white marble, dark stone, glass bricks and plate glass, it will be distinctly modern. Walls on the ground floor will be mainly of glass so that passers-by on 53rd Street will see temporary exhibitions as in store windows. Upper floors will be exhibition

rooms of the most modern design, with the film library
and projection rooms on the top floor.

Also meriting mention was the dedication on September 6th of the memorial monument to Will Rogers,
American humorist. The tower memorial, conceived
and financed by Spencer Penrose, sportsman and art
patron, has been erected on a promontory of Cheyenne
Mountain, half a mile south of Colorado Springs, Colo.
The light, pink spire is located at an elevation of 9,000
feet, so high that clouds float below it, entirely shut-
ting off this "Shrine to the Sun" from the rest of the
world. At night a beacon, visible for a distance of
125 miles, guides flyers on the transcontinental air
routes. The interior of the shrine contains two murals
by Randall Davey of Santa Fe, N. M.; one pictures
the history of the Pike's Peak region, while the other
outlines the life of the lovable Will Rogers. A larger-
than-life size bust of the humorist is placed in one of
the memorial rooms, the work of Jo Davidson.

Spanish Art Saved. With war tensions up throughout the world and civil war a reality in Spain, a country of great artistic wealth, many an art lover has
wondered how the masterpieces of paintings, sculpture
and architecture fared during blasts of air bombs, ex-
plosions of heavy shells. Some facts have come to light
regarding the salvaging and protection of art works
in Spain. On August 1st, two weeks after fighting
began, the Junta of Requisition and Protection of Artistic Patrimony was organized to protect treasures in
Madrid. The famous paintings, tapestries and other
objects in the Prado were removed to Valencia and

stored in newly-constructed, double cement vaults in
the chapel of a church. Paintings in the Duke of
Alba's palace were also saved and sent to Valencia,
where they received their first public showing before
being stored in vaults, but the famous diary of Christopher Columbus and other art items were lost in the
destruction of the palace library. Another lost masterpiece is the noted El Greco painting, "The Burial of
Count Orgaz," which hung in the Church of Santo
Tome in Toledo. It was ready for packing two days
before the rebel troops captured the city, but its whereabouts have not been reported since.

Much of Spain's art has been saved, though under
pressure of military necessity many paintings may find
new homes as government officials find it expedient to
exchange them for war materials.

The universal awakening of the public to the value
of its art, the gradual increasing interest in the progress
and accomplishments of its artists, and the growth of
art appreciation in general have contributed greatly
towards making art in 1937. Honorable mention is due
the general circulation magazines, particularly *Life,*
for the colored reproductions of meritorious paintings
which they have issued from time to time during the
year.

CHAPTER XIX

THE SCORE FOR MUSIC IN 1937

Only steel and oil, among American industries out-ranked music in dollars and cents during 1937. That staggering and soothing fact could not be explained without stacking up a brace of statistics that would make extremely dull, if revealing, reading. There was the music of the radio, for one thing: in cars, restaurants, trains, ships at sea, homes, and airplanes. Music, whether you wanted it or not. Opera from the Metropolitan, *The Skaters Waltz* via short wave from a Strasbourg concert commemorating the composer's birthday anniversary, Tommy Dorsey's band screaming through a new swing arrangement, six prize-winning compositions from CBS's orchestral studios, the nine minutes of piercing harmonies and endless drum-sequences of *Sing, Sing, Sing,* chamber music from the Coolidge concerts in the Library of Congress. Musicians hired, composers fed, announcers paid, technicians handed huge sums of money for inventing new gadgets.

Gadgets. Further study of the analyses made by investigators revealed that it was indeed the radio that made the music industry a big one.

By August the 1938 radios and radio-phonographs were launched for sale. Gadgets whooped up the prices

448

to the fantastic figures of $200, $300, and higher. Buyers complained that the successful manipulation of the new radios, despite all their self-starting devices, had become so complicated that it was almost necessary to take a college course in "Tuning In"—a college course or a box of aspirin tablets and a well developed instinct for engineering. Muttering and mumbling arose from the tortured consumers. Some of them investigated radio-making, concluded that tone-quality had not improved much these last six or seven years. And that as long as tone-control buttons were built on radios, there would be damning proof that the machine was not capable of reproducing sound as it was originally created in the broadcasting studio.

Vastly superior to the machines themselves were the programs broadcast. Ten years ago radio listeners gurgled days before and after the program of a musical highlight. In 1937, especially on Sundays, there was a good chance of getting an overdose and musical nausea if one left the radio on all day. The singers, pianists, violinists, orchestras, opera companies, dance bands, and sundry musicians and musical organizations who could not be heard over the air sometime during the season were a scant lot.

Radio Opera. Even the composers, that race of forgotten men, were given their share. Competitions, fat prizes, untold millions of ears cocked radio-wise egged music writers into a frenzy unparalleled since the days of patronage by the aristocracy. Today's patrons, pointed out several of the critics, deserve high praise; it takes real intelligence and sound musical instinct to encourage contemporary creation in the stony face of tradition and ancestor worship. Early in October, at the last program of "Everybody's Music," six compositions by Americans were performed. All of them were interesting. Here and there, according to the critics, could be detected ingratiating salaams to the past along with a few hurried curtsies to the contemporary. In the group was an opera for radio, or, as it was grandly styled, an "opera minus visual stimuli." That, naturally, brought to public attention the fact that after all, and until we passed from these dark ages into the era of television, radio opera is a matter for the ears only—with an occasional passage for the feet. The opera, *Green Mansions* then took to the air in a cloak of "Babi-Yaga awe and weh." With everyone still a bit soggy with the news that Fritz Reiner had presented *Parsifal* in its uncut version (a matter of six full hours) to London Coronation audiences, *Green Mansions* seemed breathlessly short. That, in this age of digests, might or might not have been a point in its favor. The beginning was good. Much more work will probably be done in 1938 with the idea of radio opera. However, remarked several reviewers, there was not enough difference between *Green Mansions* and the half-hour offering known as "Gang Busters" (which frightened the nation's moppets well nigh witless Wednesday evenings) to warrant the announcement of a new form in music. Critics and writers on subjects musical have, however, frequently been wrong before.

Radios to the number of 2,900,000 picked up the broadcasts of the Metropolitan Opera Company early and late in the year. Figuring on a basis of three listeners to every radio, that made a grand total of 9,000,-000 ears ringing with Flagstad and Melchior in Wagnerian opera, Lotte Lehmann, Lawrence Tibbett, Richard Crooks, Gladys Swarthout, Lily Pons, Rosa Ponselle, Helen Jepson, Elizabeth Rethberg, Giovanni Martinelli, Rose Bampton, Friedrich Schorr, singing in others. Newcomers included Gina Cigna, Bidu Sayao, Jussi Björling, Erna Sack. The Metropolitan presented new operas, many old ones, and favored Wagner at the rate of two of his works to one by any other composer. These broadcasts stood as the major activities in the radio world and, if figures did not lie, in the musical world.

Swing Time. The music of the people, popular music, careened through the year nobly, bulged publishers' pockets, crowded dance floors, filled the air with horrid cries. Wonderful tunes came up during the year. Their general tone gave proof that prosperity had arrived; most were a joyous and carefree lot. The mention of any one of them would force naming a dozen more. RCA Victor made the mistake (immediately forgiven) of capturing swing music on the wing. "A Symposium of Swing," a record album, included the jam sessions of Benny Goodman and his orchestra, Tommy Dorsey and his, Fats Waller and his, and Bunny Berrigan and "his'n." Now, if swing is extemporaneous improvisation, as its masters claim, it was a mistake to impress it immemorably in wax—or wasn't it?

Swing music, said some observers, perpetuates an

evil in music— the featured performer. Football games have been lost when each man on the team sought to dazzle the stands with his own single performance. Each man in a swing band is out to out-swing his neighbor. The result is one which, if one sits near a swing band in a hotel cafe, practically maroons him as far as over-the-table conversation is concerned. And too, where the orchestra is particularly noted for its swing antics, all the space in front of the platform is frequently occupied by swing devotees who have deserted their tables and the floor in favor of listening, spellbound, to the master and his men. What it does to one's Terpsichorean capers on the floor was another matter. That, of course, was the secret of its popularity.

Tin God Conductors. The cry from today's swing to big symphony orchestras (Boston, New York, Cincinnati, Philadelphia, Chicago, Minneapolis, etc.) became increasingly less distant during 1937. Whereas none of the latter had as yet asked its men to jam up a Brahms score, they all made of their conductors gods of tin or clay. This overpopularizing of conductors, in the opinion of many, was an unhealthy development which showed no signs of abating. After all, the "hundred men" worked too. NBC realized the value of the mere men of the orchestra when they got busy snatching players from most of the leading orchestras in the United States. But the secret hopes of the most bitter opponents of this system of conductor-worship were dashed when NBC got their orchestra ready for Maestro Toscanini, who on December 25 began his series of

concerts under the generous auspices of the networks
Red and Blue. Grand concerts these certainly were
under the baton of Pierre Monteaux, Artur Rodzinski
and the Maestro himself, but it was a pity that they
were played between 10 and 11:30 E.S.T. on Saturday
nights. Saturday night is a great American institution. Most of the people up and still able to listen
to music at that late hour, were not to be found listening to Toscanini's offerings.

Music in the Movies. *A Hundred Men and a Girl,*
musical movie sensation of the year, brought Stokowski to the screen for the second time. Flagstad sang
in the *Big Broadcast of 1938.* Werner Janssen, Ar-
nold Schonberg, Igor Strawinsky, Virgil Thompson,
Artur Honegger and other top-writers were engaged
to do musical scores for movies. In the field of writing music for movies lay much opportunity for the composer. Much that is good in music would come
through the movies. As soon as the producers were
willing to allow the finished film to stand still in its
rush from Hollywood to the public long enough to allow the composers to write scores worthy of themselves
and the film, great music would be heard. But it takes
the speed of a Mozart to get the score ready in time.
The composer has little opportunity to get his composition together during the shooting of the film—he has
no idea, usually, just what the form of the whole film,
the whole music, will be.

MUSIC TODAY

A close study of musical events of 1937 is illuminating. Late winter, spring, summer, fall, and again the early winter of 1937 were seasons of such busy note-making that no music critic found time to rest between concerts. Opera, successful beyond the most optimistic guarantor's hopes, packed auditoriums in Los Angeles, San Francisco, St. Louis, Chicago, Philadelphia, and New York. Symphony orchestras had packed schedules in most cities over the hundred-thousand mark. Soloists found their booking dates well taken up. All this went on without much pump-priming. There were, for instance, no outstanding musical finds or novelties during the season: the Salzburg Opera Guild, Marion Anderson and other newcomers came not unannounced; they had broken the ice in Europe.

Some reviewers interpreted these events to mean that America had come of age, that a well-defined musical consciousness had developed, that a democracy was developing a culture, that radio and movies had not destroyed in-the-flesh performances, and that few of the present generation would live out their day minus the benefits and satisfactions of first rate music. More cautious critics pulled at the check-rein, said that the time for singing hosannas had not fully arrived. They asked for a deeper study of human needs, of social values. They warned that 1937's bloom may be only the fever flush of an inner decay.

Thus the two extremes argued. Both agreed that, were the musical events to continue as they had begun in the years 1936 and 1937, another Golden Age of Music would appear.

Whether or not musical history was made in 1937, the events in themselves were deeply satisfying: the unforgettable operatic performances at the Metropolitan, the golden anniversary concert tour of Josef Hofmann, the triumphs of the singers, among whom were Lauritz Melchior, Lotte Lehmann, Marion Anderson, Lawrence Tibbett, Kirsten Flagstad, Grace Moore, Helen Jepson, Jussi Björling, Richard Tauber, and many others; the concerts of the pianists Bauer, Rachmaninoff, Serkin, Schnabel, Lhevinne, Levitzki; the symphonic concerts in many cities throughout the country; and the brilliant violin playing of Szigeti, Menuhin, Heifetz, Kreisler.

Laymen and critics are set sharply to observe next year's music news—perhaps to find answers to certain puzzling questions: Is opera here to stay, and will the public be content to chew the cud of traditionalism or will it ask for new operas, native operas?   Will the schools train non-musician students to make music through listening a part of their personal, home, social, and vocational interests?   Will the emphasis on technique and mechanics diminish in favor of a vital concern with the idea behind music, or will swing triumph? Will the music of the films inspire new scores or will the Hollywood musicians continue to invade the publishers' files of 1920-1928 film-music?

If 1937 has been a golden year in music, what will 1938 bring!

CHAPTER XX

BOOKS AND PUBLISHING

Hangovers. In 1936 a small woman in Atlanta sat on a divan amid two gigantic piles of manuscript, and a publisher's representative was duly aghast. *Gone with the Wind* was published; Margaret Mitchell's fame and literary history were made. For months, well into 1937, nothing else in fiction mattered much; the newspapers kept the name constantly before the public: would Tallulah Bankhead play Scarlett, or would Miriam Hopkins, or Mrs. Whitney, or possibly Janet Gaynor? The book sold 25,000 copies a month, stayed near the top of the lists all through 1937, sold the unheard of total of a million and a half copies.

There were others: *Drums Along the Mohawk, Yang and Yin, White Banners,* and *Rich Man Poor Man* in fiction; *An American Doctor's Odyssey, Live Alone and Like It, How to Win Friends and Influence People, Man the Unknown,* and the *Bible* among the non-fiction items brightened the Christmas and post-holiday season and the bookseller's faces.

Criticism in a Quandry. The year was uneventful in criticism. In April Joseph Wood Krutch sought to define a good book review: "However penetrating a piece of writing may be, it is not a good review if it leaves the reader wondering what the book itself is like

456

as a whole, or if it is concerned with only some aspects of the book's quality. . . ." Other critics worried about other critics' preoccupation with form, whether or not a book measured up to standards identified and defined by literary tradition. Most of them agreed that such an approach was poor, that it did not allow the true "communicativeness" of a book to reach the public. Critical attacks on Millay and Hemingway subsequently showed the meagerness of the critics' ability to see beyond mere conformity to rule; and the year in criticism was singularly flat.

The high spot in book criticism was probably Lovell Thompson's review of the *Sears, Roebuck Catalogue: Spring and Summer 1937* in *The Saturday Review;* certainly it was the most communicative, least concerned with form, most concerned with matter, enough concerned with the reviewer's principles, esthetic and philosophical. All other book reviews paled by comparison. Compassion and detachment, with keen perception and disillusion marched so congenially together in no other critical piece.

Moods and Manners. As for the books themselves, did they reflect the mood of the period, as books should do? The Trotsky-Stalin controversy, the WPA literary activity, the wars in Spain and China, the ballet, Soviet Russia, the Supreme Court controversy, "pinko" attitudes toward our times and institutions, music for the listening masses, personal success and psychological adjustment to a changing society, abdication and coronation in England, and fabulous Mr. Samuel Goldwyn—all these and more were grist for the mill.

Dale Carnegie's *How to Win Friends and Influence People,* more than a best seller, reflected man's increasing interest in himself and his adjustment to the world, especially to the successful world. It was but one of dozens of books, profound or popular or both, on psychology, psychiatry, neuroses, even insanity; their publication was no accident, rather part of an awakening. Ten years ago Karl Menninger's *The Human Mind,* first of the popular interpretations of psychiatry to reach wide sale, really meant little save to scientists; things were different in 1937. Healthiest sign of all seemed America's willingness not only to find out about itself but also to laugh; the Carnegie opus brought forth satirical *How to Lose Friends and Alienate People,* pungent cartoons, jibes from the stage. *Be Glad You're Neurotic* and others showed people's longing to excuse or justify themselves, satisfied their inferiority and fear, their troubled curiosity about the internal workings of the mind; but beyond that, their ability to be light about themselves in all seriousness. Morbidity, honest intellectual and emotional curiosity, and guffaws marched together.

Making Best Sellers. Sixty or seventy booksellers throughout the country report sales of fiction and non-fiction books by rank weekly and monthly; from them so-called best sellers are defined, not necessarily the "best" books of the year but definitely the most often bought. Notes follow on the year's best sellers, listed chronologically, not according to size of sales. If size of sales and prevalence of newspaper, magazine, and parlor talk, and figures from bookdealers were calculated according to importance, in fiction 1937's biggest news was the publishing and phenomenal success of (1) Ernest Hemingway's *To Have and Have Not,* (2) Vaughan Wilkins' *And So—Victoria,* (3) Virginia Woolf's *The Years,* and (4) Kenneth Roberts' *Northwest Passage;* and in non-fiction, Hendrik Willem van Loon's *The Arts*—all great sellers, all topping all other newcomers to the lists. The Hemingway book caused more anticipation, subsequently more critical guff than any other book, with critics bantering and squabbling over character, form, style, and social implications. Hemingway's books, however, always have an eager public, command it by narrative skill.

FICTION BEST SELLERS

"The Late George Apley." Early in January, John P. Marquand's book mounted the best seller lists. Another attempt to portray the New England conscience, it suggested *The Last Puritan.* Bernard De Voto thought Marquand "a much poorer philosopher than Santayana, and a much better novelist," felt the book "achingly true" with "charm and depth" even though it brought the reader little sense of the wider socio-civic Bostonian background peopled by memories of Sacco-Vanzetti and Mr. Curley. It aroused Dorothy Van Doren to words of praise for its technique, the story being told through letters from father to son. "Mr. Marquand is no Marcel Proust; but he is a telling caricaturist of a set of manners that lend themselves happily to his pencil." It sold 20,000 copies in a month, stood high on the lists for several months.

"The Street of the Fishing Cat." Jolan Foldes' prize novel, distributed by a book club, sold well for several months. Mark Van Doren thought it good; Critic N. L. Rothman found it "enchanting." "The international nature of its materials is an obvious blessing." Recounting the small lives and colors of a group of refugees in Paris, it caught public fancy, very likely because of its "simple and sensuous writing. . . ."

"Cities of Refuge." Down the lists but selling well, Philip Gibbs' novel earned scant critical notice. One critic thought its design "merely bewildered," called Gibbs a sentimentalist, bewailed his lack of irony, said: "The theme itself—the creeping of an economic shadow from city to city across Europe and time—might produce an ironical and terrifying piece of writing," but this the Gibbs book somehow did not.

"The Sound of Running Feet." Playing again on her theme of minor economics, Josephine (*If I Have Four Apples*) Lawrence achieved the distinction of the lists for one month only despite the qualities of "compassion" without sneers yet without comfort which marked both of her books.

"The Sisters." Myron Brinig's book, published in February and sold promptly to Warner Bros., recounting, with "delicate analysis," the lives of Rumanian Jews in Montana, sold well for four months. Critic Gellhorn, admiring Brinig's other books more, still found it an epic with "dignity and beauty." "In *The Sisters*—it is a feminine world into which one enters.

IN THE REALM OF SPORTS

Top: War Admiral, winner of the Kentucky Derby (Life Magazine). *Bottom:* Dick Bartell, Giant shortstop, fails to tag Frey, Chicago second-sacker (Life Magazine).

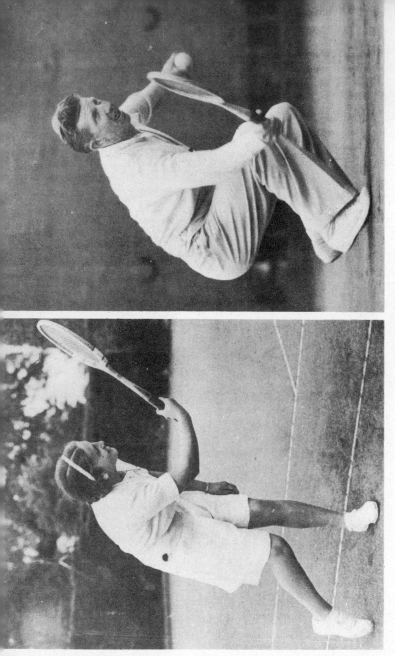

TENNIS CHAMPIONS

Left: Señorita Anita Lizana wins women's singles at Forest Hills (Life Magazine). *Right:* Donald Budge of Oakland, California, international tennis champion of the year (Life Magazine).

Hats, dresses, lovers, husbands, babies (imminent or arrived), dish-washing, slight jealousies or heroic fortitudes provide the materials out of which the epic of the Elliot family is woven."

"Theatre." The W. Somerset Maugham book won surprisingly good critical attention, sold well, its sales bolstered by book club distribution. Critic DeVoto, in one of his mellower moods, described it as "excellent entertainment, a skillful and self-conscious fantasia on vanity, cupidity, jealousy, spite, stupidity, histrionism, minor brutalities, sexual possessiveness, and the no longer secret power of personal odors to inspire passion—in short, Noel Coward without tears." Further, he thought it a "journeyman work without a flaw, as fine a specimen of the well made novel as this generation has seen . . . first-rate hammock reading for people with high I.Q.'s." Other critics, less mellow, considered it merely an advertisement for a great novel Maugham had written twenty years ago. But the story of the rise and amorous fall of a talented actress who finally throws off the shackles of an unfortunate affair by treating herself to an enormous meal appealed to a wide public. "Mrs. Siddons was a rare one for chops; I'm not a bit like her in that; I'm a rare one for steaks," Julia Lambert, the heroine, said to the headwaiter, and promptly forgot her young lover and his duplicities, remembering perhaps the Divine Sarah's penchant for Pilsener with her breakfast steak. Julia and Mr. Maugham interested the best seller buyers for five months.

"Paradise." Published late in February, Esther Forbes' New England piece stayed on the lists until June, elicited sedate praise from Critic-professor Murdock, authority on Massachusetts history: "She has written the story of a seventeenth-century Massachusetts Bay family with the emphasis on flesh and blood, not on an artifically contrived system; on drinking, eating, breeding, not on pious meditation; and on the dramatic struggle of white man and Indian ending bitterly in war, not on the tamer operations of religious zealots."

"We Are Not Alone." With the publication of this novel, it began to look as though James Hilton were perhaps only a two book novelist. On the strength of reputation made by *Good Bye, Mr. Chips* and *Lost Horizon*, the new work sold well but had mixed criticism. Author Hilton's method of understatement worked less well here where the reader needed to know the why's and wherefore's of Doctor Newcome during the events leading up to his destruction. Author Lloyd Douglas, essaying criticism, said: "The earnest reader may be amazed if not annoyed by the hapless hero's apathy while being tried on the flimsiest sort of circumstantial evidence and will find it difficult to believe that the friendly little city of Calderbury gave consent to the execution of its most useful citizen. Some may wonder, also, how a man who has placed so high a value on human life could be so drowsily unconcerned about his own."

"Of Mice and Men." With this small novel with large implications, John Steinbeck "arrived." His other books had merely toyed with the interests of Californians and literary critics. Boosted by the book clubs, it sold a thousand copies a day for a time, stayed on the lists for six months, totaled 150,000 copies, sold especially well in college towns, got a boost from Alexander Woollcott, that "most incorruptible of the oracles." Critics smiled, frowned. Dorothy Canfield Fisher took her reputation in her hands, admired it effusively if delicately in a woman's magazine, took some pains to point out the power of the story and urged the ladies to ignore the woodshed words. Mark Van Doren thought not very well of it, considered it not memorable. But Critic Canby pointed out that it was "superb in its understatements," that character and situation were inextricably entwined, that "there has been nothing quite so good of its kind in American writing since Sherwood Anderson's early stories. It is a limited kind, but close to the heart of the whole fiction business." Another critic felt that in the character of Lennie and his small tragedy "there was something of the pity and terror of classic catastrophe." A novel of social preachment in essence, the force of evil which militates for Lennie's downfall lies in "the conditions of life that keep these men bummers and vagabonds." More than propaganda, it lived as a story and sold as one. 150,000 persons had bought it by May; it stayed on the lists for six months and proved something about the 1937 taste in reading; when a true and tragic story can grip, Kathleen Norris and Mary Roberts Rinehart fly out the window.

"**The Years.**" After a succession of important books, critical recognition, and a limited public, something happened for Virginia Woolf. Considered by most critics to be one of her least distinguished books, *The Years* achieved success in its publication month, April, and in June actually outsold all other books the country over; it stayed on the lists for five months, averaged during some months 1,500 sales a day. George Stevens wrote of the world it portrayed as a "woman's world . . . made up of inner life and memory," going on to Mrs. Woolf's concern with time, her rearrangement of events in the world of "abstract experience." "This sense of time and reality is Virginia Woolf's constant preoccupation. The subject of *The Years* is our universal experience of time, the feeling that it goes faster as we grow older." He considered the book one of her "most brilliant achievements, written with imagination that is luminous and evocative." Other critics found it merely dull. Can its success be attributed to the bookbuyer's desire to be awed by the highbrow, or his longing for clarification and expression of untold deeps of common experience?

"**The Outward Room.**" In April a book club launched Millen Brand's book with 90,000 copies. A first novel, it dramatized Harriet Demuth, "a young woman who in her early twenties is partially recovering from the manic-depressive cycle into which she had plunged when an acute emotional shock made reality too unpleasant." But tracing Harriet's asylum days and those of readjustment to a world seemed to

Critic Paula Snelling accomplished in a prose style "uncharged with feeling," somewhat lacking in "its own authentic fire." In key with an interest in psychiatry and neuroses, it kept the public interest a few months, then disappeared from many counters.

"Three Comrades." Erich Maria Remarque's story of "four inconsiderable items in the back streets of Berlin, and how they lived from day to day in a small routine of hazard and panicky competition" eased itself into the top sellers for two months after its late April publication, won almost uniform good criticism, from Bernard DeVoto up or down. Remarque's conspicuous ability is "to make commonplaces evoke the profoundest emotions, to focus immensities through the smallest and simplest details." Other critics agreed on its pathos and profundity. Later the publishers dressed it up in a new gay jacket in the hope of increasing sales.

"The Wind from the Mountains." Trygve Gulbranssen ranked as a best-selling author again in 1937, his book selling 1,000 copies a week in early summer and staying for a healthy six months among the top five sellers. A sequel to *Beyond Sing the Woods*, it carried on to old age the characters developed in the other book. It "carries a nostalgia for the past where the conduct of life had at least hard, firm ideals for its guide," but, according to Phillips D. Carleton, its "manner of telling [is] much more episodic." The years, he felt, moved slowly for Adelaide, the heroine, and for the reader. "The story is told in a series of short pictures that sketch out the years, but they interlock none too well."

"Northwest Passage." When Kenneth Roberts writes an historical novel he apparently does his job to the satisfaction of both casual reader and historian; for in July *Northwest Passage* zoomed immediately to top the lists, with a prepublication issue of 136,000 copies, a second printing in July, eager book club patrons buying. By August 200,000 copies were in print. All critics agreed on its readableness, its narrative movement. Critic DeVoto traced the growth of Roberts as a novelist: "Through the earlier books Mr. Roberts steadily developed as a story teller and as an antiquarian. In the new one the antiquarian is quite willing to interrupt the story telling. . . . As a historian, Mr. Roberts is something of a revisionist. . . . As a novelist, he remains conventional in all his detailed characterization and quite uninterested in psychology." But, he concludes, "It is a first-rate job, a novel that is read with intent interest and is sure to be remembered with satisfaction. . . ." The public taste for the past romanticized but not too much was met again, and here "The soldiery, the traders, the *voyageurs,* and the first wave of pioneers are done with fine versatility."

"American Dream." In June minor best selling news was Michael Foster's restatement of the frontier spirit. Told in a series of cutbacks and written in a disillusioned journalese, the book was sired by a book club and commanded a wide if not vast audience. When a critic is hard put to say something about a book he says it "moves" or "illuminates," that despite

its faults it has "life, color, interest, and meaning."
One of the outstanding critics thus committed himself;
the public read it for three or four months.

"And So—Victoria." Whether because of Helen
Hayes' enchanting reconstruction of "Victoria the
Queen" in the theater, the interest in English royalty
and English tradition attendant on the coronation, the
insistent belief in the panoramic novel, or merely a
publisher's faith in his perception, having published
Gone with the Wind, Vaughan Wilkins' book was
launched in July with fanfares. Macmillans were not
disappointed. The public taste still coursed toward
the historical piece; *Anthony Adverse* and *Gone with
the Wind* could not have been wrong. "Have we
achieved something of a complete cycle in our fiction
fashions of late?" queries Theodore Purdy, Jr. "For
in *And So—Victoria,* a new British author pays tribute
to this return to narrative normalcy. His book is a
panorama of Regency and pre-Victorian England, a
full and exciting tale based on the adventures of one
of the innumerable Hanoverian bastards, a grandchild
of George III. There is a little of everything in the
often fascinating story of Christopher Harnish. . . ."
Some critics thought the characters two-dimensional,
but admired, as they had Maugham's *Theatre,* good
story telling and construction, feeling, as did Critic
Purdy, that "few first novels have been more facile
and technically accomplished than this book . . .
which possesses nearly all the qualities likely to please
the public." Thus it was a best seller on publication,
with an advance printing of 65,000. It sold to 115,000

by the end of August, topped the list in August, was nosed to second by *Northwest Passage,* but continued to sell. Metro-Goldwyn-Mayer bought film rights, promised production in England. If there was big news in books in 1937, *And So—Victoria* helped to make it.

"The Nutmeg Tree." The publisher of Margery Sharp's book insisted it was "capturing hearts by the thousand." In it Julia, the heroine, tries hard to be a lady but finds it not much fun. One critic found her "one of the most appealing, warm-hearted, good wenches anyone has met, in the flesh or in print or on the screen, in many months." Many more readers than critics found her so.

"The Citadel." After two months A. J. Cronin's *The Citadel* loomed as a contender for top position. "A vivid portrait of an intelligent, hard-headed young physician struggling to gain a foothold in his profession," the book brought praise from people who know, which was more than Mrs. Rinehart's *The Doctor* had earned in 1936. Dr. Mabel Ulrich admired its detachment, its lack of compromise, its cutting "through the romanticism that still surrounds the medical profession, and boldly exposes the potentialities of charlatanism and dishonesty inherent in a system whereby a large group of men must depend for economic security on the real or fancied suffering of others." Clifton Fadiman felt he "could predict the next chapter," found it machine made. Conflicting opinions attended publication: American doctors were not willing to believe that methods and conditions were sufficiently comparable in England and America to consider *The Citadel* an indictment of American practices. The layman usually did not raise the question, contented himself with the penetration and seriousness of the book; more than a hundred thousand sold by mid-October.

"The Seven Who Fled." In novel and poetry Frederic Prokosch already enjoyed recognition from press and buyer; but his new Harper Prize novel climbed into the lists in September. Critic Hassoldt Davis said of it: "A very terrible book, a book of beauty agonized through the seven passional biographies it comprehends, a book of conjury, if magic may be allowed to the evocation of the inner Asia Mr. Prokosch has taken as his scene"; but he thought that the author might well have resorted less to "putrescence and the picking of noses" to achieve his effects. Badgering Mary McCarthy thought Author Prokosch's formula "elaborated into frozen symmetry," and said: "The range of the author's sensibility is narrow, and for all his admiration of intensity the sensations themselves are not very vigorous. His book is full of 'little spasms,' 'little plans,' 'little gardens,' 'little moments.' He is a connoisseur of the gentle, the tender, the delicate, the pure, the simple, the sweet, the hesitant; and an academician of the tremor . . . a dwarf flower garden [with] the terror of the super-real." Mr. Prokosch may not have been greatly disturbed, for his book is frankly one of escape, his Asia merely his "far-off hill," his "magic mountain"; and people liked it.

"Katrina." A prize novel from Helsingfors, by Salminen, caught on, the first if not the most important of the fall books. Critic Ulrich admired its "almost childlike naïveté." Written first in Swedish by a young woman who had worked for five years in New York, it traveled from Finland to America, a success. Katrina, the heroine, leaves her father's north Finland farm to go to the Åland Island where she shall pick up "apples in the dewy grass," but where she is deserted by her lover, forced to submit to "the feudal control of the rich man of the town." The book recounts, in simple and unsophisticated manner, her "struggles and victories."

"To Have and Have Not." Critical honesty or venom, the critic's preoccupation with problems of form and the proper method of inculcating social preachment in a work of art, descended on Ernest Hemingway's first novel with an American setting. But no matter; the public's curiosity teemed. The story of Harry Morgan, boatman between Key West and Cuba, his attempts to make an honest living, his failures, his touching relationship with his wife, his not-so-touching relationships with "the haves" who cross his path, tumble on through Hemingway's gripping narrative to trace Morgan's destruction. Big news for *Time*, it got most appreciative treatment from it. *Time* reviewers pointed out the influence of Hemingway's trip to Spain, his espousal of the Loyalist cause, his growing social consciousness, his preoccupation with death. "But no matter what is to happen to Hemingway, U. S. readers last week could reassure themselves that U. S. writers still have a front rank and that he is still in it." Critic George Stevens felt that "Harry is a very simple character. There is not much about him, or about the three short stories in which he figures—to stick with you." Louis Kronenberger raised the question of the juvenility of Hemingway's thinking, quoted Goethe on Byron apropos Hemingway: "When he thinks, he is like a child," went on to point out the crudeness of the satire, its "slapdash" quality, felt he was back on the Yale campus in point of view. "As a thinking being," Kronenberger said, "he has still a very great deal to learn." As regards structure, he felt the book to be "awkward and incompetent. It is like writing a letter and then adding to it an appalling number of post-scripts." Malcolm Cowley, Hemingway partisan, was similarly disturbed by the two themes of the book never coming together, by the "serious weakness" in the characters themselves. But he summed up his opinion: "Chief among Hemingway's virtues as a writer is his scrupulous regard for fact, for reality, for 'what happened.' It is a rare virtue in the world of letters." What most critics overlooked in their quest for technical perfection and proper sympathies and completeness of presentation was merely that Hemingway is a perfectly eloquent conveyor of story-implications; even when he does not say, he suggests strongly and surely. A reader's imagination plays always when Hemingway writes, even when, as in the present case, he may write second best.

"The Rains Came." Author Bromfield took near-rank with E. M. Forster portraying aspects of the East Indian panorama being mentioned in the same critical breath with Forster's *A Passage to India*. Not that *The Rains Came* was as good as the other work, but the story is not only readable but accurate, un-romantic, rapid. Technically the book is in the pattern of recent best sellers: leisurely, broad in scope, with the house-party structure, used here to frame "the lives, the emotions, and the complications of the group of people whom Mr. Bromfield has gathered. . . ." Thematically, the story focuses on a cast-iron statue of Queen Victoria, with umbrella, which withstands Indian rain and flood, suggesting "the struggle between England's ideas of colonization and their practical workings in her colonies. . . ."

"Enchanter's Nightshade." Ann Bridge outgrew being an *Atlantic Monthly* prize winner. Although her *Pekin Picnic* had been good, her new book succeeded now again in a happy presentation of the Continent of 1905. Making no concessions to sentiment, Miss Bridge portrays uncompromisingly the young, transplanted English heroine against this "lovely" landscape and against the Vecchia Marchesa, an Italian matriarch who speaks for Miss Bridge "with the accent of life." The book was a best seller.

"The Turning Wheels" and "They Seek a Country." Two late-in-the-year entries to the lists, by authors Stuart Cloete and Francis Brett Young, these books pictured life after the great trek to South Africa in 1836, the promised land, and did so robustly. Both, Critics Morley and Charles David Abbott thought, were fine novels, accurately and vividly transcribing the "chosen" scene.

Contenders for the Lists. Selling well but not

ranking high on lists, Dorothy Sayers' *Busman's Holiday* and James Warner Bellah's *7 Must Die*, "whodunits," were the only good mystery yarns to scale even the bottom of the heights.   Phil Stong's *Buckskin Breeches* showed a tapering off of Stong's popularity. Gladys Hasty Carroll's *Neighbor to the Sky* aroused interest because of Mrs. Carroll's former popularity; but critics found it a fairly "dry syllogism."   Elizabeth Goudge's *A City of Bells*, published in February, caught on briefly in June and July. Published simultaneously with *And So—Victoria*, Cecil Roberts' *Victoria 4:30* basked in reflected glory, lasted two months as a runner up. Gabriel Chevalier's *The Scandals of Clochemerle*, several Crimefile items, Linton Wells' *Blood on the Moon*, and assorted items by Temple Bailey, Robert Briffault, Robert P. Tristram Coffin, Walter Duranty, Joseph C. Lincoln, John T. McIntyre, E. Phillips Oppenheim, Rafael Sabatini, Hugh Walpole, and P. G. Wodehouse earned good sales, faint critical praise.

Critics' and Publishers' Pets. Critics, publishers, and buyers seldom agree on book merits; but more often in 1937 than before. Relatively few novels aroused publicity enthusiasms from critics and publishers and not from buyers. The publishers seemed particularly canny: *Northwest Passage* and *And So—Victoria* skyrocketed to immediate success because of publisher publicity, as did the Hemingway opus, Hemingway being always frontpage news whether he socks Max Eastman, fishes, or writes novels.

Critics boomed Sholom Asch's *The Mother*, Jean

Giono's *The Song of the World,* Meyer Levin's *The Old Bunch,* Liam O'Flaherty's *Famine,* Jules Romains' *The Depths and the Heights,* and Lawrence Watkin's *On Borrowed Time;* the buying public turned deaf ears. H. G. Wells' *The Croquet Player,* distributed by a book club with *Of Mice and Men,* attracted less notice than did the more lauded Steinbeck book. Nevertheless this brilliant study of the world jitters reached a larger public, for this reason, than it otherwise would have reached. Critics boomed less loudly Archie Binns' *The Laurels Are Cut Down,* Johannes Steel's *Escape from the Present,* Franz Werfel's *Twilight of a World;* even less loudly novels by Richard Aldington, Lion Feuchtwanger, Robert Graves, Marquis James, Josephine Johnson, Margaret Kennedy, Compton MacKenzie, Conrad Richter, and Sigrid Undset. But of all the neglected books *Famine* was probably the most important.

NON-FICTION BEST SELLERS

"The Hundred Years." Late in January appeared Philip Guedalla's *The Hundred Years,* with book club distribution of 85,000 copies, the first non-fiction success of the new year. A panorama of the world from Victoria's coronation to the present, the book succeeded in its task because Guedalla, Critic Garrett Mattingly thought, could "put a girdle around the earth in the flick of a page." He found it particularly successful in its description of "the delightfully bogus Second Empire," but considered it "all very gay and amusing, and instructive, too . . . " Critics generally agreed with him, called it a *tour de force,* evoked enthusiasm among the book buyers.

"Present Indicative." After a full life at thirty-seven, Noel Coward turned to autobiography, the result winging its way quickly across the continent, finding immediate audience in the metropolitan centers and in Hollywood. No longer confining himself to drawing what Dorothy Parker called "people like unbaked cookies," James Thurber said: Coward "started to work and live at such high speed when he was still in short pants that by the time he was twenty-one he could look back on triumphs and failures in the theatre." The book, Thurber thought, "represents surely the most vivid picture of the theatre, from the writing of a play to the end of a long run, that has yet been done." Critics and public admired the reticence, the lack of self-consciousness of the book; some wished for more revealing comments, perhaps a spice of scandal, on Coward's friends and contemporaries, especially those who touched his life intimately; but they contented themselves with the lone brilliant observation on Gertrude Lawrence and overlooked other omissions in the whirl of grease paint and footlights. It sold strongly for months, was much talked about.

"Mathematics for the Million." In line with books which popularize, perhaps simplify, technical and scientific matters, Lancelot Hogben's treatise seemed a boon to many people, promised to be a boon to many more, with translation into all the foreign languages promised and hoped for. It remained on the lists for five months.

"Something of Myself." Rudyard Kipling became

a name and a memory to the present generation; his autobiography induced critical acclaim, especially from oldsters. Oracle Henry Seidel Canby said: "There is no place in this volume in which one cannot plunge with profit. Yet what makes it worthy of the master's hand is certainly the study of the shaping of his imagination. . . ." For a time it sold 3,000 copies a week, yet lasted but a short time among the best sellers.

"Coronation Commentary." Geoffrey Dennis' book enjoyed vast front page American publicity when published in England; it appeared in America in April and sold well past actual coronation ceremonies. Like Hector Bolitho's *King Edward VIII,* it had been written before Edward's abdication, then retouched, with chapters added on the Simpson Affair; the results were something less than satisfactory as portraits of Edward's soul, half adoration and excuse, half condemnation. George Daingerfield said: "What the two books have in common is a certain agility in the transferring of allegiance from Edward to George. Where they differ is upon the one point of interest which the abdication raised. Was the King forced off the throne, or was he not? . . . Mr. Dennis is convinced that he was." Author Dennis traces the background, the hundred years preceding, during which the Crown "lost power and gained prestige." Yet the great book about the whole matter has yet to be and should be written.

"Orchids on Your Budget." Margery Hillis rang the bell again with "advice to the luxury-lorn," telling several hundred thousand women how to "economize with gaiety and an air." Critic Agnes Rogers called the theme cutting "down your major expenses in order to have some leeway with your minor ones." Admitting the book to be a boon to smart and clever women, Miss Rogers thought that, "for their stodgier sisters it may put a very beneficial bee in their bonnets." It rose to second place in July, maintained the position in August, was strong late in the year.

"Conversation at Midnight." When a book of poetry mounts to third on a best seller list, it is more than news. Thus despite generally disappointed critical notations, Edna St. Vincent Millay's new batch of sonnets sold extremely well. The sequence records talk and chronicles character interaction among seven persons: stockbroker, painter, short storiest, communist poet, Catholic priest, petty Italian nobleman, and advertising writer. "The time is the present; the place New York; the scene is the elegant house on Tenth Avenue. . . . The men talk. In the first four parts they talk about shooting; dogbreeding; pheasant-raising; women; fads"; other matters. They get around to war and revolution. And "it is soon evident that these are not conversations, but a series of monologues in which the utterance is as haphazard as the thought. The names are tags, not characters; the lines are delivered with so little sense of individuality that the reader is continually confused. . . . At one moment Miss Millay makes her dialecticians discourse in . . . Elizabethan accent, at another she has them unconsciously imitate Ogden Nash." So fumed Poet Louis Untermeyer, going on to regret prosiness, pretentiousness, and "involved awkwardness." "Miss Millay pretends to flash light on a man's world, but it is still the world of a child—a sensitive, angry, confused child. . . ." In fact, nothing was right about Miss Millay and her book save that she might "survive" it and go on to better things. Edmund Wilson found the work "a little disappointing," "blurred," superficial, slow moving; the most serious defect seemed Miss Millay's lack of "dramatic imagination"; a secondary one the dissolution of Miss Millay's metrics. "I miss," he concluded, "her old imperial line." All the critics agreed on the lack of intensity, depth, and characterization; and the degeneration of forms.

"Life with Mother." Clarence Day's posthumous volume of reminiscences cheered Day fans; here Author Day had been able to carry on his formula of close observation, dispassion, and detached and witty charm, and repeat the success of his *Life with Father* and *God and My Father*. "Mother," it seemed to Amy Loveman, "had a way with her, and usually, too, she got her way," as had Father; and " I know of no book of the last few years so full of gaiety and sympathy, so certain to draw a chuckle, so pungent, so incisive, and yet so kindly. . . ." The "genial" book showed that the Day père and mère were intent, in their own ways, on making "the universe behave in an orderly manner. . . ." It went immediately to second place on the non-fiction lists in September, seemed destined to perpetuate the Day memory and America's sense of loss in his death.

"The Arts." Hendrik Willem van Loon's books are invariably sensational in their success; his latest was an immediate best-seller, with book club distribution of more than 150,000, weekly sales of 2,000 copies. Written as an introduction to all the arts of all time, the book aimed to make the laymen conscious "of the fascination of the arts." By means of chat, maps, and sketches, the author starts his narrative with an anecdote "of two American children seen from a train in the dreariest of American landscapes. . . . They illustrated aspiration in the midst of sordid ugliness." So wrote William Rose Benét, kinder than the technicians who reviewed the book from its various technical angles. Oliver Larkin bewailed the tapering off of discussion of sculpture; Hetty Goldman found some "misstatements and many misleading simplifications"; Henry Russel Hitchcock, Jr. felt the book would "do no one who is much interested any good . . ."; and Arthur Mendel, writing on music, found wrong things, wrong proportions. But all admitted van Loon's sincerity of intention. Artists shunned the book as they might the plague, shying at the impertience of the book as a whole, the silly drawings of great art objects. But the general public, caught by the book's essential readableness, seemed likely to buy it in ever-increasing numbers.

IMPORTANT NON-FICTION MATTERS

Other books were less important to critics or public or both; but critics uniformly praised extravagantly Mark Benney's *Angels in Undress*, as did literary men and sociologists. An autobiography of an English burglar, it seemed stylistically and psychologically as important as any book from a new writer in many moons. Less praise went to J. B. Priestley's "soliloquy in Arizona night," *Midnight on the Desert;* even less to Pitirim Sorokin's *Social and Cultural Dynamics,* generally damned by liberal critics, despite its vast scope. It brought comparisons to Pareto and Spengler. On the other hand the Lynds' *Middletown in Transition* won critical praise for its objective and statistical study of an American city, sociological and economic in its emphases. Morris Ernst's *The Ultimate Power,* studying the constitutional power of the supreme court, satisfied all the reviewers; André Gide's *Return from the U. S. S. R.* appealed to Eastman and Trotzky, not to Stalin and Malcolm Cowley; and Gene Fowler's *Salute to Yesterday* won praise for gusto.

Books by or about Thomas Benton, Cellini, Gauguin, van Gogh, and Hogarth made news; music called forth books on Frances Alda, Thomas More, Stravinsky, and Tchaikowsky; and the theater inspired comments on the WPA Theatre Project, acting methods by Morton Eustis and Boleslawsky, the mad du Mauriers, and Marie Tempest. Literature itself included works on Chekov, Elinor Glyn, the Goncourt brothers, de Quincey, Samuel Richardson, Jonathan Swift, and Walt Whitman, among others. History worked with biography and novel to produce works on Augustus, Winston Churchill, Bothwell and Mary Queen of Scots, Dreyfus and Zola, Fiorello La Guardia, young Henry of Navarre, Andrew Jackson, Joseph and Elizabeth of Austria, T. E. Lawrence, Maury Maverick, the Medicis, Napoleon, Nicholas II, Parnell, and Robespierre.

Autobiography and memoirs, with varying awareness of social consciousness and change, included revelations by the Abbe children, John Beal on his way to liberalism, Angelo Herndon, and the indefatigable Mabel Dodge Luhan. Some were embarrassing, some amusing, some valuable.

Near and far places found expression in André Maurois' *The Miracle of England,* Elliot Paul's *Life and Death in a Spanish Town,* and books on New York state, Chicago, and Minneapolis, in books on Albania, Haiti, Hawaii, India, Norway, and Peru. Not only Frederic Prokosch had his "far-off hill." Escapism in literature seemed a constant.

In poetry other than Miss Millay's conversations in sonnet form, the memory of A. E. Housman was reiterated; poems by the martyred Spanish loyalist poet, Lorca, made available in English translation; Robinson Jeffers allowed to continue his disillusioned pictures of his sensory world. And Archibald MacLeish turned his hand to poetic drama for the radio in *The Fall of the City,* made literary and radio history.

Alexander Woollcott, appearing in so many ways in the contemporary scene, essayed again to teach the reading public that his taste might be the taste of many and that anthologies will still sell, on occasion, outside campus book-stores. On the whole his *Second Reader* seemed to the critics a better selection than his first; his public bought, did not wait for critical approval: Oracle Woollcott could dictate the public taste any time and in any way he chose. That seemed to be the moral demonstrated in the flourishing sale of his book.

Mrs. Franklin D. Roosevelt's autobiography proved many things to scoffers of democracy and Rooseveltism and active womanhood; critics and public alike found her book appealing for its candor, charm, its picture of the period and society from which she emerged, its delineation of her growth of social consciousness. Most persons thought it an "important" contribution to Americana.

MISCELLANEOUS

CHAPTER XXI

HIGHLIGHTS IN THE WORLD OF SPORT

The appeal of sports in America continued its rapid growth in 1937. In part compelled by continued unemployment or part-time employment and the expanded hours of leisure, and in part fostered by completion and further expansion of WPA projects, such as swimming pools, public golf courses, recreational grounds and amusement parks, Americans from moppets to oldsters learned increasingly how to play. Thousands turned from the silly and spectacular games of 1936, such as waiter tray races and roller derbies and hog-calling contests, to more stable universal and appealing fun. Ping-pong appeared, not only in student halls in schools the country over, but in miners' and lumbermen's cabins on deal tables and in many a home from shack to mansion.

As usual, the great spectacular national public sport was baseball.

Baseball. For the second successive year a "subway series" marked the climax of the year in the "great American game." And again, as in 1936, the New York Yankees bowled over the New York Giants to win the title of baseball champions of the world. "King Carl" Hubbell pitched the Giant's to a lone victory in the fourth game, 7-to-3. Vernon ("Lefty") Gomez became the hero of the series by keeping intact his record of never having been defeated in world series competition. He won the first game 8-to-1, when his mates backed him up with a batting spree. In the fifth and last, after homers by Melvin Ott for the Giants, and Joe Di-Maggio and Myril Hoag for the Yanks, had resulted in a score tied at two-all, Gomez singled to bring in Tony Lazzeri with the winning run, crossed the plate himself a moment later with the fourth run on a double from the bat of Iron Man Lou Gehrig. The second and third games were won by scores of 8-to-1 and 5-to-1. Batting honors for the series went to the aging Tony Lazzeri, subsequently released by the Yankees to become coach of the Chicago Cubs.

Home run champion of the big leagues for the year was the sensational young Italian outfielder, Joe Di-Maggio, who was also runner up for the sports writers "most valuable player" award which went to Charlie Gehringer of the Detroit Tigers in the American League, and to Joseph "Ducky" Medwick in the National. Both Gehringer and Medwick led their leagues in batting.

As the season opened 18-year-old Robert Feller, find of the Cleveland Indians, was widely touted as the pitching sensation of the year. In his first game of the 1936 season he struck out 15 batters, one less than the American League record set 28 years before. In his third game he broke the American League record, and equaled the National record by striking out 17. But a sore arm acquired early in the spring kept him on the bench practically the entire 1937 season. The very

vocal Dizzy Dean also went lame in midseason, failed
to win the 30 games he had promised earlier. Pitching
honors for the year went to the Giants' Carl Hubbell,
who ran his winning streak, begun in July, 1936, up to
24 games before he was knocked out of the box by the
Brooklyn Dodgers early in June of 1937.

Top salary of the year was the $36,000 paid to Lou
Gehrig, a far cry from Babe Ruth's all-time high of
$80,000.

Tennis. Red-headed, 22-year-old J. Donald Budge
of Oakland, California acquired the right to call himself the greatest amateur tennis player in the world in
1937. He grand-slammed his way to an unprecedented
triple victory in the all-England singles, doubles, and
mixed doubles at Wimbledon, led the United States
Davis Cup team to its first victory in eleven years, then
came home to trim Germany's Baron Gottfried von
Cramm for the United States Men's Singles title at
Forest Hills, Long Island.

It was Budge and von Cramm all year. In the English singles championship Budge won 6-3, 6-4, and 6-2.
But in the Davis Cup interzone finals against the German team headed by the aristrocratic 28-year-old
Baron, the match between the two stars went 6-8, 5-7,
6-4, 6-2, 8-6. Budge won in what the London *News
Chronicle* enthusiastically termed the "greatest match
of all time."

In the doubles at Wimbledon, Budge teamed with
Gene Mako to bring this title to America. England's
Hughes and Tuckey bowing, 6-0, 6-4, 6-1. The mixed
doubles found Budge and America's Alice Marble de-

feating the French team of Yvon Petra and Simone Mathieu, 6-4, 6-1.

Then, late in July, Budge and his team mates, Frank Parker, Bryan ("Bitsy") Grant, and Gene Mako, brought back to the United States the Davis Cup which had remained abroad since the great William T. Tilden turned professional.

Europe fared better in women's tennis. At Wimbledon England's Dorothy Round downed the chunky Jadwiga Jedrzejowska of Poland in the finals. And at Forest Hills, U. S. women were humiliated to find two foreigners in the finals for the women's singles championship. Little Anita Lizana of Chile cut down the same burly Polish Wimbledon finalist 6-4, 6-2, to become the first foreigner to hold the title since 1930.

In the Wightman Cup matches American women redeemed their game by defeating the British team. Helen Jacobs, Alice Marble, Caroline Babcock, Sarah Palfrey Fabyan, May Sutton Bundy, and Marjorie Gladman Van Ryn comprised the United States team.

Golf. No one player dominated golf during the year as Don Budge did tennis, or as Bobby Jones and Lawson Little had in their amateur days.

At Oakland Hills Country Club in Birmingham, Michigan, Ralph Guldahl, a hard luck golfer who a short time before had given up the game in disgust to take a job as carpenter's assistant in Hollywood, burned up the course on his last round to come in with 281 strokes. Two strokes behind at 283, Sam Snead had to content himself with second money and the title of "best dressed player" in the Open tournament.

Johnny Goodman, Omaha amateur who climbed to fame after eliminating the immortal Bobby Jones in the first round of an earlier National Amateur tournament at Pebble Beach, Cal., achieved his greatest ambition by winning the amateur tournament at Portland, Oregon. He was two up on Ray Billows of San Francisco at the end of the final match.

"Hardest tournament in the world," the Professional Golfers' Association championship, was won at Pittsburgh by Denny Shute after a nip and tuck battle with Harold McSpaden. Shute thus became one of five professionals who have won the P.G.A. title more than once, the others being Gene Sarazen, Walter Hagen, James Barnes, and Leo Diegel.

Captained by the old warrior of the links, Walter Hagen, the American Ryder Cup team of U. S. professionals defeated Britian on the rainy, windswept fairways of Lancashire's famed Southport and Ainsdale course. Byron Nelson, Ed Dudley, Ralph Guldahl, Charles Lacey, Tony Manero, Gene Sarazen, and Denny Shute took all the British team of Henry Cotton, Alf Padgham, Sam King, David Rees, Percy Alliss, and Captain Charles Whitcombe had to offer, defeated them on the putting greens, 8-4. Non-playing Captain Hagen had correctly predicted the final score before the matches began.

After winning the Ryder Cup matches the American team moved on the Canoustie, the longest toughest course in Scotland, for the British Open tourney. Here they bogged down badly. Henry Cotton, British professional, won the title.

An American, Robert Sweeney, won the British amateur title, but Britons felt they had as much claim to him as the United States, since he was an Oxford man who had spent the last ten years of his life in England, later applied for British citizenship.

The U. S. women's national golf championship was won at Memphis, Tennessee by Mrs. Estelle Lawson Page of Greensboro, S. C. Runner up was 19-year-old Patty Berg, the Minneapolis youngster who flashed on the golf horizon in 1935 and was the sensation of 1936.

The Curtis Cup matches with England ended in a tie in 1937, permitting the American women's team to retain the cup by virtue of their win in 1936.

Boxing. When Joe Louis knocked out James J. Braddock in the eighth round of their championship bout at Comiskey Park in Chicago on the night of June 22, he became the first Negro to hold the heavyweight title since Jack Johnson lost it to Jess Willard in 1915. Odds were 3-to-1 against champion Braddock before he climbed into the ring against the "brown bomber." The courageous Braddock forced the fight as he had promised he would, but didn't have a chance against the murderous rights thrown at him by the methodical Louis.

For years during the twenty-two year period between Negro champions, a giant Negro named Harry Wills sought a chance at the title. Although he was better than most, and perhaps all, of the heavyweights of his period, he was never given a championship fight. In 1937, not a Negro, but a Nazi was given the same sort of runaround. Max Schmeling won the title from Jack

Sharkey in 1930 on a foul, and lost it to the same Boston Irishman on a widely disputed decision in 1932. In June 1936 he knocked out Joe Louis, making him logical contender for the title which had been won in the meantime by Jimmy Braddock. The match was made, but Braddock begged off, exhibiting an injured thumb, and the fight was postponed until June of 1937. Meanwhile a combination of the fact that Jews threatened to boycott a fight in which the Nazi was a participant, and that the independent Schmeling refused to sign over his life to Mike Jacobs, the ticket speculator who had gained control of U. S. big time fighting, caused Braddock to make the match with Louis. Schmeling's appeal to law was fruitless. And instead of being matched with Louis after the Braddock fight, the Negro champion was signed by Jacobs to a fight with Britain's plodding Tommy Farr. Staged in Yankee Stadium late in August, this match drew a small crowd of 30,000. Greatest surprise for the spectators was the fact that Farr, though badly cut up at the end, weathered the full fifteen rounds against the champion.

In other championship bouts during the year Lou Ambers beat his one-time employer, Tony Canzoneri, in defense of the lightweight crown which he lifted from Canzoneri the year before. Harry Jeffra, Baltimore ex-caddy, took the bantamweight title from Sixto Escobar. Henry Armstrong won the feather title.

Horse Racing. Horse of the year was Samuel D. Riddle's War Admiral. The delicate, undersized son of the famous Man O'War surprised even his owner, who bought him as a colt for $5,000, by becoming the fourth

horse in turf history to ride to triple victories in the
Kentucky Derby, the Preakness, and the Belmont
stakes, netting owner Riddle prizes of $144,620.

Before England's new king and queen, Mid-day Sun
won the 157-year-old classic horse race at Epsom
Downs.

Auto Racing. Germany's Bernd Rosemeyer won
the 300-mile George Vanderbilt Cup automobile race at
Westbury, Long Island, in July. And the following November Britain's Captain George E. T. Eyston broke
the automobile speed record with a mark of 311.5 miles
per hour on the salt flats of Bonneville, Utah.

Miscellaneous. Other sports events of the year
found the Detroit Red Wings winning the ice hockey
championship. Harold Vanderbilt's *Ranger* handed
four successive lickings to England's Skipper T. O. M.
Sopwith's *Endeavour II* to retain for America the "Old
Mug" symbolic of yachting supremacy. Washington
University swept the Poughkeepsie regatta, winning
freshman, junior varsity, and varsity races. Don Lash
of Indiana ran the fastest two-mile race in history, setting a record of 8 minutes 58 seconds to shade Paavo
Nurmi's indoor record by two-tenths of a second. Bad-
minton developed into one of the fastest growing games
in the United States. And Americans learned to their
surprise that not baseball or football, but bowling is
the biggest sport event in the world. Twenty-two
thousand bowlers participated in the American Bowling Congress staged in New York in March, representing the cream of the country's crop of 9,000,000
devotees.

Football. Notable for the lack of "big names" which had made Red Grange, Bronko Nagurski, and other household bywords in former years, the 1937 football schedule in America produced the following champions: In the Pacific Conference the University of California ruled supreme despite a scoreless tie with Washington, and earned the right to represent the West in the New Year's day Rose Bowl game. Minnesota won the Big Ten championship—her third in four years—but lost to non-conference Nebraska and Notre Dame teams. In the Big Six, Nebraska won top ranking. The Southeastern Conference title went to Alabama, which also won the honor of being chosen to represent the East in the Rose Bowl.[1] For the first time since 1924 the University of Colorado won the Rocky Mountain Conference title, due principally to the flashing performances of quarterback Byron "Whizzer" White, who piled up more scores than any other college football player.

In the "Ivy" league Dartmouth won top honors despite ties with Yale and Cornell. Army beat the Navy 6 to 0 in its classic annual game. Harvard won in the "Big Three" league. Pittsburgh ended its season undefeated and probably the strongest team in the country despite a tie with Fordham.

The Washington Redskins defeated the Chicago Bears 28 to 21, due to the phenomenal passing of "Slingin'" Sammy Baugh. (He completed 81 of 171 passes during the regular season for a new record.)

[1] In the Rose Bowl "classic" the score was: California 13, Alabama 0; the East-West game ended in a scoreless tie.

Even the powerful offensive and defensive work of the Bears' Bronko Nagurski, who left the team occasionally during the season to defend his wrestling championship, was not enough to offset Baugh's pitching.

Champions of Champions. As everyone suspected, the Associated Press poll of 50 leading sports writers in December revealed Donald Budge as the number one U. S. male athlete of 1937.

Swimmer Katherine Rawls won the same honor among women, and the New York Yankees were voted the outstanding team of the year.

CHAPTER XXII

DEATH AND DISASTER

HINDENBURG CATASTROPHE

Most dramatic disaster of 1937 and one that promised to rank with the starkest tragedies of all time was the destruction of the 803-foot German dirigible *Hindenburg* at Lakehurst, N. J., at 7:20 on the evening of May 6.

Just a year to the day after the giant airship made its first flight to the United States from the home port of Friedrichshafen, Germany, it moved majestically down the United States coast line on the first of 18 round trips scheduled for 1937. Commanding the ship was Captain Max Pruss, veteran of 170 transatlantic flights. On board also as adviser was Captain Ernst Lehmann, another famed lighter-than-air expert, and commander of the ship when it made its trial run to the United States in 1936. A total of 97 persons were aboard, including 39 passengers. Bad weather had delayed the *Hindenburg* on the Atlantic crossing, and when it finally arrived over Lakehurst a thunderstorm forced Captain Pruss to cruise out to sea again to wait for better landing conditions. Finally he nosed the ship up to the mooring mast while a drizzle still fell. Two lines were thrown out of the bow, and navy men and civilians from the crowd of 1,000 on hand to catch a glimpse of the ship or to welcome incoming passengers, began pulling the nose into position.

Suddenly with a splutter a long tongue of flame leaped out of the stern. With a "crack" the ship buckled, began sinking to earth, the flame rushing through the middle of the bag as it tilted at a 45 degree angle, then popping out the nose in a leaping plume. In the incredible time of 32 seconds the entire ship was in flames. The last place the fire reached was the passenger gondola. But before even the nose of the ship had reached the ground passengers and crew were jumping madly from windows, some of them to break arms and legs and be unable to avoid the inferno which settled on them. As the twisted burning mass reached the ground more persons stumbled forth. Heroic gobs dashed into the flames to save others. But most of those saved suffered fearful burns, and the dead numbered 11 passengers and 21 crew including Captain Lehmann who lived long enough to indicate that he had no idea what the cause of the explosion had been.

News of the disaster was flashed to the ship's famed designer, Dr. Hugo Eckener. He immediately boarded ship for America, arriving in time to take part in the Federal inquiry into the cause of the explosion. Weeks later the Federal Board confirmed the opinion of Dr. Eckener after the designer had seen the motion pictures of the explosion, had listened to accounts of survivors. Theories of sabotage by anti-Nazis, a broken propeller crashing into the bag, ignition by radio spark, structural failure, and lightning were all rejected in favor of a theory that the explosion had been the result of static or atmospheric electricity igniting free hydrogen which somehow had got loose on the ship.

But whatever the cause, the one fact which stood out clearly from the disaster was the failure of the highly inflammatory hydrogen as the proper gas with which to inflate such craft. The best non-inflammable gas for the purpose was known by the Germans to be helium. But the United States has a monopoly on this rare gas which made it almost impossible for another nation to buy any. Congress rushed through a bill to make it easier for Germany to purchase helium, and the German government announced that the LZ 130, sister ship of the *Hindenburg* already in construction, would be inflated with it despite its terrific cost, despite also the fact that its lifting capacity was 20 per cent less than hydrogen.

COMMERCIAL AIR CRASHES

Until the last month of December, there had only been four major crashes in 1936. Then came a series of shocking wrecks which brought the total killed in commercial planes to 59 for the year (44 passengers) —highest in aviation history. By the end of 1937 five major crashes had placed the year's toll at 52, only seven short of the 1936 record.

Early in January a United Airliner flying out from San Francisco plowed into a mountain 50 miles northwest of Burbank, California, killing two pilots, the hostess, and nine passengers. Later in the same month Explorer Martin Johnson and two others were killed in a crash of a Western Air Express plane traveling from Salt Lake City to Burbank. A big new Douglas flying for the United Airlines on the west coast plunged into San Francisco Bay in mid-February, killing all aboard. Late in March another Douglas, crippled by ice on its wings, cracked up outside Pittsburgh, killing 13 on this Transcontinental and Western plane. Then in October came the worst air tragedy of the air on a scheduled American plane. A United Airline ship, carrying 2 pilots, a stewardess, and 16 passengers, dove into a ridge of mountain in the Black Uinta Range in Utah, 17 miles off the line's normal course. Passengers and crew were scattered all over the snow-covered landscape by the force of this crash, and it was hours before the bodies could be brought down from the inaccessible spot.

Causes. Publicity attending these crashes focused the attention of the nation's legislators on the problem of doing something to improve air safety, with Chairman of the Senate Air Safety Committee Royal S. Copeland taking the lead. In February Senator Copeland called a conference of commercial airmen and other experts to investigate the matter, to determine the causes and cures. Meanwhile the air companies were pointing out that air passengers were still twice as safe as automobile passengers. And their claims were borne out when figures revealed that auto deaths in 1937 mounted considerably over those during the previous year.

According to Associate Editor Swanee Taylor, of *Popular Aviation,* "80 per cent of airplane crackups can be traced to errors in judgment, misplaced zeal, over-confidence, or out-and-out stupidity on the part of the man at the controls. . . . Bad weather used to be a popular alibi, but it doesn't go any more in best aviation circles." But many of the pilots were insisting that if not the weather, at least the lack of proper equipment, to combat weather conditions, was responsible for many of the crashes. The radio beam came in for its share of abuse, also the lack of sufficient government weather bureau stations, and the dearth of radio beacon ranges.

Out of the Copeland conference came a number of suggestions to reduce air accidents, chief among which were the following: (1) adoption of radio direction finders to supplement radio beams; (2) installation of these devices on all planes; (3) better navigation training for pilots; (4) installation of an "air-log" on all planes to record altitude, etc.; (5) installation of anti-rain-static loop antennae on all planes; (6) regulation of radio equipment by approval certificates; (7) installation of simultaneous radio ranges on all Federal airways; (8) more detailed and accurate radio maps; (9) better training for blind flying; (10) improvement of port approach lighting; (11) more safety research by the Bureau of Air Commerce.

The Bureau of Air Commerce would be charged with the job of putting these suggestions into effect. Its director, Eugene Vidal, resigned rather than bear the brunt of continued criticism, as the disastrous crashes continued through the year. He was replaced by Dr. Fred M. Fagg. (See Chapter III.) And when Dr.

Fagg handed in his resignation in the fall to return to his teaching post at Northwestern University, the name of America's foremost air hero, Charles A. Lindbergh, was being considered for the post. Lindbergh returned to the U. S. early in December to spend Christmas in this country, marking his first visit to America since his self-imposed exile to England two years before following the kidnaping and death of his infant son.

AMELIA'S LAST FLIGHT

America's foremost air heroine flew to death in the wide Pacific in the summer of 1937. Early in the spring Amelia Earhart Putnam set out on a projected world flight, but got only as far as Hawaii where her plane cracked up. Then on June 1, with Navigator Fred Noonan, she started off in the opposite direction on a leisurely jaunt around the world. She flew first to South America, then across to Africa, India, Australia. On July 1 she and Noonan left Lae, New Guinea, for the most difficult part of the trip— the 2,550 miles of ocean to tiny Howland Island, where no plane had ever been. The coast guard cutter *Itasca* heard a radio message from her hours later stating that she had only gas enough left for another hour and a half, and that land was nowhere in sight. But she gave no location. When nothing further was heard from her the *Itasca* steamed around helplessly for hours, not knowing where to look. Stormy weather forced a navy flying boat from Hawaii back after a few hours of hopeless searching. Then radio amateurs in America and in the South Pacific, as well as the radio operator of Pan-American Airways in Hawaii, heard faint signals which were attributed to Miss Earhart. All they could hear was "S O S. K H A Q Q" (the plane's call letters). But again no indication of the flyers' location was reported.

The navy dispatched the battleship *Colorado* and the aircraft carrier *Lexington* with 72 planes to the Howland Island vicinity, but no trace of the plane or its occupants was ever discovered. At home commentators pointed out that the search for the flyers was costing the Government approximately $2 50,000 a day. There was also considerable criticism of Miss Earhart's radio and direction-finding equipment, with the general feeling being expressed in aviation circles that the flight to Howland Island had been foolhardy with the type of plane and facilities used. Agitation for legislation to prevent the navy from going to the rescue of such flights was proposed by Congressmen, and finally Assistant Secretary of Commerce Col. John M. Johnson declared that, "From now on no individual will be permitted to take off on any ocean or round-the-world flight that smacks of a stunt."

Meanwhile Publisher Husband George P. Putnam refused to give up all hope, and at the end of the year was organizing an expedition to travel to the South Seas in search of his wife, on the slim chance that she and Noonan had found safety on some uninhabited coral reef.

OHIO VALLEY FLOODS

Spring floods which in 1936 made thousands homeless along the upper Ohio River and its tributaries, were
repeated with far greater severity early in 1937. Most
of the damage, however, came in the lower stretches
of the Ohio. Days of unseasonable rain—six inches
fell in parts of Ohio in 48 hours—in January and February brought untold suffering to inhabitants of the
valley, cost at least 60 lives, and did millions of dollars in damage. Pittsburgh fared better than in 1936,
but farther down the river at Cincinnati parts of the
city were under twenty feet of water. Louisville,
which was hardest hit of any city in the area, had
200,000 homeless, property damage estimated at $100,-
000,000, and was forced to invoke martial law when
flooded power plants failed to provide power and light.

At Clarksville, Tennessee, the Cumberland River
reached 24 feet above flood stage. At Cairo, Illinois,
at the junction of the Ohio and Mississippi rivers
workers frantically sandbagged the 60-foot seawall
and saved the city from destruction. But to hundreds
of other towns, villages, and farms the raging waters
brought desolation of the worst sort. CCC and WPA
workers were rushed by the thousands to help the Red
Cross with the terrific problem of caring for the homeless. The President's hopes were knocked into a
cocked hat as flood relief drained federal funds. (See
Chapter III.) At one time the Red Cross was caring
for 676,000 homeless people, had established 108 field

hospitals to care for the sick and injured and inoculate against plagues.

Only bright spot in the flood picture was the fact that it did not take its expected toll along the Mississippi. Army-built levees, combined with floodways into which the water was purposely routed, fought "Ol' Man River" to a standstill south of Cairo. But the very success of the Mississippi system roused the ire of Ohio valley residents over the fact that the Government had not similarly protected them, made it obvious that legislators in the states affected would demand more and more federal funds for this purpose in the near future.

FINIS

Headlines told of the passing of these national and world figures in a year:

Statesmen. Lawyer Elihu Root, 91, in Manhattan, Republican elder statesman. Of the 31 men who have been President of the United States only six were not, at some time of their lives, contemporaries of Elihu Root. He was Secretary of War under McKinley, Secretary of War under T. Roosevelt, Secretary of State under T. Roosevelt, U. S. Senator (1909-15), a member of the Hague Court, president of the Carnegie Endowment for International Peace, winner of the Nobel Peace Prize, one of the drafters of World Court plans.

Harry Stewart New, 78, of pneumonia, in Baltimore. One-time (1923-29) U. S. Postmaster-General, Republican National Chairman (1907-08) and Senator from Indiana (1917-23). He established the U. S.

air mail service, in 1922 made the first political campaign speech by radio.

Gaston Doumergue, 73, of an embolism, in France. One-time President of France, twice Premier.

Senator Joseph Taylor Robinson, of a heart attack, in Washington. Democratic senator from Arkansas and Senate Majority Leader. (See Chapter III.)

Robert Worth Bingham, 66, following a diagnostic operation, in Baltimore. Sportsman, lawyer, publisher, since 1933 U. S. Ambassador to the Court of St. James. Owner of *Louisville Courier-Journal* and *Times* since 1917.

Dr. Thomas G. Masaryk, 87, of pneumonia, at Chateau de Lany, near Prague. Founder and first President of the Czechoslovakian Republic.

Andrew William Mellon, 82, of uremia, bronchopneumonia, and old age, in Southampton, L. I. Multimillionaire, art fancier, statesman. Secretary of the Treasury under Harding and Coolidge. Reduced the national debt from $24,000,000,000 to $16,000,000,000. Ambassador to Great Britain. Possessor of one of America's greatest private fortunes, most of which he left to an educational and charitable trust.

James Ramsay MacDonald, 71, died of a heart attack while at sea. British Laborite. First Labor Prime Minister of England, coming into 1924, and again in 1929; in 1931 he formed the "National" government, remaining Prime Minister until 1936, when he yielded the office to Stanley Baldwin.

Philip Snowden, Viscount Snowden of Ichornshaw, 72, of a heart attack in Tilford, Surrey, England.

British Laborite. He became the first Socialist Chancellor of the Exchequer (1924, 1929-31). Along with Ramsay MacDonald, he was branded as a "traitor" to working class when he joined in the formation of the "National" government in 1931. He was knighted and retired into the House of Lords in 1932.

Nathan Lynn Bachman, 58, of heart disease, in Washington. Tennessee's Junior Democratic Senator, appointed in 1933 when Cordell Hull was drafted for the Cabinet and twice re-elected; one-time (1918-24) Associate Justice of the Tennessee Supreme Court.

Frank B. Kellogg, 80, in St. Paul, Minn. Nobel Peace Prize winner in 1930, author with Aristide Briand of the Kellogg-Briand pact to outlaw war, Secretary of State, Ambassador to Britain.

Newton D. Baker, 66, of a heart attack, in Cleveland. Wartime Secretary of War under Wilson, lawyer, and conservative Democrat.

Writers. John Drinkwater, 54, in his sleep of a heart attack in London. British poet and playwright. His best known play: *Abraham Lincoln.*

Albert Bigelow Paine, 75, after a month's illness; in New Smyrna, Florida. Biographer of Mark Twain, member of the Pulitzer Prize Novel Committee since 1929.

Edith Newbold Jones Wharton, 75, after an apoplectic stroke at her villa in France. Novelist. Her best known book: *Ethan Frome.* The book with which she won the Pulitzer prize in 1920: *The Age of Innocence.*

Sir James Matthew Barrie, 77, of broncho-pneumonia, in London. Author of *Peter Pan, The Little Minister, Sentimental Tommy*.

Journalists. Rollo Ogden, 81, of pulmonary congestion, in Manhattan. Editor-in-chief of the *New York Times* since 1922. Trained for the ministry at Andover and Union Theological Seminaries, Presbyterian Ogden preached in Cleveland and Mexico City, began in 1887 to write. At 35 he took up reporting for the *New York Evening Post*, held the editorship for 17 years (1903-20) until the *Times* lured him away.

Edgar Watson ("Ed") Howe, 84, of old age and paralysis, in Atchison, Kansas. Eternally disgruntled Kansas editor. In his Atchison *Globe* editor Howe framed catchy, pungent aphorisms which brought him the title of the "Sage of Potato Hill."

Norman Hapgood, 69, after an operation, in Manhattan. Oldtime liberal journalist, onetime (1919) Minister to Denmark. He edited *Collier's* (1903-12), *Harper's Weekly* (1913-16), *Hearst's International Magazine* (1923-25), was currently editor of the *Unitarian Christian Register*.

Actors and Actresses. Sir Guy Standing, 63, versatile British actor; of heart disease, in Los Angeles. He commanded a destroyer in the War, was knighted for service with the British War Mission to the United States in 1918. A talented pianist and marine artist, he had been ailing since a Black Widow spider bit him during the filming of *Lives of a Bengal Lancer*.

Jean Harlow, 26, platinum-blonde cinema-actress; of cerebra edema, following acute uremia; in Holly-

wood's Good Samaritan Hospital. Christened Harlean
Carpentier, reared in Kansas City, she became with
"Hell's Angels" (1930), a top-rank star and cinema's
No. 1 symbol of sex appeal. Her last picture: *Saratoga* which a double finished in her part.

Mrs. Leslie Carter, 75, of heart trouble and pneumonia, in Santa Monica, California. For 16 years
(1890-1906) David Belasco's leading lady.

William Gillette, 81, of pulmonary hemorrhage, in
Hartford, Conn. Oldtime actor-playwright (Sherlock
Holmes).

Scientists. Guglielmo Marconi, 67, of a heart attack in Rome. Italian-Irish inventor of wireless communication, Nobel Prize winner (1909). Italian marquese and senator, president of the Royal Academy
of Italy.

Dr. Alfred Adler, 67, after collapsing in the street,
in Aberdeen, Scotland. Viennese psychologist, founder
of the school of "individual psychology," originator of
the phrase "inferiority complex," professional enemy
of Dr. Sigmund Freud, his old teacher.

Capitalist. John Davison Rockefeller, 97; of hardening of the heart muscles; at "The Casements," Ormond Beach, Florida. Founded the Standard Oil Company and with it an enormous fortune. Lived to see
the public conception of him change from a mental picture of the "most hated" man in the United States
(because of his bludgeoning business methods and
monopolistic practices in the last quarter of the nineteenth century), to a kindly old philanthropist who

gave millions to educational and research foundations, bright shiny new dimes to chance acquaintances.

Militarist. Erich Ludendorff, 72, after an operation for a bladder ailment, in Munich. Germany's ruthless domineering Wartime Chief of Staff. In later years he became a militant atheist, was reconciled with Hitler only a few months before his death.

INDEX

AAA, 98

Abbe children, 480

Abbott, Charles D., 472

Abdication of Edward VIII, 458, 475

Adler, Alfred, 505

Adult education, in New York City, 184 f.

A. F. of L., drafts counter-offensive against C.I.O., 70 f.; rivalry with C.I.O., 71 ff.

Africa, 194 f.

Agriculture, Farm Tenant Act, 97; share croppers, 96 f.; Seed Loans, 96; Farm Credit Act, 98; Sugar-Control, 98 f.

Air transportation, improvements in, 155

Airplane crashes, 495 ff.

Airplanes, wing de-icers, 155

Alba, Duke of, 296

Alda, Frances, 480

Aldington, Richard, 474

Alfonso XIII, ousting of, 261

Allen, Verdi, 197

Almaden mercury mines, 277

Almeria, shelling of, 285

Altmeyer, Arthur J., 110

Aluminum Co. of America, antitrust case, 40

Amateur golf tournament, 487

Ambers, Lou, 489

Amendment, 20th, 81

American Artists Congress, 444

American Doctor's Odyssey, An, 456

American Dream, 466

America, religion in, 196 ff.

Amphitryon 38, 427

Anarcho-Syndicalists in Spain, 280 ff.

And So—Victoria, 457, 467, 473

Anderson, Marion, 454

Anderson, Paul Y., 68

Anderson, Sherwood, 463

Andrews, George B., 165

Angel Island, 429

Angell, James R., 174

Angels in Undress, 479

Anglo-Belgian neutrality agreement, 410

Anglo-French, and Hitler, 321 f.

Anthony, Harold E., 165

Anthony Adverse, 467

Anti-Communism campaign, 193 f.

Arabs, and partition of Palestine, 355 ff.

Arctic, study of, by Russians, 164

Argentina, 400

Art, abstract, 435 f., 438 f.; exhibitions, 436 f.; reproduced, 448 f.; saved in Spain, 446 f.

Artist union, 444

Arts, The, 459, 478

Asch, Sholom, 473

Associated Press, 23

Asthma, treatment of, by insulin, 154

Astronomy, 162

"Atom smasher," 165

Augustus Caesar, 480

Auriol, Vincent, 363

Austria, and Germany, 316; Mussolini prevents *Anschluss,* 304

Auto racing, 490

Automobile industry, expansion, 129 f.; production, 129 f.

Ayres, Leonard P., 145

Babes in Arms, 427

Bachman, N. L., 503

Bache collection, 438

Bache, Jules S., 106, 439

Bailey, Temple, 473

Baker, Newton D., 503

Baldwin, Stanley, 340 f.

507